P9-APW-984

PERSONAL LAW

PERSONAL LAW

Norbert J. Mietus
Bill W. West

California State University
Sacramento

SCIENCE RESEARCH ASSOCIATES, INC.
Chicago, Palo Alto, Toronto, Henley-on-Thames, Sydney, Paris, Stuttgart

A Subsidiary of IBM

014690

© 1975, Science Research Associates, Inc. All rights reserved.
Printed in the United States of America.

Library of Congress Cataloging in Publication Data

Mietus, Norbert J
  Personal law.

  Bibliography: p.
  Includes index.
  1. Law—United States.   I. West, Bill W., joint
author.   II. Title.
KF385.M52   340'.0973   74-34192
ISBN 0-574-18215-2

CONTENTS

014690

required to maintain his motor vehicle in good repair? *169* □ 15 What should you do as a driver if involved in an automobile accident? *170* □ Cases, Questions, and Problems *172*

PART III
THE ECONOMIC ASPECTS OF LAW

PREFACE

The law affects practically all human relations. Its influence is expanding as population grows and clusters more and more around cities. No one can properly consider himself liberally educated without some knowledge of the law, and yet public understanding is very limited.

We have sought to help answer this need for enlightenment. It would be impracticable as well as presumptuous to attempt a complete compilation of rules and their applications. A conscientious person will learn much law from reading this book, but not enough to enable him to serve as his own attorney. We hope, however, that through this book the student will be better able to avoid legal difficulties and to recognize and deal with them when they do arise.

Even in apparently simple legal conflicts, a multiplicity of factors must be considered. The opinions of counsel and judges and the decisions of courts are conditioned upon a number of premises, qualifications, and distinctions—many that are beyond the scope of this book. Often important differences exist in applicable laws among the various states, and even at the federal level among the various court circuits. Therefore, the reader is cautioned to consult professional legal counsel when confronted by an actual legal problem of consequence.

As a practical matter to help you use this book, the notes to the text have been dealt with in two ways. Those referring to case citations are numbered and gathered at the back of the book. Those offering substantive comments are designated by symbols such as asterisks and appear at the bottom of appropriate pages.

To convey ideas with a sense of realism and relevance and to illustrate important points of law, we have relied heavily on actual cases and also on hypothetical cases with fictitious characters. Many topics are controversial; a few may even be offensive to some readers. All reflect life and law in action.

For representative legal principles we have drawn on the law of many states and on the federal courts as well. Because California is the most populous state with a reputation for progressiveness, it is often a good model of contemporary trends. We have therefore relied more heavily on the law of this state. When deemed appropriate, professors and serious students may compare the law of their own jurisdictions to the textbook presentation. Their comments and suggestions are welcome and earnestly solicited by us.

I THE
LEGAL SYSTEM
AND YOU

1

YOU AND THE CONSTITUTION

1. WHAT IS A WRITTEN CONSTITUTION?

A *written constitution* is a document defining fundamental principles for governance of the people. It may include either a grant of power or a limitation to power or both. The U.S. Constitution is basically a *grant* of power from the fifty sovereign states to the United States of America. Powers not expressly delegated (or transferred) to the federated United States by the Constitution are reserved to individual states. The United States thus possesses the *express powers* given to it; each state possesses the remaining or *residual powers*.

State constitutions include *limitations* upon state power imposed by the states themselves. Constitutional provisions generally have greater permanence, are broader in application, and concern more fundamental issues of law than do statutes enacted by the legislative branch of government or rules created by decisions of the judicial branch. Although the U.S. Constitution is a grant of power to the federal government, it contains restraints or limitations upon both federal and state action. Restrictions contained in state constitutions often overlap those in the U.S. Constitution, and apply only to the exercise of power by the respective states. Thus, in many cases, a certain act of a state government, such as arbitrary discrimination, may be prohibited by both the U.S. Constitution and a state constitution.

The U.S. Constitution does not limit the conduct of private individuals.

2. WHAT ARE THE POWERS OF THE FEDERAL GOVERNMENT?

Among the most important powers exclusively delegated to the federal government by the U.S. Constitution are those which authorize it to (1) regulate commerce with foreign nations and among the states (interstate commerce); (2) declare war and raise and support armies; and (3) make treaties and manage foreign affairs. Many additional powers are expressly conferred such as power to regulate money, to provide for bankruptcy, to regulate maritime activities, and to control immigration and naturalization. It shares with states and local governments the power to tax.

The U.S. Constitution provides that Congress shall have power to make all laws that are "necessary and proper" for carrying into execution the powers expressly granted. These are *implied powers*. Congress has passed many laws to carry out its express duty to regulate interstate commerce, for example, as found in (1) transporting oil by pipeline among the states; (2) broadcasting radio and television signals; (3) teaching students in various states by correspondence courses; (4) advertising in nationally distributed media; and (5) organizing sports activities that involve performance in multiple states.

To execute its express power to declare war, Congress has passed a variety of "necessary and proper" laws: (1) drafting young men from all states for compulsory military service; (2) authorizing recovery by the government of excessive profits made by private manufacturers under government contracts to produce wartime materials; (3) seizing the property of enemy aliens; and (4) providing a special system of justice for the military services.

If the federal government did not have the express and exclusive power to govern foreign affairs, then that power would be a residual power reserved to the states. Such reservation would permit states to make treaties with foreign countries, and these treaties might be inconsistent with each other and even adverse to the national interest.

3. WHAT ARE THE POWERS OF THE STATE GOVERNMENTS?

State governments possess all the residual or remaining powers incidental to sovereignty that have not been delegated to the United States. Thus, any state may independently regulate commercial contracts among its citizens; it may enact fish and game laws to conserve natural resources; it may regulate marriage and divorce and determine what personal conduct within its boundaries shall be considered criminal.

Congress has voluntarily taken no action in some areas where it has power to act. In such situations each state may regulate local phases of the activity until the federal government exercises its prerogative. For example, the government of New York may regulate harbor improvements in all of its ports, or the labeling of oleomargarine, or the use of interstate highways, provided the federal government has not already "occupied" these areas of activity with contrary regulations. Such occupation is called *preemption.*

Under the doctrine of federal supremacy, the U.S. Constitution (together with the laws of the United States made in accord with the Constitution) is the supreme law of the land. Any state law, or even state constitution, that is contrary to this supreme law is void. Supremacy becomes an issue only when laws conflict; usually there is no conflict. The same principle of supremacy exists between states and local governments. For example, when Oregon enacts speed laws for a state highway, that area is preempted, and no county or city may regulate it.

4. HOW IS OUR SYSTEM OF GOVERNMENT ORGANIZED?

There are three basic branches of government: legislative, executive, and judicial.

Legislative Branch

The function of the legislative branch is to *enact* laws. This is accomplished by vote of legislators to enact, amend, or repeal specific laws. Once the legislature enacts a law, its job is done. Someone else must apply the law and, if necessary, determine whether it is compatible with the pertinent state or federal Constitution.

Because of the complexities of modern life, the state and federal legislative branches cannot provide all necessary or desirable law. Furthermore, many technical matters requiring regulation are beyond the understanding of most legislators in the limited time usually available to them for consideration. For example, how can one person be expected to cast intelligent votes during a crowded legislative session when perhaps thousands of proposed bills (that is, laws) are under consideration: maximum speed and minimum altitude limitations for commercial aircraft; limitations on the chemical composition of fertilizers and insecticides; salary requirements and job standards of hundreds of civil service personnel; limiting bullfrog hunting; and proper safety equipment standards for two-wheel vehicles?

Obviously, the legislative branches must delegate some of their legislative power in order to cope with the volume and detailed specialization of problems requiring legal solutions. Most of these delegated powers devolve upon *administrative agencies.* Federal agencies include the Civil Aeronautics Board, National Labor Relations Board, Federal Maritime

Commission, and the Internal Revenue Service. State agencies may include a Public Utilities Commission, a Workmen's Compensation Board, a Real Estate Board, and a Board of Professional and Vocational Standards. Typical local agencies are planning commissions, housing and redevelopment agencies, and school boards. These agencies have the power to make laws, called *rules,* within the area of expertise defined by the legislative branch. Violation of these rules may result in civil or criminal penalties.

All voting members of the legislative branch of government—federal, state, and local—are elected by the people, whereas most members of administrative agencies are appointed by the executive branch (sometimes subject to legislative approval) because of the need for expertise. Legislators communicate with constituents to determine needs for legislation; they conduct investigations to reveal the merits and defects of proposed laws. For example, Congressional investigation of the Watergate scandal, which involved criminal action and abuse of power during the administration of President Richard M. Nixon, may result in new legislation concerning conflicts of interest, campaign contributions, official behavior, and the like.

The legislative branch does not intrude upon the judicial branch by determining the constitutionality of laws it has enacted. Nor does it give orders to employees of the executive branch such as the military, the police, or the Federal Bureau of Investigation.

Executive Branch

The executive branch of government is headed by the President at the federal level, by the governor at the state level, and usually by a mayor at the city level. Its function is to *execute* the laws enacted by the legislative branch. As in the case of the legislative branch, many of the powers of the executive branch are delegated to independent administrative agencies. For example, the Civil Aeronautics Board may require airlines to install and use radar equipment for navigation, and may impose penalties for violations. The law or rule involved was prescribed by the Board under the broad regulatory powers delegated to it by Congress. Thus, the Board has legislative, executive, and judicial functions.

Under the broad mandate of a legislated statute, the executive branch of government also may give detailed orders on day-to-day matters and thereby actually make laws. In an emergency, orders to the military from the President are made without prior approval of Congress. Arrests are made, contracts signed, fires extinguished, committees formed, moneys spent, persons fired and hired, all without prior specific legislative approval.

The President, governors, and mayors are elected by the people. Many members of the administrative agencies are appointed by these elected officials. However, the vast majority of government civilian employees who are members of the executive branch, are hired on the basis of merit under civil service laws, which are designed to eliminate political favoritism and nepotism, and to assure job security even when administrations change.

Judicial Branch

The judicial branch of government determines the facts underlying legal controversies and resolves the disputes in the light of applicable law. When necessary, it decides whether or not a law, or its application to the facts, complies with the applicable state or U.S. Constitution.

The power of the U.S. Supreme Court to declare laws enacted by the Congress unconstitutional is not spelled out in the Constitution. This power was logically assumed by the Court early in our history in the landmark case of *Marbury* v. *Madison*. Chief Justice John Marshall, in his opinion, stated:

> Certainly all those who have framed written constitutions contemplate them as forming the fundamental and paramount law of the nation, and consequently, the theory of every such government must be that an act of the legislature repugnant to the constitution is void. This theory is . . . one of the fundamental principles of our society. . . . Courts, as well as other departments, are bound by that instrument.[1]

The judicial branch is composed of courts, and functions only while acting as a court hearing a controversy.

> Don Martin was negotiating with Bob Huntley to buy his hot rod. In their conversation, Don asked whether Bob guaranteed the mileage to be only 28,000 miles as indicated by the odometer. Bob replied that the law made him, as seller, guarantor of the mileage shown. Don questioned this legal opinion and suggested they telephone a local judge for a ruling on the point. Bob agreed, Will the judge provide such a ruling?

No. The judicial branch of government is composed of courts, not judges. Moreover, courts administer justice in properly presented cases involving actual, specific controversies. Thus, if the legislative branch should enact a law prohibiting persons without high school diplomas from voting, it would not be declared unconstitutional by the judicial branch until someone brought a specific case to determine his or her right to vote. Courts will not rule on a hypothetical controversy, nor speculate on the constitutionality of a proposed law.

In situations where parties face the strong possibility of a serious legal controversy, however, either may petition a court for a *declaratory judgment* before any loss is suffered. This might be appropriate, for

SORRY FELLAS, IT'S UNCONSTITUTIONAL

JUDICIAL

example, when a person, at considerable expense, plans to divert the flow of a stream of water on his land, thus directly affecting his neighbors. The court orders nothing but indicates whether he would violate the neighbor's rights if the anticipated action were taken.

The Overlap of Powers

In accord with the idea of checks and balances among the three branches of government, the President may veto legislation; the Supreme Court may declare a law unconstitutional; Congress may effectively curtail the power of the executive branch through its control of taxation and the appropriation of funds. Ultimately, the citizens control through their voting power to elect officials who presumably will, if pressured by enough people, change the law and even amend the Constitution. Administrative agencies have been delegated the power not only to make certain laws, and to execute them, but also to adjudicate certain controversies. Thus, the Workmen's Compensation Board has the power to determine, for example, whether or not a certain person suffered his injury on the job or at home. Only courts, however, may impose fines or sentence to prison.

Perhaps the most complicated area of government concern, and hence one in which authority is commonly delegated, is that of taxation. The Internal Revenue Service enacts detailed rules about taxes (a legislative function); investigates cases, collects taxes, and administers its rules (an executive function); and makes determinations on tax liability in many disputed cases (a judicial function). A question of the constitutionality of a tax (or its application to a certain case) is, of course, resolved by the courts.

The concept of judicial review of action of the executive branch of government arose in 1974 when the U.S. Supreme Court ordered the President to produce certain tape recordings of his confidential conversations with aides. The tapes had been subpoenaed for use in the trial of seven individuals charged with conspiracy to defraud the United States and to obstruct justice, among other offenses. The President claimed *absolute executive privilege* for all presidential communications, insisting that he could not be compelled to disclose any of the information involved.

Chief Justice Warren E. Burger, in his opinion, acknowledged the existence of absolute privilege in our system of justice. He agreed that presidential communications are presumptively privileged; however, the unanimous decision of the court turned upon another argument, one that uses principles set forth by Chief Justice Marshall in *Marbury*.

> The twofold aim of criminal justice is that guilt shall not escape nor innocence suffer. . . . The very integrity of the judicial system depends on full disclosure of all the facts, within the framework of the rules of evidence. It was not for the President, representing the Executive branch, but for the Court to decide whether

privilege existed here. Any other conclusion would be contrary
to the basic concept of separation of powers and the checks and
balances that flow from the scheme of a tripartite government
. . . We therefore reaffirm that it is "emphatically the province
and the duty" of this court "to say what the law is" with respect
to the claim of privilege presented.[2]

5. WHAT IS POLICE POWER?

Police power is the inherent power of a sovereign to govern—that is,
to subject individual rights to reasonable regulation for the health, safety,
morals, or general welfare of the public. Police power resides in the federal
and state governments, and has been granted by state constitutions to
counties and cities.

Regulations under police power involve, for example, (1) prohibition
against possession of potentially dangerous property, such as a sawed-off
shotgun, or potentially harmful property, such as opium, unless under
a medical permit; (2) prohibition against subdividing land unless in compliance with rules for orderly development; (3) specification of permitted
sizes and location of billboards; (4) specification of permissible building
heights, setback lines, and construction quality; (5) prohibition against
gambling, or operating houses of prostitution; (6) specification of land
uses by zone; (7) limitation of interest rates; (8) requirements concerning
vaccination; (9) requirements concerning food sanitation; (10) licensing
of pharmacists, attorneys, barbers, and many others; (11) regulation of
utility rates; and (12) prescription of minimum standards for conditions
of employment.

In general then, police power is the power to regulate in the public
interest for the general welfare, even at the expense of an individual
or group. However, regulation is limited by the U.S. and state constitutions. Government cannot forbid construction of a house by an avowed
communist under the guise of its police power because such a restraint
would constitute a violation of the equal protection clause of the U.S.
Constitution. But government could destroy valuable, evidently healthy,
yet possibly infected cattle to prevent the spread of hoof and mouth
disease, and it would not be obliged to compensate the owners (although
it usually does). Unless the disease is contained within a given geographical area by such drastic action, presumably it would soon envelop
the sacrificed animals and many others as well.

6. WHAT IS EMINENT DOMAIN?

Eminent domain is the inherent power of the government to take private
property for public use. Unlike the exercise of the police power, property
can be taken by government for a public use only upon payment of
just compensation to the owner.

J. B. Spalding was the owner of sixty acres of property on the outskirts of Chicago, which he had purchased for $1,500 per acre in 1955. The state needed twenty acres of J. B.'s property to construct a freeway. In 1968, a regional shopping center was constructed only one mile from J. B.'s property. As a result, his land was worth $10,000 per acre in 1974. Once the freeway was constructed, the remaining forty acres would be worth only $2,500 per acre, since its highest and best use would necessarily be changed from subdivision to mixed agricultural and residential use. How much money must Illinois pay J. B. as just compensation?

The state must pay $200,000 for the twenty acres taken and $300,000 for severance damage to the remaining forty acres. In this situation, just compensation is $500,000. *Severance damage* occurred because the value of the remaining forty acres was reduced from $10,000 per acre to $2,500 per acre. The concept is perhaps better illustrated by imagining the state taking only the elevators from a ten-story office building. The remaining portion of the building would have sustained severance damage.

Determination of the correct amount of just compensation is made by the judicial branch of government, generally with the benefit of a jury trial if either side so desires. Property may not be taken by government, regardless of the payment of just compensation, unless there is a present or contemplated future *public use and necessity* for such acquisition.

The newly elected City Council of Midvale decided that no new development should be permitted in the southern portions of town in order to preserve the existing agricultural environment. However, the area was already dotted with subdivisions; several utility trunk lines had been constructed and the city had collected property taxes based on subdivision values for years. Many landowners in the area had constructed streets, sidewalks, and storm drainage systems. Do the landowners seeking to subdivide have any legal recourse?

Yes. Under the doctrine of *inverse condemnation,* government, such as Midvale, must pay for property "taken" even though purportedly there is no exercise of eminent domain. "Taken" means damaged in that a substantial loss in market value occurs because of the governmental interference. The landowners may sue in inverse condemnation and recover damages equal to the loss in the value of their property. Although government may regulate development in order to protect the environment, it must pay damages caused when it disrupts development already in progress.

7. WHO IS A CITIZEN OF THE UNITED STATES?

> Herman Marshall was born in Ohio in 1970, the only son of Karl and Beatrice Marshalloff, resident aliens who had emigrated to the United States in full compliance with applicable immigration law. Is Herman a United States citizen?

Yes. The Constitution provides that all persons born or naturalized in the United States are citizens thereof, and of the state in which they reside. Thus, Herman need not be naturalized, a process whereby aliens, such as his parents, become U.S. citizens. Like any other citizen, however, Herman may lose his citizenship through *expatriation*. This may occur by (1) naturalization by or oath of allegiance to a foreign country; (2) service in foreign armed services; (3) employment by a foreign government; (4) voting in a foreign election; or (5) draft avoidance, desertion, or treason.

> Jacobo Hernandez Rodriguez, born in Mexico, is residing in San Antonio, Texas, as a lawful permanent resident alien. Is Jacobo entitled to vote in elections?

No.[3] The *franchise,* or right to vote, is limited to citizens of the United States. This discrimination does not violate the due process and equal protection provisions of the U.S. Constitution because the classification is considered reasonable. The alien still owes allegiance to a foreign power, and may lack the minimal knowledge appropriate for participation in democratic government. He can qualify for citizenship by routine *naturalization*.

8. WHAT FUNDAMENTAL PERSONAL RIGHTS ARE RECOGNIZED BY THE FIRST AMENDMENT TO THE U.S. CONSTITUTION?

In the U.S. Constitution, restraints upon the power of government are found principally in the Bill of Rights and the equal protection and due process clauses of the fourteenth amendment to the Constitution. (See figure 1–1.) The *Bill of Rights* is composed of the first ten amendments to the Constitution. It was adopted a few years after the Constitution because of a realization that the Constitution itself did not explicitly protect the individual from possible government abuse. The U.S. Constitution and state constitutions identify and protect specified fundamental rights of each individual.

Freedom of speech, the press, and assembly are among the fundamental rights recognized in the First Amendment, and applied to the states under the due process clause of the Fourteenth Amendment. They are essential

THE BILL OF RIGHTS AND OTHER SELECTED AMENDMENTS
TO THE UNITED STATES CONSTITUTION

I

Congress shall make no law respecting an establishment of religion, or prohibiting the free exercise thereof; or abridging the freedom of speech, or of the press; or the right of the people peaceably to assemble, and to petition the Government for a redress of grievances.

II

A well-regulated militia, being necessary to the security of a free State, the right of the people to keep and bear arms, shall not be infringed.

III

No soldier shall, in time of peace be quartered in any house, without the consent of the owner, nor in time of war, but in a manner to be prescribed by law.

IV

The right of the people to be secure in their persons, houses, papers, and effects, against unreasonable searches and seizures, shall not be violated, and no warrants shall issue, but upon probable cause, supported by oath or affirmation, and particularly describing the place to be searched, and the persons or things to be seized.

V

No person shall be held to answer for a capital, or otherwise infamous crime, unless on a presentment or indictment of a grand jury, except in cases arising in the land or naval forces, or in the militia, when in actual service in time of war or public danger; nor shall any person be subject for the same offense to be twice put in jeopardy of life or limb; nor shall be compelled in any criminal case to be a witness against himself, nor be deprived of life, liberty, or property, without due process of law; nor shall private property be taken for public use, without just compensation.

Fig. 1-1. The Bill of Rights and other selected amendments to the U.S. Constitution

VI

In all criminal prosecutions, the accused shall enjoy the right to a speedy and public trial, by an impartial jury of the State and district wherein the crime shall have been committed, which district shall have been previously ascertained by law, and to be informed of the nature and cause of the accusation; to be confronted with the witnesses against him; to have compulsory process for obtaining witnesses in his favor, and to have the assistance of counsel for his defense.

VII

In suits at common law, where the value in controversy shall exceed twenty dollars, the right of trial by jury shall be preserved, and no fact tried by a jury, shall be otherwise re-examined in any court of the United States, than according to the rules of the common law.

VIII

Excessive bail shall not be required, nor excessive fines imposed, nor cruel and unusual punishments inflicted.

IX

The enumeration in the Constitution, of certain rights, shall not be construed to deny or disparage others retained by the people.

X

The powers not delegated to the United States by the Constitution, nor prohibited by it to the States, are reserved to the States respectively, or to the people.

XIII

Section 1. Neither slavery nor involuntary servitude, except as a punishment for crime whereof the party shall have been duly convicted, shall exist within the United States, or any place subject to their jurisdiction.

Section 2. Congress shall have power to enforce this article by appropriate legislation.

Fig. 1-1. *(continued)*

XIV

Section 1. All persons born or naturalized in the United States, and subject to the jurisdiction thereof, are citizens of the United States and of the State wherein they reside. No State shall make or enforce any law which shall abridge the privileges or immunities of citizens of the United States; nor shall any State deprive any person of life, liberty, or property, without due process of law; nor deny to any person within its jurisdiction the equal protection of the laws.
(Sections 2, 3, 4, 5, refer to technical matters.)

XV

Section 1. The right of citizens of the United States to vote shall not be denied or abridged by the United States or by any State on account of race, color, or previous condition of servitude.
Section 2. The Congress shall have power to enforce this article by appropriate legislation.

XIX

The right of citizens of the United States to vote shall not be denied or abridged by the United States or by any State on account of sex. Congress shall have power to enforce this article by appropriate legislation.

XXIV

Section 1. The right of citizens of the United States to vote in any primary or other election for President or Vice-President, for electors for President or Vice-President, or for Senator or Representative in Congress, shall not be denied or abridged by the United States or any State by reason of failure to pay any poll tax or other tax.
Section 2. The Congress shall have power to enforce this article by appropriate legislation.

XXVI

Section 1. The right of citizens of the United States, who are eighteen years of age or older, to vote shall not be denied or abridged by the United States or by any State on account of age.
Section 2. The Congress shall have the power to enforce this article by appropriate legislation.

PROPOSED AMENDMENT—EQUAL RIGHTS FOR WOMEN

"Equality under the law shall not be denied or abridged by the United States or by any State on account of sex."

Fig. 1-1. *(continued)*

for a democratic society, for without them the electorate cannot be informed, issues cannot be raised and thoroughly examined, and candidates for office and government officials cannot present their views or be subjected to proper public scrutiny. Justice Hugo Black, a staunch civil libertarian, once declared:

> I do not believe it can be too often repeated that the freedom of speech, press, petition, and assembly guaranteed by the First Amendment must be accorded to the ideas we hate or sooner or later they will be denied to the ideas we cherish.[4]

Freedom of Speech

> Mac Cooper was slumped in his seat near the back of the dark and crowded movie theater. He was bored with the comedy on the screen; no one was laughing. He started to leave, but in a sudden fit of humor, he decided to stir up the lethargic audience. Instead of quietly walking to the rear, he ran down the aisle to the front and out the emergency exit, loudly shouting "Fire! Fire! Fire!" There was no fire, but in the ensuing stampede for the doors, an elderly woman died of a heart attack and ten persons were badly injured. When Cooper was prosecuted later for a variety of crimes, his defense was that he meant no harm and was exercising his constitutional right to free speech. Decide.

Guilty. Freedom of speech is not an absolute right; liberty is not license. The law, however, provides no effective *prior restraint*. In most situations, a fool or fiend can violate the rights of others before he can be subdued or restrained.

The hypothetical case is based on these often-quoted words of U.S. Supreme Court Justice Oliver Wendell Holmes, Jr.:

> The most stringent protection of free speech would not protect a man in falsely shouting fire in a theater and causing a panic . . . The question in every case is whether the words used are used in such circumstances and are of such a nature as to create a clear and present danger that they will bring about the substantive evils that Congress has a right to prevent. It is a question of proximity and degree.[5]

To avoid a "clear and present danger," the U.S. Supreme Court in 1951 upheld conviction of eleven leaders of the Communist Party of the United States who had been charged with advocating the overthrow of the U.S. government by force and violence. Chief Justice F. M. Vinson noted:

> Whatever theoretical merit there may be to the argument that there is a "right" to rebellion against dictatorial governments,

it is without force where the existing structure of the government provides for peaceful and orderly change.[6]

In another case, the U.S. Supreme Court found no clear and present danger of criminal action when a speaker apparently provoked some members of an ultra-conservative audience into throwing rocks. To avoid a riot, police ordered him to stop speaking, and when he refused they arrested him for a breach of the peace. He was convicted, but the U.S. Supreme Court reversed his conviction, Justice William O. Douglas declaring:

> A function of free speech under our system of government is to invite dispute. It may indeed best serve its high purpose when it induces a condition of unrest, creates dissatisfaction with conditions as they are, or even stirs people to anger. Speech is often provocative and challenging. It may strike at prejudices and preconceptions and have profound unsettling effects as it presses for acceptance of an idea. That is why freedom of speech, though not absolute . . . is nevertheless protected against censorship or punishment, unless shown likely to produce a clear and present danger of a serious substantive evil that rises far above public inconvenience, annoyance or unrest.

Justice Robert H. Jackson dissented strongly and was joined by three colleagues in the 5 to 4 decision:

> The Court has gone far toward accepting the doctrine that civil liberty means the removal of all restraints from these crowds and that all local attempts to maintain order are impairments of the liberty of the citizen. The choice is not between order and liberty. It is between liberty with order and anarchy without either. There is danger that, if the Court does not temper its doctrinaire logic with a little practical wisdom, it will convert the constitutional Bill of Rights into a suicide pact.[7]

Freedom of the Press

Because of the costs of producing modern metropolitan newspapers, many communities have only one major paper. Critics often complain that opinions contrary to the publisher's are not presented. Theoretically, everyone is free to start his own paper, and the government will not compel a publisher to provide others with space. However, the Federal Communications Commission requires radio stations and television stations to give equal time to the opposition party whenever a political speech is presented at no charge. This is understandable because only a limited number of broadcast channels are available and all are assigned under government licenses.

When newspapers do print stories, normally they may be sued for libel if what they say is defamatory and false.

The *New York Times* published a paid advertisement that told of alleged maltreatment of black students by police in Montgomery, Alabama. The ad stated that after students sang "My Country 'Tis of Thee" on the state capitol steps, their leaders were expelled from school; armed police surrounded the Alabama State College campus; and after protesting to state authorities, their "dining hall was padlocked in an attempt to starve them into submission." The police commissioner claimed libel, and a jury awarded him $500,000 in damages. The *Times* appealed. Decide.

Judgment for the *Times*. The U.S. Supreme Court granted special protection to persons who criticize public officials, even when what is said may be false. The court declared:

> The constitutional guarantees require . . . a federal rule that prohibits a public official from recovering damages for a defamatory falsehood relating to his official conduct unless he proves that the statement was made with "actual malice"—that is, with knowledge that it was false or with reckless disregard of whether it was false or not.[8]

Does this liberal rule on criticism of public officials extend to others who are famous or notorious and in the public eye? Yes. When a football coach sued the Curtis Publishing Company and a former army general sued the Associated Press, the Court denied relief even though statements printed were libelous.[9]

How to treat printed materials or films that are or may be considered by some to be obscene or pornographic has been a problem for the U.S. Supreme Court. In 1957, Justice William Brennan, speaking for the majority of a divided court, declared:

> Implicit in the history of the First Amendment is the rejection of obscenity as utterly without redeeming social importance . . . We hold that obscenity is not within the area of constitutionally protected speech or press . . . However, sex and obscenity are not synonymous. Obscene material is material which deals with sex in a manner appealing to prurient interest. The portrayal of sex, e.g. in art, literature and scientific works, is not itself sufficient reason to deny material the constitutional protection of freedom of speech and press. Sex, a great and mysterious motive force in human life, has indisputably been a subject of absorbing interest to mankind through the ages; it is one of the vital problems of human interest and public concern.[10]

As attitudes toward sex and its display became more liberal or relaxed in society, the Court was confronted with case after case that could not be neatly disposed of under a blanket rule for the entire country. In

1966, it stated that for material to be deemed constitutionally obscene, all of the following must be established.

1. The dominant theme of the material taken as a whole appeals to a prurient interest in sex.
2. The material is patently offensive because it affronts contemporary community standards relating to the description or representation of sexual matters.
3. The material is utterly without redeeming social value.

In 1969, the court held that private possession of obscene materials, involving no commercial sale on the open market, was permitted and protected by the First Amendment. Justice Thurgood Marshall stated:

> If the First Amendment means anything, it means that a state
> has no business telling a man, sitting alone in his own house,
> what books he may read or what films he may watch.[11]

In 1973 the Supreme Court made another attempt to provide a usable, reasonable guide as to what is obscene without doing violence to freedom. It said that regulation of obscenity must be limited to works that depict or describe sexual conduct as specifically defined by the applicable state law. Moreover, three new tests would be applied.

1. Whether the average person applying contemporary community standards would find that the work, taken as a whole, appeals to the prurient interest
2. Whether the work describes in a patently offensive way, sexual conduct specifically defined by the applicable state law
3. Whether the work, taken as a whole, lacks serious literary, artistic, political, or scientific value.[12]

To guide legislatures, the court gave two examples of materials that could be outlawed: "(a) patently offensive representations of ultimate sexual acts, normal or perverted, actual or simulated; and (b) patently offensive representations or descriptions of masturbation, excretory functions, and lewd exhibition of the genitals." Although the Court held that state community standards could be used as the gauge, within a year it overturned a Georgia conviction of a theater manager for violating the state's public decency law by showing the film *Carnal Knowledge*. The problem of what is constitutionally obscene has obviously not been resolved.

In 1971, the *New York Times* published portions of the Pentagon Papers. The documents were classified top secret by the executive branch of government, which requested the U.S. Supreme Court to issue an injunction preventing any further publication of their contents. Never before had the United States sought to enjoin a newspaper from publishing information in its possession. Is restraint of publication of military documents different from restraint of publication of obscene documents?

Yes. Justices Peter Stewart and Byron White noted:

> The only effective restraint upon executive policy and power in the areas of national defense and international affairs may lie in an enlightened citizenry—in an informed and critical public opinion. . . . Yet it is elementary that the successful conduct of international diplomacy and the maintenance of an effective national defense require both confidentiality and secrecy. Other nations can hardly deal with this nation in an atmosphere of mutual trust unless they can be assured that their confidences will be kept.[13]

9. HOW HAVE THE FIFTH AND THE FOURTEENTH AMENDMENTS BEEN INTERPRETED BY THE SUPREME COURT?

The Fifth Amendment contains the following profoundly important and broadly applicable clause forbidding actions by the federal government that violate the integrity of any person, be he citizen or not:

> No person shall be . . . deprived of life, liberty, or property, without due process of law.

After the Civil War, the Fourteenth Amendment extended this vital clause to possible actions by state governments, and added these significant words:

> No state shall make or enforce any law which shall abridge the privileges or immunities of citizens of the United States, . . . nor deny to any person within its jurisdiction the equal protection of the laws.

In recent decades, the U.S. Supreme Court has relied on these principles in deciding a variety of cases:

1. Establishing the rights of blacks to attend integrated schools[14]
2. Rejecting the railroad practice of providing different accommodations for white and black passengers[15]
3. Invalidating a poll tax (a tax of a specified standard amount on each head) as a prerequisite for voting in a state of Virginia election.[16] (The Twenty-fourth Amendment has expressly abolished the poll tax for both federal and state elections.)
4. Effectively striking down restrictive covenants, or clauses, in real property deeds whereby private owners could refuse to sell their

homes to nonwhite buyers.[17] (The U.S. Supreme Court ruled that state courts could not issue orders enforcing such a covenant against anyone who violated it.)

Other cases have involved the rights of persons accused of criminal actions:

1. Whereas the federal courts had long excluded from trials illegally obtained evidence, in 1961 it extended this rule to all the states, even in noncapital offense cases.[18]
2. It established the right of an indigent defendant to legal counsel even in noncapital offense cases.[19]
3. It required that police inform a suspect of his right to remain silent, to have legal counsel present during interrogation, and to be told that any statement he makes may be used in court against him.[20]
4. It held that although electronic surveillance, eavesdropping, or "bugging" could be used by police, a warrant must first be obtained (even for use in public places).[21]

Some critics think that the court has gone too far in protecting the rights of the accused. However, prosecutions and convictions have not declined under the new rules, although police work has become more difficult.

Relying on the Fourteenth Amendment, the U.S. Supreme Court also initiated necessary moves to end what Justice William O. Douglas referred to as "the 'rotten borough' system, notorious in the Western world."[22] Chief Justice Earl Warren observed that in Alabama, for example, ". . . there had been no reapportionment of seats in the Alabama legislature for over sixty years." In calling for a "one-man, one vote" standard, he pointed out:

> Legislators represent people, not trees or acres. . . . By holding that as a federal constitutional requisite both houses of a state legislature must be apportioned on a population basis, we mean that the Equal Protection Clause requires that a State make an honest and good faith effort to construct districts, in both houses of its legislature, as nearly of equal population as is practicable.[23]

10. IS FREEDOM OF RELIGION A FUNDAMENTAL RIGHT?

> John Lambe, a Union High School senior, asked Ms. Jean Torre, the school librarian, to purchase a Christian Bible for the school library. She refused, declaring that under the doctrine of separation of church and state the school could not require students to salute the flag if this violated their religious beliefs. By the same reasoning, a public school purchase of the bible would be unconstitutional. Is Ms. Torre correct?

014690

No. It is true that pupils cannot be required to participate in the ceremony of saluting or pledging allegiance to the American flag in a public school. However, the "establishment of religion clause" means that government may not set up a Church; it may not pass laws that aid one religion, aid all religions, or prefer one religion over another. No person can be punished for entertaining religious beliefs or for refusing to salute the flag because of religious convictions. No tax can be levied to support any religious activities or institutions. However, the purchase of a bible for a school library is simply providing a literary classic for the educational benefit of all students and is not prohibited. Religious belief is an important internationally manifested cultural phenomenon and is therefore an appropriate subject for study.

The line of separation is not clearly drawn, however. Exemption of church buildings and parochial schools from real property taxation has traditionally been held not to violate the "establishment of religion clause." Donations to religious organizations may be deducted as charitable contributions in income tax returns.

11. WHEN ACCUSED OF A CRIME, WHAT ARE YOUR FUNDAMENTAL RIGHTS?

The legislative branch of government decides what activities are criminal and therefore prohibited. Commission of a proscribed act is a crime. Of course, the legislative branch of government has no power to prohibit that which the constitution protects. The executive branch of government, in turn, has the responsibility of arresting persons reasonably thought to have committed criminal acts; and the judicial branch has the responsibility of conducting trials of the accused. In the process, it is conceivable that the executive branch or the judicial branch could treat those accused of crime in an unfair manner, thereby increasing the possibility that innocent persons may be convicted.

To minimize this possibility, certain fundamental rights are guaranteed by the U.S. Constitution, as well as by state constitutions, to every person so accused. He (or she) is presumed innocent and must be proven guilty beyond a reasonable doubt. He has a right to (1) have a speedy trial, (2) have a trial by an impartial jury, (3) be represented by a qualified attorney, (4) not testify or be a witness against himself because this could be incriminating (that is, show his involvement in a crime), (5) compel attendance of witnesses on his behalf, (6) confront all adverse witnesses, and (7) have adverse witnesses cross-examined by his counsel.

Unfortunately, the enumerated rights are not always scrupulously respected. Trials are sometimes delayed because of the sheer volume of work at hand; a poor person who cannot raise the prescribed bail may thus languish in jail for weeks or months even though he may eventually be found innocent. The jury may be prejudiced. The defendant's attorney may be incompetent or ineffective, especially if assigned to the case by the judge and required to serve with little or no compensation. Needed witnesses may not be available or may forget or misrepresent the facts. The defendant may lack the financial ability or sophistication to conduct a suitable pretrial investigation. Nevertheless, most judges and attorneys, under some prodding by decisions of the U.S. Supreme Court, have sought to translate the listed rights into reality and they are usually upheld in practice.

Before Arrest

> Officer Dick Bruno observed a van equipped with bright polka-dotted curtains. He "just knew" that hippies who smoked marijuana rode around in such vehicles and so he stopped the van. While searching it, he found a tin of marijuana in the glove compartment. He arrested the driver, Russell Rondan, for illegal possession of marijuana. Is Russell guilty?

Russell is guilty of illegal possession of marijuana. However, the U.S. Constitution prohibits unreasonable searches and seizures. A search is unreasonable unless it is made with probable cause that a crime has been or is about to be committed, and the exigencies of the situation preclude prior application to a proper judge for a search warrant. The presence of curtains on a vehicle does not constitute probable cause, and the search by Officer Bruno was therefore unconstitutional. Although Russell is guilty, the law will not permit evidence obtained in such an illegal search to be used against him in a trial. The purpose of this law is to discourage unlawful searches by the police, but the result here will be that Russell will not be convicted. It is better to protect the many innocent persons against unreasonable searches and seizures by the police, than occasionally to capture and convict a criminal by such means.

> Don Miller was convicted of possession of marijuana. Police officers had found him asleep in the front seat of his automobile, which he had parked in an abandoned private parking lot, after running out of gas in the early hours of the morning. He was arrested on an outstanding traffic warrant revealed by a radio check. The officers observed electronic and musical equipment on the back seat. Miller refused the officer's request for permission to take the property into custody for safekeeping. Nevertheless, the officers took the goods to the police station and searched the pockets of his coat, discovering marijuana in one of them. Was the search constitutional, or should the conviction be set aside?

The California Supreme Court reversed the conviction and set defendant Miller free.[24] The Court held that the U.S. Constitution compelled the officers to honor Miller's stated desire that they leave the property in the car undisturbed and, further, that even a proper taking for safekeeping would not have justified a search of the coat's pockets, an area within the zone of defendant's *reasonable expectation of privacy*. In order to justify a search and seizure without a warrant, the "exigencies of the situation" must render the search "imperative." Thus, individuals generally are free from search and seizure by police or any other arm of government unless and until a search warrant is obtained from the judicial branch of government represented by a proper judge. Presumably he examines the facts in a calm, dispassionate manner and authorizes search and seizure only for good and compelling reasons.

In a significant expansion of the police power to search without a warrant, the U.S. Supreme Court recently ruled that after a lawful arrest, the person and his vehicle may be searched without a judge-granted warrant. If evidence (such as contraband drugs) is found of unrelated and possibly more serious offenses, the driver may be cited for the more serious offense. Formerly, under the Fourth Amendment to the Constitution, which prohibits illegal searches and seizures, such evidence would be barred in court as illegally obtained. Civil libertarians have criticized the new decision as an unwarranted extension of police power to harass the innocent, who outnumber the guilty.

Before Trial

> Juan Corona was convicted of the murder of twenty-six migrant farm workers in California. Before his conviction, what protections were guaranteed him under the Constitution, pending determination of his innocence or guilt?

Unlike the accused in certain less serious offenses, Juan Corona was unable to gain freedom pending trial by posting bail. In 1972 the California Supreme Court ruled that bail may be denied whenever an individual is accused of a particular type of crime thought by the legislative branch to warrant or justify such denial. Although the applicable law is in transition, criteria thought to justify the refusal of bail would include the reasonable possibility that the accused would flee or commit additional serious wrongful acts while awaiting determination of guilt or innocence of the original crime.

A person accused of committing a crime may obtain a *change of venue* (to transfer the case to another county or judicial district) if, in the judgment of the court, he cannot receive a fair trial where the alleged crime was committed because of local publicity and aroused public opinion. This right was successfully asserted by Juan Corona, but the jury of the distant county subsequently found him guilty of committing the multiple murders.

A celebrated murder trial lasted more than six months. Is this a denial of the constitutional right to a speedy trial?

No. The guarantee of a speedy trial pertains to its commencement, not its duration. State legislatures have generally prescribed the maximum permissible delay in criminal cases. In Illinois, for example, the basic time is 120 days, unless the court grants the prosecution an added sixty days to complete its investigation or unless the defendant asks for more time. If not prosecuted within the time limits, he must be released and may not be again prosecuted for the particular crime.

Former Chief Justice Earl Warren once stated that "Justice delayed is justice denied." He urged legislative funding for additional courts to help handle the staggering case loads caused by increased population, more crimes, more automobile accidents, more divorces, more consumer complaints about products and services such as medical care, more criminal appeals, and more civil rights disputes. Further delays may originate with growing demands on the limited time of skilled counsel and because of time-consuming pretrial investigations. Often defendants in criminal cases seek delays to allow the public to lose interest in the matter as aroused emotions subside. In many places, however, unwanted and undesirable delays of a year or more before trial are common.

At Trial

As noted, the U.S. Constitution gives every person accused of a crime the right to a trial by an impartial jury. Hopefully a jury protects the accused from oppression by the government as represented by a possibly corrupt or overzealous prosecutor, working closely with a cruel, compliant, or biased judge. It interposes between the accused and his accuser the commonsense judgment of a group of laymen. Conviction has traditionally required the unanimous agreement of twelve jurors. In May, 1972, the U.S. Supreme Court held that states may provide for conviction by less than unanimous verdict.[25] The court did not disturb the unanimity requirement in federal courts. Subsequently, the Supreme Court affirmed a state conviction based upon nine votes of twelve jurors.[26] No minimum number of jurors is required by the Constitution in state or federal cases and the trend has been to reduce the number in the interests of speed and economy.

Gino Ferolli was arrested for going 120 miles per hour on Highway 15 in his sports car. He told the judge that he was without funds and desired representation by an attorney. Is he entitled to the assistance of a public defender or other court-appointed attorney?

Yes, but only if he is indigent and cannot afford to hire his own attorney. As interpreted by the courts, the U.S. Constitution and state constitutions require that the government provide, at public expense, representation for persons accused of crime, whether a felony or misdemeanor. There is no right to any particular attorney, however. Nor does this right extend to civil actions.

After Conviction

The U.S. and many state Constitutions prohibit cruel and/or unusual punishment of persons convicted of a crime. The California Supreme Court has held that the death penalty is both cruel and unusual.[27] Pointing out the declining number of executions in the United States (1963, twenty-one; 1964, fifteen; 1965, seven; 1966, one; 1967, two; 1968 through 1971, zero), it concluded that the death penalty had become unusual. Moreover execution was deemed to be cruel because it "degrades and dehumanizes" all who participate in the proceeding.

Critics insist that capital punishment is not a deterrent to crime. Moreover, they cite statistics showing that most persons sentenced to die in recent years have been poor, male, and members of minority groups. This argument was especially important in the decision of the U.S. Supreme Court banning capital punishment.[28] However, many observers concluded from this that the court would permit a state to utilize the death penalty if it were made mandatory for all persons convicted of defined crimes, such as multiple murders or the killing of another by someone serving a life sentence in prison. Consequently, more than twenty states have reinstituted mandatory capital punishment for specified crimes. The validity of these statutes must eventually be decided by the U.S. Supreme Court.

12. MAY A PERSON BE JAILED FOR FAILURE TO PAY HIS DEBTS?

Upon dissolution of their marriage, the court ordered Albert Gregory to pay his wife, Denise, support in the amount of $250 a month for two years. Albert failed to make his third payment and Denise wrote him a reminder. She added that if payment were not received soon, she would have him jailed. Albert disregarded the threat because he recalled from a class in law that one cannot be imprisoned for nonpayment of a debt. Is he correct?

Albert is generally correct. However, nonpayment of support ordered by the court is a violation of the court's order, which is a *contempt,* and may be punished by either imprisonment or a fine. Of course, Denise could not "have him jailed." A court hearing would be scheduled and Albert would have an opportunity to show that his nonpayment was not voluntary or wrong because he was unable to pay. A person unable to pay support cannot be held in contempt for failure to comply with a court order to pay.

13. IS THERE A FUNDAMENTAL RIGHT TO TRAVEL BETWEEN THE STATES AND LIVE IN ANY OF THEM?

The U.S. Constitution provides that no state may abridge the privileges or immunities of citizens of the United States. The purpose of the privileges and immunities clause was to help weld the United States into a unified whole. No state can treat citizens of other states differently than it treats its own citizens. Current controversy concerning the privileges and immunities clause revolves around qualifications for welfare and voting when persons move from state to state. The trend of decisions of the U.S. Supreme Court has been to reduce the residency requirement for voting to a minimum number of days required for recordkeeping. With welfare applications, there is a similar trend.

14. IS THERE A FUNDAMENTAL RIGHT NOT TO BE DISCRIMINATED AGAINST?

The U.S. Constitution provides that neither the federal government nor any state government can deny to any person the equal protection of the laws. State constitutions contain similar language. This clause requires that persons under like circumstances be given equal protection and security in the enjoyment of their property, their persons, and their liberty. Persons similarly situated must receive equal treatment from government. If persons are not similarly situated, it is constitutional for government to treat them differently. Thus it is not discriminatory to draft men only into military service; or to tax persons in different income brackets on a progressive scale. Neither the U.S. Constitution nor the state constitutions prohibit discrimination by private individuals in their strictly private relations with each other.

Race

> Charles Crawford and Rosemarie Reed decided to marry. When applying for their license, they were informed by the County Clerk that they could not legally marry because Charles was Caucasian and Rosemarie was not. Is the County Clerk right?

The County Clerk is wrong. There is a fundamental right to marry the person of one's choice; classification by race to determine eligibility for marriage is unreasonable. Thus, any law prohibiting such marriage violates the equal protection clause and is unconstitutional. However, if the law prohibited marriage between members of the same sex, the classification of sex would be reasonable and, hence, would not violate the equal protection clause.

> The charter of the Benevolent and Protective Order of Elks prohibits the membership of black persons. Is this discrimination unconstitutional?

No. The constitution limits only government, not private individuals. The Elks are not a part of the state government nor is state government participating in the discrimination. Therefore, the constitutional guarantee of equal protection is not violated. However, a government may discourage such discrimination by refusing to issue licenses for the sale of intoxicating liquor in lodges where such discrimination exists.

The Poor

> Joe Barnes was involved in an auto accident while uninsured. Furthermore, he was unable to post a cash bond to guarantee the availability of funds to the injured person if he, Barnes, should later be found liable. Therefore, in compliance with state law, his driver's license was suspended. Joe asked his attorney whether the state could constitutionally discriminate against poor persons by suspending their licenses because they cannot afford to *post a bond*. What would his attorney answer?

The law is constitutional. Singling out poor persons for special restrictive treatment is not generally valid. Here, however, involvement in an accident rather than economic status is the basis for the classification. Moreover there is an overriding public concern to promote safe driving by financially responsible drivers. Before revocation of his license, a fair procedure must be followed to establish that it is at least reasonably probable that Joe was liable.

> The California Supreme Court held that the imprisonment of a traffic violator because of his inability to pay the fine violated the equal protection clause.[29] The reasoning of the court was that an indigent who would pay his fine if he could must be given an option comparable to an offender who is not indigent. Does that rule of law mean that nobody can be jailed for failure to pay a fine?

No. If the sentence prescribed by statute is simply jail, so that either a rich person or poor person could be jailed, no violation of equal protection occurs. It is only when the sentence may be "Jail or a $100 Fine" that discrimination against the indigent occurs.

Women

A tavern owner challenged the constitutionality of a California statute that prohibited women from working as bartenders. The California Supreme Court ruled that "the saloon days of the Wild West are long gone," and a bartender need not be strong enough to resist inebriated customers. Hence, a law restricting women from such an occupation, while not restricting men, is discriminatory and violates the equal protection clause. The court continued:

> Women, like Negroes, aliens, and the poor, have historically labored under severe legal and social disabilities. Like black citizens, they were, for many years, denied the right to serve on juries in many states. They are excluded from or discriminated against in employment and educational opportunities. Married women in particular have been treated as inferior persons in numerous laws relating to property and independent business ownership and the right to make contracts. Laws which disable women from full participation in the political, business and economic arenas are often characterized as "protective" and beneficial. Those same laws applied to racial or ethnic minorities would readily be recognized as invidious and impermissible. The pedestal upon which women have been placed has all too often, upon closer inspection, been revealed as a cage.[30]

Would this court require the Philadelphia Eagles professional football team to accept a female fullback candidate? Not likely. Where the discrimination is reasonable, it is permissible. Interestingly, in 1974, the Little League admitted girls to full membership for amateur baseball competition.

Residency

> Fairview, the home of a major state university, adopted an ordinance requiring candidates for the city Council to be residents of the City for at least three years. The local citizenry feared the election of students if students were enfranchised (i.e. given the vote.) Joe Portman, president of the inter-fraternity council, decided to run for a seat on the Council. Joe, a resident for only one semester, had never paid any property tax, and admittedly knew nothing about city government. Is Joe entitled to be a candidate?

Yes. The U.S. Constitution prohibits as unnecessary and unreasonable a requirement that one must be a resident of the state for as long as ninety days in order to hold public office.[31] The Court did not specify an acceptable minimum period and this time has been set at thirty days in California, for example. It is deemed irrelevant that new residents may happen to know less about state and local issues than old residents.

1. Ms. Jan Griffiths, an alien from the Netherlands, was refused permission to take the Connecticut bar examination. She was refused the opportunity to become licensed as an attorney solely because of her alienage. Is such denial constitutionally permissible?

2. Miss Barbara Papish, a graduate student in a state university in Missouri, was expelled for distributing a newspaper containing "indecent" speech. The newpaper contained a political cartoon depicting policemen raping the Statue of Liberty and the Goddess of Justice. The caption read "with Liberty and Justice for All." Also included was an article entitled "Mother .... (expletive deleted) Acquitted." Was her expulsion lawful?

3. The Miami Herald editorially assailed the personal character of Pat Tornillo, candidate for the state legislature. Florida law required newspapers, in such circumstances, to print the candidate's reply.
   a. Does the Florida law violate the First Amendment?
   b. Does a law requiring publication of a retraction when falsehoods are published also violate the Constitution?

4. Massachusetts prohibits the contemptuous treatment of the U.S. flag in public. Valarie Goguen wore a small U.S. flag sewn to the seat of her pants. Was this "contemptuous treatment" and as such a crime?

5. The California constitution disenfranchises felons—that is, deprives them of the political rights and privileges of free citizens, notably the right to vote and to hold public office.
   a. Is that law valid when applied to a felon who has "fully paid his debt to society?"
   b. Would a state be justified in disenfranchising a bigamist or polygamist?

6. Can a city limit its demographic and market growth rate in housing and in the immigration of new residents in order to maintain or improve the quality of urban life by avoiding the congestion, pollution and expense that result from expanded population? Suppose such a plan "happened" to exclude blacks by effectively excluding proposed low-cost housing projects?

7. California pays money to disabled workers. However, payments are denied females who are "disabled" because of pregnancy. Is such exclu-

sion arbitrary and discriminatory and therefore unconstitutional? Does it make any difference that any disability of a male results in payment?

8. Does a female have a constitutional right to have an abortion; that is, to cause termination of her pregnancy?

9. Should the U.S. Constitution be amended to:
   a. Permit the state to require recitation of a prayer in public schools?
   b. Permit the use of illegally obtained evidence if the judge reviews it before submission to the jury and decides that it should be used?
   c. Require that bail be imposed, if at all, on a sliding scale related to ability to pay, and that a person without money be released on his own recognizance except in very serious crimes?
   d. Require that newspapers and magazines provide equal space to a political opponent whenever they print an editorial in opposition to his candidacy for office?
   e. Require that the loser in a civil action that goes to trial pay not only all court costs but also reasonable attorney fees of the winning party (who otherwise normally must pay his own way, and thus may be victimized)?
   f. Abolish the right of any person to own a hand gun unless licensed under strict controls?
   g. Abolish the death penalty for all crimes?
   h. Require election of the President and Vice-President by direct vote of the people rather than through the electoral college as now?
   i. Give equal rights to women?
   j. Limit the rate of income tax that may be imposed on any person or corporation?
   k. Establish the right to life of the unborn after conception unless abortion is necessary to save the life of the mother?

10. In September, 1974, President Gerald Ford granted former President Richard M. Nixon "a full, free, and absolute pardon . . . for all offenses against the United States which he . . . has committed or may have committed or taken part in during the period from Jan. 20, 1969 through Aug. 9, 1974." President Ford acted pursuant to the pardon power conferred upon the President by Article II, Section 2 of the Constitution. In justification of this unprecedented action he said:
   a. "Serious allegations and accusations hang like a sword over our former President's head, threatening his health as he tries to reshape his life, a great part of which was spent in the service of this country. . . ."
   b. "Many months and perhaps years would have to pass before Richard Nixon could hope to obtain a fair trial by jury. . . ."

c. "A former President, instead of enjoying equal treatment with any other citizen accused of violating the law, would be cruelly and excessively penalized either in preserving the presumption of his innocence or in obtaining a speedy determination of his guilt in order to repay a legal debt to society."

d. "During this long period of delay and potential litigation, ugly passions would again be aroused, our people would be polarized in their opinions, and the credibility of our free institutions of government would again be challenged at home and abroad. In the end the courts might well hold that Richard Nixon had been denied due process and the verdict of history would be even more inconclusive with respect to those charges arising out of the period of his Presidency. . . ."

e. "My conscience says it is my duty, not merely to proclaim domestic tranquility, but to use every means I have to insure it."

f. "I do believe . . . that I, not as President, but as a humble servant of God, will receive justice without mercy if I fail to show mercy."

g. "Finally, I feel that Richard Nixon and his loved ones have suffered enough, and will continue to suffer no matter what I do. . . ."

Many critics objected that President Ford's action violated the concept of "equal justice under law"—the words engraved above the entrance to the U.S. Supreme Court building in Washington. They said he should have postponed any decision on clemency or pardon until a determination of Mr. Nixon's guilt or innocence had been reached by trial as in the cases of all other Watergate defendants. Do you agree? Review each of President Ford's arguments; can each be applied to all the Watergate defendants? Could they be applied to draft evaders and military deserters involved in the Vietnam War? To many other persons accused or convicted of crimes? Should anyone, unless he be a dangerous criminal inclined to violence, be sent to jail?

2

YOU, LAW, AND THE COURTS

1. WHAT IS LAW?

Law is a body of principles and detailed rules of conduct that can be enforced in courts. In the United States, the application of these principles to human behavior to achieve order and justice in society is the responsibility of the judicial branch of government.

Criminal Law and Civil Law

The legislative branch deems certain conduct to be injurious to the people in general and therefore prohibits it. Such conduct becomes a crime—a public offense—and the applicable law is called *criminal law*. Armed robbery, for example, is a crime. In most crimes, the victim (not the public) is directly wronged. Theoretically, he may seek damage from the criminal; usually prosecution is undertaken by the state and conviction gives nothing to the victim.*

Civil law is the body of principles applicable to conduct between individuals where the public is involved only incidentally or not at all. In the case of marriage, for example,

---

* California has an unusual law which permits needy victims who are injured in crimes of violence to collect up to $10,000 from the state for medical expenses, up to $10,000 for lost wages, and up to $3,000 to finance a retraining course if the victim is injured so badly he or she needs to learn a new occupation.

rules are established for the creation, continuation, and dissolution of the relationship. But normally only in case of divorce or death does court action become necessary.

By no means is the law, either criminal or civil, capable of "giving every person his due," which is the classic definition of justice. However, substantial justice has been consistently realized by the American judicial system. Criminal law emphasizes the rights of the innocent to liberty. Thus, to convict an accused person, he or she must be proven guilty beyond a reasonable doubt and to a moral certainty. Under so stringent a test, doubtless some guilty people are allowed to go free, but this is deemed a low price for the added assurance that very few, if any, innocent persons are deprived of their lives or liberty or property by erroneous conviction. The civil law similarly provides reasonable and peaceful solutions to conflicts arising in modern human relationships.

Substantive Law and Procedural Law

> The sky was clear, the sun was bright, the highway was wide, and Don Martin felt exhilarated as he roared along in his sports coupe at 95 mph in a 55 mph zone. A police siren jarred him to a sudden stop. Don explained that he was hurrying to attend his wedding that evening in Tyler, Texas. The officer, unsympathetic, issued a citation for speeding and added: "Take my advice as a wedding present: slow down and you'll get there." Don arrived in time without further incident and exchanged marriage vows with Brenda Bennett before the Reverend Eugene Richards. The ceremony was performed without lights because of the energy crisis. What legal rules are involved in this drama?

One's legal rights and duties are specified and defined by the *substantive law*. A speed limit for motor vehicles is a common example of a substantive criminal law. Qualification of parties and ceremonial requirements for marriage are examples of substantive civil law.

Procedural law dictates the mechanics of administering the substantive law, as when it provides a speeder with the option of either submitting to on-the-spot arrest and confinement in jail, or promising to appear in court at a future time. One may or may not be guilty of the substantive criminal law which forbids speeding, for example. Procedural law provides a mechanical framework through which substantive law is applied.

Laws enacted by Congress and interpreted and applied by the federal courts, are called federal laws. State laws are enacted by state legislatures and interpreted and applied by state courts. In the next section we shall see how legislatures carry out their law-making responsibility and how courts can sometimes function to create laws.

2. HOW IS LAW CREATED?

The primary function of the legislative branch of government is to determine what laws ought to be enacted or amended or repealed and to act on them by voting. As we saw in our chapter 1 discussion of the legislative branch, administrative agencies are sometimes created to help with the work load, especially in areas that require technical expertise.

The body of laws enacted by the legislative branch is called the *written law*. Those of federal and state legislatures are called *statutes;* those of local governments, such as cities and counties, are called *ordinances*.

Although the role of enacting law is constitutionally delegated to the legislative branch of government, the judiciary may also, in effect, "make" law by virtue of its obligation to determine the constitutionality of the law and to apply such law to the facts of a given controversy. In 1896 the U.S. Supreme Court upheld a Florida statute requiring Negroes to sit at the rear of railroad coaches.[1] Fifty-eight years later, the same Court overruled its prior decision and held that discrimination based on race was inherently unequal and, therefore, unconstitutional.[2] The Supreme Court in effect "made" new law by overruling its former decision and superseded the state law in question.

> The city council of Carmel-by-the-Sea adopted an ordinance prohibiting tree-climbing and sitting or standing upon monuments, planted areas, or fences in public parks and streets. The preamble to the ordinance cited an "extraordinary influx of undesirable and unsanitary visitors . . . sometimes known as 'hippies'." Defendant Ann Parr was convicted of violating the substantive criminal law by sitting on the grass in a park. Might a court question the constitutionality of this law?

Yes. The ordinance was declared unconstitutional as being discriminatory against "an ill-defined social caste whose members are deemed pariahs by the city fathers."[3] The court noted that it has been "consistently vigilant to protect racial groups from the effects of official prejudice, and we can be no less concerned because the human beings currently in disfavor are identifiable by dress and attitudes rather than by color." Thus, in addition to "making" law by interpreting statutes, courts create law through decisions that negate statutes or speak where legislators are silent.

> In divorce proceedings initiated by Don Martin's bride, his attorney, J. Bartholomew Slipp, contended that divorce was not possible. He argued that the marriage was already illegal, or nonexistent, since it was performed in darkness and the witnesses were unable to see anything at all! The court held, however, that the defect was not vital in that one could not witness, or see, vows

even in the light; that witnessing occurred with ears, not eyes. Thus the marriage was originally legal and divorce now appropriate. Did the court "make" law?

Yes. The legislative branch had previously enacted the written law that a ceremony must be "witnessed" in order to result in a legal marriage. Here the court interpreted the word *witness,* and the decision becomes a part of the body of law called *unwritten law,* even though it is actually written in the form of a printed court opinion. It is also frequently referred to as *common law,* a term traceable to medieval England. When the thirteen American colonies declared their independence in 1776, they decided to retain the large body of legal principles already established in England. These principles are also referred to as the common law.

In accordance with the doctrine of *stare decisis* (Latin: to stand by decided cases) a subordinate court must adhere to decisions and interpretations of higher courts. Thus, a decision by one high court, such as a state supreme court, defining or exemplifying *gross negligence* would become a part of the unwritten common law of that state. With only limited exceptions, decisions of the U.S. Supreme Court are binding upon all courts.

Stare decisis helps to make the law stable, predictable, and uniform for all who come before the courts with cases in which the facts are essentially the same. It helps lawyers to advise clients with greater confidence: "This is how the Supreme Court ruled on a similar case in the past." It helps trial judges to decide cases with greater skill and efficiency: "Give me supporting appellate cases for your point of law, counselor!" It relieves the appellate courts of the need to repeat the laborious process of establishing basic rules of law whenever similar cases arise. Yet if conditions change over the years, the Supreme Court may overrule itself for strong and compelling reasons. This it sometimes does, whereupon the new rule prevails into the indefinite future—under the doctrine of *stare decisis,* updated.

3. WHERE IS THE LAW LOCATED?

Federal written law, enacted by Congress, is located in a set of volumes called the *United States Code,* the contents of which are arranged by subject matter. Federal written law enacted by independent administrative agencies is located in a set of volumes called the *Federal Register,* also arranged by subject matter. Federal unwritten, or decisional, law is found in the written opinions of the federal courts located in volumes called reporters. U.S. Supreme Court opinions are located in the official reports of the court published by the government. They may also be found in the privately published *U.S. Supreme Court Reporter.* Opinions of the U.S. court of appeals are located in the *Federal Reporter;* those of the U.S. district courts are located in the *Federal Supplement.* All court opinions are arranged chronologically.

State written law may be found in a set of volumes called codes, the contents of which are arranged by subject matter. There is a volume for the Penal Code, for the Vehicle Code, and so forth. Written laws enacted by independent administrative agencies of the state, and typically called rules and regulations, are located in volumes called the Administrative Code and are arranged by subject matter. State unwritten, or decisional law, is found in the written opinions of the state appellate courts located in volumes called reports, officially published like their federal counterpart. In addition to official state reports, there are privately published *regional reporters* containing the decisions of appellate courts within several states. For example, the *Southern Reporter* contains appellate decisions by the courts of Alabama, Florida, Louisiana, and Mississippi. Other sections of the country are covered by other regional reporters.

Reporters for both federal and state courts are found in law libraries, which are usually located in the county courthouse. They are available to the public.

Ordinances of cities and counties are usually not published in any volume or book. Rather copies are maintained on file by the county or city clerk.

4. WHAT INFORMATION IS CONTAINED IN A CASE CITATION?

A *case citation* refers to the system of identifying published opinions of appellate courts. It consists of the name of the case (the names of the litigants), the volume number, abbreviation of the particular report or reporter, page number, and year of decision. Thus, *Mauney* v. *Gulf Refining Co.,* 193 Miss. 421, 9 So. 2d 780, 1942 reveals that the written opinion on appeal by Mauney against Gulf Refining Company is located in volume 193 of the Mississippi official reports at page 421, and also in volume 9 of the Southern regional reporter, second series (a new series begins after volume 300 is reached), at page 780. The year of the decision was 1942. The citation does not reveal the nature of the case. *Furman* v. *Georgia,* 408 U.S. 238, 33 L. Ed. 2d 346, 92 S. Ct. 2726, 1972 refers to three separate reporters, because all written opinions of the U.S. Supreme Court are separately reported three times: the first being the official report published by the government and the others being unofficial reports published by private companies.

5. WHAT IS A COURT?

A court is a tribunal presided over by one or more persons called *judges* in the case of trial courts and *justices* in the case of appellate courts.

Trial courts conduct the original trials; *appellate courts* review the results reached in prior trials conducted in inferior, or subordinate, courts. The label *inferior* does not refer to the quality of justice obtainable but to the level of the court in a series. Inferior, or lower, courts handle the bulk of all cases, but the matters in dispute involve smaller sums of money and less serious crimes.

Most cases are never appealed: the cost may be considered prohibitive in time, money and peace of mind; one has had "his day in court"; although one may not be pleased with the outcome he may be advised by counsel that there is no appealable error of law in the proceedings. Accordingly the trial is crucial, and the trial judge is the powerful and final dispenser of justice for most persons involved in litigation.

The word *court* is commonly used to describe the place where the court convenes ("I'll see you in court!"); all persons there assembled, including judge, attorneys, clerks, witnesses, parties, and public ("Court is in session."); or even the person presiding ("If the court please, may I be heard at this time?").

6. WHAT IS A TRIAL?

A *trial* is a formal procedure before a court conducted for the purpose of resolving disputed *questions of fact* or *of law,* in accordance with applicable law. Trials normally do not take place in appellate courts.

Belinda Burroughs signed up for ski instruction at Heavenly Mountain in Idaho. Eric Blond, certified ski instructor, fitted Belinda with rental skis. He then taught her how to snowplow, and in the process, obtained her telephone number. In the afternoon after her lesson, Belinda decided to show her newfound skills to Dick Bryant, a powder freak whom she had met during lunch over a mug of hot wine. However, her show was short. Belinda fell and suffered a spiral fracture of her right leg, just above the ankle. Her bindings had failed to release her boot from the skis when she fell. Belinda decided to sue Eric on the theory that he had carelessly adjusted the bindings too tightly. Who will win?

No one knows who will win because the facts have not been determined. Did Eric secure the bindings too tightly? Did Belinda, or anyone else, tamper with the bindings after they were set by Eric? Did the bindings fail because they were too tight, or because Belinda had allowed ice to accumulate beneath her boot? A trial will determine the answers to these and all other factual contentions. In the trial Belinda will be the *plaintiff,* since she is seeking to recover *damages* (money) from Eric, who is called the *defendant.* The entire proceedings, ultimately resulting in a resolution of the controversy, are frequently referred to as a *lawsuit* or *litigation.*

Trials are generally conducted as public hearings. However, attendance can be restricted for security reasons, when one or both parties request privacy, and there is no overriding reason why the public should be informed of evidentiary details of the dispute.

> In August 1971, Earl Warren, Jr., and his wife appeared in court in Sacramento, California, concerning dissolution of their marriage. The judge ruled that the dissolution proceedings would be closed to the public. Mrs. Warren contended that the court was influenced by Earl Warren, Sr., former Governor of California and Chief Justice of the U.S. Supreme Court. What good cause would justify conducting the trial in private?

Cases involving children, who might be affected unfavorably by a public hearing, may be held in private. A closed trial means that the press is also excluded, as in the Warren case which involved child custody. Closed trials are rare, and even then, the final results are made public.

7. HOW MANY TRIAL COURTS ARE THERE?

State

Every state has a basic, or principal, trial court. In California, for example, it is called the Superior Court and one is located in each county, with as many branches or departments as are necessary to conduct the business of the respective county. Sparsely settled counties may be more than adequately served by a single Superior Court judge, whereas populous counties may require dozens, or even a hundred or more, and their duties may be specialized. A court may then be referred to by the type of case it handles. That is, felony cases are handled by a criminal court; divorce matters by a divorce court; probate matters by a probate court, and juvenile matters by a juvenile court. In New York, the basic trial court is anomalously called the Supreme Court.

Generally the basic trial court hears all controversies except those of minor importance, which are handled by subordinate courts.

To facilitate the handling of large volumes of litigation, state legislatures have established courts subordinate to the basic trial court. Accordingly, in California, the Board of Supervisors for each county has divided it into judicial districts. A district with 40,000 or more inhabitants has a municipal court. In smaller districts, municipal court business is handled by a justice court. Judges of the justice court are called *magistrates*. Basically the municipal court hears cases involving $4,999 or less, misdemeanors, and traffic infractions.

California, like most states, also has small claims courts designed to provide a speedy, inexpensive, and informal method of settling civil claims up to a maximum of $500. The figure varies among the states; in most it is lower. Judges of the municipal or justice court preside. No legal documents need to be prepared other than a simple notice, which is served on the defendant. There are no rules of evidence and no jurors. In the interests of economy, simplicity and celerity, normally attorneys are not allowed to represent litigants in small claims court. Each party speaks for himself, telling his version of the dispute, and presenting any supporting documents. The judge may ask some questions and then without any elaborate argument or research, he decides. Sometimes he may do so immediately; often his clerk will mail the decision to the parties. Corporations are artificial, legal persons, and so when they use small claims courts to collect debts, they may be represented by employees who are attorneys. Some critics complain that this gives the corporate plaintiffs an unfair advantage. They also say that small claims courts were meant to help "the little guy" and yet are usually used against him by corporations seeking collection of overdue accounts.

Federal

The federal government has one basic trial court, the U.S. district court. The country is divided into ninety-three districts, each with a court. In populous areas, the geographic districts are small; in rural areas, they are large and bear no necessary relationship to state boundaries. U.S. district courts conduct trials concerning federal matters, such as federal crimes, enforcement of federal statutes, and certain civil cases between citizens of different states. U.S. district court judges are appointed by the President and confirmed by the Senate to serve for life. In settling controversies, the U.S. district court applies its own procedural law, and the substantive law of the state where it is located or the federal substantive law, whichever is more appropriate.

8. WHAT IS AN APPELLATE COURT?

An appellate court is a tribunal with power to review the decisions and proceedings conducted by lower courts. This court works from a verbatim record of what transpired in a lower court; it does not listen to witnesses, accept evidence, or have a jury.* It accepts as true the facts that were determined in the trial court, which considered all the witnesses' testimony and other evidence. Accordingly, the only function performed in the lower court that is reviewable by an appellate court is the determination of questions of law, not fact. However, the appellate judges may "weigh," or evaluate, the evidence as presented in the trial court and

---

* A notable exception exists in disputes between states when the U.S. Supreme Court does have original, or trial, jurisdiction.

then decide whether, as a matter of law, it is sufficient to justify the verdict or judgment.

Questions of law arise in the trial court whenever the judge rules on objections made by attorneys and permits or disallows certain evidence, or instructs the jury as to what legal principles ought to be applied. Of course, a question of law, not fact, arises whenever the constitutionality of a law is an issue. A jury does not decide whether a statute is constitutional.

If the appellate court determines that the trial court erroneously applied or interpreted the applicable substantive or procedural law, it may overrule the trial court, or vacate (annul) the decision and send the matter back for a new trial in compliance with the law.

9. HOW MANY APPELLATE COURTS ARE THERE?

State

The California court structure (fig. 2–1) is comparable to that of most other populous states in that there are two levels of appellate courts: the district court of appeal and the supreme court. (In New York, the highest court is called the court of appeal, but in most states this court is named the supreme court as in California.) An unsuccessful litigant in a civil or criminal trial has the right to appeal to the district court

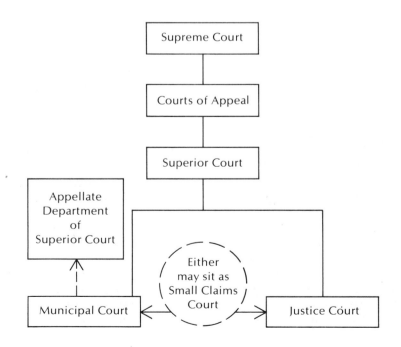

Fig. 2-1.
The California court system

of appeal, which must rule upon or decide the relevant questions of law presented. Except in certain criminal cases, the supreme court decides only the controversies that it chooses to decide. In addition to these two courts, the appellate department of the superior court has limited appellate jurisdiction. It reviews decisions of the municipal, justice, and small claims courts.

Justices of the California Supreme Court are appointed by the governor, to complete the term of the justice who has died or retired. The governor acts on recommendations of the State Bar Association, to which all lawyers licensed to practice in the state must belong. His appointment must be confirmed by a special Commission on Judicial Qualifications. When the remainder of the particular twelve-year term is completed, the justice must appeal to the electorate for confirmation for another full twelve years. If the justice is rejected, the procedure for appointment and confirmation of a new justice is followed again. Thus the political pressures of popular elections are minimized.

Justices of the California district courts are appointed and then confirmed through elections for twelve-year terms by voters within their respective districts. California is divided into five districts, each with one court of appeal with as many divisions, justices, and courtrooms as are necessary to handle their business. In California, as in most states, judges of trial courts may be initially appointed by the governor but they do run for reelection—for six year terms—and may face opposing candidates in those nonpartisan contests.

Federal

The United States likewise has two principal courts with appellate jurisdiction, the U.S. court of appeals and the U.S. Supreme Court. Although it informally reviews all matters properly submitted, the U.S. Supreme Court formally hears and decides only cases that it selects and they must involve federal law, including the Constitution, arising from either the federal or state court systems. The United States is divided into eleven circuits, or areas, each with a court of appeals, which reviews decisions of the U.S. district courts located in districts within their respective circuits. Any appeal from a U.S. court of appeals is to the U.S. Supreme Court. In addition, the U.S. Supreme Court may consider an appeal from the highest court of a state by a process called *certiorari* (Latin: to be informed), when a federal constitutional question is presented. All federal appellate court judges are appointed by the President and confirmed by the Senate to serve for life.

Figure 2–2 depicts the federal court structure, which, in addition to the principal courts, includes the court of military appeals, court of claims, court of customs and patent appeals, customs court, and tax court. Each of these is a special court restricted to hearing particular types of cases.

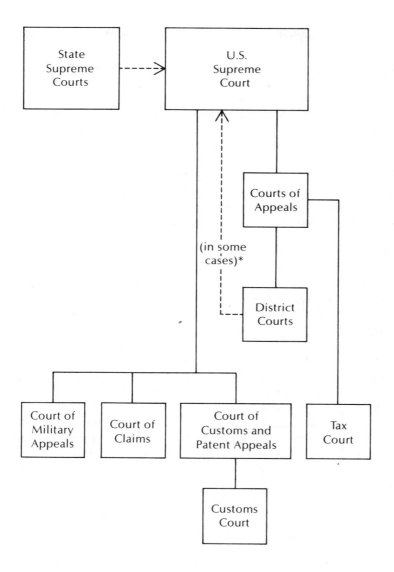

*For example, when a district court has held a federal law to be unconstitutional, and an agency of the government is a party.

Fig. 2-2.
United States Court
system

10. HOW IS A CASE BEGUN?

Civil

If Belinda Burroughs decides to sue Eric Blond for the broken leg she suffered after his ski instruction, her attorney will begin the case by filing with the county clerk a document called a *complaint.* She is the *plaintiff,* and the complaint is prepared by her attorney, who is satisfied that she has a *cause of action,* or adequate basis for suing. The complaint contains plaintiff's statement of facts, called *allegations of fact.*

County clerks maintain files, in alphabetical order, of every case started in their respective counties. These records are open to the public. A filing fee (from $15 to $50 or more) is charged at the time of filing. When the complaint is filed, the clerk issues a *summons* (prepared by the plaintiff's attorney) by endorsing it on behalf of the court. The summons states, in effect, that the defendant has thirty days to respond to the complaint and that if he fails to respond, the plaintiff will win the case by default, and a judgment will be awarded the plaintiff accordingly. (A *judgment* is a final decision of the court.)

Belinda's attorney will arrange with a process server to have a copy of the summons and complaint personally served upon the defendant, Eric Blond. (A *process server* is in the business of serving legal documents upon defendants or plaintiffs and witnesses.) If Eric cannot be found, or if he evades service of the process, he may nonetheless be "served" by a combination of mail and publication of summons in a local newspaper. The service of a copy of the summons and complaint (or publication of summons) gives Eric notice that he has been sued and gives the court *jurisdiction,* or power, to decide the controversy.

Upon receipt of the summons and complaint, Eric's attorney files with the county clerk a document called an *answer,* and mails a copy to plaintiff's attorney. In the answer, Eric admits allegations of the complaint that he feels are true, and denies the rest. He may add affirmative allegations of fact that he contends are relevant and true. Eric's attorney could elect to demur to the complaint instead of filing an answer. A *demurrer* is used when allegations of the complaint, even if true, are insufficient to state a cause of action (which exists when a court would grant plaintiff a judgment if plaintiff's allegations were true).

> In his complaint plaintiff Archibald Puny alleged that defendant "wrongfully, viciously, and wantonly stuck out her tongue at plaintiff, causing great and severe mental anguish." Has Archi stated a cause of action in his complaint?

No. Even if plaintiff's allegations were admitted by defendant, there would be no judgment for plaintiff because simply sticking out one's tongue is not against the law, or conduct that calls for legal relief. Therefore, defendant would be well advised to file a demurrer, which would be sustained by the court, and the complaint would be dismissed.

Once Belinda's complaint and Eric's answer, called *pleadings,* are on file, the factual contentions of each party have been stated, and the factual issues of the case are said to be joined. These factual disputes will be resolved at trial.

Criminal

A criminal case is formally commenced by the making of an accusation. An *accusation* can be made by the district attorney (called an *information*) or the grand jury (called an *indictment*). In misdemeanor cases, the accusation is called a *complaint;* no summons is used. The grand jury is a panel of adult citizens empaneled by the court to investigate wrongdoing in the community. It acts under the guidance of a court and with the assistance of the district attorney.

11. IS AN ATTORNEY AT LAW NECESSARY?

> Angela Davis was charged with committing the crime of assisting the Soledad Brothers in their attempt to escape from custody during a courtroom appearance in Marin County, California, in 1971. During her trial her attorney moved (requested) the court to allow Ms. Davis to act as her own attorney during certain portions of her case. The District Attorney objected on the grounds that she would "put on her attorney hat" and, in effect, would testify without taking any oath to tell the truth, and without being subjected to cross-examination. Is one compelled to utilize the services of an attorney?

No. If reasonably qualified to do so, one has freedom of choice to rely upon one's own skill of advocacy, or lack thereof. However, the problem in the Davis case was one of using an attorney for portions of the case, leaving other portions, possibly speech-making portions, to the defendant, as attorney. This problem was resolved by the court in favor of Ms. Davis. She was subsequently *acquitted,* that is, found not guilty. And she did act as her own attorney when she made the opening statement on her own behalf, without taking any oath.

Attorneys, or persons acting as attorney for themselves, are not required to take an oath to speak the truth. Generally, a defendant's intimate involvement in the case, coupled with his lack of professional legal skills, prevents him from doing a good job as his own counsel. It has been said that the man who is his own lawyer has a fool for a client. If the court believes that a defendant who participates in his own defense would prejudice his case against himself, the court may rule that he or she must be represented by an attorney.

A person is not required to engage an attorney in prosecuting or defending civil lawsuits, although it is usually advisable.

12. HOW IS AN ATTORNEY LICENSED?

The practice of law is regulated by the state and by the courts, which grant licenses to practice within their particular spheres of authority, or *jurisdiction*. An attorney at law, or lawyer, licensed to appear in all the courts of a certain state requires a different license to practice in the U.S. district courts, another license to practice before the U.S. court of appeals, and still another license to practice before the U.S. Supreme Court. In addition, the conduct of attorneys is governed by written codes of professional ethics formulated by state bar associations. For good cause, an attorney's license before any or all courts may be suspended or even revoked.

Spiro Agnew, upon resigning as Vice-President of the United States, pleaded *nolo contendere* (Latin: I will not contest) to a criminal charge of income tax evasion. At the time he was licensed to practice law in all the courts of Maryland. Can Attorney Agnew be disbarred?

Yes. Mr. Agnew's license was revoked. A suspended license would automatically reinstate after a specified period, whereas a revoked license may reinstate only upon new application, if ever. Conduct that may result in action against an attorney includes conviction of a crime involving moral turpitude, dishonesty, and corruption.

13. HOW DO YOU FIND AN ATTORNEY?

Even though the practice of law is highly regulated, it is obviously important to locate an attorney willing and able to perform the desired services for a reasonable fee. No single attorney is an expert on all questions of law or varieties of legal service. Many attorneys specialize and will handle only certain types of problems. Some attorneys do engage in a general practice and undertake to perform any conventional legal service. This approach may be satisfactory to the client so long as the attorney does not undertake to do work that ought to be performed by a specialist.

In the medical profession, if one needs the services of a dermatologist, it is a relatively simple matter not to end up with a pediatrician; the telephone directory yellow pages carry at least these distinctions. The same cannot be said for the legal profession. As in the medical profession, however, general practitioners will usually refer the individual to a specialist if his talents appear necessary. In some cases, the specialist may be brought into the case by the attorney first consulted, to serve as an associate counsel with the consent of the client.

At the outset, a person in need of legal services must rely either on the yellow pages or on word-of-mouth recommendations from friends or business acquaintances. To some extent this situation has been improved in California by regulations that permit attorneys to demonstrate expertise in taxation, criminal law, or workmen's compensation law, and to advertise these specialties with small type on their stationery and office doors and in phone books.

14. HOW DO YOU RETAIN AN ATTORNEY?

Once you have found an attorney and met with him, you need to decide whether to hire him. It is entirely proper and usually prudent to ask in advance (as when telephoning for an appointment), what a preliminary consultation will cost. Some attorneys charge nothing, especially if they are hired to do further work. Most will ask a modest fee. This can be a wise expenditure, especially when it provides useful advice for avoiding some legal difficulty. It is reassuring to get to know and trust a "family attorney," so that he will be consulted without hesitation when legal problems arise.

If you do decide to hire him, he will work for you as an *independent contractor,* a person engaged to exercise his own judgment and skill in performing a specific task. Although the client may not control the actions of his attorney, the latter is in a special *fiduciary relationship* with his client. This means that he is obliged to perform his services with scrupulous good faith and honesty toward his client. He must make a full disclosure of all relevant and material (important) information that comes to his attention. The relationship is also confidential; the attorney is committed to professional secrecy. He may not disclose to a third party, not even to a judge in court, what his client has revealed to him. (A rare exception would be where such disclosure is necessary to avoid a fraud on the court.)

An attorney may be hired by oral agreement. Preferably, it should be done by written agreement, so that both parties know what is to be done and on what financial terms. Either way, the services to be performed, including various possible contingencies of outcome or procedure, the time within which they are to be performed, the channels of communication the client may expect, the probable amount of court costs and method for paying them, and the legal fee should be clearly understood by both attorney and client. An attorney may have a hundred or more clients at any given time. Each problem, or case, will typically involve telephone calls to the client, the court, opposing attorneys, and witnesses. These can consume a substantial part of the day. Since the attorney obviously must spend some time researching the law and drafting documents, it is no wonder that communication problems with clients sometimes arise.

15. HOW IS AN ATTORNEY PAID?

Attorney fees are normally agreed upon in private by the attorney and client. Generally there is no maximum when the client is an adult. Fees charged for services rendered to, or on behalf of, a minor are subject to approval by the court. If a fee charged an adult, however, is so exorbitant and disproportionate to the services performed as to "shock the conscience" of a court, it will be uncollectible and may even justify disciplinary proceedings against the attorney.

State legislatures have placed maximum (but not minimum) fee limitations upon attorneys for performing certain services, such as probate. (Probate here refers to services in connection with handling the estate of someone who dies.) The federal government regulates the maximum fee that may be charged for certain legal services, such as Social Security disability claims (which involve eligibility for disability payments).

Attorney fees tend to be higher in metropolitan areas than in either rural or suburban areas. In large cities, hourly rates for consultation or service may range from $35 to $75. Higher hourly rates may be expected in New York City, Washington, Chicago, and Los Angeles, especially when consulting large, prestigious firms.

When litigation may result in the receipt of money by the client, as in automobile accident cases, a contingent fee may be preferred by both parties. In such an arrangement, the attorney may receive from 25 percent to 50 percent of any recovery (for example, 25 percent upon filing action, 33⅓ percent if the case is tried, 40 percent if it is appealed). If there is no recovery, the attorney receives nothing. In a clear-cut case, a client theoretically may be better off financially if he hires an attorney for a fixed fee or lump sum, usually paid in advance, or on an hourly basis rather than on a contingent fee basis. However, rarely is a negligence case sufficiently clear-cut to make this alternative financially attractive to the client.

Where the services are more or less routine, a flat fee may be in order. For example, uncontested divorces frequently are obtained on such a basis for $300 to $500. Some clients *retain* an attorney for a certain payment per month or per year without regard to the amount of routine work, if any, performed. This procedure permits easy access to the attorney for advice and consultation and may result in maximum mutual benefits. The client is always responsible for paying court costs, notably filing fees and jury fees.

Persons who cannot afford the services of an attorney for a civil matter frequently will find such services available through a local Legal Aid Society for free or for a nominal charge. The person who cannot afford to engage the services of an attorney for a criminal matter may have a public defender or private attorney assigned to his or her defense, by the court, without charge. The U.S. Constitution requires that a state provide, at no expense, the services of an attorney at law in serious criminal cases. Contrary to what one might assume, public defenders tend to be extremely competent and aggressive defenders of the poor who are accused of crime. They are usually more experienced in handling criminal matters than are most private practitioners.

Having been hired by the client, an attorney may be fired for any reason at any time. Upon discharge by the client, the attorney is entitled to be paid a reasonable fee for services rendered to the date of discharge. This allocation problem is most acute in the cases of contingent fee contracts since it is impossible to measure the impact of initial work upon the final outcome of the case which measures the fee. A thoughtful attorney will discuss this possibility at the time of employment and will include a provision in the agreement providing for some method of allocation in advance of any misunderstanding.

16. WHAT PRETRIAL PROCEEDINGS ARE THERE?

Civil

Once a civil lawsuit has commenced, it may be a year or more until the date of trial. During this period each party has the right to engage in certain *discovery* practices designed to (1) educate each party as to the facts surrounding the controversy; (2) promote voluntary settlement of the controversy by revealing strengths and weaknesses in each case; and (3) eliminate surprises that might arise at the trial and lead to a miscarriage of justice.

depositions

> Belinda Burroughs hired Tak Sharpe as her attorney in her case against Eric Blond. Tak had drafted a complaint, and caused the summons and complaint to be served upon Eric. The defendant hired Perry Darrow as his attorney, and an answer had been prepared and filed. In his answer Eric admitted that he had adjusted Belinda's bindings but alleged that he was not negligent and had done it properly. He also alleged that Belinda was guilty of contributory negligence in that she was drunk at the time of her injury, and had allowed ice to form beneath her boots. The pleadings were in and the issues of fact joined. What is the status of the proceedings?

Tak seeks to recover a money judgment against Eric to compensate Belinda for her injury on the theory that Eric was *negligent,* or careless. Perry, on behalf of Eric, is contending that Eric was not negligent and that even if he was, Belinda was also careless of her own safety and, for both reasons, should be denied any money judgment. Both Tak and Perry needed more information in order to prepare their respective cases properly.

Tak wanted to know the exact setting Eric had used in adjusting Belinda's bindings; then he could seek expert advice as to what the proper setting should have been. Tak could simply mail a notice of taking *deposition* to Eric's attorney requesting that Eric appear in Tak's office in ten days to be questioned under oath with a court reporter present. During this deposition, which Eric must attend, Tak could simply ask him what setting he had used. Of course, Eric's attorney may wish to take Belinda's deposition at the same time.

> At a deposition of Belinda, Perry asked the following question: "Miss Burroughs, do you use birth control pills?" Tak immediately objected, shouting that he would not allow his client to be humiliated by the seemingly suggestive question of Perry. Must Belinda answer the question?

At the taking of the deposition, Perry cannot force Belinda to answer a question if she simply refuses. His remedy is to obtain a court order requiring her to answer if the question is deemed proper by the judge. If she then refuses, her entire case may be dismissed or other appropriate sanction imposed. (Perry is interested in the answer to this question because one possible side effect of birth control pills is that bones may become more easily subject to fracture. If Belinda suffers from such an effect, then perhaps a jury would find her contributorily negligent for skiing under the circumstances.)

written interrogatories

> After the depositions, Perry remembered some questions that he forgot to ask at deposition. He therefore sent the following written interrogatories to Belinda through her attorney:
>
> 1. Please state in writing the address of Dick Bryant.
> 2. Please state in writing each date you visited a doctor and the total amount of medical bills you have incurred.
> 3. Please state whether or not your medical bills are being paid by some insurance company, and if so, what is its name and the applicable policy number?
>
> What will happen if Belinda fails to answer the written interrogatories?

Again, the court may dismiss Belinda's case. This is the ultimate power of the court to compel the parties to comply with discovery procedures. Should Eric fail to participate in discovery, the court would strike his answer leaving the complaint unanswered. This would pave the way for Belinda to obtain an uncontested judgment, called a *default judgment.*

request for admission of facts   To avoid the necessity of proving medical expenses during trial, Tak assembled all the medical bills and mailed a document to Perry called a *request for admission of facts.* It contained the following statement:

> Plaintiff requests defendant to admit that the total medical expense incurred by Belinda in connection with her fractured leg was the sum of $378.64.

Perry decided to admit the alleged facts as stated, by forwarding an "admitted" response to Tak because he believed that Attorney Tak was ethical and would not submit forged medical bills. If Perry had refused, the court could assess a penalty against Eric equal to all expenses Tak incurred in proving the sum during trial.

motion to produce

> Perry believed that Belinda's diary would prove something of importance. He therefore filed a *motion to produce* with the court. It requested an order compelling Belinda to deliver her diary to Perry for inspection. Will the motion be granted?

Not unless Perry can demonstrate to the court specifically what may be contained in the diary that would be relevant to the issues in the case. For example, if Belinda denied taking birth control pills in her responses to written interrogatories, the following entry in her diary would be meaningful in the litigation.

Dec. 23

Dear Diary,
    I began taking birth control pills today because I'm going skiing next week.

Of course, it is doubtful that Perry would ever learn from a reliable source the existence or alleged contents of Belinda's diary. The motion to produce would be more effective, for example, if two or more parties had seen a document and thereafter one party refused to relinquish it.
    After the trial has begun, either attorney may ask the court for a *subpoena* (Latin: under penalty), a written order directing a person to appear in court and testify as a witness. If it is believed that he has

books or documents needed for a full disclosure of the facts, the court may issue a *subpoena duces tecum* (Latin: under penalty bring with you), under which he must bring the identified documents to court.

Criminal

In a criminal case, discovery is more limited because of the *privilege against self-incrimination*. This privilege, as a very general proposition, means that a defendant cannot be compelled to testify in a criminal case because he might incriminate himself. The prosecutor, however, has no need for such privilege. Therefore, the district attorney must allow examination of his evidence against the defendant, including names of witnesses, prior to trial. Physical evidence, such as weapons, clothing, stolen goods, and the like, may be impounded (seized and held) by the district attorney pending trial. But the defendant has the right to inspect all such evidence prior to trial.

17. WHEN DO PARTIES HAVE THE RIGHT TO TRIAL BY JURY?

Any party to a lawsuit has the right to trial by jury in cases "at law." There is no right to trial by jury in cases "in equity." The distinction between these two comes down through English history from medieval times when certain cases were determined by chancellors, as a matter of good conscience and equity or fairness. The chancellors were often clergymen who were aides of the king and trusted by the people. When a person could obtain no relief from a regular court, he would appeal to the king, who would refer him to the chancellor. In most cases, the aggrieved person would seek and obtain relief from a regular king's court, where a judge would decide possibly with the assistance of a jury. As a general proposition, the chancellors would decline to become involved in criminal cases and civil cases where money, or damages, were sought.

Today a given trial court may grant either legal or equitable remedies, but the formal pleadings are different. Some civil cases that are at law include (1) an action to recover money for injury possibly caused by negligence of the defendant; (2) an action for money for loss of earnings possibly caused by defamation of character by the defendant; (3) an action to recover money lost as the result of the defendant's alleged deceit; and (4) an action to recover money for profits lost due to alleged breach of contract by the defendant.

Some civil cases in equity are (1) an action for dissolution of marriage; (2) an action requesting the court to order the defendant to comply with his contract by performing as promised, and (3) an action requesting the court to award custody of a minor child. Note that basically no money damages that a court of law could award are sought. Thus, the remedy at law is unavailable or inadequate. No criminal cases are in equity. There is no right to trial by jury in equity cases, but the judge in most states may use an advisory jury, whose advice he is not obliged to take.

Since Belinda's case against Eric is at law, either party may demand that the trial be by jury. If neither party demands a jury, it is deemed waived and trial proceeds with the judge determining all factual contentions.

18. HOW IS A JURY SELECTED?

Prospective jurors usually are selected at random from voter registration lists in the respective counties. Those selected appear in court for *voir dire* (Old French: to say the truth) which is a process of questioning prospective jurors to ascertain whether or not they have any bias that would make difficult or unlikely their impartiality. Each attorney will naturally try to seat jurors who appear to be sympathetic to his client's position. Thus, a stern accountant may not be welcomed by the defendant in a criminal trial; a clerk who earns a low salary may not be wanted by the plaintiff in a civil action where damages sought for loss of future earning power exceed a million dollars.

In large cities, profit-seeking private companies provide voting records of jurors to attorneys who may face the same persons as prospective jurors in later cases. In major trials, where the stakes are high, sociologists and psychologists have been hired by lawyers to analyze the backgrounds and personalities of prospective jurors on the basis of available data about themselves and their communities, as well as their personal appearances. The idea is to predict their probable conduct in the forthcoming trial. The introduction of such new influences, if effective, can unfairly tilt the scales of justice—even though there is no certain way of predicting human behavior.

> On behalf of Belinda, Tak demanded a jury trial. On the day set for trial, Tak and Perry met with Judge Eagleton in chambers. Tak requested permission to personally voir dire the prospective jurors. Perry did not object. Will Judge Eagleton grant this request?

Probably. Judges have discretionary power to conduct voir dire themselves or to allow the attorneys to do so.

> Judge Eagleton granted Tak's request and ordered that the voir dire be conducted by the two attorneys. One of the questions Tak asked each prospective juror was whether he or she had ever been a ski instructor. One person answered yes. Is this sufficient evidence of bias, and what recourse does Tak have?

Bias is not necessarily bad; indeed everyone possesses some bias consistent with his heredity, education, family background, experience, and so forth. What matters is whether a bias would render a person undesirable as a juror in a particular case. If such a bias were established to the satisfaction of a judge, he would excuse the prospective juror *for cause*. Probably a prospective juror for Belinda's trial who was once a ski instructor would not be as impartial as someone without this experience. The judge could then excuse him for cause.

Even if no bias were demonstrable, each attorney in a civil action can challenge peremptorily and thereby excuse from service a limited number of prospective jurors (six, for example, in civil actions and more in criminal actions). The purpose of *peremptory challenges* is to permit parties to eliminate some prospective jurors for any reason or for no reason whatsoever.

> Perry observed Mr. Frank Josephs, a prospective juror, winking at Belinda in the hallway during a recess. When voir dire resumed, he asked Mr. Josephs the following question: "Mr. Josephs, I saw you wink at Miss Burroughs during recess. Did she wink back?"
>
> "No, sir."
>
> "Did you hope she would?"
>
> Tak objected. Judge Eagleton asked Perry the purpose of the question. Perry explained that if Belinda appeared particularly attractive to the prospective juror, such bias would tend to impair his impartiality. Was the question proper?

Probably not. Sex appeal is not a bias likely to cause a juror to lose his impartiality. However, Perry may be well advised to exercise one of his peremptory challenges!

Once the peremptory challenges are either exhausted or waived (given up or unused), the twelve seated jurors are sworn to discharge their duty faithfully and the trial begins. If it is expected to last very long, sometimes one or two extra jurors are also selected; they remain throughout the trial, but are included and asked to vote only if a regular juror withdraws because of illness or dies.

19. WHAT DOES A JURY DO?

In a trial by jury, the jury determines questions of fact that are disputed. The judge rules upon all questions of law and instructs the jury as to what law is to be applied to the facts. This proposition is the same in civil and criminal cases. If the jury returns a *verdict* in favor of Belinda Burroughs, it in effect is determining that the essential facts alleged by Belinda are true and those alleged by Eric are false.

A jury normally consists of twelve jurors, and in civil cases a verdict is reached when at least nine jurors are in agreement. In criminal cases in most states, the verdict must be unanimous. Any jury that cannot reach a verdict because not a sufficient number of jurors are in agreement is said to be *hung*. When a jury hangs, no verdict has been reached, and a new trial is necessary just as if no trial had been conducted.

There is a trend to reduce the size of juries and to reduce the number of jurors that must agree to arrive at a verdict in both civil and criminal cases.

20. WHAT IS THE ADVERSARY SYSTEM?

In the adversary system, the parties (generally acting through legal counsel) are truly opponents, each producing in the trial evidence that supports his position. In short, each party is openly slanted for himself and against the opponent. Each party earnestly asserts every conceivable reason why he should win. Every theory revealed and asserted is a theory considered. Truth depends upon openness. Deceit depends upon concealment.

Like the adversary system, the jury system is designed to help reveal the truth. Perhaps the best argument for the jury system is that a group of laymen can think of and consider much more than can a single individual. Also, plaintiffs in civil accident cases may expect more generous understanding of need from a jury; defendants in criminal cases may hope for greater compassion from at least one juror, which would suffice to bar conviction. The jury, observing an adversary trial, has the opportunity to consider every aspect of the entire case before reaching a decision. Although fewer than twelve jurors are used in selected civil and criminal trials in various states, no responsible observers propose abolishing the system itself, even though a smaller number would permit savings of time and money.

Whether or not a jury is used in the trial, the adversary system is the backbone of what is probably the most just legal system the world has known.

21. HOW IS A TRIAL CONDUCTED?

After the jury is impaneled in a civil case, the plaintiff through his attorney proceeds first because he has the *burden of proof*. In a civil case, the burden of proof is a mere preponderance of the evidence. If the jury feels that more likely than not the plaintiff is right, then they must return a verdict in his or her favor. In a criminal case, however, the burden of proof is much greater. The plaintiff is the State, represented by a *prosecutor,* who has the burden of proving the guilt of the defendant beyond a reasonable doubt and to a moral certainty.

On the day Belinda Burroughs broke her leg and while she was in the hospital, she told her father that Eric Blond, during the ski instruction, had fondled her each time she fell. This incensed Timothy Burroughs, Belinda's father, who demanded that Eric be prosecuted for attempted rape. The case came to trial months before the civil case and the jury found Eric not guilty. Does this mean that Belinda will lose her civil case?

No. Belinda's civil case concerns negligence in adjusting ski bindings. The criminal case concerned later physical acts. In some situations the identical act can result in civil liability and criminal penalty. For example, if Eric had deliberately struck Belinda in the face, damaging her two front teeth, he would have been civilly liable for damages and criminally responsible for *battery*. Theoretically he could win the criminal case and lose the civil case, or vice versa. The rationale for this result is in the different burdens of proof involved; moreover, the trials take place at different times with different personnel. Thus, there is no *double jeopardy,* or being tried twice for the same offense, which would be unconstitutional.

The procedures by which a criminal trial is conducted are substantially the same as in a civil case. However, in a criminal case, the defendant cannot be compelled to testify. The opposite is true in a civil case, unless his testimony would tend to incriminate him and possibly subject him to prosecution for some crime.

Figure 2–3 shows a floor plan for a typical courtroom. The procedures involved in a trial are depicted in figure 2–4.

Opening Statements

The plaintiff's attorney begins the trial by making an *opening state-ment*—a summary of what the plaintiff expects to prove in the ensuing trial. Thereafter, the defendant's attorney may, but need not, make an opening statement describing what he expects to prove.

Case-in-Chief

After the opening statements, the plaintiff puts on his *case-in-chief.* This consists of calling witnesses and introducing into evidence documents, photographs, or whatever bears upon the issues. *Evidence* is everything that the finder-of-fact (the jury, or judge when there is no jury) is entitled to consider in arriving at a determination of the facts. For example, the oral testimony of witnesses presented under oath is evidence; remarks of the attorney are not. He has not sworn to tell the truth because he is not a witness. Rather he elicits evidence, comments on it, and argues about its significance. Of course, if he is persuasive, the jury will be influenced by his interpretation of the facts presented by the witnesses.

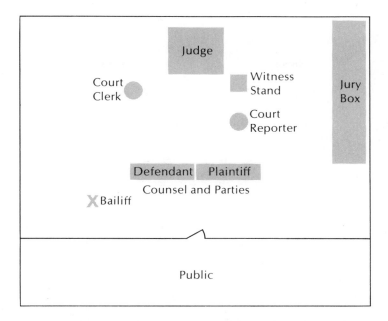

Fig. 2-3.
Floor plan for a
typical courtroom

The judge rules on all questions of what constitutes proper, or admissible evidence, since this is a question of law.

> Tak called Belinda as his first witness. She recited her story and Tak turned her over to Perry for cross-examination.
> "Isn't it a fact, Miss Burroughs, that immediately before you fractured your leg you got drunk on wine with some flake you picked up in the bar?"
> Tak objected to the question as argumentative and irrelevant. Will the objection be sustained or overruled?

The objection will probably be sustained. It improperly infers from her testimony that she got drunk and makes improper assumptions about her partner and how they met. Since these factors had not been shown to have a bearing on the issues under consideration, Perry will probably be instructed to rephrase or drop the question. (The judge has ruled on a question of law.)

> "Isn't it a fact, Miss Burroughs, that immediately before you fractured your leg you were drinking wine?"
> "Yes, sir."
> "With whom were you drinking wine?"
> "Dick Bryant."
> "And did you know him previously?"
> "No."

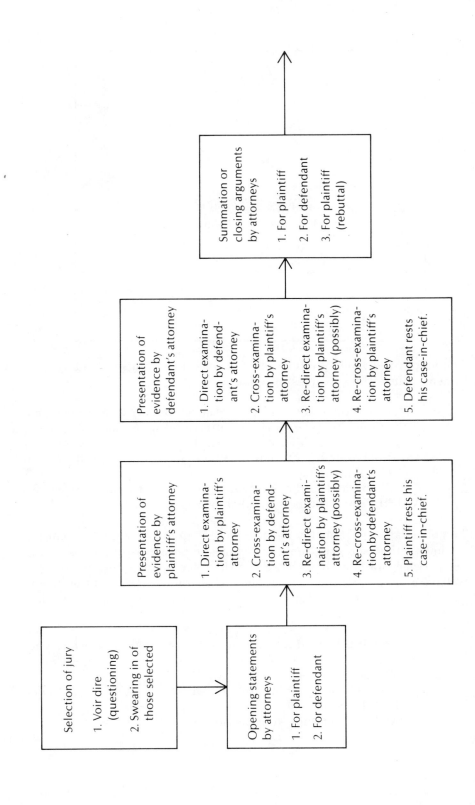

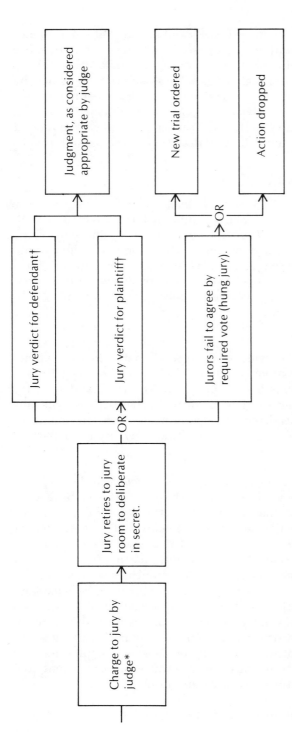

Charge to jury by judge*

Jury retires to jury room to deliberate in secret.

— OR →

Jury verdict for defendant†

Jury verdict for plaintiff†

Jurors fail to agree by required vote (hung jury).

Judgment, as considered appropriate by judge

— OR —

New trial ordered

Action dropped

*A judge may direct a jury to return a certain verdict when, if all testimony on one side were believed, the other party would be entitled to win.

†In rare cases, a judge may grant a judgment *non obstante veredicto* (J.N.O.V.), setting aside the jury's verdict because in his opinion it is wrong as a matter of law.

Fig. 2-4. Steps in a civil jury trial

After the plaintiff has called his witnesses and introduced into evidence all of his documents, he will rest his case. The defendant may move to dismiss the case, claiming that the plaintiff has failed to establish a *prima facie* (Latin: at first sight) case. If this motion is denied by the judge, the defendant may then make an opening statement (provided that it was not made earlier). He will begin his case-in-chief by calling his witnesses. Of course, the plaintiff has the right to cross-examine all witnesses of the defendant immediately after their direct examination.

Motion for a Directed Verdict

When each party has rested his case-in-chief, either one may ask the judge to decide the matter by making a motion for a directed verdict. The judge could, for example, properly direct a verdict in favor of the plaintiff if, despite the evidence presented by the defendant, a jury would still be required to find for the plaintiff. This situation is unusual. Even if the evidence appears to the judge to be legally conclusive for one party, he normally allows the jury to provide its independent opinion.

Summations

In most cases, after all the evidence is in, each party in turn argues his case before the jury. In other words, each may tell the jury (through his attorney) what he thinks he has proved in the trial, and thus try to persuade the jury to agree. The plaintiff begins with an opening argument, followed by the defendant's argument, then the plaintiff's concluding argument. Belinda's attorney, Tak, may argue in part as follows in his summation:

> Ladies and gentlemen of the jury, you have heard all the evidence. It is now your duty to determine the facts. If you believe by a preponderance of the evidence that the accident was caused by Mr. Blond, you will return a verdict in favor of Miss Burroughs.
>
> You are reminded that the medical bills of Miss Burroughs were $378.64 and that she missed one month of work, at her rate of pay of $700, and that for six months she was required to wear a cast from her waist to her toes, all because the defendant, this careless ski instructor Eric Blond, fastened the bindings down on the foot of Miss Burroughs with unprofessional disregard for her welfare. The evidence was clear: he was not thinking about bindings. He had other base and vile ideas on his mind and did not pay attention to his business. He was clearly negligent, and so it is your duty to return a verdict in favor of my client.

Perry might argue to the jury along these lines:

Ladies and gentlemen, it is our duty to pierce the veil of passion with which counsel is attempting to surround us, and look at the facts. The facts are: Miss Burroughs was not thinking about skiing; she was more interested in impressing her "date" after spending a good part of the day drinking wine. She was injured not because of any negligence of Mr. Blond. She is lucky she didn't break her neck by falling off a bar stool. Bindings won't work if they are all iced up, and if she had been sober she would have seen the ice when she put her skis back on. She was negligent and is trying to reap a bonanza at the expense of my client, a hard-working, sincere, and very professional gentleman. It is your duty to return a verdict for the defendant.

Instructions to Jury

Following the summation, Judge Eagleton will instruct the jury on the law to be applied to whatever facts the jury accepts as true. The instructions might include the following:

> You are instructed that statements of witnesses, sworn to tell the truth, constitute evidence that you may consider. Comments of the attorneys are not evidence.
> You are instructed that if defendant carelessly secured the bindings too tightly, he was negligent.
> You are further instructed that if the accident was caused by ice between the boot and ski, and not by the bindings, defendant was not negligent.

Deliberation and Outcome

After the instructions, the jury will retire to a jury room to deliberate, and by three-fourths vote, return a verdict. In criminal cases in most states, a guilty verdict requires unanimous agreement of the jurors. However, there is no constitutional requirement that the verdict be unanimous even in criminal cases; in some states conviction does not require unanimity. In cases where there is no jury, either because it was waived or the case is "in equity," the judge will perform the role of the jury, as well as the role of the judge. Of course, the outcome is then decided by one vote, the judge's.

If the jury comes back with a verdict that the judge considers wrong as a matter of law, he may render a contrary judgment, sometimes called a J.N.O.V., or a judgment *non obstante veredicto* (Latin: notwithstanding the verdict). In effect, the judge is the thirteenth man on the jury: he has the power to veto their decision and to substitute his own.

After a verdict that he disapproves, he may also entertain and grant

a *motion for a new trial* made by the losing party. To avoid the costs and uncertainties of another trial, the parties may compromise and agree to a modified award of damages.

22. HOW IS AN APPELLATE COURT CONDUCTED?

Procedures before an appellate court, federal or state, differ widely from trial court procedures. Appellate courts hear appeals from trial courts and do not conduct trials.* They operate from partial, or complete transcripts of the trial and accept as true all facts found by the trial court to be true. The only open question on appeal, as a general proposition, is whether or not the law was applied correctly during the trial proceedings. If so, the appeal is denied.

> The jury found Jack Malum guilty of possession of marijuana. During trial the judge instructed the jury, in part, as follows: "I instruct you that a crime is committed when one attends a party at which marijuana is being smoked regardless of whether or not the defendant did participate in such activity." Will an appeal by Mr. Malum likely succeed?

Yes. An appellate court would conclude that the court's instruction to the jury was an erroneous statement of the law. Mr. Malum did not receive a "fair" trial because mere attendance at a party is not in itself a crime. Yet the jury was instructed to the contrary. On appeal Mr. Malum would be called the *appellant* and the state would be the *appellee,* or *respondent.*

Appellate courts consist of three or more judges, called *justices.* Most of the justices' work is done in private and consists of reading *transcripts* (official copies of the proceedings in the trial court) of pending cases on appeal, studying law, and examining briefs filed by the attorneys for the appellant and appellee. A *brief* is a written legal argument addressed to the appellate court discussing or arguing why the judgment from below ought to be affirmed or reversed, or perhaps modified. Before a decision is made by an appellate court, oral arguments by the attorneys usually are scheduled. Oral arguments are sometimes not presented when the briefs on file adequately set forth the parties' contentions.

23. HOW IS A CASE ENDED?

The concluding pronouncement of a court is its *judgment.* A judgment may declare a status (e.g., divorced), order one to do or not do something

---

* The U.S. Supreme Court has limited jurisdiction to conduct original trials, as in controversies between two or more states.

(e.g., pay money damages or transfer title to land), impose a sentence (e.g., go to jail), or otherwise resolve a controversy.

> In an auto accident case, the jury became convinced that plaintiff Mary Hughes should be compensated for the leg she lost through amputation due to injury caused by the negligent operation of a truck by the defendant E. Ryder. The jury returned its verdict in her favor for $30,000. Is the verdict the voice of the court?

No. The *verdict* is the expressed opinion of the jury. Based upon the verdict the court may issue its judgment declaring Mr. E. Ryder to be the judgment debtor of Mary, the judgment creditor. This would be a judgment for damages. As noted earlier, if the court differs with the jury verdict, it can prevent a miscarriage of justice by ordering a new trial, or by simply entering judgment in favor of the loser.

In divorce proceedings the judgment of the court will be termination of the marriage. In a *paternity* case the judgment of the court will be a declaration that the defendant is or is not the father. In a suit to prevent someone from building a home in violation of zoning laws the judgment of the court will be an *injunction*. In a suit to compel someone to do that which was promised, the judgment of the court will be an order of *specific performance*.

In criminal cases the verdict will be guilty or not guilty. The judgment of the court must correspond to a verdict of not guilty; however, to avoid a miscarriage of justice, the court may overrule a jury and acquit a person declared guilty or may order a new trial.

Once a party has a judgment, the judicial branch of government has completed its work, unless the matter is appealed. Sometimes, a party to the action may return to the court if its orders are not obeyed. In divorce, for example, after support payments have been ordered, either party may return and request an increase or decrease because of changed circumstances and modified needs or ability to pay.

The winner—the judgment creditor—must secure enforcement of the judgment. This is accomplished by the executive branch of government. Assets of the loser—the judgment debtor—may be confiscated and delivered to the judgment creditor in satisfaction of the debt. An order of the court directing the sheriff to confiscate property of the defendant is called a *writ of execution*. Such a writ may be used to garnish (confiscate) part of the wages earned by the judgment debtor. After the judgment creditor has been paid in full, he must provide the judgment debtor with a *satisfaction of judgment*—proof that the debt has been paid.

The steps in a civil case are set forth in figure 2–5.

A criminal trial is procedurally very similar to a civil trial. The distinctions between the two are explored in the next chapter. Trial procedures in the U.S. district courts are governed by the Federal Rules of Civil and Criminal Procedure and closely resemble state procedures.

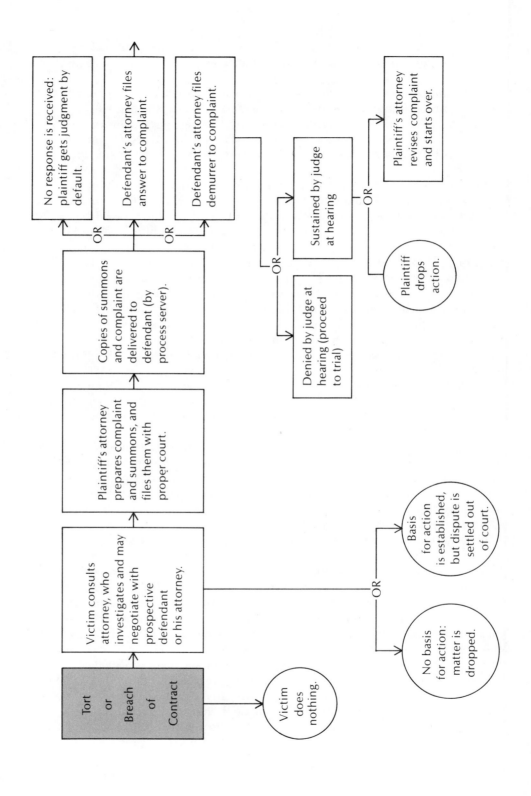

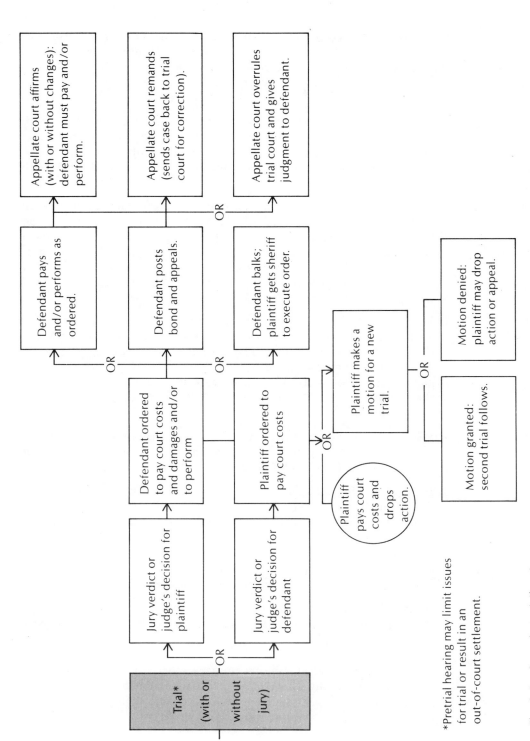

Fig. 2-5. Steps in a civil action

Trial*
(with or without jury)

OR

Jury verdict or judge's decision for plaintiff

Jury verdict or judge's decision for defendant

Defendant ordered to pay court costs and damages and/or to perform

Plaintiff ordered to pay court costs

OR

Defendant pays and/or performs as ordered.

Defendant posts bond and appeals.

Defendant balks; plaintiff gets sheriff to execute order.

OR

Appellate court affirms (with or without changes): defendant must pay and/or perform.

Appellate court remands (sends case back to trial court for correction).

Appellate court overrules trial court and gives judgment to defendant.

OR

Plaintiff pays court costs and drops action.

Plaintiff makes a motion for a new trial.

OR

Motion granted: second trial follows.

Motion denied: plaintiff may drop action or appeal.

*Pretrial hearing may limit issues for trial or result in an out-of-court settlement.

**CASES,
QUESTIONS,
AND
PROBLEMS**

1. In selecting a jury for a criminal trial, the judge ruled that the defense attorneys could not personally conduct voir dire. Rather, the judge insisted on personally interrogating all prospective jurors. Has the judge committed an error? Why might an attorney desire to conduct voir dire personally? How could voir dire be abused?

2. George Lewis, without provocation, hit Sam Fletcher in the mouth, knocking out his front teeth. What are the legal consequences, civil and criminal? Are the remedies involved mutually exclusive? Could George be civilly liable to pay damages and yet not be criminally responsible?

3. An indigent defendant in a criminal case is entitled to free representation by an attorney. This fundamental right is derived from the federal constitution. Does the Constitution treat defendants in civil cases differently? Do the rich always win because they can afford to hire very talented and very expensive lawyers? Should poor defendants be assigned the most experienced and most effective attorneys, who usually command the highest fees?

4. During a murder trial, the defense attorney moved for an order authorizing the court to convene the following day at the scene of the alleged unlawful killing. The stated purpose was to improve the jury's comprehension of the physical setting. May a trial, or any part of it, properly take place outside its regular courtroom? Are there objections to such procedure? What circumstances might justify the request?

5. What factors should an attorney consider in establishing the fee he intends to charge a particular prospective client? Should the services of an attorney be provided by one's employer as a fringe benefit?

6. In an action for dollar damages arising from an automobile accident, the plaintiff demanded that the trial be conducted without a jury. The defendant demanded a jury trial. Will a jury be empaneled? Is the right to a jury trial a valuable safeguard from oppression by the executive branch of government? Is a jury trial worth its cost in time and money or is efficiency more important? What considerations are involved in answering such a question?

7. In cases where a jury is a matter of right, would a jury consisting of five persons be more, or less, satisfactory than a jury of twelve?

8. There are many definitions of law. How would you define this term?

9. In your opinion, what are the proper objectives of law? Are order and stability among them? Can a society such as Nazi Germany provide order and a measure of stability without justice?

10. Law is considered a major instrument or force of social control in our society. What are other instruments, institutions, or forces that greatly influence human behavior, usually with no legal sanctions?

11. The Supreme Court has remained a small group of justices for almost 200 years despite the nation's tremendous growth in population and litigation. Should the Congress add more members, which is possible under the Constitution? Should the work of the Court be divided into civil and criminal branches? Should the ultimate court of appeal for designated cases be a lower court? If so, for what types of cases?

12. Litigation consumes time and money. Can you suggest ways to avoid it?

13. How are prospective jurors selected in your community? For what reasons are persons excused from service? What fees are paid for service? Do most employers keep their workers on the payroll while on jury duty?

14. Prepare a chart outline of the court system of your state and compare it with the system (for California) illustrated in the text.

15. Visit a local court and report to the class on what you observed. Spend a full day there, if possible. Ask an attorney friend or judge for suggestions as to when and where to visit. How do the proceedings differ from the typical television or motion picture presentations of trials?

II THE
SOCIAL ASPECTS
OF LAW

3

YOU AS VICTIM OR ACCUSED OF CRIME

1. WHAT IS A CRIME?

Most wrongful behavior, such as injuring another through carelessness, is a private offense between the persons involved. It is called tortious conduct, or simply a *tort.* Certain wrongful behavior, however, is deemed by the legislative branch of government to be so offensive as to be also injurious to the people in general and is, therefore, punishable in accordance with written law. Violation of such law is a *crime,* or public offense.* Many crimes are also torts: a person who burglarizes a home, for example, is guilty not only of theft, but also of disturbing the public peace, of trespassing, and of wrongfully converting another's

---

* Even in the absence of written law, *contempt of court* is punishable as a crime. In general, disorderly, contemptuous, or insolent behavior in the presence of the court, willfully violating its orders, or otherwise interfering with the judicial process is a criminal contempt. There is also civil, or quasi-criminal, contempt such as willful failure to pay child support as ordered by the court. The right to trial by jury extends to criminal, but not to quasi-criminal contempt. Contempt involves the inherent power of a court to enforce its process, rules, procedures, and respect. Most states have codified contemptuous conduct and they classify it as a misdemeanor.

property to his own use. Of course, the victim seldom sues a criminal in a civil action for damages, because recovery is so doubtful.

Under the U.S. Constitution, criminal statutes must describe the forbidden conduct clearly and precisely, so that all persons may know what is prohibited. Moreover, the courts will then construe or interpret the statutes strictly; and if all the elements of the crime as described are not present, the defendant must be found innocent. If found guilty, he may be placed on probation—that is, released under a suspended sentence for a period of time during which he is supervised by a probation officer and must maintain good behavior. (This is especially common for juvenile first offenders.) If not placed on probation, he may be required to pay a fine to the state; he may lose his liberty by being incarcerated in a county jail or state prison or other detention facility; he may even lose his life by being executed, although the constitutionality of the death penalty has not been definitively resolved by the U.S. Supreme Court as of this writing.*

With the exception of certain types of regulatory offenses and criminally negligent conduct, all crimes require a *criminal intent* or *mens rea* (Latin: guilty mind). There is no precise definition of criminal intent; the term includes felonious intent, malice aforethought, guilty knowledge, malice, and similar concepts signifying an evil state of mind. Intent does not mean *motive,* which is a need or desire that causes a person to act. A prosecutor need not prove the existence of a motive, and a good motive can never justify a criminal act (Robin Hood notwithstanding).

Criminal negligence is conduct that is without criminal intent, and yet is sufficiently careless or reckless to have criminal penalties prescribed for it by the legislature. Driving a vehicle while under the influence of drugs or alcohol, when injury or death results, is an example of criminal negligence. Violation of food quality regulations is an example of a *regulatory offense,* in which criminal intent is irrelevant (that is, not applicable) and therefore need not be proved.

> Preble Stulz desired to murder his wife, Evelyn. Mentally, he developed an elaborate plan to commit the crime. Has a crime occurred?

No. Criminal intent in the absence of any supportive overt act is not a crime. This proposition is true even if one confesses to such an intent.

---

* The U.S. Supreme Court held, in *Furman* v. *Georgia,* 408 U.S. 238 (1972), that the death penalty was unconstitutional when applied arbitrarily. The California Supreme Court held, in *People* v. *Anderson,* 6 C.3d 628 (1972), that the death penalty was cruel and unusual punishment as applied. The California legislature has reinstated the death penalty under certain limited circumstances, such as murder by a paid assassin. Presumably this legislation will satisfy the constitutional mandate of certainty in application of the penalty. (See California Penal Code Sect. 190, 190.1, and 190.2.) At this writing, constitutionality of the death penalty as newly reinstated has not been determined.

In furtherance of his plan, Preble asked his lifelong friend, Patrick Barnes, to assist him in murdering his wife. Has a crime occurred?

Yes. Regardless of the response of Patrick, Preble is guilty of the crime of *solicitation*.

Patrick Barnes responded that he would be happy to assist in the plan. Has another crime occurred?

No. An agreement to commit a crime, standing alone, is not a crime.

Patrick then purchased a pistol and ammunition, which were delivered to Preble. Has another crime occurred?

Yes. Preble and Patrick are now guilty of the crime of *conspiracy*. An agreement to commit a crime becomes a criminal conspiracy once some substantial act is performed by one or more of the conspirators in furtherance of their plan. Purchasing a gun and ammunition is such an act.

Early that evening, while his wife was preparing supper, Preble aimed the loaded gun at her through the kitchen window. But she kept moving, providing a poor target. Have any more crimes occurred?

Yes. Preble has now committed the crime of *attempt to commit murder*. Since conspirators share each other's guilt, Patrick is also guilty of that crime. As a practical matter, neither is likely to be prosecuted because, if no evidence occurs, the authorities will probably remain ignorant of the plot. Indeed, even when harm is inflicted, there is no certainty of arrest, conviction, or punishment. The typical criminal is like a guerrilla: he strikes from hiding when he has the advantage in strength and surprise, and he flees before his victim can respond.

Stealth and deception are also tactics used in so-called white-collar crimes, which involve no violence—defrauding an employer, swindling customers, fixing prices illegally, evading taxes (which forces others to pay more), selling securities that are worthless, or getting illegal kickbacks from suppliers. The injury to society may be enormous, but because there is no bloodshed, judges and juries tend to be more lenient in meting out punishment. In any event, if the test of the "perfect crime" is that the criminal escaped, probably most crimes are perfect, be they of the blue-collar or white-collar variety.

Angela Davis was accused of conspiracy to commit the crime of assisting the Soledad Brothers in attempting to escape from custody during a courtroom appearance in Marin County, California. She allegedly did overt acts in pursuance of the conspiracy, both by supplying guns and ammunition and by helping plan the escape while visiting one of the Soledad Brothers in prison. She was not present at the scene of the abortive escape attempt in which several persons died, including a judge held as hostage. Would Ms. Davis be guilty of the crime of conspiracy if she committed the alleged acts, even though she was absent from the scene of the murders?

Yes. If two or more persons agree to commit a crime, such as effecting the escape of a prisoner, and, in accordance with such an agreement, the accused performs an overt act, the crime of conspiracy has occurred, regardless of the whereabouts of the conspirators. In the case of Angela Davis, the jury unanimously agreed that she did not, in fact, agree to commit the crime as charged.

2. WHO ARE THE PARTIES TO A CRIME?

The actual perpetrator of a crime, such as a bank robbery, is guilty as the *principal,* or chief actor. All persons who encourage or assist him—as by ordering or inciting action, by giving advice, by standing guard, or by driving the getaway car—are sometimes called *accessories before the fact* but are guilty as principals (although to a second degree in some states and subject to a lesser punishment). After a crime has been committed, any person who harbors, conceals, or otherwise aids a principal in escaping arrest or punishment—knowing that such principal committed, or is charged with committing, such crime—is an *accessory after the fact* and is punishable as such.

> In a famous case in 1971, Charles Manson was charged with the murder of the pregnant Sharon Tate and others. He was not present at the scene of the crime. Is Manson a principal or an accessory?

Because of his involvement in planning and inciting the murders, he was an accessory before the fact and was properly convicted as a principal and sentenced to death.*

Accomplice is a broader term that includes the principal and all accessories before the fact.

---

* The death sentence of Charles Manson was reduced to life imprisonment as a result of the abolition of the death penalty in California by the case of *Furman* v. *Georgia,* 408 U.S. 238, 1972. Although the death penalty was thereafter restored by statute, its effect is prospective and does not purport to affect the sentence of Manson.

3. WHAT IS THE CORPUS DELICTI?

The *corpus delicti* (Latin: body of a crime) is not the body of the deceased. The term refers to two elements of every crime: (1) any occurrence of harm, and (2) the probable evidence of a criminal act.

> A body was washed up on a beach near Coos Bay, Oregon. An autopsy indicated that death had occurred by drowning. It was a widely known fact that the decedent was hated by Orval Swenson. Can Swenson be tried for murder?

No. There is no clear evidence that a crime has occurred and the corpus delicti cannot, therefore, be established. The drowning could have been accidental. However, if the corpse had a head injury apparently inflicted by a weapon, Swenson might be investigated and, if there were corroborating evidence, he could be accused of murder and tried.

It is possible to convict a person of murder even though no human corpse is ever discovered. In such cases, the corpus delicti may be established by other evidence that a harm occurred (for example, the testimony of an eyewitness). In any crime, the corpus delicti must be established before criminal prosecution can take place against the accused.

4. WHAT IS THE DIFFERENCE BETWEEN A FELONY AND A MISDEMEANOR?

Crimes are classified as felonies and misdemeanors, and in some states as infractions. A *felony* is a crime that is punishable by death or by imprisonment in a state prison for a year or longer. Statutes may declare that a certain crime, such as murder, is a felony. If the statute is silent, but incarceration in a state prison is the prescribed punishment, the crime is a felony. Where a statute prescribes punishment as imprisonment in either a state prison or a county jail, the actual punishment ordered by the judge decides the issue. A *misdemeanor* is a crime that is punishable either by fine or by incarceration in a jail for less than a year or by both. An *infraction* carries no moral stigma, and is punishable only by fine. A parking violation is a common infraction.

A *felon,* the person convicted of a felony, typically suffers suspension of all civil political rights, such as the right to vote. The suspension becomes permanent upon a sentence of life imprisonment when a person becomes "civilly dead." Loss of civil rights does not mean loss of constitutional rights. A sentence for a felonious crime may be suspended on condition that the felon serve probation for a specified period of time. Upon successful completion of probation, the right to vote is automatically restored. The punishment prescribed for a crime may be more severe if the defendant has previously been convicted of a felony. Furthermore, conviction of a felony also justifies loss or suspension of professional licenses. Conviction of a felony involving moral turpitude is usually sufficient ground to revoke the license of an attorney, a doctor, a dentist, a pharmacist, or a real estate broker. Architects, professional engineers, contractors, and accountants may lose their licenses only if the particular felony is connected with their professional activities.

5. WHAT IS A CRIME AGAINST THE PERSON?

Murder and Manslaughter

> Harold Turner was drinking whiskey in the U-2 Bar and was boisterously commenting upon the Vietnam War. Jesse Johns, a veteran, became enraged and, without warning, stabbed Harold with a pocketknife. Harold died later in the emergency section of the local hospital. Is Jesse guilty of murder?

Jesse unlawfully took the life of Harold Turner, and is therefore apparently guilty either of murder or of manslaughter unless he was insane at the time. *Murder* is the unlawful killing of a human being with *malice aforethought,* the highest degree of mental culpability or blameworthiness. A killer for profit, and the person who hired him, clearly exemplify such a state of mind. *Manslaughter* is the unlawful killing of another without malice aforethought. Generally, if there is a manifest and deliberate intention to kill, with no provocation, the killing will be murder of either the first or the second degree. Murder perpetrated by explosive device, or by poison, or while lying in wait is *first degree murder* punishable by life imprisonment or, in some states, by execution. Murder committed in other circumstances, such as during an unjustified rage, is *second degree murder,* commonly punishable by five years to life in prison. Jesse Johns apparently reacted to Harold's comments about the Vietnam War without malice aforethought and, if that is true, he is probably guilty of manslaughter.

> Harry Gore, intending to murder his arch-competitor, Frank Brook, wired a bomb to the ignition system of Brook's pickup. The next morning Frank happened to loan the pickup to his neighbor, Pat Heald, who was killed in the explosion which followed. During his trial for murder, Gore contended that he could be guilty only of manslaughter because he did not intend to kill Pat. Is his contention sound?

No. The law transfers the intent to kill from the intended victim, Frank Brook in this case, to the person killed. This is the *doctrine of transferred intent.* In addition to first degree murder, Harry is also guilty of the separate crime of attempt to commit murder with regard to his competitor.

> During a heated quarrel, Lil Kadett finally screamed at her husband, Carl, that it was true: she had been having an affair with their neighbor. In a rage, Carl struck Lil on top of her head with the heavy magazine he had nervously rolled into a tight wad. Lil's skull was fractured and she died the following day in the hospital. What crime has occurred?

Carl is guilty of manslaughter.* Such a killing may be of the first degree, called *voluntary manslaughter,* or of the second degree, called *involuntary manslaughter.* The degree of manslaughter, like the degree of murder, refers to the degree of mental culpability. Generally, manslaughter during a heat of passion is voluntary, and manslaughter through accidental conduct is involuntary.

> Bill Tell aimed his target rifle just over the head of his neighbor, Charles McDonald, in order to frighten him. Bill did not intend to fire the rifle and did not intend any harm. The firearm accidentally discharged, killing McDonald. What crime has occurred?

Bill is guilty of involuntary manslaughter because the killing occurred due to carelessness. However, when conduct involves a strong probability of death or serious injury to another, it may justify the implication of malice and a resultant charge of murder. Other examples of involuntary manslaughter include a case wherein a "face rejuvenation" practitioner used so much carbolic acid to remove wrinkles and pockmarks that the patient died; a case wherein the defendant struck one fatal blow to the face of the victim for repeatedly calling him a "son of a bitch"; and a case wherein a mother, upon giving unattended birth to an illegitimate child, allowed it to die through neglect.[1]

> Hugo Splash was driving on the freeway at 125 miles per hour when his front left tire blew out. The car careened across the center divider causing a multi-vehicle crash which resulted in many injuries and two deaths. Splash was under the influence of narcotics at the time of the accident. What crimes have occurred?

---

* The notion that a husband, upon learning of his wife's extramarital affair, has a license to kill either his wife or her paramour or both is incorrect. However, discovery of such unfaithfulness generally constitutes sufficient provocation to reduce the killing from murder to manslaughter.

Deaths caused in connection with the use of motor vehicles are generally treated separately from unlawful killings caused by other means. If a person operates a vehicle with *gross negligence* and a death ensues, the crime committed is a special category of manslaughter in most states and the punishment is less severe than in other types of manslaughter. If the vehicle is operated with *simple* or *ordinary negligence,* the crime is still called manslaughter but is regarded as a misdemeanor rather than a felony. Splash was probably driving with gross negligence and is therefore guilty of the crime of felonious manslaughter. Of course, he may be guilty of a narcotics crime as well as of a speed limit violation.

Extortion and Kidnapping

> Richard M. Alday telephoned the father of a seven-year-old boy to say that he had kidnapped his son. Alday demanded $15,000, threatening that the child would be "hurt bad" unless the money was paid. Before the payment of any ransom, it was discovered that the boy had not been kidnapped but had become lost when he wandered away from the family summer cabin. Alday was arrested. During his prosecution for extortion, his attorney argued that no crime had been committed because no kidnapping had occurred. Did a crime occur?

Yes.[2] The *extortion* (obtaining money or property by threatening injury to the victim or to his family) took place when the defendant posed as a kidnapper. No actual kidnapping need occur; it is not a part of the corpus delicti. *Kidnapping* is the unlawful seizure and secret confinement of a person without his or her consent. It is a form of false imprisonment, aggravated by moving the victim and seeking to extort ransom. Under the Lindbergh Law (enacted by Congress in 1932 after the famous aviator's son was kidnapped and murdered), the Federal Bureau of Investigation may officially enter the investigation of any kidnapping twenty-four hours after it takes place. After that time, it is presumed that the victim has been taken from one state to another and so, under the interstate commerce clause of the Constitution, federal intervention is permissible.

Rape and Mayhem

> Max Mashe and six other "Devil's Angels" were motorcycling on a country highway. Along the way Mashe picked up hitchhiker Maryanne Patts, aged sixteen. Against her will, she was taken to a deserted cabin for "initiation" by the group. During the ritual, she was repeatedly raped and permanently disfigured. What crimes have occurred?

Mashe and all of his accomplices are guilty of the felonies of rape and mayhem. *Rape* is the act of unlawful sexual intercourse without the true consent of the victim. Consent obtained by threat, by trick, or through the use of intoxicants or narcotics is not true consent. Every person who maliciously maims or disfigures another is guilty of *mayhem,* but some states require a specific intent to maim or disfigure. Furthermore, any killing that occurs during commission of mayhem is automatically murder of the first degree.

> Stephanie Willson, aged sixteen, voluntarily had sexual intercourse with the very wealthy C. J. Haarm, aged fifty. Stephanie's father, Arthur, became enraged when she disclosed her romance. Deciding to capitalize on the situation, and being in need of funds with which to support his family, Arthur called Haarm and threatened to file a complaint with the police for statutory rape unless C. J. paid $5,000. What crimes have occurred?

Arthur Willson is guilty of extortion, which includes threatening another with criminal prosecution to induce the payment of money. Additionally, the crime of *statutory rape* has occurred because Stephanie was not capable, by reason of her minority, to give legal consent to sexual intercourse. The age of consent is eighteen. In Miss Willson's situation, resistance is irrelevant because a girl of such youthful age is considered incapable of making an informed decision. In many states one exception is made when, given the circumstances, the male participant could not reasonably be expected to have known that the girl was younger than eighteen. In such cases, her consent becomes legally sufficient. The rape of a male by a female is legally possible.* The crime of rape may also be committed by a female, conspiring with a male who personally performs the criminal act upon a female victim.

> One evening Joe Twist received a telephone call. Afterwards, he informed his wife, Harriet, that he was needed at the office to handle an emergency. Thirty minutes after Joe left, Harriet responded to a knock at the door and admitted Bartley Field, seemingly an encyclopedia salesman. Bartley threatened to kill Harriet unless she submitted to his sexual advances. Harriet submitted. Unknown to Harriet, Joe and Bartley had agreed to carry out this weird course of events. Has a forcible rape occurred?

Yes. A woman is not required to fight for her life in order to demonstrate

---

* Dorothy Hernandez, armed with a rifle and with threats of bodily harm, forced her innocent and unwilling husband to commit an act of sexual intercourse with her friend. Dorothy was convicted of the rape of her husband. *People* v. *Hernandez,* 18 C.A. 3d 651 (1971).

her lack of consent. Submission in response to a threat of serious injury is sufficient. Although sexual intercourse by husband with his wife against her will is not a crime, Joe Twist is guilty of rape as an accessory before the fact for his role in aiding and encouraging the principal, Bartley Field. An unlawful killing of the victim during rape is automatically classified by statute as murder of the first degree.

Assault and Battery

Lawrence Lath, while a passenger in a car traveling on Highway 99, was shooting his .22 caliber pistol at road signs when he noticed a parked auto at the side of the road. He took a couple of shots at it. Unknown to Lath, one of his shots hit Michael Binson in the foot. Binson happened to be talking with Barbara Jones at the side of the road. When tried on a charge of assault with a deadly weapon, Lath contended that he could not be convicted because he had no intent to commit a battery. Is his contention sound?

No.[3] An *assault* is an unlawful attempt, coupled with present ability, to commit a violent injury on the person of another. In other words, it is an attempted battery. A *battery* is the unlawful infliction of injury on the person of another. Therefore, the "intent" necessary for an assault with a deadly weapon is the intent to attempt to commit a battery. Technically Lath would appear to be correct. However, when an act inherently dangerous to others is committed with a conscious disregard of human life and safety, the requisite intent to commit a battery is presumed. If Lath's shot had killed Binson, he would have been guilty of voluntary manslaughter because he was recklessly engaging in an activity that was conspicuously dangerous to human life. The classic example of an assault is a left hook that just misses. A right cross that connects is a battery.

6. WHAT IS A CRIME AGAINST PROPERTY?

Jake Jacobsen and Joyce Marchant went camping in the Great Smoky Mountains. They packed a tent, among other things, and rigged it at Lost Lake. While they were exploring the area, Tom Trammpel, a hiker in the vicinity, decided to steal anything of value he could find. He therefore surreptitiously entered the tent. To his chagrin he found nothing worth stealing and so he left empty-handed. Has a crime occurred?

Yes. Tom is guilty of burglary. The entry of a home, apartment, or temporary abode, such as a tent or a vehicle (if its doors are locked), with intent to commit a crime therein is a *burglary,* a crime against property. *Robbery* is the felonious taking of property from the person of another by force or by threat. It involves a dual offense against both person and property.

Theft is also a crime against property and is of two varieties: grand theft (a felony) and petty theft (a misdemeanor). *Grand theft* is the stealing of personal property worth a sizable amount (such as $200 or more), except that theft of farm produce is often deemed to be grand theft even if it reaches a lower value (such as $50). Likewise, theft of most varieties of farm animals is commonly grand theft regardless of value, no doubt because farmers are so vulnerable to attack. The specific values vary among the states. *Petty theft* is the theft of personal property of a value less than that necessary to qualify the crime as a felony. Shoplifting is usually petty theft.

> Joe Swift, a freshman at Central Community College, was stretched out on the lawn, meditating in the sun, when George Fence, a complete stranger, rode up on a new fifteen-speed bicycle. Fence offered to sell the bike for $15. Swift said, "Great," and paid for it on the spot. He then asked, "By the way, is this bike stolen?" Fence winked and walked off. Has a crime occurred?

Yes. Joe is guilty of the crime of receiving stolen property and, if the bike is worth $200 or more, it is a felony. George, of course, is guilty of the crime of selling stolen property and possibly of related crimes.

Arson is the unlawful burning of a building or other personal property. As with any other crime, the motive of the arsonist is irrelevant. That is, a thrill fire is arson just as much as is the burning of a business for the purpose of collecting insurance proceeds. The seriousness of this crime is reflected in the fact that any unlawful killing that occurs during commission of the crime of arson is first degree murder. A fire caused by negligence or carelessness is not arson.

7. WHAT IS A CRIME AGAINST PUBLIC HEALTH, SAFETY, AND WELFARE?

> Joe Moreno was walking along Main Street. Reacting to a campaign poster for reelection of the governor of the state, he spat on the sidewalk. A police officer observed the incident and placed Moreno under arrest for the spitting, which violated a city ordinance. When brought before the judge, he pleaded not guilty. He claimed that the right to spit in response to a political sign was safeguarded by the constitutional guarantee of free speech. Does Moreno win or lose?

He loses. Freedom of speech has nothing to do with spitting on the sidewalk, which was a misdemeanor in that town. Spitting on the sidewalk is a crime against the public health, and cannot be justified as a kind of communication.

> Derrick Thiessen was an avid deer hunter. He had a license, and on opening day was driving along Highway 89 when he saw a buck near the road. He stopped, took his loaded rifle from his plainly visible rifle rack, leaned against the hood of his pickup, and shot the deer. A game warden observed the activity and promptly placed Thiessen under arrest. Of what crime, if any, is he guilty?

Thiessen is guilty of transporting a loaded firearm in a motor vehicle as well as of firing a weapon on or near a public highway. Concern for public safety is the principle underlying enactment of this type of misdemeanor statute.

> On April 26, 1968, Paul Robert Cohen appeared in the Los Angeles County Courthouse wearing a jacket on which were printed the plainly visible words, "Fuck the Draft." Cohen's purpose was to inform the public of the "depth of his feeling against the Vietnam War and the draft." Among the public receiving his message were women and children in the courthouse. Was Cohen guilty of a crime?

Yes, but only temporarily! Cohen was convicted of disturbing the peace with his "offensive conduct." Despite Cohen's contention that his message was a communication of ideas protected by the first amendment (free speech) to the U.S. Constitution, the California Supreme Court allowed the conviction to stand. However, the U.S. Supreme Court, recognizing that "we are often 'captives' outside the sanctuary of the home and subject to objectionable speech," held that "words are often chosen as much for their emotive as their cognitive force," and both modes are protected by the first amendment. "For . . . one man's vulgarity is another's lyric." The three dissenting justices asserted that Cohen's "absurd and immature antic . . . was mainly conduct and little speech."[4]

Other crimes against public health, safety, and welfare include (1) motor vehicle offenses; (2) violation of laws regulating food, liquor, drugs, and cosmetics; (3) narcotics violations; (4) corporate securities violations; (5) licensing violations by attorneys, accountants, and other professionals; (6) illegal employment practices; (7) violation of natural resources and fish and game laws; (8) violation of civil rights; (9) gambling violations; (10) allowing animals with known vicious propensities to be loose; (11) abandoning iceboxes with doors intact; (12) adulterating candy with laxatives or other chemicals; (13) cutting public shrubs; (14) failing to yield use of a party telephone line for an emergency call; and (15) selling alcoholic beverages during off hours.

8. WHAT IS A CRIME AGAINST PUBLIC DECENCY AND MORALS?

> Harry Hackett and his wife, Margaret, on their wedding night and at Harry's insistence, engaged in oral copulation. Thereafter, Margaret reported the matter to the district attorney, who charged Harry with a crime against public decency and morals. Can Harry be prosecuted?

Yes. Although in recent years some best-selling books on sexual conduct have maintained that oral copulation (fellatio or cunnilingus) is a natural form of heterosexual gratification and should be legalized, many states regard it as a felonious crime. In California it is punishable by incarceration for up to fifteen years in a state prison. If Margaret willingly participated and later decided to report the matter to the district attorney, she would discover that a willing participant is equally guilty. Harry is guilty of a crime called *sex perversion,* which includes sodomy and lewd or lascivious acts with a child. Conviction of sex perversion, or of any other crime involving lascivious activity, such as rape, pimping, or prostitution, results in a continuing duty in some jurisdictions to register with the local police as a sex pervert. *Contributing to the delinquency of a minor* is a catchall misdemeanor referring to any conduct by an adult that involves assisting a person under eighteen years in any unlawful activity.

Some people say that undue and unnecessary amounts of public law enforcement money and police attention are devoted to what they call "crimes without victims": deviant sexual behavior, homosexuality between consenting adults, prostitution, criminal abortion, illegal gambling, drunkenness in public, drug abuse—especially when involving the use of marijuana. Other people seek to justify the battle against each of these offenses. Deviant sexual behavior and homosexuality are said to be unnatural and, if carried to the extreme under a tolerant policy, would endanger the survival of the human race. Prostitution debases women and contributes to epidemic levels of venereal disease in our sexually permissive society. Criminal abortion threatens maternal life as well as destroying fetal life. Illegal gambling not only diverts funds from food and other necessities but commonly involves tax evasion. The alcoholic is arrested for his own protection and "drying out." Hard drugs are physically and mentally ruinous; although the full effects of marijuana remain to be determined, some research indicates serious negative effects. Moreover, when individuals fall by the wayside because of one or more of these abuses, society is forced to finance their care and rehabilitation.*

---

* For further information on this controversial subject, read: Edwin M. Schar, *Crimes Without Victims* (Prentice-Hall: Englewood Cliffs, N.J., 1965); Edwin Kniester, Jr., *Crimes With No Victims* (Alliance For A Safer New York: New York, 1972); Gilbert Geis, *Not the Law's Business?* (National Institute of Mental Health, Rockville: Maryland, 1972).

Delbert Brock, a civil engineer, consented to the artificial insemination of his wife. When "their" child was three, Delbert abandoned the family. Has a crime occurred?

Yes. Delbert is guilty of the misdemeanor of failure to support his child unless excused by economic inability. He is also guilty of the misdemeanor of abandoning his wife—if she is destitute and provided his abandonment was not justified by her conduct. Generally speaking, both parents are equally responsible for the support of their children. In this regard, adoptive children and children conceived through artificial insemination are treated in the same way as natural children.

In the tenth year of their marriage, Oxnard Fickle and his wife, Ozzie, decided to take separate vacations. While alone in Colorado Springs, Ozzie met and became infatuated with Charles Davidson, a bachelor playboy with whom she engaged in sexual intercourse. Oxnard had hired a detective to follow his wife, and, upon receiving his report, went to the district attorney and demanded that Ozzie and Charles be charged with adultery. What should the district attorney do?

Nothing. The best advice for Oxnard and Ozzie might be to visit a marriage counselor. *Adultery* is a misdemeanor, but casual acts of sexual intercourse are not sufficient to constitute the offense, although one experience suffices as grounds for divorce in most states. To complete the offense, the married adulterer must *cohabit* (live together) with another in an open and notorious manner. Illicit intercourse by an unmarried adult is generally not a crime. However, some states hold that unmarried persons who engage in intercourse are guilty of the misdemeanor of *fornication*. Prosecutions for these offenses are rare in today's society with its greatly relaxed standards of morality.

9. WHAT ARE SOME EXAMPLES OF OTHER CRIMES?

There are many miscellaneous crimes. Some examples are (1) abusing animals; (2) conducting cockfights; (3) altering telegrams; (4) "beating" vending machines or pay telephones; (5) removing articles from a corpse; (6) loitering around public schools; (7) offering a "dead or alive" reward; (8) tattooing a minor under eighteen; (9) harassing another by telephone; (10) carrying a switchblade knife; (11) perjury, which is lying while sworn to tell the truth, and subornation of perjury, which is getting someone else to commit perjury; (12) killing protected species of birds; (13) bribing, which is paying money to a public official in return for some special consideration; and (14) defacing public property.

This list shows the diversity in criminal laws deemed necessary to maintain peace and order in a politically organized society. There are thousands of miscellaneous crimes "on the books," including many silly ones that are never enforced, but ignorance of the law is not a defense. If it were, no doubt most persons accused of crime would plead such ignorance. Generally, the rules are reasonable and conform to standards of good conduct. The human conscience, or one's innate knowledge of what is sometimes called "natural law," normally provides a workable guide to what is right and lawful and what is wrong in the eyes of society and, hence, a crime.

10. WHAT IS THE DIFFERENCE BETWEEN FEDERAL AND STATE CRIMES?

As previously noted, a crime is an action that is proscribed by a law enacted by the legislative branch of government (or, technically, the failure to do some act that is mandated). Most of the examples thus far in this chapter have demonstrated violations of laws enacted by state legislative bodies as contrasted with those enacted by Congress.

> In July 1971, Muhammed Ali, formerly known as Cassius Clay, defeated Jimmy Ellis by a TKO in ten rounds. The Internal Revenue Service immediately after the fight took $200,000 of the anticipated $800,000 purse as a prepayment of estimated income taxes. Muhammed contended that his constitutional rights were violated because the IRS does not confiscate everyone's estimated taxes in advance. Is Muhammed correct?

No. Congress has authorized the Internal Revenue Service to confiscate taxes in advance when there is a danger that, unless so secured, the taxes may not be paid. This technique has also been applied to big winners at keno (a game of chance). Willful failure to pay federal income taxes is a federal crime punishable by fine or by imprisonment in a federal penitentiary or by both. Willful failure to pay state income taxes is a state crime punishable by fine or by imprisonment in a state prison or by both.

Other common examples of federal crimes are (1) transportation of contraband across state lines; (2) bank robbery; (3) forgery of a federal check; (4) failure to obey draft laws; (5) violation of certain civil rights protected by federal laws; (6) transportation of females across state lines for immoral purposes; and (7) wrongful interference with or theft of mail.

11. WHAT PROCEDURES LEAD UP TO A CRIMINAL TRIAL?

Arrest

To *arrest* is to take into custody in order to charge with commission of a crime. Actual restraint of the person is involved. Arrest may be accomplished by a police officer acting in compliance with a *warrant,* which is the written authorization of a judge or magistrate to arrest a specific person. A judge will not issue a warrant unless someone files a written statement, called a *complaint,* that contains detailed facts indicating both that a crime was committed and that the person to be arrested probably committed it. Arrest may also be made by a police officer acting without a warrant: (a) when a felony or misdemeanor is committed or attempted in his presence; or (b) when he has probable cause, or reasonable grounds, to believe both that a felony has been committed out of his presence and that the suspect is the guilty party. The reasonable grounds could be an accusation by a private citizen. To require less would be to violate the Fourth Amendment ban on unreasonable seizures.

In about twenty states, private citizens are also authorized by law to make arrests—without warrants, of course—for any felony or misdemeanor committed in their presence. Most other states permit citizens to arrest only for felonies or misdemeanors involving a breach of the peace either attempted or committed in their presence. Such "citizen's arrest" is generally not advisable because of the problem of restraining the suspect, the possibility of his violent reaction, and the hazard of mistake, which could lead to a civil suit for damages for the tort of false arrest. Even police officers may be sued for false arrest.

Booking

After an arrest, the accused may be booked. *Booking* involves fingerprinting, photographing, blood testing for alcohol, and reasonable related activities. The accused has certain rights following arrest, including the right to obtain an attorney (a telephone call must be provided for this purpose); the right to remain silent; the right to be promptly taken before a judge or magistrate; the right to be allowed bail; and the right to have a blood test taken.

Promptly after booking, an accused must be taken before a judge or magistrate. This requirement limits the possibility of unreasonable police interrogation and affords an opportunity for the accused to have bail set and to have his rights explained.

Bail

Bail refers to the security given to the court by the accused to assure his later appearance for trial, in order to obtain his immediate release. The amount of bail must be specified in the warrant, or if arrest is without warrant, the judge will set bail following the arrest. The amount depends on the seriousness of the offense, the wealth of the accused, and the likelihood of his becoming a fugitive.

The bail may consist of a specified amount of money; or it may be a *bail bond* purchased at considerable expense (typically 10 percent of the amount of the bail) from a bail bondsman, and under which the accused and his bondsman or surety agree to pay the full amount if the accused fails to appear as promised. In such event, the bail is forfeited and a warrant is issued for his rearrest. The bondsman usually suffers no loss, because he requires security (such as stocks, bonds, jewelry, or other valuables) in order to protect himself in the event of the bail posted being forfeited because of the continued absence of the accused.

Because every accused person is presumed innocent until proven guilty beyond a reasonable doubt, he is entitled to release on bail unless the charge is a capital offense and the evidence of guilt is very clear. Under the eighth amendment, the judge may not demand "excessive bail," but any amount may be beyond the financial means of a poor person. Accordingly, at the federal level and in a number of progressive states, reforms have been enacted to permit release of the poor as well as the prominent and wealthy on their own *recognizance,* whereby the accused person simply promises in writing to appear for the trial. His failure to do so would lead to rearrest, and may involve an obligation to pay a specified sum of money to the court.

Accusatory Pleading

An accused in not formally charged with a crime until there has been an *accusatory pleading,* which specifies the crime committed and accuses the defendant of its commission. There are three types of these documents: information, indictment, and complaint. In felony cases, either an *information* is filed by the district attorney or an *indictment* is brought by the county grand jury. This is generally a group of twelve to twenty-three citizens impaneled by the court to investigate wrongdoing in the community under the guidance of the superior court and with the assistance of the district attorney; they will issue an indictment only after conducting a deliberative hearing at which at least twelve of them agreed to it. In misdemeanor cases in the municipal court, the accusatory pleading is called a *complaint.*

When accusation is by indictment, the accused necessarily has already had a deliberative hearing before the grand jury. When accusation of committing a felony is by information, a *preliminary hearing* must be scheduled at which a judge will determine whether or not there is sufficient cause to hold the accused for trial. During a preliminary hearing, the district attorney presents witnesses and other evidence to demonstrate sufficient "probable cause." Obviously, he must prove a corpus delicti. Otherwise, the judge will dismiss the charges. Defense attorneys frequently engage in lengthy cross-examination of prosecution witnesses during the preliminary hearing in order to learn as much as possible about the case. Some states still require that all felony accusations be made by grand jury indictment.

Arraignment

After an accused is formally charged with a crime by the filing of an accusatory pleading, he or she must be *arraigned*—that is, called into court, informed of the charge, and given an opportunity to make a response, or *plea:* either guilty, not guilty, nolo contendere, or not guilty by reason of insanity. A plea of *nolo contendere* in the criminal law is comparable to a plea of guilty. The only real distinction justifying its use is that a guilty plea can be used against the defendant as an admission in subsequent civil litigation, whereas a plea of nolo contendere cannot. A guilty plea standing alone presumes that the defendant was sane at the time the crime was committed. Hence, the question of insanity must be raised by special plea, namely "not guilty by reason of insanity."

Trial will follow the defendant's plea unless the plea is guilty, in which event sentencing will follow.

Misdemeanors

The procedures for misdemeanors are somewhat different. For example, upon arrest for a misdemeanor traffic offense, the accused must be taken before a magistrate only if he or she refuses to give a written promise to appear in court or if continued operation of the vehicle is unsafe because the accused is under the influence of alcohol or some drug. The notice to appear, or "ticket," constitutes the complaint to which the defendant may plead guilty or not guilty. Prior to the time specified for appearance, the accused may post bail, the "fine" that will be declared forfeited if the defendant fails to appear in person. There is no formal proceeding after such forfeiture.

Many states authorize a citation procedure similar to traffic citations for violations of city and county ordinances, such as failure to pay a business license fee or failure to keep a suburban lot free of trash and weeds.

12. IS LACK OF MENTAL CAPACITY A DEFENSE?

Insanity (irrationality) at the time of committing an offense is a defense. To be held criminally responsible, one must be rational and possess freedom of will. In most states a person is insane if he or she is unable to distinguish between right and wrong because of a diseased mind. The insanity need not be permanent. In some states an *irresistible impulse* to commit a crime, caused by a diseased mind, is a defense even though the accused understood that the act was wrong.

The most widely accepted test of legal insanity today is the "substantial capacity" test proposed by the American Law Institute and included in the Model Penal Code, Section 4.01:

> A person is not responsible for criminal conduct if at the time of such conduct as a result of mental disease or defect he lacks substantial capacity either to appreciate the criminality (wrongfulness) of his conduct or to conform his conduct to the requirement of the law. The terms "mental disease" or "defect" do not include an abnormality manifested only by repeated criminal or otherwise antisocial conduct.

In California the issue of insanity, raised by a plea of not guilty by reason of insanity, is determined in a separate trial following the principal trial. Insanity at the time of trial is not a defense to a crime commited during a prior time of sanity. However, a trial cannot proceed until the defendant is sane because a "fair" trial, as guaranteed by our constitution, contemplates a rational defendant. Nor can a criminal sentence be served by an insane convict. In general terms, insanity suspends judicial proceedings so long as it continues. However, the defendant may be committed to a state institution for the insane. Should he regain his sanity, the criminal proceedings may resume.

Voluntary intoxication from alcohol or drugs is generally not a defense. However, this condition may be used by a defendant to prove lack of a specific intent when a particular crime (such as assault with intent to commit murder) requires such intent as a part of its corpus delicti.

> Valerie Dawn Kelly had used drugs ever since she was fifteen. When she was eighteen, and a repeated user of LSD and mescaline, she was found wandering in a daze at the Los Angeles International Airport. Her parents were called and took her home. While Mrs. Kelly was preparing breakfast, Valerie entered the kitchen and repeatedly stabbed her mother with an array of kitchen knives. At her trial, Valerie pleaded "not guilty by reason of insanity." The trial court held that the defense was not applicable because the evidence showed that Valerie was only temporarily unable to perceive right from wrong. Was the court's ruling correct?

No. The California Supreme Court observed that temporary insanity is as fully recognized as a defense to a crime as is permanent insanity.[5] Valerie Kelly was so incapacitated through prolonged use of drugs as to be insane at the time of the crime. A subsequent recovery did not vitiate her defense.

> Sirhan Bishara Sirhan was convicted for the first degree murder of Senator Robert Kennedy. In his defense, he contended that

the crime was committed during an emotionally charged moment connected with the Senator's promise to supply jets to Israel with which to kill thousands of Arabs. Accordingly, due to his "diminished capacity," he could not be convicted of first degree murder and the death penalty could not be decreed. Was this contention correct?

No.[6] It is true that a defendant cannot be convicted of first degree murder if, at the time of the alleged offense, he had a mental disability (not amounting to legal insanity) that prevented him from acting with malice aforethought or with premeditation and deliberation. However, Sirhan was unable to substantiate such a diminished capacity during his trial.* *Diminished capacity* is a defense to the existence of specific intent, such as is required for first degree murder or assault with intent to commit murder. The diminished capacity may be caused by delusion, narcotics, alcohol, or even a political rage such as contended by Sirhan. Any claim of lack of mental capacity must be substantiated with evidence.

13. WHEN IS VIOLENT CONDUCT LEGALLY JUSTIFIED?

Violent conduct, which would otherwise be criminal behavior, is justified when used in defense of oneself or of others. All states recognize some form of the privilege of self-defense.

> Harry Holland and his girlfriend Shirley Snow were listening to records in her apartment. A noisy party was under way next door. Suddenly there was a banging on Shirley's unlocked door and it was flung open. There stood Butch Meen, table knife in one hand and beer bottle in the other. Harry's first thought was to retreat with Shirley out of the back door. But Shirley grabbed her pistol from the table drawer, aimed it at Butch's heart, and stared him right in the eye. When Butch took a menacing step toward her, Shirley killed him with a single well-aimed shot. Was the killing unlawful?

No. When confronted with a genuine and reasonable fear of imminent danger of great bodily injury, the *privilege of self-defense* arises. Deadly resistance is justified when the imminent peril is great. Since Butch held a knife and bottle, Shirley's fear of great and imminent harm, including

---

* Subsequently, the California Supreme Court declared that the death penalty was unconstitutional and was "cruel and unusual punishment." Sirhan, and a number of other convicted criminals who were awaiting execution, are now confined to prison for life. In California, a person sentenced to life imprisonment is eligible for, but not necessarily entitled to, parole after seven years; few actually die of old age behind prison bars.

possible death, was reasonable and her defense was reasonable. If Butch had stepped backwards, the killing would not have been justified and Shirley would be guilty of manslaughter. If Butch had stepped toward Harry alone, the killing would still be justified because she was entitled to defend Harry as well as herself. Generally, the right to self-defense extends to members of one's immediate family or household and to others whom one is under a legal or socially recognized duty to protect.[7]

These general principles would apply even if the events had occurred in a public park. The fact that the acts transpired in Shirley's apartment increases the scope of the privilege of self-defense. Defense of habitation is rooted in the ancient principle that a man's home is his castle. It does not mean that a killing is justified merely because it takes place in the home of the accused. However, he is not obliged to retreat, whereas outside his home (or apartment) he might be required to do so if possible without added risk. Even in the home, the killing must be in defense of life or to prevent grievous bodily injury, such as rape.

Deadly force may not be used in defense against nondeadly force, such as slapping. Nor may it be used in defense of property when life is not threatened. Thus, one may not set a deadly spring gun to go off if a door or window is broken into when one is not at home. If an intruder is hurt or killed, the person who set the gun may be guilty of manslaughter and may also be liable in tort for the injury or wrongful death.

The mere refusal of a house guest to leave can never justify killing him. Reasonable force to eject such an obnoxious person would be in order, although a telephone call to the police might be more effective. If, in response to reasonable force or a telephone call, the "guest" produced a knife and threatened the life of the host, a killing in reasonable defense against such violence would be justified. However, the privilege of self-defense is never a "license" to kill. If force less than a killing is all that is reasonably required, then a killing in defense becomes unlawful and punishable as a crime.

14. WHAT IS ENTRAPMENT?

> Joe Shapiro, operating on Whidbey Island, Washington, negotiated with Richard Russell and others for the purchase of homemade methamphetamine, or "speed." Russell needed the very scarce, but legal, chemical phenyl-2-propanone to prepare the drug and this was supplied by Joe. When the batch was prepared and delivered, Russell was advised that Shapiro was an employee of the Federal Bureau of Narcotics. Arrest and trial followed in due course. Had Russell been constitutionally entrapped?

No. *Entrapment* occurs only if the government agent implants the criminal design in the mind of the defendant. The U.S. Supreme Court held that Russell had a predisposition to commit the crime, and the mere affording of opportunity by Shapiro was not entrapment.[8]

15. IS CONSENT BY A VICTIM A LEGAL DEFENSE?

Generally speaking, a crime has a dual impact. It may be an offense against both the person and the public, and therefore consent of a victim to the commission of a crime is not a defense available to an accused.

> Max Pugger and Butch Cassidy decided to earn a little money by staging a bare-knuckle fistfight. Admission of five dollars per spectator was charged. The police learned of the event, appeared during bloody round one, and promptly placed Max and Butch under arrest. Is there any legal defense available to them?

No. Engaging in a bare-knuckle prize fight is a misdemeanor in many jurisdictions, and the fact that each participant consented to the activity is not a legal defense.

In some instances, lack of consent is an element of the crime.

> George Harper met Maryanne Montgomery in the Elegant Barn bar. After some conversation, George accompanied Maryanne to her nearby apartment. They had been drinking heavily. One thing led to another and, in the early morning hours, they commenced an act of intercourse. During it, Maryanne changed her mind and demanded that George leave her alone immediately. George disregarded her demand even though she physically attempted to regain her liberty. The following day Maryanne filed a formal complaint of rape against George. What factors will the district attorney consider in deciding whether or not to prosecute?

The district attorney must decide whether or not all elements of the crime of rape are present. One element is the lack of consent of the victim. If the victim initially consents, as Maryanne did, can that consent be withdrawn so as to legally characterize further intercourse as rape? Assuming the answer to that question is yes, what if George did not believe that consent was really withdrawn? Regardless of these questions, do the facts justify the conclusion that there never was any legal consent because Maryanne was too intoxicated to make an effective decision? But had she not willingly joined in the drinking, knowing what the aftermath might be? Does the fact that Maryanne waited until the following day to make her complaint shed any light on the question of her consent or lack of it?

These are difficult questions and there are no clear-cut answers. Suffice it to say that lack of consent of the victim is a necessary part of the crime of rape, and the determination of what constitutes consent may vary widely from state to state, and even from community to community as well as from case to case.

16. WHAT IS THE STATUTE OF LIMITATIONS?

A *statute of limitations* is a legislative determination that legal proceedings in connection with various types of civil and criminal acts may not be commenced beyond specified periods of time. Accordingly, it may be a valid defense for the defendant. The purpose of the statute is not to shield defendants from the law; it is to prevent stale prosecutions in which witnesses' memories may have faded, and so a "fair" trial would be exceedingly difficult, if not impossible, to obtain. Criminal courts in metropolitan areas are already overcrowded. Moreover, witnesses and principals may move, or get sick and die; evidence may be obscured or lost. Society is better served if wrongdoers resume a normal, productive, law-abiding life, without the omnipresent psychological burden of possible arrest.

The period of time specified in a statute of limitations commences upon commission of the offense. An *accusatory pleading* (indictment, information, or complaint) must be filed within the period prescribed. The statute is suspended, or "tolled," by the absence of the defendant from the state and there is no statute of limitations for certain crimes, such as murder. The limitation period for misdemeanors is usually one year; for most felonies, it is three years. If the crime is either a misdemeanor or a felony, depending upon the sentence ultimately to be imposed, the limitation period is three years. A different statute of limitations is applicable to civil cases and is described in the next chapter.

17. WHAT ARE THE CONSTITUTIONAL RIGHTS OF AN ACCUSED?

Searches

Stephen V. Scott and his three-year-old son were observed by Highway Patrol Officers Schultz and Ellis urinating on U.S. 101 in Marin County, California. They advised Mr. Scott, who appeared intoxicated, that thumbing on the freeway was illegal. The officers volunteered to give Scott and his son a ride into San Francisco, but advised him that, for their own protection, a pat-down search was necessary. Scott obliged. During the search Officer Schultz felt something soft in Scott's pocket, which turned out to be marijuana. Arrest followed immediately. A further search disclosed two beers and some LSD tablets. Thereafter Scott moved the court to suppress all the evidence of narcotics on the grounds that the search was illegal. Did the search constitute an unreasonable and therefore unconstitutional search?

The U.S. Constitution prohibits government, usually acting by and through its police officers, from unreasonably searching its citizens or lawful residents. Determining the validity of a search is one of the most perplexing legal problems. It involves weighing the interest of the state in preventing crime against the interest of each person in maintaining his liberty.

It is widely believed and probably true that police officers, under the strain of daily action with dangerous and disagreeable suspects, are not always scrupulously considerate of the constitutional rights of the persons they search and arrest. Police can be and sometimes are sadistic bullies, guilty of brutal and illegal behavior, but courts are reluctant to believe the stories of arrested persons when flatly denied by officers. Comparatively few defendants have the means or the inclination to challenge the propriety of police procedures. The situation is improving with rising salary scales, which attract better educated, higher caliber personnel. Increased public respect for the men and women who engage in this necessary but difficult work can help even more.

In the case cited, Mr. Scott felt that his search was unreasonable and that therefore any evidence discovered was tainted with illegality and should not be used against him in a criminal prosecution. However, whenever a person is to be transported in a police vehicle, a pat-down search is justified. In Mr. Scott's case, "something soft" could not be a weapon, and a complete search following the pat-down was not justified.[9] It might have been justified if, for example, the marijuana had been plainly visible. (Technically, Scott was guilty of the misdemeanor of urinating on a freeway but that charge was not pressed by the district attorney.)

Children of tender years are not capable of formulating criminal intent, and so Scott's son is, of course, innocent. At common law, an infant under seven has no criminal capacity; between seven and fourteen he is presumed incapable of committing a crime but this is rebuttable. Statutes have modified this rule in some states, as in California where the Penal Code states that a child under fourteen is incapable of crime "in the absence of clear proof that at the time of committing the act charged . . . [against him, he] knew its wrongfulness."[10] The presumption of innocence for persons under seven years of age remains conclusive.

Referring back to the example in chapter 1 of the police officer who searched a curtained van because he knew hippies drive such vans and smoke marijuana, a search is unreasonable if it is made without probable cause that a crime has been or is about to be committed, and if the exigencies of the situation preclude prior application to a qualified judge for a search warrant. The presence of curtains on a vehicle does not constitute such probable cause, and the search was therefore unconstitutional. The law does not permit evidence obtained in an illegal search to be used against someone.

A police officer may, in appropriate circumstances and in an appropriate manner, approach a person to investigate possible criminal behavior, even though there is no probable cause to make an arrest, and *temporarily detain* him for that investigative purpose. The definition of which circumstances are appropriate differs from situation to situation. But before any such detention may take place, there must be an objectively reasonable suspicion that something out of the ordinary has taken place, and that the person detained is connected to that unusual event. Police officers cannot randomly detain and question persons, and certainly cannot conduct pat-down or any other type of search without some justifiable reason. If it can be proved that police officers have violated these principles, evidence obtained during such wrongful detention or search is not allowed as evidence in any criminal prosecution against the person wrongfully detained or searched.

A special rule exists when an officer desires to enter a house to investigate. To protect the fundamental right of privacy of dwelling occupants and to ensure the safety of police, innocent bystanders, and occupants who may be injured as a result of violent resistance to unannounced entries, an officer must demand admittance and explain his purpose before forcible entry. He must, of course, also possess a search warrant issued by a judge or a magistrate. As with most rules, there are exceptions. An officer may forcibly enter a dwelling without a search warrant and without first demanding entrance in the case of a violent felony committed in his presence or sight, or in the hot pursuit of a felon. If the officer merely has probable cause or reasonable grounds for arresting a person suspected of committing a crime, he may go to that person's home and enter it without a warrant, provided he first knocks (or rings the doorbell) and indicates his purpose. Then if refused admittance, he may forcibly enter to make the arrest.

Trials

In chapter 1 we discussed a defendant's constitutional right to a speedy trial. A defendant charged with a misdemeanor can demand trial within thirty days if he or she is in custody, otherwise within forty-five days. As a general proposition, delay favors the defendant since witnesses may disappear or suffer a fading memory. Of course, there are exceptions: for example, the defendant may be best served by an immediate trial before a missing witness can be found.

The U.S. Constitution requires that persons accused of a "serious" crime have the opportunity for a trial by jury. It does not prescribe a minimum or maximum number of jurors; conviction has traditionally required the unanimous agreement of twelve. In May 1972, however, the U.S. Supreme Court held that states may provide for conviction by less than a unanimous verdict.[11] The Court did not disturb the unanimity requirement in federal courts. One state conviction based upon nine votes of twelve jurors has been upheld by the Supreme Court.[12]

The purpose of a jury is said to be to protect a person from oppression by the government, from a corrupt or overzealous prosecutor, and from a biased or eccentric judge. A group of laymen interpose between the accused and his accuser their common sense judgment. Critics of the jury trial system do not attack its historical ability to achieve substantial justice, but they claim it is too expensive and unwieldy. These are arguments of expediency.

An accused is presumed innocent at all stages of the criminal proceedings prior to conviction; the prosecutor has the *burden of proof*. Accordingly, he must prove every element of the crime and every material link connecting the defendant *beyond a reasonable doubt and to a moral certainty*. It is not enough that a defendant "probably" is guilty. The jury must be so convinced that no "reasonable" doubt lingers in their minds after all the evidence is heard. If there is such a doubt, the accused must be acquitted. In civil cases, there is no presumption that the defendant is or is not liable.

No accused can be compelled to be a witness against himself. Furthermore, no person need answer a question if to do so could tend to prove him guilty of a crime. These rights are variations of the *privilege against self-incrimination*. Many defendants exercise this privilege by refusing to take the witness stand in their trial. This forces the prosecutor to prove his case beyond a reasonable doubt without the benefit of the defendant's personal testimony.

Obviously the privilege, when exercised, may be a double-edged sword. The jurors may wonder why the accused chose not to testify. They may reason that an innocent man would want to declare his innocence as openly and strongly as possible. In certain situations, the district attorney may grant immunity from prosecution to an accused in order to force him to testify against another defendant. An accused with immunity possesses no privilege against self-incrimination and therefore may be compelled to testify. Thus, after Richard M. Nixon was granted a full pardon by President Gerald Ford in 1974, he could be required to testify in the criminal trials of other persons involved in the Watergate affair. A refusal to testify under such circumstances would be a continuing contempt of court punishable by imprisonment until the person agreed to comply with the court order to testify.

In addition to these constitutional guarantees, a defendant in a criminal trial has several rights: to be present in court; to be assisted by counsel at all stages in the proceedings; to confront and cross-examine all adverse witnesses; to have a public trial conducted by an impartial judge in an impartial community; to subpoena witnesses on his own behalf; and to have a "fair" trial generally.

18. WHAT PUNISHMENT DOES THE CONVICTED FACE?

Imprisonment and imposition of a fine are the two basic forms of punishment. Either or both may be used, depending on what the law requires and what a judge decides. Misdemeanants are confined in county jails, and felons are incarcerated in state prisons.

For Misdemeanors

> Ripley Offenbach tried to shoplift a pair of jeans from a department store. He was caught, entered a plea of guilty in the municipal court, and was sentenced to sixty days in jail. While confined, can Ripley simply loaf, eat nourishing food, and—in some jails— watch television?

No. County jail prisoners can be made to work on public roads and trails or on other jobs for the benefit of the public. Some counties have road camps for such purposes. However, commitment to such a camp, called the "farm," is selective and Ripley may or may not be selected. In any event, a prisoner is entitled to be fed, to receive medical care, and to be kept free from physical abuse by prisoners or guards. In some states, under work furlough programs, a prisoner in a county jail may work at regular outside employment during working hours and remain in confinement at other times. Assignments to the farm for work are made by the sheriff or other designated agency, whereas work furlough may be ordered by the sentencing judge. Under such a program, the sheriff collects the misdemeanant's earnings; withholds the cost of his board, personal expenses, and administration; and may, by order of the court, have to pay the surplus, if any, to appropriate dependents.

Commonly, a county jail sentence imposed by the court may be shortened for good conduct—for example, five days for each month of such behavior. Additional time off may be granted for satisfactory completion of work assignments, and for blood donations made to a blood bank.

For Felonies

Confinement in the state prison for a felony is declared to be imprisonment for life or for a specific period of years up to a maximum prescribed by the legislature for certain crimes. California and Washington have adopted an indeterminate sentence law that provides for a range (one year to life, for example) rather than a specific period. Such a law eliminates the power of a judge to set a prescribed period as a sentence. Instead, the sentence is "confinement for the period prescribed by law," as determined by an agency within the executive branch of government.

The indeterminate sentence was introduced as a liberal experiment to encourage speedier rehabilitation by offering prisoners the possibility of earlier release. In fact, most prisoners resent it deeply because of the psychological burden of uncertainty, and because they feel insecure and helpless before the reviewing board (the Adult Authority in California, for male prisoners, and the Board of Trustees of the California Institution for Women, for female prisoners). The sheer volume of their work makes it impossible for them to give adequate time to each case as it comes up for annual review, and they are forced to rely heavily on reports and recommendations of prison guards and officials. This further alienates the prisoners.

In most states, the legislative branch of government establishes either (1) specified periods of confinement, or (2) minimum-maximum ranges for specified offenses. A specified minimum sentence is automatically increased when certain aggravating circumstances are present. For example, in California, when the defendant committing a felony is armed with a deadly weapon (such as a blackjack, a billy, a sandbag, metal knuckles, a dagger, or a firearm), the minimum prison sentence otherwise applicable is increased by two years, and the statutory maximum is increased by up to ten years.

Where a prior conviction exists, California has established additional minimum sentences of two years. Thus a "two-time loser" who was armed would face a combined minimum of four years' confinement (two for the prior conviction plus two for the deadly weapon) plus up to ten years on top of the maximum period prescribed for the particular offense. What would have been one to five years becomes five to fifteen years. Increased sentences are also typically imposed where grand theft and narcotic offenses are involved. In California, a three-time loser may be declared a habitual criminal and sentenced to life imprisonment. Other states have similar laws.

Prior arrests not resulting in conviction may not be used against an accused during trial or in fixing sentence.

19. WHAT ARE PAROLE, PROBATION, AND CLEMENCY?

Either a felon in a state prison or a misdemeanant in a county jail may be paroled. *Parole* suspends a sentence after incarceration has started, as distinct from probation, which suspends the sentence before incarceration. Parole is decided by officials designated under legislative authority; probation is granted by a judge. The liberty of a parolee is conditional and may be suspended or revoked unilaterally for violation of conditions specified, such as avoiding certain company or activity.

The purpose of *probation* is to aid in rehabilitation. After conviction and before sentencing, a probation officer will, at the court's discretion, thoroughly examine the defendant's background and circumstances. A recommendation to grant or deny probation will be made to the court before sentencing. There is no absolute right to probation; it is a matter of discretionary decision for the judge. Once probation is granted, the probation officer will supervise the defendant. Probation may depend upon many events, such as compliance with all laws, search for gainful employment, restitution or return of stolen property or its value, abstention from using intoxicants, and submission to periodic tests for drug addiction.

In many states, the privilege of probation is limited by statutes. Thus, probation cannot be granted to a defendant in California who was armed with a deadly weapon during commission of forcible rape, murder, kidnapping, escape, or train-wrecking. Nor is probation possible for a defendant who has two prior felonies.

When probation is granted, either the sentence is suspended pending successful completion of probation, or the imposing of any sentence at all is suspended during probation. In either case, probation will be revoked if the defendant violates its terms or conditions. The original sentence may then become operative. However, revocation may occur only after a hearing is conducted to establish the fact of the violation. A defendant has the right to refuse probation and accept the sentence in its place, but this seldom happens.

In addition, there are three types of executive clemency: *reprieve* (stay of execution of judgment), *commutation* (reduction of punishment), and *pardon* (release from punishment).

20. CAN A DEFENDANT'S RECORD BE CLEARED?

Once probation is successfully completed by a defendant, the court will, upon motion, vacate the plea or finding of guilt and dismiss the accusation or information. Thus, most disabilities arising in connection with the conviction are legally erased. However, the conviction will still stand and be counted as a prior offense. A defendant who was under twenty-one at the time of conviction for a misdemeanor may, upon completion of probation, obtain an order of the court sealing all records pertaining to the conviction. Although the records are officially sealed in this manner, some applications for professional licensure inquire whether or not records have been sealed and, if so, what circumstances surrounded the crime.

21. CAN A PROFESSIONAL PERSON BE PUNISHED ONLY WITH LOSS OF HIS OR HER LICENSE?

Loss of a professional license may follow conviction for a crime but not as a substitute for a fine or imprisonment. It is an additional penalty that a professional person may suffer as the result of committing a particular crime.

Lisbeth Doe, an elementary school teacher, and her husband joined a private club called "The Swingers" and attended a Christmas party. Undercover agent Ricardo Tracy was also in attendance, as were about twenty other persons. During the party Tracy observed Lisbeth commit fellatio upon three different men. Following her arrest she pleaded guilty to the misdemeanor of outraging public decency. Thereafter, the State Board of Education revoked her teaching credential on grounds of unfitness to teach. Was Lisbeth unfit to teach?

Yes. According to testimony, Lisbeth would be unable to set a proper example for her pupils or to teach moral principles to them.[13] This rule has been applied to an alcoholic teacher; a teacher advocating use of marijuana; a teacher who was found in a compromising position with a student and, upon discovery, assaulted a police officer and resisted arrest; and a teacher who made a homosexual advance to a police officer at a public beach.[14]

22. WHAT IS JUVENILE COURT?

Commission of an unlawful act by a minor younger than eighteen is not a crime. A *juvenile court* has jurisdiction not only to adjudge such a minor a ward of the court but also, typically, to reprimand, to commit to a home or camp, to assign to a probation officer for guidance, or even to incarcerate in certain penal-type institutions. The juvenile court is staffed by a judge of the superior court assigned by the presiding judge.

The juvenile court judge, with heavy reliance on social workers, seeks to protect and to rehabilitate rather than to punish the minor. Procedures are less formal than in a regular trial; there is no jury, and no publicity in the press. The judge is expected to exercise the wisdom of Solomon with patience and with compassionate parent-like concern for the welfare of the young defendants.

In reality, juvenile court often falls short of this ideal. On the one hand, many delinquents are street-toughened repeaters; they appear to be confirmed "hards," irrevocably and defiantly set in their antisocial ways. Often they are "hooked" on drugs, and this addiction complicates salvage efforts. Whatever the cause of their predicament, they appear to be incorrigible. On the other hand, judges assigned to juvenile duty may be ill-prepared for the work, both educationally and emotionally; they may be quite unsympathetic to the needs of the people who appear in court. There is never enough time for in-depth analysis and follow-up, and under pressure to get the job done, there have been flagrant denials of due process of law.

The Youth Authority in California and appropriate agencies in other states are given great discretion in confining and treating juveniles. They examine and study each inmate, and may confine him or her in a special institution designed to rehabilitate through education and training. They may compel vocational and physical activities conducive to rehabilitation, and may require work in forestry camps, public parks, and the like. In California, the sentence of such an offender ends when, in the judgment of the Youth Authority, there is a reasonable probability that he can be given full liberty without danger to the public. However, in the case of a misdemeanor conviction, release must occur within two years or upon attainment of the twenty-third birthday, whichever is later. For felonies, an offender must be released before the age of twenty-five, unless he has been transferred to a regular state prison. An incorrigible could be rejected and returned to court for sentencing to a regular state prison.

23. HOW ARE JUVENILE COURTS CHANGING?

In the state of Arizona, Gerald Gault, aged fifteen, was adjudged a juvenile delinquent and placed on probation for being in the company of a boy who had stolen a woman's wallet. While on probation, Gerald was arrested on the basis of an oral complaint by a woman neighbor who accused him of telephoning her and using obscene language. After an informal hearing in the judge's chambers with Gerald, his mother, his older brother, and two probation officers, Gerald was committed to the State Industrial School until reaching maturity. This meant confinement for maybe six years; the penalty for the same offense if committed by an adult would be a fine of $5 to $50 or jail for up to six months. Arizona law did not permit appeal of a decision by a juvenile court judge, and so Gerald's parents sought his release by hiring an attorney who filed a petition for a *writ of habeas corpus* (Latin: you have the body). Denied in the state courts, they appealed to the U.S. Supreme Court on grounds that Arizona's juvenile court laws violated the due process clause of the Fourteenth Amendment to the U.S. Constitution. Decide.

In a landmark decision, the judgment of the Arizona Supreme Court was reversed and the case was sent back for further proper proceedings. The U.S. Supreme Court declared that "neither the fourteenth amendment nor the Bill of Rights is for adults alone."[15] In juvenile proceedings where commitment to a state institution may follow, due process makes requirements as follows:

a. Adequate notice must be given to the child and his parents "sufficiently in advance of the hearing to permit preparation."
b. In such proceedings, the child and his parents must be advised of their right to be represented by counsel. If they are unable to afford a lawyer, one must be appointed by the court.

c. The child has the constitutional privilege against self-incrimination. "An admission by the juvenile may not be used against him in the absence of clear and unequivocal evidence that the admission was made with knowledge that he was not obliged to speak and would not be penalized for remaining silent. It would indeed be surprising if the privilege against self-incrimination were available to hardened criminals but not to children."

d. In the absence of a valid confession, a juvenile in such proceedings must be afforded the rights of confronting witnesses against him and of having the sworn testimony of such witnesses available for cross-examination.

Recognition of a juvenile's right to trial by jury must await further corrective legislative or judicial action. As it is, an apathetic and some-times militantly unsympathetic public, along with a stern and tradition-bound judiciary, have delayed and thwarted the full implementation of the *Gault* decision in many parts of the country.

24. WHAT SHOULD YOU DO IF ARRESTED?

1. Do not strike an officer or resist arrest. If he is abusive, get his badge number and (if possible) his name.
2. Do permit the officer to search you and your car and to pat down your body.
3. Do permit fingerprinting when booked.
4. Do request (if not offered) the right to make a telephone call and use it to contact someone (parents, relative, friend) who can get a lawyer. (If too poor to hire a lawyer, later ask the judge to provide such legal assistance.)
5. Do not respond to detailed questions beyond such harmless basics as name, address, telephone number—until and unless you are ad-vised to answer by your attorney. You cannot be penalized for remaining silent.
6. Have your attorney take steps to obtain your release, with or without further proceedings. Sometimes bail is required.
7. Be frank and honest in explaining in confidence to your attorney exactly what happened. He is bound to respect this confidence, and he will be better able to represent you if he knows all the facts.
8. When applicable, do immediately mention any physical condition requiring medication, such as multiple sclerosis, epilepsy, or diabetes.

1. Defendant Robert J. Adami was under investigation for selling narcotics. He became acquainted with undercover agent Thomas Dell'Ergo and made several sales of cocaine to him. During their business, Adami expressed an interest in getting rid of his wife, because he feared she would "rat" to authorities about his drug business. Dell'Ergo said he knew an assassin who required a $500 deposit and a photograph of the victim. He arranged a meeting with the "assassin," who was really undercover agent King. The deposit was paid and the photograph supplied.

    a. Is Adami guilty of attempted murder?

    b. Is the defense of entrapment available?

2. In a federal criminal court, defendant Richard J. Taylor was being tried for selling cocaine. During the trial he was free on bail. Mr. Taylor failed to show up for trial on the third and succeeding days during which the trial concluded with a conviction. On appeal Mr. Taylor argued that he had been convicted without confrontation with adverse witnesses as guaranteed by the U.S. Constitution. Should the conviction be affirmed or reversed?

3. In Coweta County, Georgia, a list of "intelligent and upright citizens" representing a "fair cross-section of the county" is prepared. From this list jury commissioners "select the most experienced, intelligent, and upright citizens"—not to exceed 40 percent of the whole number selected to serve as grand jurors. Population of the county is 28 percent eligible blacks, 53 percent eligible women, and 26 percent eligible young adults aged eighteen to thirty. The basic list contains 2,138 names, of which only 10 percent are blacks, 16 percent are women, and 3 percent are young adults. Of the 400 determined to be "most experienced," only 14 percent are black, 4 percent are women, and 1 percent are young adults. Defendant White, indicted by the grand jury, challenged the jury array as discriminatory. Will the challenge prevail?

4. When divorced, Teresa Keeler was already pregnant by her friend Ernest Vogt. A few months later her former husband accosted her in a rage, said he was going to "stomp it out," and proceeded to shove his knee into her abdomen. A Caesarian section was performed and the fetus was delivered stillborn. Cause of death was a skull fracture. Mr. Keeler contended that he was not guilty of murder because a fetus, although viable (alive), is not a "human" and murder is the unlawful killing of a human with malice aforethought. Decide.

5. When a police officer observes a traffic violation and stops the motorist for the purpose of issuing a citation, is a pat-down search for weapons permitted as part of the arrest?

6. May an officer conduct a pat-down search of a hitchhiker's sleeping bag?

CASES, QUESTIONS, AND PROBLEMS

3 YOU AS VICTIM OR ACCUSED OF CRIME / 103

7. If an officer conducts an improper search, what remedy does the accused have?

8. a. Is the sentence of five years to life for a conviction for sale of marijuana unconstitutional as being cruel and unusual punishment?
   b. Would your answer be different if the offense were public drunkenness?

9. a. Is the sentence of life imprisonment for a second conviction of indecent exposure unconstitutional as cruel and unusual?
   b. Would your answer be different for a sentence of fifty years for unlawful intercourse involving a girl of seventeen?
   c. What factors should be considered in setting a sentence for any crime?

10. If a person voluntarily becomes so drunk, or so "freaked out" from drugs that he or she cannot distinguish right from wrong, is the defense of insanity available?

11. Suppose that *A* hits *B* on the head with a wine bottle and leaves him unconscious in the street, but alive and capable of recovering. A car driven by *C* runs over and kills *B*.
    a. Is *A* guilty of murder?
    b. Would your answer be different if *C* were driving while under the influence of alcohol? If *A* were not guilty of murder, of what crime would he be guilty?

12. a. If a judge had reason to believe that a forthcoming rape/mayhem trial would attract an audience of persons whose only motive in attending would be to satisfy their morbid taste by listening to narratives of indecencies and obscenities, could he exclude the public and conduct the trial in private?
    b. Would your answer be different if the defendant agreed to this procedure?
    c. Should the press have a right to attend a trial even if the public generally does not?

13. a. Should prison and jail sentences be abolished except for persons convicted of violent crimes?
    b. Should prisoners be permitted to go home at night, or to have private visits by their spouses and children?
    c. Should sentences for crimes be increased or decreased in length?
    d. Should the use of a gun in the commission of a crime automatically double the punishment?
    e. Are so-called victimless crimes really victimless? If so, should they be decriminalized?
    f. Should nonviolent white-collar crimes be punished as severely as other crimes?

g. Should prisons be designed to punish criminals or to rehabilitate them? What differences would there be between these two types of prisons?

h. If prisoners learn useful trades, what should be done with their products? If sold on the open market, would that be unfair competition for outside companies and their workers?

i. Should prisoners be paid a living wage for work done behind bars? Consider whether their savings might make it less likely that they would resort to crime in order to live immediately after release.

j. Should indeterminate sentences be abolished?

k. Should every accused person be released on his own recognizance before trial?

l. What is a proper definition of *legal insanity?*

m. Should the statute of limitations be changed or abolished?

4

YOU AS TORTFEASOR OR VICTIM

1. WHAT IS A TORT?

A *tort* is a wrong, committed by one person (the *tortfeasor*), that injures another person and for which the law allows the victim the legal remedy of collecting monetary damages from the wrongdoer. A tort is either *intentional* (in the sense that the act causing the injury was intended) or *negligent* (in the sense that the injury was caused by the carelessness of the wrongdoer). It is unlike crime, which is a wrong against the public at large and for which the state will prosecute. In many cases, a given act will be both a tort and a crime, as when a criminal steals your wallet; both society and you are hurt.

2. WHAT ARE DAMAGES?

Damages refer to the *injury or loss suffered by a victim,* whether monetary (doctor bills), physical (loss of an arm), mental (pain and suffering), or potential (expectation of future monetary, physical, or mental loss). The tortfeasor is required to pay the victim, and the money awarded is called *compensatory damages. Special damages* cover out-of-pocket expenses, such as medical costs and lost wages. They flow naturally but not necessarily from the injury. Thus, not all persons under similar circumstances suffer the same special damages. *General damages* cover intangibles that generally accrue to all persons similarly victimized. These include pain and suffering, and mental and emotional distress.

The civil law punishes certain tortfeasors by assessing *punitive,* or *exemplary, damages* in addition to compensatory damages. These are extra monies awarded to a plaintiff in order to punish an especially blameworthy defendant, such as a corporation that has callously defrauded the plaintiff. They make an example of the defendant and try to deter others from committing similar torts.

> Elvin Kadeno, a newspaper carrier, rang the doorbell of Joe Smith's apartment in the early evening to collect for the newspapers he had delivered during the past month. He had come by weekly and Joe was never at home. This time Joe opened the door, Elvin dunned him for the money, and Joe (a strapping six-footer) busted Elvin in the mouth with a strong right. Elvin's two front teeth were knocked out and his gums severely cut. Unfortunately, Elvin was a hemophiliac and spent two months in a hospital receiving many blood transfusions. In addition, he could not be fitted with false teeth because of the injury to his gums. During his stay in the hospital, he was fed intravenously, lost several pounds, and became highly nervous and depressed. What are Joe's legal responsibilities?

Joe is responsible for compensatory damages payable to Elvin for all past, present, and prospective monetary losses, such as medical expenses and lost wages, plus a sum to compensate for pain and suffering. These damages could be substantial, especially since Elvin may be permanently injured. A jury could base general damages on the estimated pain, physical and mental, suffered each day. If Elvin has a life expectancy of sixty years, and if a jury believes that $10 a day is a reasonable compensation, the verdict could exceed $200,000. Special damages would equal Joe's out-of-pocket expenses. In addition, Elvin may seek punitive damages to punish Joe for his maliciousness in committing the battery.

Of course, winning a lawsuit does not assure collection of damages. Joe could prove to be *judgment-proof,* meaning that he has insufficient liability insurance (if any) and lacks other resources to pay. However, such a judgment survives for years (up to twenty in California), and so earnings and other assets he obtains during the life of the judgment would be subject to confiscation in partial satisfaction of it. Sometimes debtors "skip," leaving town with no forwarding address, or they die, with few or no assets available for creditors. Moreover, a judgment debtor can discharge his debt by going bankrupt. However, a judgment of punitive damages, as distinct from compensatory damages, is not dischargeable in bankruptcy.

If an injured husband's wife must quit her job in order to nurse him, the family may recover the value of the nursing service (whether more or less than the wife's salary). Furthermore, if a husband must quit work in order to perform household tasks usually done by his wife, their community may recover compensatory damages equal to the value of such services. Generally, recovery may be had for any related loss of *consortium,* which is the right of companionship and affection of each spouse for the other.

Wrongful-death statutes allow the surviving spouse, and each heir of a person who is killed by the wrongful conduct of another, to recover damages from the tortfeasor for loss of financial benefits being received at the time of death as well as those reasonably expected in the future. States are divided on the recoverability of the monetary equivalent of loss of comfort, society, and protection. Usually, wrongful death cases involve death of a spouse and recovery by the surviving spouse of lost future wages of the decedent. Thus, the wrongful death of a high-income-producing person normally results in a large recovery. The wrongful death of a small child normally results in a modest recovery because his future earnings are speculative and uncertain. However, parents sometimes recover for the intangible emotional shock they have suffered.

3. WHAT IS AN INTENTIONAL TORT?

Assault and Battery

> Molly MacNeil was sleeping with her head on a table in the Kennedy High School library when Jim Schlock leaned over and kissed the back of her neck. She awoke to the laughter of other students and, when told of his action, went from surprise, to annoyance, to tears, to illness. While vomiting in the restroom, she ruptured her spleen. Has a tort occurred?

Yes. Jim has committed the intentional tort of *battery,* which is the harmful or offensive touching of another person without justification or excuse. Of course, it usually involves an attack more violent than a kiss.

A related intentional tort is an *assault,* which is the wrongful creation of apprehension, in the mind of the victim, of some immediate peril. Hence, a left hook that misses is an assault, not a battery, if the victim saw it coming. It is an assault to shake a fist or to point a weapon at a person, provided these actions are seen by the intended victim.

> Officer Ted Sloan stopped Al Johnson, who was speeding along Parkway Boulevard in his sports coupe. When Sloan asked Al for his driver's license, Al shoved him violently and tried to escape. What torts have occurred?

Al has committed the intentional tort of battery. In addition, Al has committed the crime of assaulting and battering a police officer.

> Stewart Head, employee at Roger's Jewelry Store, decided to find someone to rob the store, using information about easy entry that he would supply. He met Skip Rogue in a local tavern, and they agreed that the following evening, with Head's advice about the alarm system, Rogue would burglarize the store. Rogue said he would carry a gun to "scare the hell out of anyone who might come along while I escape." Stewart replied, "Don't tell me the details; now you know how, just bring me my half of the goods tomorrow night after you finish." During the burglary, Rogue was observed from the street loading gems into a gunnysack. The police came and during the ensuing melee Officer Clifford Jones was shot and killed. His widow later sued Stewart Head for the wrongful death of her husband. Will she win?

Yes. Although Head was nowhere near the scene of the battery upon Officer Jones, he had conspired to commit the theft and is therefore liable for all the torts committed by his co-conspirator. *Conspiracy* simply means agreement. If two or more persons agree to commit a tort and, while the tort is being committed by one or more of the conspirators, an injury occurs, each participant in the conspiracy is liable for the entire damages. Thus, in a conspiracy, all who conspire are equally liable for all resulting damages. Mrs. Jones did not need to sue Skip Rogue because each conspirator is liable for the entire loss. In her case, each is also guilty of a crime.

In all states, if a judgment is obtained by a plaintiff against two or more tortfeasors who together are responsible for a tort, each is fully liable. However, the plaintiff may recover only once. In many states, if he collects all damages from one tortfeasor, that tortfeasor is not entitled to any contribution or partial payment by the others. This is the old common law rule. A large and growing number of states do permit contribution: some divide the damages equally; others divide it according to degree of fault. Some states—including Texas, New York, Michigan, and California—allow contribution only among defendants against whom a joint judgment has been rendered; others—including Virginia, Pennsylvania, New Jersey, and Minnesota—allow contribution even if the joint tortfeasor was not formally joined in the action as a defendant.

Intentional Infliction of Mental Disturbance

Some intentional conduct is outrageous, although not involving physical touching or placing another in apprehension of an immediate wrongful touching. Here are examples of such conduct:

1. A practical joker lies to a woman by saying that her husband has been crushed to death in an accident at the steel mill where he works.
2. Someone spreads a false rumor that a neighbor's son has hanged himself.
3. Another practical joker puts a gory dead rat in a loaf of bread belonging to a person known to have delicate sensibilities.
4. One tortfeasor mutilates a dead body and thus offends surviving relatives.
5. A creditor attempts to collect a debt by repeatedly threatening arrest and ruination of the debtor's credit, making telephone calls day and night, and using other objectionable techniques.

Activities such as these are classified as the tort of *intentional infliction of mental disturbance or distress*. They are characterized by outrageous conduct that causes mental, if not physical, suffering by the victim.

> On March 13, Jean McCormick died. Thereafter, the office of Dr. Haley, her physician, mailed a letter to Mrs. McCormick saying, "A check-up will keep you smiling . . . missed you!" An heir of Mrs. McCormick sued Dr. Haley for invasion of her right of privacy. Has she stated a legal cause of action?

Yes.[1] Each person has a right of privacy and may maintain an action for a wrongful invasion thereof. A wrongful invasion includes the intrusion into one's private activities in such a way as to outrage or cause mental suffering. However, invasion of right of privacy is an intentional tort, and if Dr. Haley were only negligent in the operation of his office, there could be no recovery.

Conversion

> Freddy Bennedy surreptitiously removed Errol Goldmuth's textbook from his briefcase and sold it to the school bookstore. Has a tort occurred?

Yes. Freddy has committed the intentional tort of *conversion,* which is the wrongful exercise of rights of ownership over someone else's personal property. He has also committed the crime of petty theft. Deliberate destruction of another's personal property would likewise be a conversion. The injured person is entitled to recover the converted goods or their value from the thief or from the innocent buyer, such as the bookstore. Real property cannot be converted but may be the subject of a wrongful trespass.

Defamation

> Thomas Mitchell called Aurelia Contento a "bitch," "thief," and "dirty whore" in the presence of other persons. These statements were not true. Ms. Contento sued for damages. Will she win?

Ms. Contento won because Mitchell committed the intentional tort of slander, for which damages are recoverable.[2] A spoken defamatory statement is *slander;* a written defamatory statement is *libel.* Courts have ruled that it is slanderous for one falsely to say that the plaintiff has syphilis; that the plaintiff, a used car dealer, is a "son-of-a-bitch"; that the school principal allows children to pet in hallways; that a baseball player is "temperamental, uncooperative, and underproductive"; that the plaintiff is a Communist Party member.[3]

Both libel and slander are variations of the intentional tort of *defamation,* which occurs when a false statement reflects unfavorably upon the reputation of the victim. There can be no defamation without publication, which is simply a communication to a third person. There can be no damage to reputation if nobody else is ever aware of the statement, and, after all, the plaintiff knows it is false. Some comments, otherwise defamatory, are *privileged* and can be made without fear of successful lawsuit. The victim is simply left without any remedy because some higher social purpose is thereby served or protected.

> Judge Osker Basel was deeply prejudiced against blacks, who appeared in his courtroom infrequently since they were a minority in the local community. When sentencing one black for a serious felony, Judge Basel remarked from the bench, "You are a rotten nigger, and I'm giving you the maximum sentence of life imprisonment as an example to the rest of your family and friends who are no better than you." Does the defendant have a cause of action against the judge for defamation?

No. Neither the defendant nor his family and friends may sue the judge for defamation, even if the remark was false, viciously racist, and motivated by personal ill will, because judges are absolutely privileged while acting in their official capacity. Witnesses and attorneys are similarly protected while in court during a trial. The same is true of members of the legislative branch of government when in session and speaking on the floor of the assembly. Certain members of the executive branch, such as the President, cabinet members, and department heads, enjoy similar protection when acting officially. The purpose of the privilege is to guarantee the freedom of government officials to function without fear of tort actions for defamation while performing their duties. They should seek and speak the truth as they see it, for the general welfare of all. Obviously, this privilege can be, and sometimes is, abused.

The *right of retraction* is a defense favoring certain publications, such as newspapers. Even if a newspaper defames someone, publication of a retraction or admission of error generally serves to reduce damages. In some states, if the libel is published innocently, the plaintiff must demand the retraction and be refused before he can collect more than special damages. California takes the extreme position that, even if the libel was maliciously published, a full retraction is a complete defense.[4]

Other privileges exist, such as *"fair comment"* on matters of public concern (for example, the competence of leaders in the Vietnam War, the honesty of persons involved in a political scandal, and the level and propriety of oil company profits). Truth is the traditional and complete defense to any action for defamation.

Deceit

> Calvin Gradd told his widowed grandmother, Sadie Stover, that the most secure and safe investment for her savings was not the local bank, but the stock of the Sark Company. Sadie thereupon invested her life savings of $50,000 in Sark. Unknown to Sadie, Sark was a corporation owned completely by Gradd. It had no assets and was, in fact, created solely to cheat Sadie out of her money. Have any torts occurred?

Yes. Cal has perpetrated the tort of *deceit* upon his grandmother. This tort is frequently called *misrepresentation* and *fraud*.

Other Common Intentional Torts

False imprisonment is wrongful detention of the victim. Most states have enacted statutes allowing store owners to detain a person reasonably suspected of shoplifting. Otherwise, such a detention would be a false imprisonment if he proved to be innocent. *Malicious prosecution* occurs when a sham lawsuit is filed against a victim for the purpose of vexing or harassing him. *Trespass* is the wrongful interference with the real or personal property of another. The intentional breaking of a window is a trespass.

4. HOW ARE DAMAGES FOR AN INTENTIONAL TORT DETERMINED?

The jury determines the amount of damages to be awarded, because the amount of loss suffered is a question of fact, not of law. Also, when punitive damages are appropriate, the amount necessary to discipline a particular defendant is a question of fact. If no jury is involved, because both parties have waived such trial, then the judge acts as finder of the facts and sets the amount of damages. Even when the jury sets the

amount, the judge may reject its verdict as either grossly inadequate or grossly excessive.

In determining the amount of punitive damages, if any, the jury considers the wealth of the defendant and the gravity of his intentional misconduct.

5. WHAT DEFENSES ARE THERE TO AN INTENTIONAL TORT?

A victim of an intentional tort may not complain if he consented to its commission.

> Jack Rodie, quarterback, lost several front teeth on the goal line when smashed in the face by the outstretched arm of Big Al Ortiz during a professional football game. Can Rodie collect?

No. Rodie implied his consent to being battered. However, if Ortiz had used brass knuckles to inflict injury, there would be no implied consent and he would be liable for damages. Similarly, if Rodie had been tackled, the whistle had blown, and then an opposing player had stepped up and deliberately kicked him, a battery would have been committed.

> Marvin Manuver was parked on the American River levee, about two in the morning with his girlfriend, Mildred Waterfield. Suddenly, the car door on Mildred's side was jerked open and Harry Dank stuck a zip gun in her face and said, "Look, buddy, all I want is your girl . . . you just sit still and there'll be no trouble. Otherwise, I'll mess up your friend." Mildred fainted, and in dragging her from the car Dank dropped his zip gun. As he stooped to pick it up, Marvin came across the front seat with a tire iron and laid Harry out with a blow on the head. While waiting for the police, Marvin, in a rage, occasionally kicked Harry, who was lying unconscious. What torts have been committed?

Harry Dank committed the tort of assault by brandishing the gun. He battered Mildred in seizing and dragging her from the car. Both Marvin and Mildred had the right to defend themselves, or each other, by using reasonable force to overcome their assailant. Hence, Marvin was legally permitted to batter Dank with the tire iron and no tort or crime occurred, even if the blow proved to be fatal. However, after Harry was unconscious, there was no further threat. Accordingly, Marvin committed a tort of battery upon Harry when he kicked the unconscious body. The right of self-defense, or defense of another, is limited to the necessary use of reasonable force. Whether or not force was necessary and reasonable, if used, are questions of fact for the jury.

6. WHAT IS A NEGLIGENT TORT?

Everyone has a duty, imposed by law, to behave as a reasonable person under the circumstances at a given time and place. Whether or not the particular conduct of a person is reasonable is a question of fact for a jury. Thus, the standard of care everyone owes to everyone else is an objective standard, that of a hypothetical "reasonable man." If one behaves less than reasonably—that is, negligently—and such behavior causes injury or loss to another, the victim may recover damages from the actor for his negligence.

> Ms. Edith Simmons, a senior citizen, onetime civic leader and highly respected community leader, was driving to her home from church. In preparing to turn left, she inadvertently allowed the right wheels of her car to edge about twelve inches over the white line into the right lane. Contact was thereby made with the front left side of Dave Biller's car, which veered to the right, hitting and killing a pedestrian, Pete Koster, a construction worker. Has Edith committed a negligent tort?

Yes. A reasonable person would not allow the right wheels of an automobile to move into the right lane while preparing to turn left. Edith's conduct was less than that expected of a hypothetical reasonable person, and she is therefore responsible for all reasonably foreseeable damages caused by her negligence. She must pay damages to Pete's family by replacing the income, society, and comfort they lost as a result of his death. She must pay for damages to Dave and his automobile. However, punitive damages are not assessable against Edith because she did no intentional wrong.

> After an appendectomy, Beverly Barton had to have additional surgery to remove a small clamp and a sponge from her abdomen. It was not ascertainable whether the hospital staff nurses, the doctor performing the operation, the doctor's assistant, the anesthesiologist, or the person who sterilized various instruments had been negligent. Beverly certainly didn't know, being unconscious throughout the operation. It was ascertainable only that (1) sponges and clamps are not left inside the patient after surgery unless someone has been negligent; (2) the negligent act must have taken place while Beverly was under the exclusive control of the medical people involved; and (3) Beverly could not have been responsible or contributed negligence to the event. Can Beverly recover damages against all the medical persons involved in the operation?

Yes. Under the doctrine of *res ipsa loquitur* (Latin: the thing speaks for itself), she is not obliged to prove who was at fault. The inference of negligence is all that is required. This special doctrine protects innocent victims who, by reason of the circumstances, are otherwise unable to recover for their loss. However, the doctrine applies only when (1) some person must have been negligent; (2) the negligent act must have been caused by an instrumentality within the exclusive control of the defendant; and (3) the plaintiff was faultless.

The Liability of Children and Parents

Children generally are liable for torts they commit. As with criminal conduct, however, a minor under seven is conclusively presumed incapable of negligence. Between seven and fourteen he is presumed incapable, but the presumption is rebuttable; over fourteen, he is presumed capable, but he may sometimes prove his incapacity. The standard of care, as always, is reasonable care, but for minors "it is that measure of care which other minors of like age, experience, capacity, and development would ordinarily exercise under similar circumstances."[5] This "lack of capacity" defense does not apply to intentional torts.

Parents generally are not liable for the torts of their minor children unless they direct or condone the wrongful conduct. They may also be liable if they give a child a *dangerous instrumentality* (such as a gun) and fail to instruct him or her in its proper use and the child hurts someone with it. Similarly, parents are liable if they fail to restrain a known *dangerous propensity* of their child, such as a habit of throwing rocks at trains or poking sticks at friends. Some statutes make parents liable up to a certain amount for willful and malicious conduct by their children. Other statutes may require that parents obtain minimum insurance coverage for children as a prerequisite to licensing as drivers.

The Liability of Insane Persons

Insane persons generally are liable for intentional torts when they can and do formulate the necessary intent to act. They can also be liable for negligent torts, although this seems strange in the light of the emphasis on a standard of reasonable care.[6] No doubt the law assumes that if an insane person hurts another and can pay, he should do so. Why should the innocent suffer without compensation?

7. WHAT LIMITATIONS ARE THERE ON DAMAGES FROM NEGLIGENT TORTS?

Brent Starr was negligently driving his car at ninety mph on a clear highway when he lost control and hit a high voltage electricity pole. This caused a short circuit and power failure in the Barstow General Hospital a hundred miles away. Just as the power failure occurred, surgeon Paul Young was making an incision near Beatrice Johnson's heart during open-heart surgery. As a result of the darkness, the incision went too deep and Beatrice died on the table within minutes. Is Brent Starr liable for Beatrice's death?

No. The duty to act as a reasonable man does not extend to being responsible for harmful results that are exceedingly remote. In other words, once a negligent act is committed, the actor is responsible only for injuries that are the "proximate" result of the act. Brent's conduct may have been the actual cause of Beatrice's death, but his act was not the proximate or legal cause because the injury was so remote. The law places no duty upon a person to protect others from consequences that are said to be unforeseeable. Where the line is drawn is a question of fact for the jury.

Brent, after shearing off the power pole, caromed into the brush, striking and killing Tom Sneed, who was dove hunting. Brent had no idea of his presence in the area. Is he liable for Tom's death?

Yes. Although Brent was unaware of Tom's presence, everyone is expected to know that a car out of control can cause harm to persons in the vicinity. In other words, injury occurring in the vicinity of a car is foreseeable and is not exceedingly remote. Since Tom's death was foreseeable by a reasonable man, it was the proximate result of Brent's negligence.

Dayton Duncan was driving down a suburban street. He noticed a large cardboard box in the road ahead and decided to run over it. He did. Thereafter, to his dismay, he discovered that Kathy Wellington, aged three, had been walking on the curb holding the box over her head when she stumbled into the street and fell with the box covering her entirely. Kathy's parents seek to hold Duncan liable for Kathy's death. Will they prevail?

No. Although Kathy was certainly in the vicinity of the automobile, her presence was not foreseeable. While it is foreseeable that a pedestrian may be in the vicinity, even in remote areas, it is not foreseeable that a person will be inside a cardboard box in the street. It is possible that a jury would find Duncan negligent in running over the box. However, his negligence was not the proximate cause of Kathy's death, and he is therefore not liable to her parents.

8. HOW ARE DAMAGES FOR A NEGLIGENT TORT DETERMINED?

As with intentional torts, damages caused by negligence are determined by the jury. However, punitive damages are not recoverable in an action based upon negligence because the elements of aggravated blame-worthiness (such as malice, violence, and fraud) are lacking.

9. WHAT DEFENSES ARE THERE TO A NEGLIGENT TORT?

A defendant is liable for damages proximately caused by his negligence unless the plaintiff's injury was in part caused by his own negligence. In such an event, the plaintiff cannot recover anything from the defendant because of the plaintiff's *contributory negligence*.

> Albert Henderson was driving his car, although he knew it had faulty brakes. He intended to have them fixed the next day. Jim Cook carelessly made a left turn in front of Albert's oncoming car. Albert tried to stop but could not. In the resulting collision, Albert was seriously injured and later sued Jim. Jim also was injured and sued Albert. Who wins?

Nobody. Jim was negligent in making his left turn. However, Albert was contributorily negligent in that, if his brakes had been fixed, he might have avoided the full impact. Hence, Jim cannot be found liable for damages: the other party's contributory negligence is considered to be a complete defense, even if such negligence is slight and the defendant's negligence is great.

> Linda Connoly was playing golf. While putting, she was struck on the head by a golf ball hit off the tee by Judy Ramsi, who failed to wait until the fairway was clear of all players. Linda sued Judy for negligence. Who wins?

Judy wins because Linda, in playing golf, implicitly assumed the risk of being hit with a golf ball. *Assumption of risk* is a defense to an action for negligence. The doctrine has been applied to spectators at ball games, hitchhikers who know their driver is intoxicated, and operators of cars who know of defects in their vehicles. The plaintiff is barred from recovery because he has willfully acted with full knowledge of the risk involved.

> Lillian Horn was in an automobile wreck in which the horn cap was dislodged. This exposed three metal prongs that the impact of the crash thrust her face into. As a result, she was seriously injured. The defense offered to produce expert testimony that if she had been wearing a seat belt, her face would not have struck the prongs. Should the court allow such testimony?

Yes. Failure to wear a seat belt may be contributory negligence if its use would have avoided or minimized the plaintiff's injuries. In an appropriate case, evidence may be submitted to show that a seat belt may have aggravated the injury, although this is less likely. Thus, proper evidence is admissible in support of either theory.

10. WHAT IS THE STATUTE OF LIMITATIONS FOR TORTS?

The *statute of limitations* is a defense, the purpose of which is to outlaw stale claims. Many courts, especially in metropolitan areas, are crowded with current problems. The difficulties of determining the truth are multiplied by the passage of time, as evidence is lost and witnesses move, forget, or die. Moreover, it is psychologically bad and against accepted judicial procedure to keep a potential lawsuit hovering over a person indefinitely.

Commonly, an action to recover damages for tortious injury must be begun within one year from commission of the intentional or negligent tort. If the victim dies, the one-year period begins with the date of death rather than with the date of the wrongful act. In the event of negligence by a physician or attorney, the one-year period begins when the victim first discovers, or reasonably should have discovered, the wrongful act. The statutory period for fraud or deceit generally is three years from the time of discovery.

To prevent a defendant from avoiding a lawsuit by leaving the state until the action is barred by the statute of limitations, the clock is stopped while he is absent. The statute generally does not begin to run against minors until they become adults. However, their parents would be well-advised to get court permission to sue on their behalf as soon as practicable, while evidence is fresh and defendants as well as witnesses are more readily available. The parents are named guardians *ad litem* (Latin: for the suit). Any judgment recovered for the child is held in trust for him until he attains majority.

11. WHAT IS PRODUCTS LIABILITY?

Doug Kalnow purchased a Poca-Pola in the local Quikee-Mart. When he applied a bottle opener to the lid, the bottle exploded. Doug lost the vision of his left eye as a result of the glass fragmentation. The bottle had been manufactured in New York and the contents in New Jersey. It had been filled in Atlanta by a bottling company and had been on the Quikee-Mart shelves for five years. Can Doug reasonably expect to prove someone's negligence?

He cannot. If negligence were the sole basis of relief for Doug, he would doubtless lose. It would be practically impossible to prove how the product was manufactured, so long ago and so far away, and especially difficult to establish that someone was negligent during the making. Because many consumer products are manufactured in distant places and used years later, the law has developed a remedy against sellers for consumers who are injured by defective products, regardless of who (if anyone) is negligent. In short, the seller of a defective product is strictly liable for injury caused thereby, regardless of negligence or intent. Hence, Doug can recover against the most readily available defendant, Quikee-Mart, which can sue the bottling company in Atlanta, which in turn can sue the manufacturer in New York. Alternatively, Doug can sue any processor in the marketing sequence, including bottler and bottle maker.

The cost of product injury is shifted from the injured consumer to the manufacturer and middlemen, who absorb these losses by buying insurance and adding to the sales price. The ultimate burden (along with other costs of production and distribution such as labor, materials, and overhead) properly falls on all consumers of the product. It is, of course, to the advantage of the producer to reduce his costs and gain a competitive advantage over other producers; he may try to do so through more careful product design, better testing, more thorough inspection, and conscientious servicing and follow-up. (Note the massive recalls of new automobiles to repair discovered defects.) No field of tort law is expanding more rapidly today, as consumers aggressively assert their rights. A realistic remedy does exist for the consumer.

In a products liability case, the injured plaintiff must prove three things: (1) that he was injured (2) by a defective product (3) manufactured, distributed, or simply sold by the defendant. A product is defective only if there is something wrong with it that makes it unreasonably dangerous. The explosion of a soda pop bottle is strong evidence that it was defective. The routine explosion of a bullet in a gun is no evidence of defect (even though someone may have been hurt) because that is what the product was designed to do.

12. WHAT DUTY DOES AN OWNER OF LAND OWE THE PUBLIC?

The possessor of land, who by his possession is in control of it, owes society the duty of reasonable care. He must exercise the care of the hypothetical reasonable man. The amount of care a reasonable man owes to a member of the public depends on the relationship of that member to the land; the least care is owed a trespasser—someone who enters another's property without permission.

Trespassers

Martin Networth owned a cabin near Lake Winnebago. He feared that, while he was at work in Milwaukee, vandals would break into his retreat, consume his supplies, and mess up the place.

He knew that breaking into his cabin would be a crime. In self-defense against such a crime, he rigged three shotguns so that if a door or window were opened, a string to the trigger of a gun would discharge buckshot into the would-be trespasser. One cold November evening, Wadsworth Wilkins and his teenage gang approached Martin's cabin, broke down the door, and were sprayed with buckshot. Wadsworth lost his eyesight and brought an action against Martin for battery. Who wins?

Wadsworth Wilkins wins his case. Although an intruder who enters the property of another without his consent has no right to expect a safe place to trespass, such a trespasser does have the right not to be intentionally injured or trapped. The landowner can use reasonable force to expel a trespasser and need not give warning of extremely dangerous conditions, but he does not have a license to kill or trap a trespasser.

When a child of tender years trespasses because he was lured by an "attractive nuisance" or potentially "dangerous instrumentality," such as a swimming pool or an unattended tractor, a special duty arises for the landowner. He must anticipate, and use ordinary care to protect trespassing children, as through construction of a suitable fence.

Licensees

Following a path, Albert Frisk took a shortcut across Farley Granger's lot to a party at Maryann Mather's. Suddenly he fell into a hole, which must have been dug by some children, and broke his ankle. He got up and hopped to Maryann's, a short distance away, to get a ride to a doctor. While hobbling up the flagstone path to Maryann's house, he tripped over a garden hose and broke his other ankle. Albert hired an attorney to sue Farley and Maryann. Who will win?

Not Albert. Existence of the path constitutes consent, or license, to use it. Likewise, a social invitation amounts to consent to approach and enter the premises. Thus, Albert was not a trespasser; he was a *licensee*. The owner of land must use appropriate care in protecting a licensee; he must warn him, for example, of known dangerous conditions. But unless Albert can show that Farley knew of the hole and that it was dangerous, he will be out of luck. Likewise, unless Maryann knew or should have known of a danger inherent in the placement of the garden hose, she is not liable.

Business Invitees

Sybil Martin had a kitchen utensil sales party at her home. If she could sell $50 worth of merchandise, she would receive a free gift. She sent invitations to twenty friends, all of whom attended. While examining some merchandise, Pam Middlebrook slipped on a throw rug on the shiny wooden floor and cracked her skull. She sued Sybil for negligence. Who wins?

Pam. She was not a trespasser, nor was she a licensee. She was present in and upon the property of Sybil as a *business invitee*. Since the land occupier expects to make money from business invitees, the law imposes the greatest degree of care. Although the occupier is not an absolute guarantor or insurer of the safety of a business invitee, Sybil has a responsibility to inspect the premises and to correct any condition that might reasonably be expected to cause harm, such as a loose throw rug on a well-waxed floor. All retail customers are business invitees and are owed such care by retail merchants.

Mary Mauser was entering a department store by walking up a sloping tile ramp. The ramp was wet from rain and she slipped, fell, and injured her back. Can Mary recover damages from the store owners?

Yes, if a jury determines that the wet ramp was an unreasonable hazard and that the defendant knew, or should have known, of its condition. Mary is a business invitee and is entitled to reasonable care from the store owner, including a reasonably safe entrance. If the ramp were no more slippery or dangerous than other walkways wet with rain, the jury would probably decide that the injury was caused by Mary's carelessness in the face of an obvious hazard, and would deny recovery.

13. MAY FAMILY MEMBERS SUE EACH OTHER FOR TORTIOUS CONDUCT?

Sally Font and her husband, Harry, were driving home in the early hours of the morning from a New Year's Eve party. Neither was intoxicated, but she had fallen asleep and his head was nodding with fatigue. Suddenly their car crashed into a telephone pole. Sally was badly injured. May she successfully sue her husband for damages because of his negligence?

Yes, under the preferred rule today. Historically, an *interspousal immunity* existed in order to avoid any disruption of family harmony caused by lawsuits between family members. Since, in some situations where litigation would have resulted if the litigants had not been family members, little family harmony remained anyway, the historical reason for the rule became suspect. Moreover, in many modern cases, as in automobile accidents, the real defendant who pays the damages is an insurance company. People buy automobile liability insurance to indemnify—that is, make good the losses of—others who may be hurt because of the insured's negligence. Certainly they would want such care to include members of their own family, even if this requires an increase in premiums. The modern rule disapproves of interspousal immunity and permits actions for negligence or intentional torts between married persons.

> E. W. Roller raped his fifteen-year-old daughter, Lulu. He was convicted and sentenced to a term in Walla Walla State Penitentiary. Lulu sued her father, seeking $2,000 in damages. What resulted?

Lulu lost because the court felt that family peace and harmony would be irreparably destroyed if such a lawsuit were permitted.[7] In most states today, Lulu would win because of a wide rejection of the doctrine of *parental immunity* in tort actions.

Some states, such as Wisconsin, immunize parents if a negligent act involves an exercise of ordinary parental discretion.[8] California, and another group of states, immunize parents if their conduct involves "reasonable parental discipline."[9] Other states that have abolished parental immunity are Alaska, Arizona, Illinois, Kentucky, Minnesota, New Hampshire, New York, and North Dakota.

14. IS AN EMPLOYER RESPONSIBLE FOR HIS EMPLOYEE'S TORTS?

> Barbara Zane, a suburban housewife, hired Darin Dammon, her seventeen-year-old neighbor, to mow her lawn. She was watching him closely, often instructing him on areas he had missed, how to care for the power mower, and the like. Suddenly Charley Brown, a twelve-year-old neighbor, fell while running across the yard. Darin, looking over his shoulder at Barbara who was yelling at him to hurry up, ran the mower into Charley's left foot, severing the big toe. Is Barbara liable to Charley?

Yes. Barbara was the employer of Darin, who was negligent in not looking where he was directing the mower and running into Charley. An employer is liable for injuries caused to third persons by their employees, who are both negligent and acting in the course and scope of their employment. The rule holding employees responsible in tort is called the doctrine of *respondeat superior* (Latin: let the superior answer).

> In a metropolitan furniture store a salesman, Ivan McDonald, invited a pretty customer, Doris Doan, upstairs for an exclusive showing of the latest arrivals of merchandise in an isolated storage area. Once there, he grabbed her roughly and made amorous

advances. She screamed, broke away, and ran down the stairs. McDonald was fired and Doris later sued General Stores for battery under the doctrine of respondeat superior. Will she win?

No. An employer is not responsible for all acts of an employee. The battery was not committed in the course and scope of Ivan's employment, even though it occurred during store hours upon store premises. The employer had no reason to anticipate such an event nor had he means to prevent it.

Generally, an employer is responsible for all negligent acts of employees done upon the work premises, but is responsible for intentional torts only if closely related to the job. For example, the driver of a delivery truck who gets into an argument with a customer and hits him in the mouth, renders his employer liable for resulting damages. Or, if a service station attendant flicks a lighted cigarette while pouring gasoline for a customer and the station blows up, the owner will be liable for the substantial resulting damages.

15. MAY AN EMPLOYEE SUE HIS EMPLOYER FOR JOB-RELATED INJURY?

> Buster Ampeer was an electrician working at the Bear River dam site for Inter-Network, a utility company. Gary Gref was a crane operator for the General Contracting Company, which was also working at the dam site. Gary somehow moved the crane too near high voltage power lines, causing a bolt of electricity to leap through the crane, striking Buster and inflicting serious injury. May Buster sue his employer for his injury?

No. Buster may not sue Inter-Network even if his injury was caused by the negligence of a fellow employee. In such a case Buster would be compensated under the *workmen's compensation law*. Under this law, every employer is required to carry insurance to cover employee injuries caused by co-employees, working conditions, or the employee himself. Buster's injury, however, was caused by a third party, Gary Gref, acting as an employee of General Contracting. Therefore, Buster can sue General Contracting under the doctrine of respondeat superior, and will not receive workmen's compensation benefits.

When appropriate, workmen's compensation insurance pays for various types of injuries suffered, as specified in the insurance contract. No payment is made for pain and suffering. There is no right to a jury trial in obtaining workmen's compensation benefits, and attorney fees for assistance are minimal and regulated by law.

Workmen's compensation, when applicable, is payable regardless of fault, and so it is a form of *absolute liability*. Some activities are inherently so dangerous that absolute liability is imposed upon the actor for all injuries he causes. The keeping of a wild animal or the storage and use of explosives in a residential area are examples of such activities.

16. IS GOVERNMENT LIABLE FOR TORTS?

Under the fiction that "the king can do no wrong," government historically has not been liable for its torts. This principle is called the *doctrine of sovereign immunity*. In the United States, although we have no king, it was theorized that a successful lawsuit against the government could endanger its stability and continuity; this would be intolerable. In fact, all citizens, through the taxing power of their government, can better afford to absorb a loss than could an unfortunate victim of a tort committed by a government employee.

Congress adopted the Federal Tort Claims Act in 1946, which waives sovereign immunity in cases involving negligence. Thus, a federal employee who carelessly operates a government vehicle in the course and scope of his employment may subject the government to liability for injuries he causes. However, the federal government remains immune to injuries caused by the intentional conduct of its agents and employees.

States, cities, and counties are also protected by the doctrine of sovereign immunity. State statutes do normally allow recovery for negligence of such governmental entities in operating and maintaining public streets, buildings, and grounds and in operating motor vehicles. The trend of the law is to treat government, as regards its liability for torts, the same as any other employer.

17. IS A TORTFEASOR PROTECTED BY INSURANCE?

The purpose of liability insurance is to protect the insured against certain tort claims asserted by persons he injures. The most common variety is automobile liability insurance.

> Harold Prince bought a policy for automobile liability insurance covering claims of any one person up to $10,000 and claims arising from any one accident up to $20,000. In addition, it provided $5,000 for property damages, and $2,500 collision coverage. One afternoon, Harold was driving down a country road along a river with his girlfriend, Sally Brandon. They had been drinking wine. Suddenly Harold passed out, ran off the road and into the river, and rammed a passing boat. Joe Pyle, John Jones, and George Jackson were fishing from the deck of the cabin cruiser sunk by Harold's vehicle. John was drowned, George lost his right arm, and Joe suffered a skull fracture. Sally had internal injuries and Harold was unhurt. To whom is Harold liable, and for how much?

Harold is liable to everyone, except Sally who assumed the risk of injury by voluntarily riding with Harold and joining in his drinking. Juries may award John's family, George, and Joe considerably more than $20,000. If this is the case, Harold must cover any excess from his own resources. Harold's collision insurance will pay for damage to his car up to $2,500, since that type of coverage has nothing to do with fault. Likewise, the medical coverage will pay medical expenses of Harold and Sally without regard to fault. Damage to the boat will be paid in accordance with the property damage clause, up to $5,000.

Liability insurance does not reimburse a tortfeasor for liabilities he incurs through his intentional wrongful conduct. The victim of such conduct must look to the personal assets of the wrongdoer. Even if insurance companies were willing to assume the high risks of insuring against losses caused by deliberate wrongful conduct, they could not do so because it would be contrary to public policy and bad for the general welfare of society.

CASES, QUESTIONS, AND PROBLEMS

1. At three in the morning state police trooper Kellogg observed Donald Schanbarger walking along a public street in the township of East Greenbush, where there had been several burglaries recently. Schanbarger was carrying a large bag. When stopped by Kellogg, he refused to reveal his name, destination, or address and was promptly arrested for loitering. He was booked and released on $20 bail. Does Schanbarger have a cause of action against Kellogg for false arrest?

2. John Ryan, aged three, was playing in the backyard of his neighbor, Jerry Preston, aged eight. Jerry ran over John's hand with a power mower and cut it severely. John's mother was a guest in the Preston home at the time of the accident. John sued his mother for negligence in supervising himself. He asked for $500,000 in damages.
   a. Who wins?
   b. Is Jerry responsible for his own negligence? Are Jerry's parents responsible?
   c. Could John's cause of action be barred because of his own contributory negligence?

3. Can a parent who vigorously spanks his child be sued by the child for battery? Suppose the child is locked in a closet; does a cause of action for false imprisonment arise? May the parents be prosecuted by society for the crime of child abuse?

4. Nick Dekker went into the Black Oak Restaurant for dinner. When leaving, he mistakenly took George Walton's hat from the coat rack and walked out the door. Walton observed the incident, ran outside,

and yelled "Stop thief!" just as Dekker was driving out of the parking lot. Walton jumped into his own car and gave pursuit. He overtook a car driven by a man who looked like Dekker, although it was really Ferdinand Sinzant. Walton pulled alongside, and forced Sinzant onto the shoulder of the road by easing his car along the front left side of Sinzant's car. When the cars stopped, Walton leaped out and smashed Sinzant in the mouth, knocking him unconscious. He put Sinzant into his car and drove back to the restaurant, where he phoned the police. When the squad car arrived, Sinzant regained consciousness, and Walton said "Arrest this man, he's a thief." The police refused to make the arrest because they had not observed any crime. However, they advised Walton that if he made a citizen's arrest, they would book Sinzant. Walton thereupon placed Sinzant under arrest. Meanwhile, Harry Hightower ran into the left rear of Sinzant's car, which was protruding slightly into the street with its lights out. At the time of the accident, Hightower was under the influence of marijuana. What torts have occurred?

5. Carolyn Webster was the victim of a rape by Victor Store, a casual acquaintance. Victor was prosecuted, convicted, and sentenced to six months in the county jail, but the sentence was suspended and probation granted. Carolyn was pregnant by Victor. She filed a lawsuit for battery against Victor seeking damages measured by (1) all prenatal and delivery expenses; (2) $150 a month for eighteen years as normal child support; (3) $50,000 for her mental anguish, grief, and embarrassment; and (4) $50,000 punitive damages.
   a. Is Victor liable to Carolyn for any damages? If so, what is the proper measure of damages?
   b. Would Victor be legally entitled to visit his child?
   c. Could Carolyn obtain a legal abortion even though Victor objected?

6. Alonzo Mobry held up Charley Smith at gunpoint and robbed him of his wallet containing $300. Mobry was apprehended after he had spent all of the money. He was tried, convicted, and sentenced to a year in the county jail. Upon his release, Smith sued him for $300 in compensatory damages and $500 in punitive damages. Mobry contends the lawsuit would be double jeopardy and unconstitutional. Is Mobry correct?

7. A woman's daughter who had been born out of wedlock sought damages for the wrongful death of her stepfather, whom the mother married after the child's birth. The plaintiff had not been adopted. May the daughter recover although she is not an heir?

8. Torts are legally recognized wrongs. Is every tort a moral wrong? Are all moral wrongs legal wrongs? Does society require everyone to be a good Samaritan and to go to the aid of neighbors in distress?

9. When a country loses a war and is required to pay reparations to the victorious power, is the process analogous to any tort action?

10. In most states, a plaintiff's contributory negligence in an accident, even though it may be a small percentage of the total involved, completely bars recovery of damages. Some states, such as Wisconsin, follow a rule of comparative negligence and permit the person who has contributed the smaller percentage to recover damages (reduced by the percentage of his negligence). Which is the better rule, and why?

11. Much has been said in recent years about no-fault automobile insurance, under which all parties involved in most automobile accidents would recover damages from their own insurance companies, regardless of fault. Damages would be limited but certain, as with workmen's compensation. No trials would take place, except perhaps when injuries are very serious. Should no-fault insurance be adopted in all states or at the federal level? Some have suggested extending the idea to strict product liability cases. Do you agree?

12. Should governments (federal, state, and local) be held as fully responsible for their torts as are private citizens?

5

YOU
AS STUDENT

1. IS A FREE PUBLIC EDUCATION A BASIC RIGHT GUARANTEED BY THE U.S. CONSTITUTION?

Nothing in the Bill of Rights or in subsequent amendments to the U.S. Constitution prescribes a free public education as a basic right of everyone. Nor does the Constitution specifically grant the federal government power to provide schools and schooling. But Congress has established West Point and the other military academies as necessary and proper under its authority "to provide for the common defense"[1] of all the states, "to raise and support armies," and "to provide and maintain a navy."[2] Under its broad power "to lay and collect taxes . . . and provide for the . . . general welfare,"[3] Congress has the implied authority to spend money for educational purposes. This it has done.

Over the years, the federal government has provided a wide variety of financial support for public schools. The Ordinance of 1785 reserved, for the support of public schools, every sixteenth section (one square mile) of public lands surveyed into townships. More recently, billions of dollars have been appropriated by Congress to assist schools at the elementary, secondary, and higher levels. The Civil Rights Act of 1964, designed primarily to eliminate discrimination in employment, has also been used to outlaw discrimination in schooling where federal funds are provided.

2. WHAT LAW BARS DISCRIMINATION IN PUBLIC EDUCATION?

The Fourteenth amendment outlaws discrimination in public education when state or local government agencies provide this service. The crucial section 1 of the Fourteenth Amendment reads as follows:

> All persons born or naturalized in the United States, and subject to the jurisdiction thereof, are citizens of the United States and of the state wherein they reside. No state shall make or enforce any law which shall abridge the privileges or immunities of citizens of the United States; nor shall any state deprive any person of life, liberty, or property, without due process of law; nor deny to any person within its jurisdiction the equal protection of the laws.

The Fourteenth Amendment was adopted in 1868, shortly after the Civil War, and was directed against possible abuse of persons by states. Persons had already been protected against abuse by the federal government under the Fifth Amendment (adopted in 1791) which reads in part:

> No person shall be . . . deprived of life, liberty, or property, without due process of law; nor shall private property be taken for public use, without just compensation.

Supreme Court Interpretations

> James Hinkee campaigned for the governorship of his state on the pledge: "Separate but Better Schools for Blacks. Treat Them Right, but Keep Them in their Place!" He proposed to keep all public schools segregated but to make ghetto schools models of efficiency through liberal financial support well beyond the level for other schools. Is his proposal legal?

No. Hinkee's proposal is unconstitutional. The U.S. Supreme Court has not always interpreted and applied the Fourteenth Amendment as it does today. Thus, in the famous (or infamous) case of *Plessy* v. *Ferguson* (163 U.S. 537, 1896), the Court upheld the constitutionality of a controversial Louisiana law that provided for "equal but separate accommodations for the white and colored races." It referred directly to passenger coaches in trains but was applied to other facilities, including schools. The majority of the Court were persuaded by the argument that the law properly upheld absolute equality for all. In the reality of daily living, this was not true; facilities were not equal, and to bar certain persons from any public or quasi-public facilities is obviously to discriminate against them illegally.

Nevertheless, fifty-eight years passed before the U.S. Supreme Court unanimously overruled *Plessy* v. *Ferguson* in the landmark case of *Brown* v. *Board of Education* of Topeka, Kansas (347 U.S. 483, 1954). The Court now held that when a state undertakes to provide education in public schools, the opportunity becomes a right that must be made available to all on equal terms under the Fourteenth Amendment; all are entitled to equal protection of the laws. To segregate children in public schools solely on the basis of race deprives the minority members of equal educational opportunities, even if physical facilities may actually be of equal quality. The raw fact of segregation may have negative psychological effects on developing personalities and interfere with proper education. Such separation, the Court said, "generates a feeling of inferiority as to their status in the community that may affect their hearts and minds in a way unlikely ever to be undone."

During the following year the Court ordered the federal district courts to "enter such orders . . . as are necessary and proper to admit to public schools on a nondiscriminatory basis *with all deliberate speed* the parties. . . ."[4] The italicized words were construed by different authorities differently, and delays in implementation resulted. Later court decisions made it clear that the language used was not intended to encourage or permit avoidable delays in desegregation.

De jure (Latin: by law) *segregation* in public schools is clearly illegal and intolerable. *De facto* (Latin: in fact) *segregation* in public schools is a reality in many cities, and reflects the neighborhoods and the economic levels of the residents; it has been considered legal and is tolerated. One judicial trend suggests elimination of school district lines as through consolidation where their effect is to permit de facto segregation of pupils on a racial basis. Another approach is the construction of larger schools, serving more territory and a wider diversity of income groups and racial classes. The U.S. Supreme Court has called upon school district officials to work out system-wide desegregation plans, but as of this writing it has not categorically condemned de facto segregation.[5] Nor has it extended to private schools its orders for desegregation. The Court has, however, struck down, as violating the Fourteenth Amendment, efforts in Virginia to finance segregated but private schools with state funds.[6]

State Court Interpretations

Recent decisions in state courts in California and elsewhere promise some improvement by requiring essentially equal financial support of all public schools on a state-wide basis. When fully implemented, this should tend to equalize the quality of schooling in all districts. Of course, the intangible psychological distinctions that flow from segregation would remain.

Critics point out that in a recent year (1968–69) the Beverly Hills (California) school district could tax property with an assessed value of $50,885 per pupil, whereas the nearby Baldwin Park school district could tax property worth only $3,706 per pupil. Even after being augmented by state and federal aid, the total funds available per pupil were $1,232 in Beverly Hills and only $577 in her sister city. In *Serrano* v. *Priest,* the California Supreme Court relied on the equal protection clause of the U.S. Constitution and also on the state constitution in calling for equalization.[7] Subsequently, the U.S. Supreme Court held that the federal Constitution does not require "absolute equality" in financial support of schools, or "precisely equal" educational advantages. Speaking for the majority in the 5-to-4 decision, Justice Lewis F. Powell, Jr., said:

> Education, of course, is not among the rights afforded explicit protection under our Constitution. Nor do we find any basis for saying it is implicitly so protected.[8]

He added that this does not mean approval of the status quo and suggested that "the ultimate solutions must come from the lawmakers and from the democratic pressures of those who elect them." Thus, the problem of gross inequality in school financing must be solved by the people of each state and by their legislatures.

Busing and Other Suggested Solutions

In Metropolis, a large group of Mexican-Americans (Chicanos) resides in their own neighborhood (barrio), a substandard area along the railroad tracks on the south side of town. They have their own public elementary schools and public high school. Although these schools have produced many championship athletic teams, their academic reputations are not good. Manuel Morales and a group of his fellow citizens want pupils from the barrio to be bused from one to seven miles to Anglo schools on the other side of the tracks in an exchange with pupils now enrolled there. Will a court support this demand?

Not necessarily. As of this writing, the desegregation debate revolves around proposals to bus school children, especially at the elementary level. The issue has not been judicially resolved by the U.S. Supreme Court, although decisions at the trial court level have supported the concept of compulsory busing. In a 5-to-4 decision in 1974, the U.S. Supreme Court disappointed advocates of speedy desegregation when it ruled that busing pupils across school district lines in Detroit was improper. Lower courts had upheld a plan to bus children between the inner city schools, which were 65 percent black, and the suburban schools, which were 90 percent white. The majority opinion concluded that the evidence did not show that acts of the outlying districts "affected the discrimination found to exist in the schools of Detroit," and sent the case back to the lower court for an appropriate decree "directed to eliminating segregation found to exist in Detroit city schools." Chief Justice Warren Burger said courts should not become "a de facto 'legislative authority' to resolve these complex questions and then the 'school superintendant' for the entire area." But, he warned:

> No state law is above the Constitution. School district lines and
> the present laws with respect to local control are not sacrosanct
> and, if they conflict with the Fourteenth amendment, federal
> courts have a duty to prescribe appropriate remedies.[9]

Many parents are adamant about having their children attend nearby
neighborhood schools. They do not want to have them transported to
distant schools, which may be inferior and which are located in what
they believe is a hostile or even dangerous environment, in order to achieve
a better racial balance among the pupils. Yet, because the races are in
fact segregated geographically in many cities, unless pupils are bused,
public schools cannot be desegregated. In his dissent in the Detroit busing
case, Justice Thurgood Marshall declared:

> Our nation, I fear, will be ill-served by the court's refusal to
> remedy separate and unequal education, for, unless our children
> begin to learn together, there is little hope that our people will
> ever learn to live together.

Special financial support has been suggested for ghetto and barrio
schools, but this solution appears to return to the discarded *Plessy* v.
Ferguson doctrine of separate but equal facilities for minorities. Obviously, if neighborhood housing can be desegregated, neighborhood
schools will automatically be desegregated. For that to happen, however,
jobs must be desegregated, and, in turn, education must be desegregated
to prepare minorities for more responsible and more lucrative employment. Thus, it is a vicious circle. In a society dedicated to freedom and
justice for all, it would appear that changes must be made at all three
critical points: housing, employment, and education. If not accomplished
under the nagging of conscience, the changes will probably be accomplished
under the pressure of law.

3. MUST PUBLIC COLLEGES AND UNIVERSITIES DESEGREGATE?

> James Meredith, twenty-nine-year-old Negro, was an Air Force
> veteran with academic credits from several universities. His grades
> were "good to superior." When he applied for admission to the
> segregated University of Mississippi at Oxford, Mississippi, the
> university refused, citing a variety of reasons: he did not present
> the required alumni certificates; he was a "troublemaker"; and
> he had registered falsely for voting. Meredith appealed to the
> federal district court for an injunction to compel the university
> to admit him. Decide.

Meredith wins and must be admitted.[10] He had been denied admission
solely because he was black, and this is unconstitutional. Other reasons
cited lacked substance, or were not valid nondiscriminatory bases for

rejection. For example, to require certificates of approval from alumni of a school that never admitted a black student might effectively maintain that status quo forever.

Meredith's troubles were not over. The Governor of Mississippi issued a proclamation calling for the arrest of any federal official interfering with state officers who followed orders to bar Meredith from the university. The President of the United States met this challenge to the supremacy of federal law by taking command of the state National Guard, and by ordering the Secretary of Defense to remove all obstructions to justice in the state. Four hundred U.S. marshals and sixteen thousand federal troops moved onto the campus and surrounded the area. There was rioting and bloodshed; two men died. But in the end the federal law prevailed: segregation in schools of higher education ended. Meredith was enrolled.

On college campuses throughout the country, the climate of tolerance and acceptance has dramatically improved since the Meredith confrontation in 1962. Enrollment of minorities has increased substantially. Many such students have graduated and are already making significant contributions to the nation's productivity and well-being.

> Marco De Funis was one of 1600 applicants for the 150 openings in the freshman class of the law school of the University of Washington. He was a superior student and scored within the top 7 percent of those taking the entrance exam, but he was rejected. Thirty minority applicants, however, most of them black, were admitted even though some had grades and test scores below the normal minimal standards. De Funis asked a state court to order the school to admit him. Decide.

The trial court ordered the law school to follow the law of the famous *Brown* v. *Board of Education* case, and to admit De Funis. Brown made race irrelevant in school admission decisions.

The university appealed the decision and won. In May 1973, Justice Marshall Neill of the state supreme court declared that the Brown case "did not hold that all racial classifications are per se unconstitutional, but only those that stigmatize a racial group with the stamp of inferiority."[11] Only invidious discrimination is bad. Discrimination can be desirable and necessary to achieve legitimate social goals—for example, to give minorities "equal representation within our legal system." This means that minorities must be provided with professional legal education. In dissent, Justice C. J. Hale argued that inequalities cannot be solved by "shifting inequities from one man to his neighbor."

De Funis appealed to the U.S. Supreme Court and meanwhile was belatedly admitted to the University of Washington School of Law. When the case came up for consideration in April 1974, the Court ruled that it was *moot*—that is, it had become an abstract and theoretical question, hence not appropriate for decision, since De Funis was scheduled to graduate shortly (in June 1974). He would presumably do so "regardless of any decision this Court might render on the merits of this litigation."[12] Similar cases are moving toward the top court as this is written, and so a definitive ruling on this issue of "reverse discrimination" may be expected soon.

4. HOW LONG MUST ONE GO TO SCHOOL?

> Joe Machold was six feet five inches tall and weighed 210 pounds. He shaved regularly and looked at least ten years older than his fifteen years. Attending school had become a bore and an embarrassment for him, and so he left home and attempted to enlist in the U.S. Marine Corps under an assumed name. The Corps ultimately sent him back home. Must he return to school?

Yes. The predicament of Machold dramatizes the way many students feel sometime during their seemingly endless years of formal schooling. They want out. "Experts," however, say that the very future of our civilization and of our democracy depends in large measure on an educated citizenry, and so society insists that the young attend school. Many opportunities are also provided for lifelong learning by adults.

California's school attendance laws are representative of those found in most states. Unless exempted, every person between the ages of six and sixteen years is subject to compulsory full-time education.[13] Exempt from compulsory attendance in public schools are children who

a. are instructed in a private full-time day school by persons capable of teaching

b. have physical or mental conditions that prevent school attendance or render it inadvisable

c. are mentally gifted and are instructed in a full-time day school where as much as 50 percent of the instructional time may be taught in a foreign language

d. are being properly instructed by a private tutor with valid credentials

e. are blind or deaf and for whom no appropriate public schools are available[14]

In the case of Machold, his principal could recommend that, as a minor over fourteen, he be assigned to a vocational course at some place of employment in lieu of the regular school course.[15] Alternately, he might attend a special continuation school where emphasis is given to individualized instruction with an occupational orientation, or he might be given a combination work-study schedule. Such specially designed programs of individualized instruction and intensive guidance are geared to meet the needs of pupils with "behavior or severe attendance problems."[16] Pupils who have appeared in juvenile court are also commonly assigned to continuation schools.

In 1973, a national commission sponsored by the Kettering Foundation concluded that "compulsory attendance laws are the dead hand on the high schools."[17] It found that daily attendance in many inner-city schools runs less than 50 percent of the enrollment. "The harm done to the school by the student who does not want to be there is measured not only by the incidence of vandalism and assault, but also by a subtle and a continuous degradation of the tone of the educational enterprise." The commission urged expanding vocational and work-study programs, and lowering the age of compulsory attendance from sixteen to fourteen.

5. MAY PARENTS REFUSE TO SEND THEIR CHILDREN TO PUBLIC SCHOOLS?

Yes, but only if they provide an acceptable equivalent—usually attendance in a private school, privately financed. Most private schools are also parochial schools, established and financed by members of religious denominations (commonly, but far from exclusively, the Roman Catholic church).

In 1922, the Oregon legislature enacted a law requiring all children between the ages of eight and sixteen to attend public schools. To no one's surprise, the law was promptly challenged as a violation of the Fourteenth Amendment to the U.S. Constitution. In *Pierce* v. *Society of the Sisters of the Holy Names,* the U.S. Supreme Court upheld the right of parents to send their children to qualified private schools, which also provide education in a sectarian religion not available in public schools. The court declared:

> The fundamental theory of liberty, upon which all governments of this Union repose, excludes any general power of the state to standardize its children by forcing them to accept instruction from public teachers only. The child is not the mere creature of the state; those who nurture him and direct his destiny have the right, coupled with the high duty, to recognize and prepare him for additional obligations.[18]

> Herger, Wendel, and Scheu were parents of children of high school age and devout Mennonites, or Amish (named after Jacob Ammann, a Swiss Mennonite who lived in the seventeenth century). They wanted to remove their children from a local public high school in Wisconsin because they feared that such education, if continued, "would gravely endanger if not destroy the free exercise of . . . [their] religious beliefs." They did not intend to send the children to a parochial private school, but proposed to substitute their own on-the-farm, informal, agricultural, voca-

tional education, emphasizing manual physical labor and self-reliance. Can the Amish parents be compelled to send their children to a public (or private) school until the age of sixteen, as required by Wisconsin law?

No. The U.S. Supreme Court has held that enforcement of the state's requirement of compulsory formal education after the eighth grade would gravely endanger, if not destroy, the free exercise of the religious beliefs of the Amish. Moreover, the alternative they proposed appeared to be adequate. In the words of Chief Justice Warren Burger, the Court warned, however, that "nothing we hold is intended to undermine the general applicability of the state's compulsory school attendance statutes or to limit the power of the state to promulgate reasonable standards. . . ." In other words, for most parents and children, the compulsory attendance law still applies. The Court noted that "few other religious groups or sects could make . . . [such a] convincing showing."[19]

> Lon Jennings and his wife disapproved of their local public high school, but could not afford to send their teen-age daughter to a private school and did not want to send her to a sectarian parochial private school. Therefore, they enrolled her in a full program of high school courses by correspondence with a mail order school in Chicago. They planned to help their daughter with her academic work. Would this program exempt her from attending a public high school?

No. The law does not recognize correspondence courses as equivalent to full-time day school.[20] Parents who are laymen do not qualify as professional tutors. Moreover, certain studies that are prescribed for all elementary and secondary pupils may not be available by correspondence.

6. MAY THE GOVERNMENT PROVIDE FINANCIAL SUPPORT FOR PRIVATE OR PAROCHIAL SCHOOLS?

The answer is a qualified no, if actual practice is the criterion. The first amendment to the U.S. Constitution explicitly states that "Congress shall make no law respecting an establishment of religion, or prohibiting the free exercise thereof." The founders of our national government were aware of abuses resulting from alliances of church and state in ancient and medieval societies in Europe. They also knew that many colonists had come to America in search of a place where they could freely exercise their religion. The Bill of Rights neatly handled the religion question by barring legislation that either supports or interferes with any religion. Thus, when religious doctrine and practice are not immoral or contrary to public safety, health, or welfare, the government theoretically remains neutral. In fact, the government provides property tax exemption to all religious sects—a form of impartial support to which some atheists and agnostics object. Government deviates from absolute neutrality in other ways, such as providing military chapels and chaplains; granting income tax concessions for contributions to charities, including religious societies; and imprinting the words "In God We Trust" on coins and paper currency.

In the area of schooling, the problem of separation of church and state is confused by the fact that pupils in parochial schools are citizens as well as members of religious sects. Their parents pay taxes for support of free public education, and could, if they chose, send their children to these schools. Critics of private schools say that they are divisive. The parents respond with the argument that public schools necessarily are not universal in their teaching and must neglect religious instruction, which can help prepare better citizens; moreover, diversity is essential for experimentation, comparison, and progress. Should not their children therefore receive the benefit of government programs that do not directly support religious instruction?

On that rationale, governments have provided parochial schools and their pupils with free or subsidized lunches, health services, science instruction equipment, secular library books, and textbooks. Even costly busing services have sometimes been furnished. In the leading case of *Everson* v. *Board of Education* of Ewing Township, the U.S. Supreme Court held that use of public funds by school districts in New Jersey for transportation of pupils to private schools did not violate the U.S. Constitution (First or Fourteenth Amendments).[21] However, the state legislature must specifically authorize such transportation. Most states do not do so; in the state of Washington, for example, such transportation is regarded as a violation of the state constitution.[22]

In the words of Chief Justice Warren Burger of the U.S. Supreme Court, "while some involvement and entanglement are inevitable [between religion and government], lines must be drawn." In the case of *Lemon* v. *Kurtzman,* that line was drawn when Pennsylvania attempted to reimburse nonpublic elementary and secondary schools for the cost of teachers' salaries, textbooks, and instructional materials, and Rhode Island tried to pay a 15 percent salary supplement to teachers in nonpublic elementary schools. Both statutes were held to be unconstitutional; the "entanglement" with religion was "excessive." "The Constitution decrees," said Chief Justice Burger, "that religion must be a private matter for the individual, the family, and the institution of private choice."[23]

It is significant that since World War II, moneys have been provided to veterans for their education. In each case, the veteran selects his school, public or private. Some observers assume any mass support of private education in the future would use the same approach: payments would be made to students (or parents) followed by their choice of institution. Others have proposed tax credits under which taxpayers with children in private elementary and secondary schools would write off part of their tuition payments against their federal income tax liability. Critics say this breaches the constitutional barrier against government support of religion. They point out that it could be abused by segregationists to establish a system of nonsectarian private schools barred to blacks in defiance of the spirit of the *Brown* v. *Board of Education* ruling.

In 1973, in a series of decisions from New York and Pennsylvania, the U.S. Supreme Court struck down state laws that granted tax deductions to parents of nonpublic school students, as violating the first amendment ban on establishment of religion. Other forms of aid will probably also be challenged and forbidden in the future—although the court stated that "not every law that confers an 'indirect,' 'remote,' or 'incidental' benefit upon religious institutions is, for that reason alone, constitutionally invalid."[24]

7. MAY THE RECITATION OF A PRAYER BE REQUIRED BY LAW IN A PUBLIC SCHOOL?

No. In New York, the state Board of Regents composed what they considered to be an innocuous and unobjectionable prayer and recommended it to all school districts of the state for daily recitation. It read:

> Almighty God, we acknowledge our dependence upon Thee, and we beg Thy blessings upon us, our parents, our teachers, and our country.

Some parents objected, contending that the prayer was contrary to their beliefs and practices and to those of their children; moreover, it violated the first amendment to the U.S. Constitution, which extends to state laws, as here, by virtue of the Fourteenth Amendment. The justices of the Supreme Court agreed. Speaking for the Court in *Engel* v. *Vitale,* Justice Hugo Black said that "daily classroom invocation of God's blessings as prescribed . . . is a religious activity" and "in this country it is no part of the business of government to compose official prayers."[25] He went on to say that the purpose of the establishment of religion clause, which was violated by the official prayer, "rested on the belief that a union of government and religion tends to destroy government and to degrade religion." Justice Black later pointed out that the decision did not indicate hostility toward religion or prayer. The framers of the Bill of Rights "knew that the first amendment, which tried to put an end to governmental control of religion and of prayer, was not written to destroy either." Efforts to amend the U.S. Constitution to permit such prayers have been unsuccessful.

Carl Nevin was principal of a public elementary school in which all of the children happened to be Muslims. In keeping with their culture and religious beliefs, he ordered his teachers to begin every class with a short reading from the Koran, the sacred book believed by Muslims to contain revelations of Allah (God) to Mohammed. No pupils or parents objected to the practice; indeed, many wrote letters of commendation. Nevertheless, the superintendent of the school district told Nevin to stop the practice immediately; the readings violated the law. Is this true?

Yes. In an analogous case involving the reading of the Bible, the U.S. Supreme Court found the practice unconstitutional, even though any child, on written request of his parents or guardian, was excused from the compulsory reading. Public schools are not barred, however, from offering classes in the Koran or the Bible or in any religious doctrine and practice, if presented in voluntary classes as part of a secular program of education in literature, social studies, or philosophy. In some states, parents may have their children excused from regular public school classes for religious and moral instruction, or from participation in religious exercises away from school.

Lyn Beinecke was known to be an imaginative and enterprising teacher of the eighth grade at the Willow Run Public School. Among the many projects she had her class engage in was a four-phase production entitled "Man Worships God." As part of the social science studies, at appropriate religious feast times during the school year, pupils prepared displays of Christian, Jewish, Muslim, and Buddhist art. Karl Thomas, an agnostic, and Abner Perry, an atheist, were parents who objected to the project and sought a court order to end it. Will they succeed?

Probably not. The project was not designed to propagandize or proselytize for any religious sect. It appears to be a proper part of the social studies program. Religion is important in the history of man, and religious beliefs are reflected in temples, cathedrals, shrines, sculptures, and paintings.

8. MAY THE STATE REQUIRE THAT CERTAIN SUBJECTS BE TAUGHT TO ALL CHILDREN IN THE PUBLIC SCHOOLS?

Yes. Courts have upheld the right of public schools to offer subjects of their choice as well as subjects prescribed by state law. In California, for example, even at the college and university level, students must either demonstrate competence in certain areas or successfully complete prescribed courses: U.S. history and Constitution, American ideals, and California state and local government. For lower levels of instruction, a statute added in 1968 prescribed that "instruction in the social sciences shall include the early history of California and a study of the role and contributions of American Negroes, American Indians, Mexicans, persons of oriental extraction (added in 1970), and other ethnic groups to the economic, political, and social development of California and the United States of America."[28]

Under the Education Code, the adopted courses of study must also provide instruction at the appropriate elementary and secondary levels in:

a. personal and public safety and accident prevention
b. fire prevention
c. protection and conservation of resources, including the necessity for the protection of the environment
d. health, including the effects of alcohol, narcotics, drugs, and tobacco upon the human body[29]

All pupils in grades 7 through 12, except those excused for physical reasons or because of participation in interscholastic athletic programs, are required to attend courses of physical education. During grades 9, 10, 11, and 12, pupils may be excused for a limited time to participate in automobile driver training.

Reciprocally, the state may prohibit the teaching of certain materials in public schools. The teaching of religion for purposes of indoctrination is forbidden, as discussed earlier. Although the facts about communism may be taught, "no teacher giving instruction in any school . . . shall advocate or teach communism with the intent to indoctrinate or to inculcate in the mind of any pupil a preference for communism."[30]

9. MAY THE STATE REQUIRE THAT PUPILS ATTEND CLASSES IN SEX EDUCATION?

The Durlands and the Foshays were shocked by the promiscuity in contemporary patterns of sexual behavior among adolescents. The Durlands were determined to shield their children (aged nine, thirteen, and fifteen) as much as possible from what they considered "corrupting influences." Their neighbors, the Foshays, were of the opinion that appropriate family life instruction, including sex education at all grade levels, was the best available solution. When the local school board in San Francisco introduced a program of sex education in grades 5 through 12, the Foshays cheered and the Durlands groaned. Must the Durland children attend the sex education classes?

No. California's legislature is explicit in declaring that "no governing board of a public elementary or secondary school may require pupils to attend any class in which human reproductive organs and their functions and processes are described, illustrated, or discussed, whether such class be part of a course designated 'sex education' or 'family life education' or by some similar term, or part of any other course which pupils are required to attend."[31] When such classes are offered, the parents must be notified in writing and must be given an opportunity to request that their children not attend the classes. It is noteworthy that the statute does not apply to descriptions or illustrations of human reproductive organs in textbooks (adopted in conformance with law) on physiology, biology, zoology, general science, personal hygiene, or health.

In Hawaii, parents challenged sex education classes at the fifth- and sixth-grade levels as both invasions of privacy and a violation of their religious freedom. The state Supreme Court denied their request for an injunction. On the first argument, it quoted the U.S. Supreme Court from a case in which a Connecticut statute that made the use of contraceptives a criminal offense was held invalid (because it was an invasion of marital privacy): "The state may not, consistent with the spirit of the first amendment, contract the spectrum of available knowledge."[32] Sex and family life education, after all, are part of the "spectrum of available knowledge." On the second argument, the Hawaii court pointed out that the public schools had an excusal system, whereby parents or guardians could withhold or withdraw their children from the program.[33]

10. MAY ELEMENTARY AND SECONDARY PUBLIC SCHOOLS REGULATE THE WAY PUPILS DRESS?

Schools may outlaw dress styles that are deemed to be immodest, offensive to community standards of good taste, or disruptive of reasonable standards of school discipline. Obviously these are matters of judgment and degree. Nevertheless, courts are inclined to support school authorities and to give them wide discretionary powers to maintain order and discipline. Of course, the very existence of such rules is an affront to some and a challenge to others. The old may object to the restraint as an unwarranted limitation on personal freedom of action; the young, as they mature, may see extremism in dress and grooming as a means of testing and taunting their elders in the natural and normal struggle for emancipation and independence.

Hair Length

In recent years, hair length—especially for boys—has been a focal point for heated discussion and litigation. The problem has eased as more and more men, including no less a personage than the late Lyndon B. Johnson, have allowed their hair to grow into long, flowing locks. Meanwhile, the American Civil Liberties Union has intervened on the side of the young in a number of cases, suggesting that certain principles of freedom of action transcend the immediate issue of how long is too long.

> Benny Benware was the class clown: a good student, but always good for a laugh. When he and several friends allowed their hair to grow to their shoulders, they were warned by their high school principal and were finally expelled because their hair length violated a published regulation. With their parents, they went to court to have the regulation declared unconstitutional and to get an injunction against its enforcement. Will they win?

Probably yes, depending on where they live. In a typical case, which reached the Massachusetts Supreme Court, the judges upheld the decision of school authorities, noting that the boy's hair (grown well over his ears) "could disrupt and impede school decorum."[34] But that was in 1965, before such appearance became commonplace. In 1970, the First Circuit Court of Appeals superseded the state Supreme Court on the basis of the due process clause of the Fourteenth Amendment to the U.S. Constitution. It held that:

> Within the commodious concept of liberty, embracing freedoms great and small, is the right to wear one's hair as he wishes. . . . [There is no] outweighing state interest justifying the intrusion . . . We see no inherent reason why decency, decorum, or good conduct requires a boy to wear his hair short. Certainly, eccentric hair styling is no longer a reliable signal of perverse behavior. We do not believe that mere unattractiveness in the eyes of some parents, teachers, or students, short of uncleanliness, can justify the proscription. Nor . . . does such compelled conformity to conventional standards of appearance seem a justifiable part of the educational process.[35]

Similarly, the Seventh Circuit Court of Appeals ruled in favor of long hair in a Wisconsin case.

> The right to wear one's hair at any length or in any desired manner is an ingredient of personal freedom protected by the United States Constitution . . . within the penumbras of the first amendment freedom of speech . . . or as encompassed within the ninth amendment as an "additional fundamental right" . . . and is applicable to the states through the due process clause of the fourteenth amendment. . . . Discipline for the sake of discipline and uniformity is indeed not compatible with the melting pot formula which brought this country to greatness.[36]

In contrast, in a case from a high school in Tennessee, involving two boys who were members of "The Purple Haze" combo band, the Sixth

Circuit Court of Appeals upheld board of education hair length regulations as constitutional. The long hair disrupted classroom atmosphere and decorum, caused disturbances and distractions among other students, and interfered with the educational process. A teacher complained that the boys were "constantly combing, flipping, looking in mirrors, and rearranging their hair."[37]

The U.S. Supreme Court has refused to grant certiorari on any of the hair length cases to resolve the conflict among the circuit courts. Any young man of high school age who would like really long hair had better first check local regulations.

11. MAY PUBLIC SCHOOLS BAR PREGNANT OR MARRIED STUDENTS FROM ATTENDING CLASSES?

> When Lucy Larkin appeared in her high school class in a maternity dress, her classmates learned for the first time that she was five months pregnant. After extended discussions with her and her parents, the principal prohibited her further participation in physical education classes or competitive athletics. After two more months he asked her to take a leave of absence until after the baby arrived. When she refused, he expelled her officially. Was he acting within his legal authority?

Yes, if she lives in some states; no, in others. As with the matter of hair length, local courts are divided and the U.S. Supreme Court has never considered the issue. Schools in metropolitan areas, such as New York City, permit class attendance by pregnant high school students, whether married or unmarried. New York City also provides special schools that expectant mothers of high school age may attend.

Clearly, a principal or school board may not bar a pupil from class on a permanent basis simply because he or she may be married; in the words of one court, the state of matrimony is honorable, even though the school board may contend that married students are "detrimental to the good government and usefulness of the school."[38] However, courts have held that high school students who marry may be barred from attendance for a limited time (such as the remainder of the school year) because of the confusion and disorder that usually result immediately and during the period of readjustment.[39] An Ohio court supported the school board which suspended from classes a married girl during her pregnancy, expressing concern for her well-being as well as for the morale and order of the student body generally.[40] Ironically, courts generally hold that a married student is emancipated and cannot be compelled to attend school.

In Massachusetts, a federal district court upheld the right of an eighteen-year-old, unmarried, pregnant senior to attend regular classes.

In summary, no danger to petitioner's physical or mental health resultant from her attending classes during regular school hours has been shown; no likelihood that her presence will cause any disruption of or interference with school activities or pose a threat of harm to others has been shown; and no valid educational or other reason to justify her segregation and to require her to receive a type of educational treatment which is not the equal of that given to all others in her class has been shown.[41]

Students in colleges and universities are generally permitted much greater freedom of action. Unique and even bizarre appearances and life styles are tolerated and even encouraged by some. Since World War II, when many mature veterans returned to school, married students are commonplace; many campuses have special housing facilities to accommodate them and their children. Extraordinary hair and dress styles have become ordinary. Nonconformity is a mark of new conformity—and the republic endures despite it all.

12. MAY A TEACHER ADMINISTER CORPORAL PUNISHMENT TO A PUPIL FOR MISBEHAVIOR?

Yes, with qualifications. The practice is generally confined to the elementary grades where presumably persuasion and alternative sanctions or inducements are sometimes not effective. If used, corporal punishment must be reasonable; it should be administered without malice or cruelty, should not leave permanent marks or cause serious injuries, and should be appropriate to the pupil's size, age, and sex. The teacher and his employer may be liable in tort for assault and battery if the punishment is unreasonable.

Traditionally, teachers have stood *in loco parentis* (Latin: in the place of a parent) during school hours, and have therefore assumed a right to use reasonable punishment with misbehaving youngsters. But many parents today themselves reject corporal punishment as a sanction within the home and become very upset if their children are so punished in school, no matter how badly the child may have behaved. Accordingly, most schools emphasize affirmative incentives to good behavior (for example, interest-stimulating programs of study, grading, honor rolls, and parent-teacher conferences). If negative action becomes necessary, they tend to rely on *suspension* from class, or *expulsion* from the school in extreme cases. Suspension is typically effected by the teacher, perhaps with the cooperation of the principal, and usually lasts no more than the remainder of the day. Expulsion may be permanent and usually requires action by the school board. After expulsion from a regular full-time public day school, the pupil may be enrolled in a special continuation school or possibly in a private school.

Listed on the next page are representative grounds for suspension or expulsion from public schools:

Continued willful disobedience, habitual profanity or vulgarity, open and persistent defiance of the authority of the school personnel, or assault or battery upon a student upon school premises or while under the authority of school personnel, or continued abuse of school personnel, assault or battery upon school personnel, or any threat of force or violence directed toward school personnel, at any time or place shall constitute good cause for suspension or expulsion from school; however, no pupil shall be suspended or expelled unless the conduct for which he is to be disciplined is related to school activity or school attendance.[42]

In some school districts, smoking or having tobacco on school premises constitutes good cause for suspension or expulsion. Similarly, a student may commonly be suspended or expelled for use, sale, or possession of narcotics or hallucinogenic drugs or substances on school premises or elsewhere.

13. IS IT UNLAWFUL FOR PUPILS IN ELEMENTARY AND SECONDARY SCHOOLS TO JOIN SECRET SOCIETIES?

Yes. Many states have enacted specific laws barring pupils in elementary and secondary schools from organizing or joining secret fraternities, sororities, or clubs. In others, school boards have frequently taken steps to ban or closely regulate societies that arbitrarily restrict admission and have secret rituals. "Doubtless these organizations have many redeeming features . . . [but] they tend to engender an undemocratic spirit of caste, to promote cliques, and to foster a contempt for school authority."[43]

Generally, the sanction used for enforcement is to deny secret society members the right to participate in athletics and other extracurricular activities, although suspension or expulsion could also be used. It matters not that meetings are held off campus, outside of school hours, and possibly with parental consent. The divisiveness and discord that such organizations generate in elementary and high schools are said to justify the repressive controls.

At the college level, this is less likely to be true—probably because the community is larger; the students are more mature, self-reliant, and mutually tolerant; and their interests are served and satisfied by a greater variety of activities and groups. Nevertheless, even at the college level, secret sororities and fraternities may be barred by school authorities under legislative authorization.

In a case involving membership in a fraternity at the University of Mississippi, it was argued that a state law barring fraternities obstructed the individual's pursuit of happiness and deprived him of rights guaranteed by the Fourteenth Amendment. The U.S. Supreme Court rejected this plea saying that attendance at a state university is not an absolute right. The legislature may enact such disciplinary measures, presumably "induced by the opinion that membership in the prohibited societies divided the attention of the students and distracted them from the singleness of purpose which the state desired should exist in its public educational institutions."[44]

14. IS THE PUPIL PERSONALLY LIABLE IF HE WILLFULLY DAMAGES SCHOOL PROPERTY? ARE HIS PARENTS ALSO LIABLE?

Yes, the pupil is liable. Yes, within statutory limits, his parents are also liable. "Trashing," or willfully defacing or destroying the property of others, has increased in recent years. Schools are prime targets of disturbed, embittered, frustrated, or otherwise maladjusted children, as well as of those who are inconsiderate of the rights of others because of their own faulty ethical standards of conduct. Wrongdoers may never consider whether their actions will inconvenience or deprive their fellow pupils, or whether their parents and other taxpayers may be burdened even more heavily by having to pay for repairs or replacement of vandalized property. If such ideas are entertained, by twisted reasoning they may actually reinforce the vandal's decision to destroy.

Under general principles of tort liability, the willful wrongdoer is liable, even if he is a minor. His parents are generally not liable unless they have in some direct manner encouraged or approved the misbehavior. However, by statute, parents can be made liable. In a representative state (California):

> any minor who willfully cuts, defaces, or otherwise injures in any way any property, real or personal, belonging to a school district is liable to suspension or expulsion, and the parent or guardian shall be liable for all damages so caused by the minor. The parent or minor shall also be liable for the amount of any reward paid (by a local government agency for information leading to the apprehension of the wrongdoer).[45]

In that state, parents having custody or control of minors who commit an act of willful misconduct that results in injury or death of another, or injury to his property, are "jointly and severally liable with such minor for any damages resulting from such willful misconduct." However, the parental liability in such cases is limited to $2,000 for each tort; and in the case of injury to a person, the parental liability is further limited to medical, dental, and hospital expenses, not exceeding $2,000.[46]

15. IF A PUPIL IS INJURED DURING A SCHOOL ACTIVITY, IS THE SCHOOL DISTRICT LIABLE?

Probably, yes. Formerly, school districts were protected from liability for torts of their agents and employees by the common law rule that "the king can do no wrong," meaning that the government could not be sued for its own torts unless it consented to be sued. However, both at the federal and state levels, the sovereign immunity doctrine has been modified through statutes and court decisions. Although limitations remain, in many cases today government can be successfully sued for wrongs committed by its employees and agents, especially when they are performing some *proprietary function,* such as running a bus line. It is also increasingly true when they are performing a traditional *governmental function,* such as providing police and fire protection.

> Tommy O'Neil was conducting a chemistry experiment during his regular chemistry class laboratory session at Encinal Public High School. The teacher had given very brief instructions, saying, "Check your workbook if in doubt." Then he busied himself in preparation for another demonstration experiment. O'Neil became confused but was afraid to disturb the instructor, and so he proceeded, with the aid of another pupil. Suddenly, the beaker exploded. Tommy was permanently blinded. Is the school district liable?

Probably, yes. A teacher is required to maintain reasonable supervision of all activities. Where danger of injury is great, as in chemistry laboratory experiments that can involve explosions, he must exercise special care. If he fails to do so, he is liable to anyone injured, as is his employer (the school district) under the doctrine of respondeat superior.

16. MAY A TEACHER BE DISMISSED FOR MEMBERSHIP IN THE COMMUNIST PARTY?

No. Membership without proof of intent to further the unlawful aims of the Communist Party (such as the overthrow of the government by force) is not enough to bar a person from employment as a teacher.[47]

In our society, everyone enjoys freedom of thought and expression, but teachers and students—especially in higher education—tend to use these freedoms in new areas of inquiry more frequently. The U.S. Supreme Court has declared:

> The essentiality of freedom in the community of American universities is almost self-evident. No one should underestimate the vital role in a democracy that is played by those who guide and train our youth. To impose any straitjacket upon the intellectual leaders of our colleges and universities would imperil the future of our nation. No field of education is so thoroughly comprehended by man that new discoveries cannot be made. Particularly is that true in the social sciences, where few, if any, principles are accepted as absolutes. Teachers and students must always remain free to inquire, to study and to evaluate, to gain new maturity and understanding; otherwise our civilization will stagnate and die.[48]

17. MAY FREEDOM OF SPEECH AND ASSEMBLY BE LIMITED ON A COLLEGE OR UNIVERSITY CAMPUS?

On campuses and in classrooms especially, students and teachers on the one hand and legislators and judges on the other are generally anxious to maintain a climate and an environment of free inquiry. U.S. Supreme Court Justice Louis Brandeis has said:

> Although the rights of free speech and assembly are fundamental, they are not in their nature absolute. Their exercise is subject to restriction, if the particular restriction proposed is required in order to protect the state from destruction or from serious injury, political, economic or moral. . . . No danger flowing from speech can be deemed clear and present, unless the incidence of the evil apprehended is so imminent that it may befall before there is opportunity for full discussion. If there be time to expose through discussion the falsehood and fallacies, to avert the evil by the processes of education, the remedy to be applied is more speech, not enforced silence.[49]

More than a decade later, U.S. Supreme Court Justice Hugo Black summed up in these words:

> What finally emerges from the "clear and present danger" cases is a working principle that the substantive evil must be extremely serious and the degree of imminence extremely high before utterances can be punished.[50]

On a college or university campus, when there is a clear and present danger that a speech or assembly will injure others, campus authorities (with outside police and even military help, if necessary) may legally take steps to protect persons and property. This happened often in the late 1960s during anti-Vietnam-War demonstrations. In some cases, there was probably overreaction on both sides. Thus in 1970, at an allegedly illegal anti-war demonstration at Kent State University in Ohio, four students were killed when National Guardsmen fired into a large group of protesters and curious onlookers. At Jackson State College in Mississippi, two students were shot to death by state patrolmen. In mass meetings and violent demonstrations, tear gas and bullets do not always distinguish between the innocent and the blameworthy. Fortunately, American military disengagement in Vietnam, coupled with the end of the draft, cooled heated tempers and restored a measure of tranquility to the campus scene.

> Students Al Monroe and Ed Hudson led a mass meeting of fellow students to protest the denial of tenure to a popular young instructor. In response to their eloquent urgings, the large group blocked all traffic on the public highway in front of the campus, ripped down the campus gates, and smashed plate glass windows in the administration building. A police car was overturned and

burned, and a battle of rocks and tear gas ensued. Monroe and Hudson were subsequently expelled by the president of the college for violating the school rule against unruly and unlawful gatherings. Was the rule in violation of the U.S. Constitution?

No. Such regulations are generally deemed reasonable and necessary and "relevant to the lawful mission of the educational institution," in the words of the U.S. Court of Appeals for the Eighth Circuit.[51] Note that restraint is imposed only when words and acts interfere significantly with the proper operation of the school or threaten the rights of other persons.

On this basis, a guest speaker may be barred from a campus when it appears likely that he will advocate overthrow of the government; willful destruction or seizure of school property; forcible disruption or impairment of regular classes or other educational functions; physical harm, coercion, intimidation, or other invasion of lawful rights of school officials, teachers, or students; or other campus disorder of a violent nature.[52] Surveys have shown that student activists who are philosophically committed to the use of violence as an acceptable means of achieving desired change are a very small minority. Even they appear to have concluded that violence in a democratic society is unnecessary and usually counterproductive.

> In a strongly worded editorial, Gabriel Mercado, editor of his college weekly newspaper, condemned the legislature and ridiculed the governor for failing to provide "adequate financial support" for the school and for boosting tuition and fees. The president received a phone call from the irate governor, then promptly expelled Mercado, and suspended publication of the paper. Were these valid actions?

No. Student reporters and editors enjoy the protection of freedom of the press under the First Amendment to the U.S. Constitution. School officials may not interfere or infringe on this right of free and unrestricted expression where the exercise of such right "does not materially and substantially interfere with requirements of appropriate discipline in the operation of the school."[53] Here the college president overreacted.

In a significant Alabama case, the court held that a student has a right to *procedural due process of law*. Specifically, in university disciplinary proceedings where the charges can lead to suspension for a period of time or to outright expulsion, a student has a right to notice ("a statement of the specific charges and grounds which, if proven, would justify expulsion") and to a fair hearing.[54] The judges did not prescribe the nature of the required hearing other than to say that it would depend on the circumstances of the particular case. Clearly, the student should have a fair opportunity to present his side of the dispute, and he should not be disciplined unless there is substantial evidence to support the sanctions.[55] Elementary justice also requires that "the rules embodying standards of discipline be contained in properly promulgated regulations . . . [and they should be] reasonably clear and narrow."[56]

The American Association of University Professors has published a "Joint Statement on Rights and Freedoms of Students."[57] In it, they support the policy that normally, when a student is accused of misbehavior, he shall not be barred from classes pending a hearing where he has a fair opportunity to state his defense. However, he may be barred summarily without hearing, according to the AAUP, if his emotional safety and well-being require it, or if the safety and well-being of other students and faculty or the security of university property require it.

18. MAY SCHOOL AUTHORITIES OPEN AND SEARCH A STUDENT'S LOCKER, OR DORMITORY ROOM, WITHOUT HIS PERMISSION AND WITHOUT A WARRANT?

Yes, at the high school level. The Fourth Amendment affirms the right of the people "to be secure in their persons, houses, papers, and effects, against unreasonable searches." However, this amendment protects against unreasonable searches by police and similar government agents; it does not apply to searches by private persons. School teachers and administrators are not considered to be government officials within the meaning of the Fourth Amendment. They stand *in loco parentis* with a duty to supervise at all times the conduct of children on the school grounds.

> The vice-principal of Ponderosa High School learned from a student that the defendant, another student, had sold her "speed" or methedrine pills. The vice-principal, without a warrant or consent, searched the seller's locker and found marijuana. The seller was found guilty of violating the state Health and Safety Code. On appeal, he claimed that search and seizure were illegal and therefore the evidence should not have been admitted. Decide.

Conviction affirmed. The court held that for the protection of other students "a pupil who has on school premises or elsewhere used, sold, or been in possession of narcotics, may be suspended or expelled."[58] The search and seizure were legal under the circumstances.

At the college and university level, the rules on search and seizure are not as clear. The *in loco parentis* argument usually does not apply, and in the words of a New York court "the price of modern education is not the waiver . . . of constitutional privileges." Specifically, the court did not rule out the possibility and propriety of a reasonable search by university officials for university purposes. However, it condemned a search without warrant by police, even though they were accompanied by two university representatives.[59]

A federal district court in Alabama also held illegal a search without warrant instigated by the police at Troy State University, again even though university officials cooperated. The two students in whose rooms incriminating evidence was found were therefore released from prison under writs of *habeas corpus* (Latin: you hold the body). The fact that marijuana was found is immaterial. "The results of the search do not prove its reasonableness."[60]

The same federal district court in Alabama upheld the right of officials of the same college to enter student rooms for inspection purposes when reasonably necessary for the orderly operation of the school. If police are involved, their role must be secondary or incidental.[61]

CASES, QUESTIONS, AND PROBLEMS

1. Booker persuaded several other black parents of pupils at Central Public High to join him in a demand that Swahili be taught in the school. They insisted that it was just as appropriate as the French, German, and Spanish courses already offered. Must Swahili be taught?

2. The Blatows of Los Angeles, both Ph.D.'s and college teachers, conceived a son after twenty years of marriage. The child was precocious and probably a genius. He could read, write, operate a digital calculator, and play the piano by the age of five.
   a. Must they wait another nine months before he may be admitted to the first grade of a public school?
   b. Must he remain with his peers until high school graduation twelve years later?

3. Cheryl Shrine was a child star of radio, television, and motion pictures at the age of six. Her crowded production schedule and multiple personal appearances made it impossible for her to attend regular full-time day school classes. Therefore, with her parents' consent, her employer, the Colossal Colorama Features Corporation, engaged a qualified full-time tutor to teach her. However, she was spoiled by public adulation and simply would not study anything seriously, except her lines for shows. Are her parents violating the law?

4. For $25, Arnoff obtained a Doctor of Divinity degree from a small private mail-order school in New York upon completion of a simple two-page objective examination. He then rented an empty garage and opened his new church, The Universal Church of Transcendental

Equanimity and Tranquility. Krondome and Allohead were his first "converts," and they withdrew their five children from local elementary public schools so that the children could devote full time to "education through meditation." Is this legal?

5. Stuart was greatly disturbed by man's inhumanity to man as he observed it while serving in the U.S. Army in Vietnam. Upon his release, he vowed to do what he could to rectify matters. Accordingly, he applied for G.I. benefits (subsidy) for schooling and enrolled in the divinity school of a sectarian Christian college in order to become a minister. Is this government payment for religious education in a church school a violation of the first amendment to the U.S. Constitution?

6. After the U.S. Supreme Court outlawed de jure segregation in public schools, Graham and a group of twenty like-minded individuals withdrew their children from their desegregated public school. Instead, they hired qualified teachers and opened a private school open only to whites. Is this legal?

7. Galvin, a public high school science teacher, discussed Darwin's theory of evolution in his class on zoology. A state law explicitly forbade such instruction. Was the state within its powers in enacting such a law and in dismissing Galvin for violating it?

8. Gail Trecida was only twenty-three and in her first year of employment as an elementary school teacher. Many of the boys in her eighth grade public school class were considerably larger, faster, and stronger than she. "Knuckles" Knox was a consistent troublemaker. When Armstrong, another pupil even more powerful, suggested that he could thrash some sense and manners into Knox, Trecida agreed to let him try. In the fight after school, Armstrong gave Knox a black eye and a broken nose and knocked out two of his front teeth. His shirt and trousers were torn. Knox and his parents sued the school district for damages. Is it liable?

9. Sammy Savage was the class troublemaker and bully in the tenth grade of Crescent Public High in a California city. He frequently rolled marbles across the floor of the large homeroom, banging the metal desk legs. Often he tripped fellow students in class and in the corridors. In the cafeteria he threw three fruit pies against the ceiling. He avoided detection by school authorities and threatened his victims into silence. One day he started an unprovoked fight in the school yard with Arthur Fielden, who was a good student, shorter and twenty pounds lighter than Savage. Savage stomped on Fielden's glasses and beat him badly, breaking his jaw. What, if any, legal remedies are available to Fielden?

10. Parker was a member of the Order of De Molay, a Masonic organization for young people, which could be classified as a secret society. He was also captain of their championship close-order drill team. A rival at the public high school he attended sought to have Parker disqualified from competition for the coveted job of drum major of the school band because he allegedly belonged to a secret society. Should he be disqualified?

11. In 1965, to symbolize and publicize their objection to the Vietnam War and their support for a truce, John Tinker, aged fifteen, and his friend Chris Eckhardt, aged sixteen, decided to wear black armbands at their high school. Mary Beth Tinker, aged thirteen, did the same at her junior high school. School officials had previously ruled that students wearing such armbands would be suspended. All three defied the order and were suspended. Other students noticed and discussed the bands, but there was no important disruption of classwork or substantial disorder. Now, through their fathers, the three students seek a court injunction restraining the officials from enforcing the rule. Decide.

12. In 1966, when the Berkeley campus of the University of California was much astir with protest meetings and movements, plaintiff Eisen was a law student and an officer of a fully qualified organization which was "engaged in the advocacy of dissident ideas." A member of the general public sued the university regents demanding disclosure of the names of the officers and the stated purposes of all registered student organizations. When the university announced its intention to comply, plaintiff Eisen sought a court order barring such disclosure. He claimed that disclosure would violate the First and Fourteenth Amendments because it would have a detrimental effect on his rights of free speech and association. Decide.

6

YOU
AS OWNER OR
DRIVER OF A
MOTOR VEHICLE

1. WHY DOES THE LAW REQUIRE THAT MOTOR VEHICLES BE REGISTERED?

The Importance of Automobiles

Automobiles are probably the most valuable personal property owned by many Americans. As with real property, ownership of autos, trucks, and motorcycles is required by law to be on public record.

The worldwide energy shortage, which reached crisis levels in 1973, has caused some reduction in the use of motor vehicles for pleasure and even for business. But for ground transportation, most Americans continue to rely on gasoline-powered cars and trucks. In 1972, there were more than 121 million such vehicles on the roads of this country. They were driven by 118 million licensed drivers. The manufacture, fueling, and servicing of these vehicles, coupled with highway construction, constitute one of our largest industries.

No contrivance of man—not even weapons of destruction—has killed or wounded more Americans. In 1972, the total number was 56,000 fatalities and 2,100,000 disabling injuries from motor vehicle accidents. In every year since 1966, more than 50,000 Americans have died as a result of such accidents. The energy crisis, however, led to reduced speeds and to some reduction in travel. According to the National Safety Council, these factors were the primary causes of a 24 percent drop in auto accident fatalities during the first four months of 1974, compared with the same period in 1973.

In 1972, the cost of the carnage was estimated by the National Safety Council to exceed $19.4 billion in wage losses, property damages, medical expenses, insurance administration, and claim settlements. Not included are losses where no recovery was obtained by victims, related costs of police and courts, damages awarded in excess of direct costs, indirect costs to employers, and so forth. It is easy to see why ownership and operation of motor vehicles is a matter of prime economic, social, and political concern, the subject of a large body of law, and the cause of much litigation.

Advantages of Registration

To be properly registered, the vehicle must comply with minimal safety standards governing brakes, lights, and so forth. Registration of ownership also assures orderly transfer of title. By requiring production of the certificate of ownership and signature of the seller, the buyer has better assurance that he is getting good title. If the car is stolen, the certificates of ownership and of registration facilitate identification and restitution to the true owner. If a vehicle is involved in an accident in which property is damaged and persons are injured or killed, license numbers help trace the vehicle to the party responsible and facilitate follow-up measures. Periodic renewal of the certificate of registration also serves as a convenient means of raising revenue for construction and maintenance of highways and for other purposes.

In Relation to Accidents

> Cal Carson was carefully riding his new imported English motorcycle along a city street, when Stuart Berolz negligently lost control of his automobile and crashed into Cal. Berolz now claims Carson was guilty of contributory negligence because he failed to register his motorcycle as required by law. Is it considered negligent to drive an unlicensed motor vehicle on a public road?

No. Carson's failure to register his motorcycle had nothing to do with Berolz's negligence, and will not prevent him from recovering damages for his injuries.[1] However, failure to transfer title to a new owner when delivering possession of a car may leave the original owner still liable to third parties injured by the car in subsequent accidents.

Very commonly, the certificate of ownership lists two owners: the *registered or equitable buyer-owner* and the *legal creditor-owner,* who advanced the money or sold the car on credit and holds a security interest in the vehicle until it is paid for in full. The legal creditor-owner is generally not responsible for the manner in which the registered equitable-owner uses or misuses the vehicle. The legal owner is concerned only with getting paid, and so he will insist that the equitable owner who is using and enjoying the car carry adequate collision and comprehensive automobile insurance.

Licensing and Registration Procedures

States issue two certificates to the owners of motor vehicles: a *certificate of ownership,* or title, showing who owns the vehicle, and a *certificate of registration,* which is a license permitting operation of the vehicle on the highways of the state. License plates, or annual renewal tags, are also issued in conjunction with the certificate of registration.

A car is licensed in the state where it is usually used. When you drive into another state, your vehicle registration generally remains valid for a limited period of time (thirty to ninety days), whereupon a local license is required. Special regulations also govern vehicle and driver when traveling in foreign countries, and these regulations should be checked with a knowledgeable travel agent before departure.

Many counties and cities require the registration and periodic licensing of bicycles. Money thus raised is commonly used to maintain records that facilitate recovery and return of stolen bikes.

2. WHY DOES THE LAW REQUIRE THAT DRIVERS OF MOTOR VEHICLES ON PUBLIC HIGHWAYS BE LICENSED?

> Arthur Ingersoll's driver's license had been revoked for proper cause. He resented this interference with his need for a convenient means of transportation, and so he decided to defy the court order and to drive anyway—but with extra care to avoid any trouble. As luck would have it, while he was driving legally and safely, another motorist negligently ran a red light and rammed into his car. Would his lack of a driver's license have any effect on the ensuing civil and criminal court proceedings?

No and yes. Unless there is some cause and effect relationship between the lack of the driver's license and the accident-caused injury, lack of license is immaterial. In itself, it is not evidence of negligence.[2] Ingersoll's rights in a civil action for damages resulting from the accident are not affected by his lack of a driver's license. However, he would be liable in a criminal action for the offense of driving without a license, and for this he could be fined and/or imprisoned.

Some years ago in a television series called "Highway Patrol," actor Broderick Crawford used to remind his audience that when "you're behind the wheel of a car, you're not merely driving an automobile; you are aiming a weapon!" This is painfully true when the driver is careless, intoxicated, or otherwise unfit to drive. But legally, motor vehicles are not considered dangerous instrumentalities as are explosives and wild animals. Ordinary people can safely drive them, and drivers are not held to extraordinary standards of care.[3] Nevertheless, for their own safety and that of others, prospective drivers are required to demonstrate at least minimal ability to drive in traffic and minimal knowledge of the rules of the road.

Driving is a privilege, not a constitutionally protected right. The license to drive may be suspended or revoked for violating rules of the road, or even for inability to demonstrate financial responsibility after an accident. In some states, computers may be used to record all convictions for moving traffic offenses. Demerit points may be assigned, and a person's license may be suspended or revoked if he accumulates too many too fast. An accident in which he is responsible may be reckoned as one point; reckless or drunken driving, two points; causing property damage by hit-and-run, two points—and a total of four points in one year may terminate the license.

In California, which has more vehicles and more drivers than any other state, any adult may qualify for a driver's license. A minor between sixteen and eighteen may also qualify by doing all of the following:

a. completing an approved classroom driver education course, devoted mostly to the rules of the road
b. completing a driver training course, primarily concerned with actual handling of automobiles on the highway
c. passing a written test on rules of the road
d. passing an eye (vision) test and a driving test
e. having his parents sign and verify his application whereby they become responsible for any civil liability he incurs while driving upon a highway*

Fortunately for parents, their liability is limited to $15,000 for injury to or death of any one person as a result of any one accident in which their minor child is legally responsible.

Note that the law on liability of parents for torts of their children committed while driving motor vehicles deviates from the general rule. Parents are generally not liable for their children's torts not done at their command or in the course of parental business. The minor, as

---

* California Vehicle Code 17707. If only one parent is living or has custody, he or she alone signs; if neither parent is alive or has custody, the minor's guardian or custodian signs.

tortfeasor who caused the injury, would himself be liable; but he usually lacks resources, and in cases of negligence, he could ultimately free himself of any heavy judgment by going bankrupt.

3. WHAT STANDARD OF CARE DOES THE LAW PRESCRIBE FOR DRIVERS?

The law requires that, whether on or off the highway, every person refrain from injuring every other person or his property, or otherwise infringing upon any of his rights. This broad duty may be violated willfully or negligently. Comparatively few people injure others willfully, with deliberate intent to harm. Such conduct is often criminal, and makes the wrongdoer liable for punitive damages as well as the usual compensatory damages. In one case, the court said:

> Here there is testimony from which the jury could find that defendant saw plaintiff 196 feet away in the paved portion of the roadway, and neither slowed nor sounded his horn. There is also the testimony that defendant's car swerved toward plaintiff immediately before the impact. Thus the evidence could support a jury finding that defendant was guilty of willful or wanton misconduct.[4]

From time to time most of us behave negligently. That is, we fail to exercise reasonable care. We do not behave as an ordinary, prudent man or woman or child of comparable age would behave under the same or similar circumstances. If someone is injured as a result of our negligence, we are generally liable, unless the other party is himself guilty of contributory negligence.

It is possible, of course, to injure another when acting without negligence or willful intent to harm; then there is no legal liability. This could happen in a pure accident, a casualty that is unexpected, unforeseeable, unplanned—perhaps the result of an unknown cause or the unprecedented result of a known cause. This might be true of a natural calamity where a violent storm is the moving force. This might also be true where the victim alone was careless and at fault—for example, a person is reading a paper as he walks and steps off a curb into a stream of traffic.

To be liable for negligence, three elements are essential: (1) a *duty* under the law to exercise reasonable care under given circumstances, (2) a *breach of duty,* and (3) an *injury proximately caused by the breach of duty*. In this context, proximate cause is part of a natural and continuous sequence. It produces the injury, and without it the effect would not have occurred. There must be no intervening cause that breaks the chain of causation.[5] The consequence or result must have been foreseeable by an ordinary, reasonable man.

Gus Shikel, an expert in first aid, was driving along a lonely country road when he came upon the scene of a one-car accident. The wrecked vehicle had collided with a utility pole. Inside were two adults and a child, either unconscious or in shock. One was bleeding profusely. Not wanting to get involved, Shikel drove on. Was he legally obliged to stop and render aid?

No, in most states. The victims were strangers to whom he legally owed no duty. Generally, the law does not require us to be good Samaritans. Of course, had Shikel in any way caused or contributed to the accident, he would be criminally liable if he failed to stop. In any event, if he stops—and one hopes that most drivers would—and renders first aid, he must do so with reasonable care. Conceivably, the injured persons could later sue him for failing to exercise such care and thus aggravating their condition. Such lawsuits are extremely rare, and the authors are aware of none succeeding before a jury.

Hank Kirkeby was driving along a freeway with his girlfriend at his side, bragging to her about the car and about himself as a hot driver. Suddenly, without notice to her or signal to other drivers, he accelerated within seconds to 95 mph. Visible ahead, moving at different speeds in the three lanes, were about a dozen other vehicles. He rapidly passed them all, weaving skillfully from outside to inside lanes and back again. There were no highway patrolmen in sight, he was not arrested, and he did not cause an accident. Has he breached any legal duty?

Yes. He has breached his general duty to drive as an ordinary prudent man with reasonable care, respecting the rights of his date and all others on the highway to the safety of their lives and property. He has breached specific duties to drive within the speed limits, to refrain from weaving in and out of traffic lanes, and to signal before changing lanes. Unfortunately, most breaches of duty that are crimes go unpunished; fortunately, most breaches of duty cause no injury to others.

Kirkeby, still speeding illegally, pulled alongside Dan Riley, who was driving at the legal limit of 55 mph, and then swerved as close as possible in front of him. Riley, seeking to avoid the collision he reasonably thought was imminent, slammed on his brakes. His car skidded off the highway, spun around, and struck a heavy guard rail and post. He was injured and his car was badly damaged. Is Kirkeby liable?

Yes. Kirkeby's negligence was the proximate cause of injury to Riley. When ordinary negligence causes injuries to another, or even death, it often happens that no citation is issued for violation of traffic laws.

The driver at fault may be civilly liable for compensatory damages in a tort action, but not criminally liable. However, if the negligence is extreme, or gross, verging on the willful or deliberate, punitive damages may be added to the compensatory damages, and criminal charges are more likely to be filed against the wrongdoer.

4. SPECIFICALLY, WHAT IS A DRIVER LEGALLY EXPECTED TO DO WHILE ON THE ROAD?

Every driver of a motor vehicle on the public highway is legally expected to observe certain rules.

a. Be alert and awake at the wheel. (If drowsy, he should park and sleep, or let someone drive who is not fatigued.)
b. Obey all rules of the road, such as regulations regarding speed and the right of way.
c. Watch for official highway signals, such as stop signs, and comply as appropriate.
d. Maintain a careful lookout—ahead and to all necessary directions before turning, and to the rear, especially when backing. Constant vigilance is the price of safety.[6]
e. Anticipate the presence of others, be they motorists, pedestrians, or cyclists.
f. Keep the car under such control that he can avoid hitting other cars driven with reasonable care, particularly the car immediately ahead. He should not tailgate.
g. Give proper signals of lane changes, turns, and stops.
h. Drive with extra caution when visibility is obscured by darkness, rain, sleet, fog, snow, dust, or anything else, and when road traction is reduced as by rain or snow. He should use headlights when appropriate, being careful not to keep the high beam lights on when approaching other vehicles.
i. Always operate the vehicle with due regard for traffic volume, highway conditions, visibility, time of day or night, and other relevant factors.[7]

> Jeremy Harper was driving on the wrong side of a two-lane highway when he was involved in a head-on collision with Frederick Bowden, who was legally proceeding in the opposite direction. Is Harper guilty of negligence per se (Latin: of itself) because he was apparently violating a statute at the time?

Not necessarily. Proof of violation of a relevant statute raises a *prima facie* (Latin: at first sight) presumption or inference of negligence. If the plaintiff proves that the statute was violated, and no contrary evidence is introduced by the defendant, it is concluded that the defendant was negligent. A prima facie presumption of negligence can, however, be rebutted or overcome by proof of excuse or justification. Here possibly Harper's car was diverted suddenly by conditions beyond his control (such as an object in the road, sudden unforeseeable failure of his steering mechanism, sudden heart attack that he could not have anticipated, or illegal action by another car squeezing by on his right side).[8] It should be noted that in some states, violation of a relevant statute is negligence per se, and the defendant is not permitted to prove the contrary.

5. IS THE OWNER LIABLE IF HE LENDS HIS CAR TO ANOTHER WHO NEGLIGENTLY INJURES SOMEONE IN AN ACCIDENT?

Yes. In order to protect innocent third parties from the careless use of automobiles, the California legislature made the owner liable "for death or injury to person or property resulting from a negligent or wrongful act or omission in the operation of the motor vehicle, in the business of the owner or otherwise, by any person using or operating the same with the permission, express or implied, of the owner."[9] The owner is not liable for punitive damages, and his liability is limited to $15,000 for the death of or injury to one person in any one accident, and $30,000 to more than one, as well as to $5,000 for damage to property in any one accident. If the driver is an employee of the owner, and is acting within the scope of his employment, the owner-employer is liable without limit under the doctrine of *respondeat superior*. The driver is always liable for his own torts, and so is also liable without limit; but he may be judgment-proof.

Since most car owners are insured against liability, Indiana approached the problem with a statute requiring that every automobile policy contain a clause insuring the owner against liability caused by any person using the vehicle with the owner's permission. Such protection is commonly provided in automobile insurance policies today. Also, when an insured person drives another owner's car with permission, his own insurance generally covers him.

> Kirtley Mellon parked his car in the street and ran into the post office to mail a parcel. In his haste, he forgot to remove the ignition key. When he returned, the car was gone. Later the police reported that the person who stole his car collided with a motorcycle, injuring the rider, John Denton. Denton later sued Mellon. Is he liable?

No. Leaving the key in an unattended car is negligence and, in some states, a violation of a statute. But the owner has no duty to protect the general public from unexpected and illegal activities of thieves, or from their more remotely possible negligent use of stolen property.[10] Some courts, however, would hold Mellon liable under the stated facts.

6. IS THE DRIVER LIABLE FOR INJURIES TO GUESTS IN HIS CAR?

Generally no. When passengers are members of the driver's immediate family (husband or wife, children or parents), most states bar any lawsuit because it would allegedly tend to disrupt domestic tranquility. California is among the states that consider this to be nonsense, especially since the payment for injuries is likely to come from an insurance company, not from the relative who was negligent. Of course, the plaintiff's attorney is not permitted to mention in the presence of the jury that the defendant carries liability insurance, or to state the amount of coverage.

Distantly related or unrelated passengers are also barred from collecting damages if they are guests of the negligent driver. (An exception is made when the plaintiff can prove that death or injury proximately resulted from intoxication or willful misconduct of the driver.) In other words, guests who have accepted the driver's hospitality cannot sue for recovery for ordinary negligence. This limitation also prevents possible fraudulent claims by guests who may be the only witnesses to a single-car accident. But here, too, California takes a contrary position. Its supreme court has held that justice is better served by permitting guests to sue a driver who causes injury through his negligence.

> Alvin Kretan was driving his convertible on a clear night, with four friends as his guests. As he approached a railroad crossing visible more than 400 feet away, he could see the locomotive's powerful headlight throwing a beam 800 feet ahead. The crossing bell was ringing and the engineer had sounded two long horn blasts some 1500 feet from the crossing. Kretan decided to try to beat the train to the crossing. He lost. Could his guests or their heirs sue him for the injuries they suffered?

Yes. His behavior under the circumstances was willful misconduct, and the guest statute will not shield him from liability.[11] Other examples would include racing on a winding uphill road at twice the prudent speed; driving at night at 50 mph in a fog so dense that lighted street lamps were hardly visible; driving at 80 mph on a two-lane road past oncoming traffic.

7. WHO QUALIFIES AS A GUEST UNDER THE GUEST STATUTE?

Where guest statutes are in effect, the key question in deciding whether a person is an *ordinary or business passenger* (who can sue the driver if he is injured) or a *guest* (who cannot, unless the driver is guilty of intoxication or willful misconduct that causes the accident and resulting injury or death) is simply: Did the rider confer a benefit on the driver in exchange for the ride?[12] If the driver receives money or other tangible benefit and this motivated him at least in part to provide the transportation, his rider is a passenger, not a guest. Psychic income from companionship, pleasure of conversation, satisfaction from doing a favor, simple kindness, or friendship are not deemed to be compensation.

> Corabel Lanier was considered by everyone to be the most gorgeous, most personable, most vivacious, and most entertaining girl in the senior class. After ten unsuccessful attempts to get a date with her, Kenton Maynard finally succeeded. As they drove off from her palatial home in his sports coupe, the question uppermost in his mind was: Is she a passenger or a guest in my car?

She is a guest. The euphoria he may enjoy from her company is not tangible compensation such as would make her a passenger in the eyes of the law. If a trip is of a purely social nature, the friendly sharing of expenses or even full payment for gas and oil ("I'll provide the car; you give her a drink if she gets thirsty") does not constitute compensation. The same is true for sharing the driving on a pleasure trip. But if the transportation is furnished on condition that the rider do the driving or share in this duty, then he becomes a passenger and the owner is compensated—and may be liable for damages if he negligently causes injuries in an accident.[13] Thus, members of car pools who rotate in using their cars to get each other to work are not guests but business passengers. When a real estate salesman drives you about town to show you houses that are for sale, you are a business passenger.

On a business trip, if auto expenses are shared, but the rider goes along for his own pleasure and contributes to the cost as a matter of reciprocity and social amenity, he is probably a guest. But if both driver and rider have a mutual business interest in the trip, and the latter contributes money as his fair share of the cost of the journey, he is a passenger for compensation.

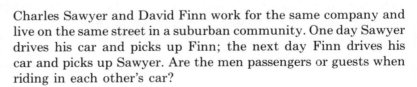

> Charles Sawyer and David Finn work for the same company and live on the same street in a suburban community. One day Sawyer drives his car and picks up Finn; the next day Finn drives his car and picks up Sawyer. Are the men passengers or guests when riding in each other's car?

Passengers. Consideration is the reciprocal ride, which reduces the cost of transportation for each.[14]

When boys or girls go to scout camps in vehicles owned by members or by their parents, courts have held them to be guests. No monetary or other tangible benefit motivates the owner or operator of the vehicle to drive them.

8. WHAT IS THE FINANCIAL RESPONSIBILITY LAW?

> Both Bill Searle and Bob Ranney drove their cars to college in San Francisco. As they rushed to get to their 8:00 A.M. classes, they collided at the main entrance to the campus. The resulting traffic jam caused almost half of all students to miss the first class. Many regarded the event as a festive occasion, because no one was hurt. But damage to each car exceeded $500. Searle and Ranney notified their respective insurance companies and relaxed in the thought that both had adequate coverage. Have they forgotten anything important?

Yes. Automobile insurance is not compulsory in most states. But California, like most states, does have a *financial responsibility law*.[15] Under it, after any accident that causes more than $250 in property damage, or in which someone is killed or injured (no matter how slightly), each driver involved, regardless of fault, must report the accident to the state Department of Motor Vehicles. The report must be made within sixty days after the accident on a form available from any office of the Department of Motor Vehicles, the Highway Patrol, or a police department. If the driver does not have the prescribed minimum automobile insurance coverage ($15,000 for injury to or death of any one person in any one accident; $30,000 for injury to or death of more than one person in any one accident; and $5,000 for property damage resulting from one accident), he will be asked to post a cash deposit or a bond with the department for up to $35,000 for one accident. For three years, both drivers must maintain proof of future responsibility to respond to a claim for damages. These financial responsibility requirements, as the name suggests, are designed to provide some assurance that persons who use the highways and negligently injure others shall make good their losses. Obviously, damages awarded by a court may far exceed the statutory limits of the responsibility law.

If, after an accident, a driver fails to report it, his driver's license is automatically suspended for one year. If he fails to establish proof of financial responsibility, his license is suspended until such proof is established.

> Because of his negligence in backing his car and house trailer on a mountain road, Malcolm Maclede caused a major accident in which three persons were seriously injured and two $5,000 automobiles were totally wrecked. Medical expenses alone exceeded $30,000 within a year, and one victim had to be confined to a bed for the rest of his life. All three were adults with families, and none could work for a year or longer. Maclede had the

minimum insurance coverage required by the financial responsibility law. Is he in deep trouble?

Yes. Although he will not lose his driver's license or vehicle registration, he may be faced with a judgment for damages that far exceeds the statutory minima. The moral of the story is that all drivers should carry adequate public liability coverage for bodily injuries to others.

9. IS IT ILLEGAL TO DRIVE AFTER DRINKING INTOXICATING LIQUOR?

Laurence Harberson and other members of his fraternity were at the frat house celebrating the end of the school year. Beer was flowing freely. Harberson, 250-pound star tackle on the college football team, had finished a twelve-ounce can, when he opened a second. Waving the can, he jumped into his car, and burned tire rubber as he drove off to pick up his girlfriend at the airport. En route he was stopped by a highway patrolman for exceeding the posted speed limit by 10 mph. Is he also guilty of driving under the influence of alcohol?

Probably not. One beer is not likely to intoxicate a 250-pound football player. However, he could be cited for carrying an opened container of alcoholic beverage in his car. He could also be required to demonstrate his sobriety.

Excessive drinking of alcoholic beverages is a major cause of accidents on the highways, and is an ingredient in most fatal accidents. Understandably, police officers are particularly vigorous in enforcing laws against driving while drunk or under the influence of narcotics or other drugs that may interfere with normal control of a vehicle. When stopped under suspicion of intoxication, the driver is required to submit to appropriate tests of his sobriety; if he refuses—which is his constitutional right against possible self-incrimination—he may forfeit his license to drive, an option he implicitly consented to when his license was granted. He must be given a proper warning of the law's effect and is entitled to an administrative hearing on the matter before his license is revoked.

As a preliminary test of sobriety at the scene, he may be asked to walk a straight line or to stand on one foot or to perform some other suitable act. If he appears to be intoxicated, he will be taken to a police station and asked to provide a sample of his breath, blood, or urine, to be analyzed for alcoholic content. He may refuse to submit to the test, but if he does, his license may be suspended for six months. There is a presumption that, if the blood alcohol content is .10 percent or more (in some states the standard is as low as .08 percent), the individual is legally intoxicated and incapable of properly operating a motor vehicle on the public highway. This presumption is rebuttable by proof that a person has adequate control of his faculties.

Penalties upon conviction for "driving under the influence" vary widely. In California a jail sentence of from two days to six months is mandatory if one is convicted two or more times for drunk driving within five years; if the judge, in his discretion, fails to send the defendant to jail, he must write a formal opinion justifying this action. A fine of from $250 to $1000 is also assessed. If the defendant is under twenty-one and the vehicle is registered as his, it may be impounded at his expense for up to thirty days.

10. IS THE SELLER OF LIQUOR EVER LIABLE TO THIRD PERSONS INJURED BY THE BUYER WHO DRIVES WHILE DRUNK?

Yes. Laws that cover operation of cocktail lounges, saloons, and taverns generally forbid serving an additional drink to a patron who is obviously intoxicated.[16] The California Supreme Court has held that the seller can also be civilly liable for damages to third persons who are injured by the drunken driver who was obviously intoxicated when he received his last drink "for the road." This supersedes the old common law rule that, in the words of the court, "would deny recovery on the ground that the furnishing of alcoholic beverages is not the proximate cause of the injuries suffered by the third person."[17]

> Keith Lanterman was guest of honor at a party celebrating his safe return from the war in Vietnam. Sam Bercher, the host, gave each guest his first drink of alcoholic beverage and then said "The bar's open; all drinks are on the house. Serve yourself and save your time and mine." When Lanterman finally reeled out of the apartment at three the next morning, he was too intoxicated to drive safely. Within a block he crashed his car into seven parked vehicles before ramming into the front of a house. Was Bercher liable along with Lanterman for the damages?

Probably not. Bercher did not sell the drinks. Although he provided all the refreshments his guests wanted, they served themselves. Even if he had served them, he is not as well qualified as a professional bartender to know when a drinker has had enough. Indeed, Bercher might himself have been too "high" to understand what was happening. To hold him liable would be to open countless hospitable hosts to indefinite and unexpected liability. In any event, the court in the *Vesely* case cited earlier stated that it did "not decide whether a noncommercial furnisher of alcoholic beverages may be subject to civil liability."

11. IS A DRIVER REQUIRED TO EXERCISE GREATER CARE IN THE PRESENCE OF CHILDREN?

Yes. Children are much more unpredictable than adults; they tend to act impulsively, suddenly, and swiftly. Because of their youth and inexperience, they lack the mental capacity to appreciate the hazards of the highway. Although children are required by law to exercise care, it is of a degree or kind that a normal child of like age, mental capacity, and experience would ordinarily exercise in a similar situation.[18] An infant may be so young that no negligence may be imputed to him. Of course, if he is of sufficient age (and this may be a question of fact for the jury), he can be found guilty of contributory negligence, which bars recovery of damages.

> Patricia O'Donnell, a two-year old toddler, was playing with her dolls on the sidewalk. Suddenly she ran across a driveway, just as George Nielsen was backing his heavy-duty truck down the slight incline. The child was struck by the truck and was crippled for life. Was she guilty of contributory negligence so as to bar any recovery?

No. At that tender age, the court would undoubtedly hold that she was incapable of contributory negligence as a matter of law.[19] Appellate courts have made the same finding in cases involving older children: a seven-year-old boy running across the street, an eleven-year-old boy moving his bike from the shoulder of the road to the pavement without looking behind. Very young children can, however, be found negligent—for example, in using fire, which they know is hot and can burn, or knives, which they know are sharp and can cut.

A driver should anticipate the possibility of children's erratic and impulsive behavior, and should exercise appropriate vigilance to avoid injuring them. Even if he does not see the children, but as a reasonable man should have known of their proximity, he may be found liable if he injures them.[20] Around schools, when children might be expected to be on the streets, the driver must exercise special caution.

12. IS DRAG RACING ON A PUBLIC HIGHWAY PRIMA FACIE EVIDENCE OF NEGLIGENCE?

Yes. Many states expressly outlaw drag racing on public highways.[21] Violation of such statutes constitutes prima facie evidence of negligence as a matter of law, but generally any person injured thereby can recover only if he proves that the violation was the proximate cause of his injury.

> A. P. Venema and J. B. Zwiener were racing each other on a residential street, at speeds far above the legal limits. They ap-

proached a blind intersection with a stop sign, but both roared ahead. Venema just avoided colliding with a sedan entering from the right. Zwiener hit the sedan broadside. The car rolled over twice, burst into flames, and the driver was burned to death. Zwiener was strapped into his car with shoulder harness and seat belt and survived with minor cuts and abrasions. Are both Venema and Zwiener liable in damages to the victim's widow?

Yes. Both were involved in the illegal race; both violated several laws; their illegal actions led directly to and caused the fatal crash.

13. IN REAR-END COLLISIONS, IS THE DRIVER OF THE TRAILING CAR ALWAYS AT FAULT?

No. Both drivers are required to use ordinary care in the control of their vehicles. The trailing vehicle is governed by statutes that prohibit following another vehicle more closely than is reasonable and prudent, with due regard for speed and traffic conditions.[22] The leading vehicle is governed by statutes that prohibit stopping or suddenly decreasing speed without first giving the required signal to the driver immediately in the rear where there is opportunity to do so. Thus, in most such disputes, the jury must decide whether either or both drivers were negligent.

14. IS THE DRIVER LEGALLY REQUIRED TO MAINTAIN HIS MOTOR VEHICLE IN GOOD REPAIR?

Yes. One appellate court succinctly stated this generally applicable duty in the following words:

> Generally speaking, it is the duty of one driving a motor vehicle along a public highway to see that it is properly equipped so that it may be at all times controlled to the end that it be not a menace to the safety of others or of their property. The law requires that such a vehicle be equipped with brakes adequate to its quick stopping when necessary for the safety of its occupants or of others, and it is equally essential that it be maintained in such a condition as to mechanical efficiency and fuel supply that it may not become a menace to, or an obstruction of, other traffic by stopping on the road. But if the person in charge of such vehicle has done all that can be reasonably expected of a person of ordinary prudence to see that his vehicle is in proper condition, and an unforeseen failure of a part of his equipment occurs, it does not necessarily follow that he must be deemed guilty of negligence as a matter of law.[23]

Indeed, not only would the driver not be liable for injuries suffered by others from an unforeseeable mechanical failure of his automobile, but, if he is injured, he might recover damages from the manufacturer or a middleman on the theory of strict product liability. He would have to prove that the defendant placed the product (automobile or component part thereof) on the market, knowing that it was to be used without inspection for defects. He would also have to show that he was injured as a result of a defect in the design or manufacture of the article while he was properly using it, and that he was unaware that such defect made the article unsafe for its intended use.

> When Albert Ayers stopped for a cup of coffee at the Moonlight Cafe, he complained about the fact that he had a "short pedal" on the hydraulic brakes of his heavy-duty truck. He had to pump the pedal to get a braking response. Nevertheless, he proceeded up the mountain road. On his way down, the brakes failed to hold and he lost control. The truck careened over the side of the road and landed 200 feet below. Was the manufacturer of the truck or brake liable?

No. Even if the brakes were defective in design or manufacture, Ayers had notice of the condition and was negligent to go into the mountains.

15. WHAT SHOULD YOU DO AS A DRIVER IF INVOLVED IN AN AUTOMOBILE ACCIDENT?

The following suggestions are made to help protect your legal rights in the event that you have an accident while driving a car. More importantly, they may help to protect human lives, including your own.

1. If not stopped by the accident, stop. To hit and run is a serious criminal offense and morally wrong. Clear the vehicle(s) and person(s) involved out of the way of oncoming traffic if practicable; if possible, post someone to warn oncoming vehicles or place warning flares, or do both.
2. Provide first aid to the injured. Do not move any bodies needlessly, lest you aggravate injuries.
3. Call, or have someone call, for an ambulance and a doctor, if appropriate. See a doctor yourself if you have been injured.
4. Call the highway patrol or local police when anyone is injured or killed, or property damage is high (in excess of $250, for example). Get the name or number of the officer who investigates the accident.
5. Even before the police arrive, write down (or have someone else write down) the vehicle license numbers, names, addresses, and phone numbers of all witnesses (they might shortly leave the scene) and of the driver and occupants of the other vehicle. Ask for the name of the other driver's insurance company. If witnesses are willing, get brief statements from them.

6. Do not admit responsibility for the accident. You could be wrong, and yet such a statement could be an admission of fault that might be held against you later in court. If not a lawyer or judge, you are probably not qualified to make such a judgment. (If appropriate, try to get the other driver to admit his fault.)

7. Notify your insurance company, even if you have not been hurt and your car is undamaged, but the other party has been injured or his car damaged.

8. As soon after as practicable, write a memorandum with full details of what happened immediately before, at the time of, and immediately after the accident. A map or sketch of the scene may help. Note weather and road conditions, time, speed estimates, and skid marks. If you can, get pictures of the cars and of skid marks.

9. If the accident was serious, contact your attorney as soon as possible. If you have none, find one fast. He may have a professional photographer take pictures of the scene, including skid marks. Give him your memorandum of the event.

10. Notify the Department of Motor Vehicles or other designated agency, to comply with the state's financial responsibility law.

11. If an insurance claims adjuster for the other driver contacts you, refer him to your attorney. If you have no attorney, be careful not to admit any fault to the adjuster. Do not make any settlement until you are reasonably certain of the full extent of your damages—that is, until you have been released by your doctor or have received some clear indication from him of the medical outlook for your case, and have received legal advice. Remember that normally you are entitled to damages sufficient to cover (a) medical and hospital expenses, incurred and prospective; (b) damage to property (car, clothing); (c) loss of wages, actual and prospective; (d) payment for pain, suffering, and disfigurement.

When the amounts are substantial, you are usually well advised to retain an attorney. Even after deduction of his fee, you will probably receive a larger sum than the best direct offer of an insurance claims adjuster.

12. You will probably want to have your car repaired if it has been damaged. The insurance company will usually ask for two written estimates to be obtained by you from reliable repair shops, and the company will indemnify you (that is, make good your loss in cash or pay the bill for repairs) on the basis of the lower estimate. However, if it appears that a defect in the vehicle caused the accident, consult your attorney before you have anything done to the car. He will arrange to have an expert examine the suspect parts and preserve them as evidence for possible use later, should he rely on the doctrine of strict product liability in the litigation.

1. Latimer had not quite mastered the stick shift in his new car. As a result, while in a shopping center parking lot, he shifted into forward when he wanted reverse. With a sickening crunch, he rammed into the side of a new limousine, causing $1,500 in damages. His own car needed $500 in repairs. Since Latimer had paid only 10 percent down on his new car, the seller was listed as legal owner. Who is liable for the damages?

2. Darryl Galloway is fourteen years old, but he has been driving autos and trucks on his family's 6,000-acre cattle ranch for more than five years without a driver's license. Is he or are his parents guilty of violating the state's vehicle code?

3. Hugo Finch was daydreaming as he slowly backed out of his driveway, and failed to look both ways. The rear end of his car entered the residential street just when Felix Monk came racing by in his souped-up sedan at 65 mph. Monk was testing his car's acceleration and happened to be looking down at the instrument panel when Finch's car appeared. There was a collision. Monk had on his seat belt and shoulder harness and suffered no injury, but Finch was seriously injured and permanently disabled. Is Monk liable to Finch for damages suffered?

4. After a long, hard day at the office, Ludwig Belk was glad to be behind the wheel of his imported sports car, heading home. A gentle drizzle was falling in the dark as he moved on to the crowded freeway. He was soon up to the posted limit of 55 mph, and moving effortlessly from lane to lane as he passed slower-moving traffic. The drizzle suddenly turned into a cloudburst, obscuring his vision even though he adjusted his windshield wipers to their top speed. He reduced his speed to 50 mph and thought he had control of his vehicle but was unable to get around a bus and plowed into its rear end. When cited by the highway patrol, he claimed he was innocent because he had been driving within the posted speed limit. Is this a valid defense under the circumstances?

5. When Victoria Ziff needed a new car, she selected a station wagon. Then she arranged to transport to work each day eight of her fellow employees who lived in the same suburban neighborhood, charging a modest fifty cents for the round trip. All were pleased to be relieved of the burden of driving and to save money at the same time. Legally, were Ziff's eight associates guests, or ordinary passengers who could sue her if the station wagon were in an accident and they were hurt because of her negligence?

6. As Alistair Brooks eased out of the tight parking space in the underground garage under Union Square in San Francisco, his front bumper

creased the side of the adjoining parked automobile. He stopped, examined the damage, and drove off. He had decided it was an old car and the owner might not even want it repaired; even if it were repaired, it should not cost more than fifty dollars.

    a. Has Brooks violated the California financial responsibility law?

    b. Has he violated any other law?

7. After a night baseball game at the Coliseum that went into overtime, thousands of tired spectators poured out of the stadium and headed home. Most drove their own cars, but traffic was slowed by a night fog. On the main highway a chain collision involved thirty-seven vehicles before police were able to control the mess. If it could be established that Douglas Burnham, driver of the second car in line, was at fault because he rear-ended the first car, is he liable for damages to all the other vehicles involved?

8. Manuel Omera was driving carefully down a residential street where vehicles were parked at irregular intervals on both sides. Suddenly, a boy of five darted from in front of a parked truck. Omera's car struck the child and injured him. At the ensuing civil trial, counsel for the plaintiff claimed the child was too young to be guilty of contributory negligence and therefore Omera should pay damages demanded. Decide.

9. The California Highway Patrol spot-checks vehicles that are stopped at selected points along streets and highways. Those with defective lights, mirrors, tires, and so forth are cited and required to make specified corrections. Maureen Harvin's car had never been checked by the patrol, and so when she skidded into another vehicle because her tires were worn smooth and could not grip the road, she blamed them for negligence in failing to do their duty to inspect and warn her in time. Is the patrol at fault?

10. Dave Selfridge rode his ten-speed bicycle to school as his contribution to smog reduction (and also to help save money for his first car).

    a. Must he or his bicycle be licensed by the state?

    b. Must the bicycle meet any minimum standards of design and equipment?

    c. Must he observe all applicable rules of the road while riding the bicycle?

7

YOU
AS FAMILY
MEMBER

1. WHAT IS FAMILY LAW?

Family law governs the legal relations of the basic social unit, the family. For the most part, the applicable principles and rules have been established by the legislative branch of state government. Thus, there is no federal marriage or divorce law. As a family member, however, a person may become involved in a matter involving federal jurisdiction. For example, if Bruce Brown, husband and father, was caught at Nogales, Arizona, entering the United States with contraband such as marijuana, he would be involved in a federal crime. But the question of how Brown's incarceration could affect his duty to support his children would be determined by principles of family law in the state of his residence. In more than thirty-five states, conviction of a felony is grounds for a divorce; in more than ten, so too is life imprisonment.

Most principles of family law are found in the civil law; some are found in the criminal law because certain conduct involving family members is so objectionable that the public becomes concerned. Child abuse or beating is an example.

Family law, in both its civil and criminal applications, has been enacted principally to protect and enhance marriage and the family. Among the criminal laws designed to protect the family are those that proscribe adultery, bigamy, seduction accomplished by promise of marriage, and incest (which is sexual intercourse between a man and a woman who are closely related to each other within the degrees forbidden by law, such as first cousins). Incestuous unions are objectionable largely because of genetic hazards to offspring. Principles of civil law that relate to the family state that contracts made in restraint of marriage are void; that marriage by *proxy* (a person authorized to act for another) is invalid; and that upon termination of the marriage, courts may distribute the family property equitably and define the continuing rights and duties of family members.

2. WHAT IS MARRIAGE?

Joe Marston and Margaret Fuller decided to marry. However, they agreed to ignore the state marriage license laws and to create their marriage by simply declaring mutual love for one another at a beach party on the seashore in the presence of friends. Thereafter they lived as husband and wife for several years. Then Joe was killed in an auto accident. Joe's parents contended that Margaret was not Joe's widow, but merely a girlfriend; therefore they, not she, should inherit all of Joe's possessions, including the car and home he had purchased while cohabiting (living together as husband and wife) with Margaret. Are Joe's parents correct?

Yes—in most states.

In the exercise of their power to regulate marriage, state legislatures have enacted laws specifying when and how marriage may be legally created. In almost all states, a woman of eighteen may marry without parental consent; for men, the minimum age is usually twenty-one. In California, as in Michigan and in North and South Carolina, any person eighteen years of age and of sound mind is legally capable of marriage. In most states, with parental consent, a woman may become a bride at sixteen; a man may become a bridegroom at eighteen. These ages drop to fourteen and sixteen in New York, and as low as thirteen and fourteen in New Hampshire. When the parties are younger than the legal ages, in some states (such as California) a court order is necessary to permit them to marry.

All but four states (Maryland, Minnesota, Nevada, and South Carolina) require blood tests, usually thirty days or less before the marriage, to provide assurance of freedom from venereal disease (syphilis), which could be dangerous to the other spouse as well as to any children conceived. Usually the prospective bride must also be checked for immunity to German measles (rubella), likewise because of the possible hazard to the fetus (the unborn child from the end of the third month until birth; it is referred to as an embryo in the earlier months of pregnancy). A marriage license must be obtained (at a nominal cost) but is not issued if either prospective spouse is an imbecile, insane, under the minimum age, or under the influence of drugs at the time of application. The ceremony of marriage must be performed by an adult who is a judge, priest, or minister of any denomination. Joe and Margaret failed to comply with these legally prescribed requisites: their "marriage" was defective.

Nullification of Marriage

A *defective,* or *voidable, marriage* may be legally nullified by the innocent party through court action, thereby restoring both parties to the legal status of unmarried persons. Technically, a void marriage is of no legal effect; practically, a court decree of nullification is recommended and generally obtained in such cases if only to avoid uncertainty about one's status and possible future arguments over rights and duties. Children born or conceived prior to a declaration of nullity are legitimate, and both parents are equally responsible for their support.

A marriage may be defective for many reasons. Either person may have been tricked by some fraudulent representation of the other, such as concerning impotency (inability of the male to copulate) or sterility (inability of either partner to germinate or reproduce). However, a fraudulent representation by the prospective wife to the effect that she is a virgin is not enough to render the marriage defective. A marriage is also defective and voidable if contracted by force, or if either party lacks mental capacity. A person under the influence of drugs or intoxicating liquor may lack sufficient mental capacity to enter the marriage relationship. A marriage that is either incestuous or *bigamous* (where either party was already legally married) is void.

Even when a marriage is defective, some rights and duties may be imposed upon "spouses" by law. For example, if a woman, acting in good faith, is ignorant of the impediment that makes her "marriage" unlawful, she may be a *putative spouse* (from Latin *putare:* to think). Perhaps she is unaware that her "husband" is a bigamist. Therefore, she could be entitled to alimony if their relationship ends, and to a share of her "husband's" estate if he dies. In the hypothetical case of Margaret and Joe, Margaret knowingly rejected the legally prescribed procedures for valid marriage. Therefore, his parents take all of his estate.

Common Law Marriage

In some states, a *common law marriage* may exist where persons live together as husband and wife.* For a common law marriage, the parties

---

* Alabama, Colorado, District of Columbia, Georgia, Iowa, Kansas, Montana, Ohio, Oklahoma, Pennsylvania, Rhode Island, South Carolina, and Texas.

must cohabit and create the public impression that a marriage exists, and they must intend that it exist.[1] Thirty-seven states do not permit this method of establishing a marriage. However, under Article IV, Section 1 of the U.S. Constitution,

> Full faith and credit shall be given in each state to the public acts, records, and judicial proceedings of every other state.

New York and California, for example, do not permit common law marriages, but they do recognize as valid a common law marriage created in Ohio or Texas—as they do all other marriages that are valid where created.

A California Variation

In California, as an alternative to formal ceremonial marriage, persons who have lived together as husband and wife may be legally married by a clergyman, without regard to the usual requirements of health tests, waiting period, license, and witnesses. Couples such as Joe and Margaret may thus legitimize their relationship—provided that they have already assumed the rights, duties, and obligations typically associated with marriage; a premarital affair or illicit relationship would not qualify. Some people have misued this "secret marriage" law simply to avoid the expense of health tests. If either party is diseased, however, children who are conceived may become the permanent victims of such false economy.

3. WHAT LEGAL OBLIGATIONS ARE IMPOSED UPON A HUSBAND AND WIFE?

> Harry Evans and Anita Jones were married in San Diego, California, where they were both employed. Shortly thereafter, Harry decided that they should immediately move to Los Angeles, that they should invest all of their savings (including money in their joint account earned by Anita) in a speculative stock issue, and that Anita should no longer attend college in the evenings. Harry asserts that he has the legal right to make these decisions. Is he correct?

Although more and more wives are gainfully employed outside the home, although every state has given married women the right to retain property they owned while single, and although most give them clear title to what they earn or receive by gift or inheritance during marriage, nevertheless a husband still generally has the legal obligation to support his wife and minor children if he is able to do so.

In most states, a husband takes title to and manages what he earns.

When he dies, unless he leaves his wife a share that she considers fair, she may "elect" to take the portion prescribed by law had he died intestate (that is, without a will)—typically one-third to one-half of the total, depending on whether there are children who also share in the estate. A similar protection is given a husband when his wife dies first.

The husband decides where the family shall live, usually near his place of employment. If his wife refuses to join him, she may be guilty of desertion unless she has good and compelling reason for her refusal (such as her health). Normally, she is the homemaker and housekeeper, providing services worth thousands of dollars but legally not compensable because of the marriage contract. She need not accede to having any of her husband's relatives move in, nor need she live with them. Reciprocally, he need not provide room in the family home for his in-laws.

Each spouse is entitled to *consortium*—the companionship, assistance, affections, and services of the partner. Neither spouse has the right to dictate details of the other's behavior nor, for example, to prevent the other from attending school, so long as the studies do not interfere unreasonably with consortium.

> Robert Hamilton became crippled and unable to work. His wife, Sally, a trained legal secretary, had been serving as housewife and homemaker. Sally declared that she would not seek gainful employment to support her husband and would henceforth terminate the marriage. Is Sally required to go to work to support Robert if the marriage remains intact? If it is terminated?

Yes, in both instances. Although in most states the husband has the primary responsibility to support the family, if he is unable to do so this burden falls on the wife. Sally will have to apply her skills to supporting her husband whether or not the marriage remains intact. In community property states, she could be required to use her separate property for his support.

The trend of the law is to treat husband and wife as equal partners. The equal rights amendment, if ratified by all of the states, would help establish and maintain this equality.

Community Property

Community property is all property acquired by the husband or the wife during marriage other than by gift or inheritance. This legal concept is derived from the ganancial system used in medieval Spain to regulate ownership of property within marriage. It affects the laws of Arizona, California, Idaho, Louisiana, Nevada, New Mexico, Texas, and Washington. In these community property states, the earnings of husband and wife during marriage are owned equally (in the absence of contrary agreements). The husband manages the property, but upon dissolution of the marriage or upon the death of either spouse, it is divided equally. Either may will his (or her) share as he (or she) pleases.

Separate property is property, real or personal, either brought into the marriage by one spouse or acquired by one spouse during marriage by gift or inheritance. It remains separate, and earnings received from it are separate, so long as independent records are kept. If the owner treats it as community property, as by commingling it, it becomes community property.

In 1975, California modified its community property law by giving each spouse equal rights in the management and control of community property. Both must sign deeds transferring community real property; but if either solely operates a business, he (or she) normally has the sole right to manage and control it. Harry and Anita in the hypothetical case reside in California. Therefore, Harry cannot invest or squander the community savings without the consent of Anita. However, a spouse need not give his (or her) written consent each time the other spouse wants to buy or sell something. Since consent may be implied, dissipation of the community assets during family squabbles remains an unfortunate possibility. The husband, in California, is no longer the head of the family, nor can he legally prescribe the place and mode of family living. In short, marriage in California is now an equal partnership, unlike most other states, where the husband continues to have extra rights and powers.

> In Seattle, Washington, George Marichol was enamored of his secretary, Gloria Evans, and gave her an automobile purchased with earnings from his accounting business. When his wife, Betty, learned of the gift, she insisted that the car be taken from Gloria. Can this be done legally?

Yes. Whenever a husband gives away community property without his wife's consent, her remedy is to request the court to set aside the conveyance (transfer of property) and order the property returned to the community. However, if the automobile was "given" to the secretary in exchange for services legitimately rendered, then the "gift" could be in the nature of a bonus, or wage, and could not be set aside. If the gift was discovered after George's demise, only half of it could be recouped from Gloria, because Betty's interest in the community property is one-half.

> While Gary Jones was at work in Reno, Nevada, his wife, Susan, decided to drive the family automobile downtown to buy, on credit, a lot for a vacation home near Lake Tahoe and a new ski outfit for herself. In a parking lot, Susan opened the car door so vigorously that she dented the car of Jonathan Misterbye in

the adjacent parking space. It would cost $50 to repair the dent. When Gary was informed of these expenses, he declared that he was not responsible for them, and that Susan would have to take care of them on her own. Is Gary correct?

No. Community property is liable for the obligations—tortious or contractual—incurred by either spouse. The same rule applies to family property in noncommunity property jurisdictions. However, a lot is real property and its purchase requires the written consent of both spouses. If Susan had incurred these or other debts prior to their marriage, neither her husband nor his earnings after marriage would be liable for them. One does not "marry" the spouse's premarital debts.

Barbara Urbanski had $1000 in a savings account when she married Robert Jamison in Phoenix, Arizona. During the marriage, a department store sued Barbara and Robert in small claims court for the balance due on their charge account, attributable to a suit of clothes purchased by Robert months after their wedding. The department store sought to be paid from Barbara's savings account. Would this be lawful?

The savings account balance is Barbara's separate property and is liable for the debts of her husband only if the debt was incurred to purchase "necessaries" for him. If Barbara purchased the suit or if the contract opening the charge account was signed by Barbara, she is responsible because it then becomes, in essence, her individual debt, and her separate property is, of course, liable. The separate property of either spouse, as well as the entire community property, is liable for necessaries furnished.

One spouse is not responsible for the crimes or torts of the other in the sense of criminal penalty, and separate property is immune from fines or judgments against the other. Indirectly, one is damaged if the fine is paid from community property or if, as a result of confinement, community property is not earned. Of course, marriage does not shield one's separate property from his (or her) own creditors.

4. WHAT LEGAL ADVANTAGES ARE GAINED BY MARRIAGE?

Jack and Sandy Schmidt married in Indianapolis, Indiana, on December 31, 1973, when Sandy was eighteen. In April 1974, Jack was working on his income tax return for the 1973 taxable year, during which his taxable income was $20,000. In his computations, Jack used a joint income tax return for all of 1973 and also deducted from taxable income $500 as a charitable contribution, although the money was in fact never given to charity. When questioned by Sandy, Jack contended that splitting his 1973

income with a joint return was legal even though they were not married the entire year, and that although the charitable contribution deduction was illegal, he could never be caught because the law prevents one spouse from incriminating the other. Sandy finally signed the tax return with Jack. Was Jack's analysis correct?

Partly. A husband and wife may file a joint income tax return, both federal and state, applicable for any year in which they were married for any length of time. The effect of filing such a return is to split the income of one spouse over two taxpayers, thereby achieving payment at a lower tax rate or bracket. To claim the false charitable deduction is a federal crime, and both Sandy and Jack committed a criminal act by signing the return they knew was false. Although it is true that one spouse cannot be compelled to testify against the other in a criminal trial, the Internal Revenue Service can disallow any deduction that is not supported by sufficient documentary evidence, and could prosecute both Jack and Sandy without relying on such testimony.

Later Jack Schmidt was killed in an auto accident. His wife Sandy was untrained and therefore unable to earn much. What financial remedy does she have because of her marriage?

When a husband is killed by the negligence of a third person, the widow may recover damages from the wrongdoer to replace the lost earning power of her deceased husband. Damages for loss of consortium and protection are also proper. The wrongful death of a wife or child may also justify the payment of damages; however, the recovery is usually smaller, especially in the case of a child, whose future earnings cannot be known with any certainty.

If Jack and Sandy had been living together illicitly, she would have no remedy for his death. She would, however, be legally able to recover proceeds under any insurance policy he may have purchased on his life, naming her as the beneficiary. If, however, she had purchased a policy on his life, naming herself as beneficiary, she would not be entitled to the face value, since she had no insurable interest in his life.

5. WHAT NEW OBLIGATIONS ARE IMPOSED UPON THE SPOUSES WHEN CHILDREN ARRIVE?

Even before they were married, John and Nancy Stiles agreed never to have children. When Nancy announced that, by mistake, she was pregnant, John said that the child must be "put up" for adoption and he would not pay a dime. Nancy disagreed and said she would keep the child and make John provide support. Does John have to support his child?

Yes. Both parents are equally responsible for the maintenance and care of their minor children. Their obligations exist, regardless of whether the child was conceived within wedlock (even though maybe unwanted and unplanned for) or out of wedlock. Thus, a father is responsible for the support of his child unless the child is lawfully adopted by other persons, who then become legally obliged to provide the necessary care.

A husband alone cannot relinquish his child. If a child is to be put up for adoption and the parents are married, the consent of both spouses is necessary, following legally prescribed procedures. If the child is illegitimate, the mother alone may consent to the adoption. She need not be, and generally is not, told the identity of the adopting parents, nor are they supplied with her name and address. Social welfare workers who assist in the adoption carefully establish the suitability of the adopting parents and provide them with background information about the natural parents. Birth records are changed to give the child the new family name, and the relation between child and adopting parents legally becomes the same as that between natural parents and child. The natural parents are relieved of all parental duties and deprived of all parental rights toward the adopted child.

During the first trimester (three months) of her pregnancy, Nancy Stiles, in consultation with her physician, could have elected to have an abortion. This absolute right of the mother is protected, according to the court, by concepts of freedom and privacy implicit in the due process clause of the Fourteenth Amendment. Under the controversial decision, a pregnant woman of any age, without parental consent, may obtain an abortion from a licensed physician during the first trimester. The U.S. Supreme Court has refused to recognize any right of the unborn child to continued life, or of the father to intervene on the child's behalf in such a situation. However, abortions during the second and third trimesters may be restricted by state regulation.[2]

6. WHAT DISTINCTIONS EXIST IN LAW BETWEEN NATURAL AND ADOPTIVE CHILDREN?

Delbert Smith and his wife, Hedwig, died in an automobile crash. Neither left a will. They were survived by two infant children, Matilda, their natural daughter, and Roman, their adoptive son. During probate of their estates, blood relatives of Matilda contended that she was entitled to the entire estate and that Roman should be placed for adoption. Are the relatives correct?

No. The law does not distinguish between natural and adoptive children. Matilda and Roman would share the estates equally.

> Paul and Janice Robertson attempted in vain to have a child. After some years, Janice secretly arranged to become artificially inseminated. The child was born and named Charles. A few years thereafter, Paul and Janice adopted Louise. Some years later Paul and Janice were killed in an auto accident and upon autopsy it was determined that Paul had a congenital (dating from his birth) condition that made him sterile. Based on that determination, Louise brought an action to exclude her half-brother from any portion of the estates of their parents. Does she prevail?

Louise will lose her case even though she can prove medically that Charles cannot be issue of the marriage. The law regards children who are conceived during cohabitation of married persons as legitimate issue of the marriage.

Possibly Paul or Charles could have successfully pursued a civil action designed to establish lack of paternity. Once established, Charles's right to inherit from Paul would end, although Paul could voluntarily include him among the beneficiaries in his will.

7. WHAT VICARIOUS LIABILITIES ARE IMPOSED UPON PARENTS BY LAW?

> Joe Stewart, aged ten, was playing with a pellet rifle in his neighbor's backyard. The rifle was a Christmas gift from his father, who was an expert hunter and rifleman. The rifle accidentally discharged and the shot blinded Harry Moore, Joe's young friend. Harry's parents decided to sue Joe's parents. Are Joe's parents legally responsible?

Joe had accidentally discharged the rifle, and parents generally are not liable for the intentional or negligent torts of their minor children simply because they are parents. However, Joe's parents may be liable for negligence of their own because they entrusted a "dangerous instrumentality" to a minor child without properly instructing him in its use. This liability would be the same even if the rifle were entrusted to any minor of tender years, not necessarily their own child.

California, by statute, makes an interesting exception to the general rule: in the case of an intentional tort, parents are responsible for damages up to $2,000 caused by their minor child. This statute was aimed primarily at parents of children who vandalize school buildings and equipment.

Fred and Linda Hart frequently permitted their son, Flash, aged seventeen, to drive the family car, although they knew he often drank whiskey from the family liquor cabinet and suspected that he drove with a heavy foot. One evening, Flash hit and killed a pedestrian, Harold Sprock, who was survived by his wife. On that evening, Mr. and Mrs. Hart did not know that Flash was using the car. Flash was arrested and charged with manslaughter while driving under the influence of alcohol. What rights have accrued in favor of Mrs. Sprock?

Mrs. Sprock can sue Flash for the wrongful death of her husband and recover a judgment that includes compensation for the loss of her husband's earning capacity for his life expectancy. Judgments are valid and enforceable for years, the period varying among the states; moreover, they may commonly be extended. In California, for example, the initial period is ten years, which may be extended for another ten. Thus, Flash could be required to make payments until he reached thirty-eight years of age. In addition, Mrs. Sprock could probably recover punitive damages that would not be dischargeable in bankruptcy. She may be able to successfully sue Mr. and Mrs. Hart, even though a parent is not generally liable for the torts of a child. They would be liable if they either signed Flash's license application or can be proved to have "permitted" Flash to use their vehicle on that fateful night. This *owner's liability* is limited to $15,000 for injury or death to each person, and $30,000 total liability, plus $5000 property damage.

Since Mr. and Mrs. Hart knew of Flash's propensities, they were probably negligent in letting him use the car. If so, they would be responsible for the entire judgment by their own negligence. They would not, however, be vicariously responsible for the crime of manslaughter Flash committed. Crimes of children are not imputed to their parents, although parents can be implicated as accessories under certain circumstances (as when they behave like Fagin in *Oliver Twist.*)

8. WHAT LEGAL ADVANTAGES ARE GAINED BY PARENTHOOD?

Sam Fong and his wife, Lin, became parents on December 31, 1974. In preparing their tax return for that year, they took their new son as a dependent for the entire year. Is this procedure proper?

A whole exemption from federal and state income tax is allowed without allocation as to the portion of the year during which a minor child is alive. The same rule applies in the event a man marries a woman with dependent children. If the marriage is on or before December 31, full exemptions are allowed for all children.

> Hugh and Shirley Mangum have a minor son, Barry, aged seventeen, who lives at home. Although Barry is working in an aircraft factory for $150 a week, he has not offered to pay rent to his parents, who have a modest income. When his parents asked that he pay some rent, he refused, saying that they were required to support him until he becomes an adult. Is Barry correct?

Barry is correct that his parents must support him as a minor child. The parents of an unmarried minor are entitled, however, to his or her custody, services, and earnings. Therefore, Mr. and Mrs. Mangum could legally notify Barry's employer to make his check payable to them and to mail it to them. Furthermore, if Barry should be injured on the job, all proceeds from his workmen's compensation claim would be payable to his parents.

9. HOW MAY PARENTHOOD BE ESTABLISHED LEGALLY IN THE ABSENCE OF MARRIAGE?

> Carrie Sanbord, a single person, became pregnant sometime during December or January by Ronald Henderson or Ed Macchia. Carrie believed the father to be Ronald. Accordingly, her parents advised Ronald that unless he agreed to pay the prenatal and birth expenses and support the child, Carrie would sue. Ronald responded that he did not have to pay anything until after the child was born and would never have to pay anything because Ed might be the father, or somebody else for that matter. Is Ron correct?

Ronald is wrong on both counts. The person who is the father of the child can be required to pay prenatal, delivery, and postnatal expenses and support the child's mother. Paternity can be determined prior to birth or any time thereafter by a legal proceeding, regardless of who might be the father. The proceeding is brought by the mother on behalf of the unborn or minor child. Evidence of sexual intercourse by the mother with other persons during the period of possible conception can be considered by the court or jury in determining the identity of the natural father.

Parentage can also be established legally, without marriage, by adoption or by legitimation. *Legitimation* involves irrevocable acknowledgment by a natural parent that he is the father, although not married. Such acknowledgment need not be express, but can be inferred from circumstances such as treating an illegitimate child as one's own for a period of time.

10. DO THE OBLIGATIONS, LIABILITIES, AND ADVANTAGES RELATING TO PARENTHOOD DIFFER WHEN THE NATURAL PARENTS ARE NOT MARRIED?

Elmo Tabern and Patricia Jackson did not want to comply with marriage licensing laws and chose simply to live together in the hippie environment of San Francisco's Haight-Ashbury district. During their "marriage" Patricia gave birth to twins. Shortly thereafter, Elmo left her and moved to Florida. Patricia, being unable to support the children, applied for welfare. The Welfare Department wrote Elmo demanding child support payments. He responded that the children must be illegitimate and so he was not required to pay support. Furthermore, he said he liked Florida and was never returning to California. If Patricia wanted to sue him, he added, she could come to Florida. What can Patricia and the Welfare Department do?

Elmo must support his children whether or not they are illegitimate. However, there must be a prior adjudication of paternity. Since the children were conceived in California, its superior court has jurisdiction to determine paternity, even in Elmo's absence. The trial could proceed, and the appearance of the children and testimony of Patricia could be strong evidence. If the court determined that Elmo was the natural father and ordered child support, Patricia or the Welfare Department could initiate proceedings under the uniform Reciprocal Enforcement of Support Act. The district attorney in Florida would be asked to pursue collection in Florida, without Patricia's presence, and could remit the support payments as and when received.

This procedure is available to collect all support awards made in paternity or dissolution proceedings, including attorney fees and court costs, regardless of whether or not the defendant is a support fugitive. This is an interesting example of public assistance in enforcement of private claims, at public expense. When successful, of course, it reduces public welfare costs. Normally, a private creditor must himself bear the costs and burdens of collecting debts owed.

11. HOW MAY MARRIAGE BE TERMINATED?

Preble Stutz abandoned his first wife in 1960, and neither of them ever legally terminated their marriage. In 1973, Preble married Eloise in San Jose, California. In 1974, Eloise consulted an attorney for the purpose of obtaining a dissolution of her marriage with Preble because of his adultery. She also desired the return of her maiden name, recovery of her attorney fees, and support until she remarried or died. Preble contends that it was a bigamous marriage and as such is void. Therefore, he says, Eloise cannot compel him to pay anything. Is Preble correct?

No. Marriage is dissolved by death, decree of divorce, decree of dissolution (in a few states), or judgment of nullity.

In most states marriage is terminated by divorce only when one of the spouses is guilty of serious fault, such as adultery, physical cruelty, habitual drunkenness or drug abuse, nonsupport, desertion, postmarital insanity, or conviction of a felony. Mental cruelty may be sufficiently serious to justify a divorce.[3] In other states, a long-standing voluntary separation alone may justify divorce.[4]

A *decree of dissolution* is awarded a petitioner in California or Florida when irreconcilable differences have caused the irremediable or irretrievable breakdown of a marriage, regardless of fault. In Iowa and Michigan dissolution is granted when the marriage relationship has broken down and there is no reasonable likelihood that it can be restored.

In the hypothetical case, Preble's adultery is irrelevant. A *judgment of nullity* will be granted a petitioner when the marriage is either void or voidable, because of fraud, or duress, or minority. Since a bigamous marriage is void, Eloise or Preble could obtain a decree. Preble will have to pay support in accordance with Eloise's need and his ability to pay, as well as her attorney fees, because Eloise is a putative spouse. (If Eloise had known of Preble's previous marriage, she would not be a putative spouse and would not be entitled to support.) Eloise is also entitled to restoration of her maiden name.

12. WHAT IS A LEGAL SEPARATION?

Louis and Margaret Lotus lived in California and were Roman Catholics. Although their marriage seemed to have deteriorated beyond repair, they desired to remain married. Thus, they agreed to live apart and respectively provide for themselves. Louis was concerned that his future earnings would become community property unless a dissolution were obtained. Are his fears justified?

No. The California court may decree a *legal separation* on the grounds of irreconcilable differences or incurable postmarital insanity; it may, at that time, make necessary orders with respect to child custody and support, support of the wife, and division of community property the same as if dissolution were occurring. As an alternative, Louis and Margaret may privately agree in writing concerning these matters without the necessity of court adjudication. Future earnings of the spouses during legal separation become their respective separate property, just as in a divorce or dissolution, and so Louis's fears are unfounded.

Roman Catholics who have been validly married in a Christian ceremony may divorce or obtain a dissolution as a matter of legal convenience. Under the rules of their church, only if they remarry are they subject to excommunication, whereby they are cut off from communion or membership.

13. UPON DIVORCE OR DISSOLUTION, WHAT HAPPENS TO ASSETS ACCUMULATED DURING A MARRIAGE?

Joe Gilbridge and his wife, Jane, had been married twenty-five years when they sought a dissolution. They possessed the following assets and liabilities:

Cash in savings accounts, $10,000. This consisted of $1,000 that Jane owned upon her marriage, together with $2,000 contributed by Joe and $7,000 by Jane from their respective earnings while married.

Residence, fair market value of $50,000, with a note secured by deed of trust outstanding in the amount of $40,000. They acquired the home while married and made the down payment with money accumulated during their marriage.

Common stock, fair market value of $30,000, in the form of 1,000 shares of ABC Corporation. During the marriage Joe inherited 500 shares of XYZ Corporation worth $10,000 at that time. Joe traded in the stock market, tripling the value of this inheritance.

Jane contends that she should receive one-half of all these assets. Is she correct?

In common law states and in community property states other than California, the wife is not automatically entitled to one-half of the marital property. Rather, the court will make an award consistent with the wife's own industry, earnings, labor, economy, and frugality during the marriage.[5] Her fault in causing a divorce may justify depriving her of any right to her husband's future earnings.[6] Cases are handled individually, and the trial court judge has wide discretion.

Upon dissolution in California the court must divide the community property equally. With respect to the savings account, Jane will receive one-half of the community property portion ($9,000) plus the $1,000 that was her separate property, for a total of $5,500. She is entitled to one-half of the equity of the home, or $5,000.

Separate property can be converted into community property inadvertently if it becomes commingled and its source cannot be traced. In a California court, Joe could argue, with reference to the stock, that the original $10,000 of XYZ stock was his separate property, that it has grown into $30,000, and that it retains its identity as separate property. Hence, Jane should get none of it. However, Jane would likely contend that Joe devoted substantial time and effort that belonged to the community of marriage, and hence the $20,000 earned thereby in capital gains during marriage is community property, entitling her to one-half, or $10,000. The court might allow legal interest (7 percent a year) as natural growth of the original $10,000 separate property and declare all growth in excess thereof to be community property.

14. UPON DIVORCE OR DISSOLUTION, WHAT HAPPENS TO THE LEGAL OBLIGATIONS, LIABILITIES, AND ADVANTAGES OF MARRIAGE?

> While Don and Hazel Rathblock were married, she contracted a crippling disease. It appeared that she would need considerable medical attention over a period of years during which she would be unable to work. Don's parents suggested to him that the marriage should be terminated so that Don would not be forever financially burdened by doctor's bills. Can Don save money by terminating the marriage?

No. The court, upon granting a divorce or dissolution, will make such support orders as are consistent with Don's ability to pay and Hazel's need, including medical care. When the wife is healthy, her earning capacity will be considered by the court in determining the propriety of support, both as to amount and duration.

Since the California Family Law Act (which eliminated the element of guilt from divorce, renamed the action dissolution, and recognized husband and wife as equals) California courts no longer grant indefinite support to young wives. Judicial practice varies. In a representative county, support is typically awarded for half the duration of the marriage if under twelve years; if between twelve and twenty years, it depends on the education and marketable skills of the wife; over twenty years, the support is usually nonterminable.

15. UPON TERMINATION OF A MARRIAGE, WHAT HAPPENS TO THE LEGAL OBLIGATIONS, LIABILITIES, AND ADVANTAGES OF PARENTHOOD?

> While Jack and Diane Howard were contemplating dissolution of their marriage, their daughter, Melinda, aged fifteen, ran away

and joined a commune in New Hampshire. During proceedings to dissolve their marriage, Jack contended that he did not have to pay support for their daughter because of her life style, even if she returned. Is Jack correct?

He is not. The obligation of parents to support their children extends to age eighteen or earlier *emancipation,* which generally refers to financial care of oneself with parental consent. Living in a commune is not emancipation.

16. MAY THE LEGAL EFFECTS OF TERMINATION OF MARRIAGE BE CONTROLLED BY THE SPOUSES?

While contemplating marriage, Mike Evan requested Denise Konner to sign a contract to the effect that, if the marriage failed, she would not demand support for herself or for any children they might have. Denise signed the contract and they were married. He would not have married Denise if she had refused to sign the agreement. Is the contract valid and enforceable?

No. Such an antenuptial agreement is not enforceable because it violates accepted judicial procedure, which imposes upon both parents a duty to support and care for their minor children. Furthermore, it is void because it attempts to shift the responsibility of a husband to provide for his wife onto her shoulders, or perhaps to some state agency. The fact that the marriage was conditioned upon the invalid agreement is irrelevant and does not vitiate the marriage. Premarital property agreements may validly relate to the status and disposition of separate property of the spouses. They are not uncommon when rich old men marry attractive young women, and the men are doubtful about the enduring quality of the union.

Terrence and Barbara McDivott were contemplating dissolution of their marriage. They had considerable community property and three children. Mr. McDivott had interests in several real estate projects, the exact value of which would be difficult to ascertain. To minimize attorney fees, court costs, and time, they signed an agreement. They agreed that the total community property was worth $125,000, and Barbara agreed to accept a promissory note from Terrence for $62,500 as her one-half interest. Terrence agreed that Barbara should have custody of the two youngest children, and he would keep the eldest. In addition, he agreed to pay $500 a month for child support, and $500 a month for Barbara's support, for one year only. Is this agreement enforceable?

Partly. The court will award child custody and support in a manner consistent with the best interests of the children, regardless of parental agreements.[7] However, the best interests of the children may be satisfactorily expressed in the agreement. In other respects, the agreement is legal and enforceable, even if the wife might have fared better under a court determination of the value of the estate and her proper share.

17. WHAT ASSISTANCE DOES THE LAW PROVIDE FOR ENCOURAGING THE CONTINUANCE OF MARRIAGE?

> Gregory and Brenda Roanoke were having marital difficulties. Gregory threatened immediate dissolution of the marriage. Brenda felt that they once loved each other dearly and should be able to work out their difficulties as intelligent adults. Trivial annoyances had swollen into major issues because they were not communicating with each other. Can Brenda prevent Gregory from dissolving the marriage while professional marital help is obtained?

In many states, upon request of either the petitioner or the respondent, the court may postpone the divorce or dissolution proceedings pending conciliation counseling by a public or private counselor. Large metropolitan counties in California, for example, have public marriage counselors, and in such areas, participation in counseling may be ordered by the court. However, the high incidence of dissolution in that state suggests that counseling is usually of little value when the relationship has deteriorated and either party is an uncooperative participant.

18. WHAT ARE THE LEGAL IMPLICATIONS OF LIVING TOGETHER AS A FAMILY WITHOUT BENEFIT OF MARRIAGE?

> Dick Rogers and Elaine McIntosh never married, but they had two children while living together. After fifteen years, when Dick was forty, Elaine thirty-one, and the children in their teens, Dick received a million dollar inheritance and promptly abandoned the family in favor of "bright lights and the loose life." Elaine consulted an attorney who advised her that she could not expect support from Dick and that support for her children would be possible only if paternity litigation were successful. Furthermore, the children could not inherit from Dick nor be entitled to survivor's benefits in the event of his death. What action might ease Elaine's problem?

Probably the best remedy would be a legal proceeding to establish paternity. If this were successful, Dick would be required to support the children during their minority. The court might order payments to Elaine for support of the children, but Elaine could not receive support for herself, and neither she nor the children would inherit from Dick under his will unless he voluntarily included them. If there is no will, an illegitimate child is legally entitled to inherit from his mother, but not from his father. This seemingly anomalous distinction is presumably designed to forestall a multiplicity of false claims against the estates of wealthy dead men who may have developed a reputation for being libertines. Note that either parent may specifically include or exclude a child, legitimate or illegitimate, from inheritance by so stating in a will.

When a legitimate child (or grandchild, if the child is dead) is excluded from his parent's will, the law refers to him as a *pretermitted heir*—meaning omitted or neglected—and it assumes that the exclusion was inadvertent. Therefore, the child takes his share of the estate as though there were no will. To avoid this result, the parent must make some appropriate settlement (gift) on the child during life, or expressly exclude him in the will. In a few states, this special protection is not extended to children who were alive when the will was made.

CASES, QUESTIONS, AND PROBLEMS

1. Upon marriage, is a woman required by law to forfeit the use of her surname and adopt her husband's?

2. Dean Hillard is on duty with the U.S. Army in Europe. Elaborate and expensive arrangements were being made for his forthcoming wedding and reception in Kansas City, Kansas, when his leave was unexpectedly cancelled. He therefore arranged for his friend, Lyle Dakota, to appear at his wedding in his place and upon his behalf. May a legal marriage by proxy take place under these circumstances?

3. What legal rights may accrue to a woman who lives with a man for thirteen years in the absence of marriage?

4. How may parents control an incorrigible teenager who disrupts the family?

5. Is there a right to trial by jury in divorce or dissolution proceedings?

6. Persons concerned about the worldwide population explosion have proposed various solutions, including family planning through birth control and abortion. The Russian government has been a strong supporter of such activities. However, in September 1974, it was reported that the Soviet Union had initiated a system of subsidies or family allowances "to alleviate poverty and to counteract the

nation's falling birth rate." At the same time in the United States, the number of live births dropped so precipitously that this nation had a zero population growth birth rate. Should we also begin to make payments to families with young children and a low income to reverse the low birth rate?

7. It has been said that divorce is "the great American tragedy." Among measures suggested to reduce the divorce rate are: higher age requirement for marriage, computerized analysis of personalities and backgrounds of prospective spouses, longer mandatory waiting period after a marriage license is obtained, mandatory "marriage license training" (including instruction in the financial, social, psychological, and sexual aspects of marriage), trial marriage for a probationary period, and government day-care centers for infants and preschool children to free mothers from the burdens of child care. What do you think should be done, if anything?

8. For many years, illegitimate children have been called bastards and have been the objects of public opprobrium and discrimination. Some observers argue that "There is no such thing as an illegitimate child. There are only illegitimate parents." Should all laws that discriminate against illegitimate children be abolished? Would this necessarily eliminate the stigma that now marks such persons?

9. In some places an illegal black market has developed in babies available for adoption. Exorbitant fees are paid to middlemen and sometimes to unmarried mothers for the babies, desperately wanted by childless couples. Should the government and private agencies promote birth control but discourage abortion and routinely provide all necessary support for pregnant mothers and their unwanted children until they can be placed for adoption?

10. What are the prerequisites for marriage and divorce (or dissolution) in your state? Should they be changed? Should divorce be made easier or more difficult to obtain?

11. Parents are legally obliged to support their children. Should adult children be obliged to support their elderly parents, if indigent? State laws vary on this issue. What are they in your state? What should they be?

III THE
ECONOMIC ASPECTS
OF LAW

8

YOU AS CONSUMER

1. HOW DOES THE LAW RELATE TO ECONOMIC TRANSACTIONS?

Consumption of goods and services is a common denominator among all people. Food, clothing, shelter, medical care and pharmaceuticals, recreation, and transportation are but some of the many categories of items that satisfy human needs and wants. Farms, factories, stores, and offices in the United States produce a gross national product of goods and services worth more than a trillion dollars annually.

For the most part the production and distribution of these goods and services is accomplished through an intricate network of freely entered *contracts,* or legally enforceable agreements to do or not to do certain things. The law prescribes the essentials of a valid contract, and courts serve as forums for the resolution of disputes concerning the nature and performance of contracts. Most persons who make contractual agreements act honorably and keep their promises, or peacefully negotiate the settlement of disputes. Usually the product received is substantially what was bargained for and expected, and so the buyer-consumer is generally satisfied. Sometimes, however, consumers are misled by false advertising or deceptive packaging. Or they may be injured because of defective designs or disappointed because of faulty workmanship.

Ellacinder had a wonderful personality, but she thought her physical appearance left much to be desired. For the gala dance, she bought a bottle of Rainbo dye to change the color of her hair, and some new Bathsheba brand rouge to tint her face and mascara for her eyelashes. She splurged and purchased a shocking pink party gown made of imported Sternoyarn synthetic fabric. Unfortunately, the party proved to be a disaster. Her hair had two-tone streaks; as the evening wore on, her face developed a rash, and her eyes became swollen because of irritants in the cosmetics. Trying to be nonchalant, she lit a cigarette and a spark turned her gown into flames, which caused painful burns before the fire could be put out. Does she have a legal cause of action against anyone?

Probably yes—against the retail sellers, middlemen (wholesalers and brokers), and manufacturers of the products that caused her injuries. Government-prescribed standards for such products as cosmetics and fabrics make the hypothetical problem uncommon today. But when a defective or dangerous product causes injury, legal remedies are available to the victim.

The victim who turns to the courts in a suit for dollar damages or other relief may act alone or in company with others in a *class action,* whereby one or a limited number of parties can sue (or be sued) on behalf of a larger group to which they belong. This tends to encourage recourse to the courts even when the individual's potential damages are negligible and yet, collectively, a large sum is involved. Unfortunately for consumers, the U.S. Supreme Court in 1974 held that every member of the class must have a claim of more than $10,000 to join together in a lawsuit in a federal court. It does not suffice if the plaintiffs' collective claim adds up to the minimum amount prescribed for federal jurisdiction. This limit does not apply, however, to class actions brought in state courts. In California, the progressive Consumers Legal Remedies Act permits such class actions, provided there is unity of factual situation and applicable law: for example, where many persons buy what proves to be a defective electrical carving knife of a certain brand. The offending seller must be given an opportunity to correct, repair, replace, or otherwise improve the goods or services within thirty days.

As an alternative, the victim may turn to government consumer protection agencies; there are more than fifty such agencies at the federal level alone. He may lobby for new laws to create additional agencies to set standards and provide appropriate supervision in critical areas. The regulation may be aimed at a particular person-firm-industry (such as real estate brokers or television repair shops), or product (such as poultry), or transaction (such as securities sales).

2. WHAT IS CONSUMERISM?

Consumerism is a social movement that seeks to improve the status of buyers and consumers in their relations with sellers and producers. Some of its roots are traceable to the beginning of the twentieth century. In 1904, Ida Tarbell wrote her biting exposé of the original Standard Oil Company monopoly of the petroleum industry.* In 1906, Upton Sinclair censured the meat packing industry of Chicago in his classic reform novel *The Jungle.* Congress responded by passing the Pure Food and Drug Act and the Meat Inspection Act in 1906, and in 1914 it established the Federal Trade Commission (FTC). In recent years the FTC has become more aggressive in enforcing laws against false and misleading advertising, and other deceptive practices such as fictitious testimonials, "free goods" offers that are not free, and false warranties.

> I.T.T. Continental Baking Company extensively advertised Profile bread as a food that could be eaten for reducing weight. This was false. What could the FTC do about the ads?

The FTC issued a *cease and desist order* (equivalent to an injunction in equity). Violation of this final order to stop the illegal advertising could result in a penalty of $5,000 each day the violation continued. Moreover, to help correct the misleading impression already created in the public mind about Profile bread, the FTC required *corrective advertising.* For a full year, Continental had to devote 25 percent of its advertising budget for Profile bread to ads saying that Profile was not effective for weight reduction.[1]

In the mid-1930s, during the Great Depression, there was a resurgence of consumer pressure for more protection. In 1933, authors Authur Kallett and F. J. Schlink wrote their best-selling book *100 Million Guinea Pigs: the Dangers in Everyday Foods, Drugs, and Cosmetics.* But not until the early 1960s did consumerism become a major movement. Opinion leaders aroused public concern and crystallized demands for corrective action. In 1962, President Kennedy proclaimed what has been called the Magna Charta of Consumers when he stated that every consumer has four rights: to safety, to be informed, to choose, and to be heard. Senator Paul Douglas of Illinois, an economist, fought in the U.S. Congress for truth-in-lending legislation.

Consumer-advocate Ralph Nader gained fame in a confrontation with General Motors Corporation after his book *Unsafe At Any Speed* appeared

---

* Independent units of the fragmented Standard Oil Company are today much larger than the parent company was. Growth from within a company is encouraged; there is nothing illegal in sheer size alone. Some critics blame the big petroleum corporations, along with the Arab states, for the current energy crisis. They cite, for example, the high industry profits and the lack of foresight in planning for rising consumer needs.

in 1965.* One salutory result was the Motor Vehicle Safety Act of 1966, under which the federal government has established mandatory safety standards for motor vehicles, with further improvements to come. Nader recruited a select group of young lawyers and nonprofessional college student "Nader Raiders" to investigate and expose such varied sore-spots as abuses in meat and fish inspection, lassitude and indifference in the operations of the Federal Trade Commission and Food and Drug Administration, and lack of social conscience in the management of major corporations. He has taken his campaign to many college campuses through public speeches.

Today consumers are better educated, more sophisticated, and more conscious of their rights and their powers than their counterparts in years gone by. They make better use of their "dollar ballots" in the open market and of their secret ballots at the polls. Yet, paradoxically, because of the mass production and mass distribution of a proliferation of increasingly complex products, many consumers know less about their purchases than their grandparents knew, and today's consumers have greater difficulty in evaluating quality. How many people understand how their radios, television sets, or automobiles work? How many can disassemble and repair basic household appliances? How many know the ingredients of the processed foods they eat and of the drugs and cosmetics they use daily?

One may argue that consumers retain the ultimate veto power: they can refuse to buy the faulty or dangerous product. But an unscrupulous seller can make a fortune on "first and only" sales to unwary buyers. The individual buyer's loss or injury may be too small to justify a costly lawsuit with an uncertain outcome. The seller usually draws up the contractual agreement in terms that favor himself. The buyer must accept the contract as drafted or forego the purchase completely. Consumer law helps restore balance to the bargain.

3. HOW MAY A PERSON LEGALLY ACQUIRE PERSONAL PROPERTY?

Abner Wiesgie was trying to indoctrinate a young friend on how to get by for practically nothing. "In this paper and plastic age," he said, "hang loose. Live free and fancy-free. Travel light. You don't have to own a thing, and you can avoid paying for what you use. Rent a furnished pad; lease wheels. Use credit cards instead of cash. Borrow from Peter to pay Paul if Paul crowds

---

* Nader also gained fortune when General Motors paid him $270,000 in an out-of-court settlement of his lawsuit charging the corporation with invasion of his privacy. Private detectives hired by G.M. allegedly tried to involve him with prostitutes and harassed him in other ways. Company officials denied that they knew or approved of the illegal measures.

you. Borrow to pay what you borrowed to pay. Borrow, borrow, borrow. Uncle Sam does; why shouldn't you?!" Is this good advice?

Not really. The landlord who provides an apartment, like the U-Drive firm that leases a car, will expect to be paid on schedule. Debts incurred on credit cards or otherwise must eventually be paid. Lenders and sellers exchange information about borrowers and buyers. If debts are not paid, credit dries up fast. Judgments for unpaid debts hang over you for years (ten in California, for example), and they can be renewed. Interest on loans runs high. Buying goods on time costs heavily: 18 percent a year is a typical charge. Governments borrow, but even government credit may be ruined by failure to repay. Tax revenues cover most current expenses and are used to pay the interest and principal on bonded debts.

Most people like to own things, and they find ownership cheaper than renting or leasing in the long run. Under the law, one may acquire personal property as his own in a variety of ways.

1. *By gift from a living person,* in what lawyers call an *inter vivos* (Latin: among the living) transfer.
2. *By gift from a decedent's (dead person's) estate.* This may be done under the terms of the decedent's will or, if there is no last testament or will, under *intestate* law (which prescribes how his property will be distributed).
3. *By employment contract.* A worker may be paid *in kind* (that is, in goods, such as a part of a farm crop). However, most persons work for compensation paid in money, a medium of exchange used to buy other property.
4. *By accession,* or addition to property already owned, as when a horse drops a foal, or an apple tree produces several bushels of fruit.
5. *By finding.* The finder of lost property is not bound to take charge of it; but if he does, he becomes a depository or bailee for hire on behalf of the owner.* Eventually he may become the owner if the true owner cannot be found.
6. *By creative labor.* An artist owns his paintings; an inventor owns

---

* In California, if the item is worth $10 or more, the finder should turn it over to the police (or sheriff's department if found outside the city limits), which tries to locate the owner and return the goods. If no owner appears within ninety days and the property is worth $25 or more, the police publish a notice at least once in a newspaper of general circulation. If the owner still fails to appear within seven days, the finder pays the cost of publication and gets title to the property. If the property is worth less than $25, no ad is required; after a wait of ninety days title vests in the finder. Local regulations may prescribe different rules, but there must be a minimum ninety-day holding period after public notice and before public auction of the goods. If the owner claims his property, the finder may demand a reasonable charge for saving and taking care of it.

THIS IS MY PAINTING...
...BECAUSE I PAINTED IT.

his original device and may obtain a *patent* from the U.S. government (commissioner of patents), which gives the creator the exclusive right to make, use, or sell the invention for seventeen years.* An author owns the song or book he has written and can obtain a twenty-eight-year *copyright,* renewable once, which provides monopoly rights to print and publish during the stated time. Thereafter, the work is in the public domain, and anyone may print and publish it. The commissioner of patents also issues *trademarks* to distinguish by name or symbol a product used in interstate commerce. They can be registered for a period of twenty years and are renewable. An ® is printed next to the trademark.†

7. *By occupancy.* By this method, a hunter gains title to deer he shoots, or a fisherman to the trout he catches in public areas.

8. *By purchase contract (or sales contract,* if viewed from the seller's side). Most property is acquired in this manner. The law of contracts governs the buyer-consumer, seller-producer relationship.

4. WHAT ARE THE REQUIREMENTS FOR A VALID CONTRACT?

Several factors must be considered in determining whether a contract is valid. First, there must be an *offer,* generally made by the seller, and an *acceptance* by the buyer. (Sometimes the roles are reversed and the buyer makes the offer.) The offer must be definite and certain, intended to create a legal obligation, and communicated to the offeree. Most advertisements are not offers, but merely invitations to deal. In such cases, the advertiser is inviting prospects to come in and to make offers, which need not be accepted, although they usually are. The Federal Trade Commission has ruled that the seller must have a supply of goods on hand adequate to meet reasonable demands. Also, a seller may not use the "bait and switch" technique, whereby he advertises one item on attractive terms to lure a prospect who is then persuaded to buy a costlier item.

Second, if a contract is to be considered valid, it must be made *between competent parties.* Minors and insane persons are generally regarded as incompetent by the law in regard to binding contracts. Such contracts are *voidable* or subject to rescission by the minor alone at his option.

---

* Patents originally were granted to anyone who invented any "new and useful process, machine, manufacture or composition of matter, or any new and useful improvement thereof." Later, protection was extended to new and original ornamental designs for articles of manufacture (such as lamps, fabrics, appliances, and furniture) and even for new varieties of garden plants such as roses. Patents on ornamental designs are granted for three and one-half, seven, or fourteen years.

† Some famous names and marks are not registered because they have been used exclusively so long that the owners could bar imitators on general principles of unfair competition and possible deception of the public.

In *rescission,* the parties return to their status before the agreement. Normally, the minor must make *restitution*—that is, return what he received in order to get his money back, less allowance for use if appropriate. In California and some other states, if the minor cannot make restitution (as would be the case if he were in an accident and totaled a car he has purchased), he is still entitled to the full refund, even if he lied about his age to the seller.*

Some contracts of minors are valid and enforceable by either party. For example, in California, a court-approved contract to work as an actor or athlete is considered valid, as are also in New York contracts entered into by a minor engaged in business. A few types of attempted contracts entered into by minors are absolutely void and of no effect—for example, a contract to transfer real property. A minor may own such property but would have to act through a guardian *ad litem* (Latin: for the lawsuit) under court supervision to dispose of it.

> Ripley's Cycle Center sold Roy Wampler, aged seventeen, an expensive Italian ten-speed racing bicycle, on credit. When Ripley's discovered that Wampler was a minor, they decided to rescind the contract, return the down payment, and repossess the bicycle. May they do so?

No. Only a minor is legally entitled to take advantage of his minority to void a contract. Adults are expected to investigate and to refuse to sell in doubtful cases, or to insist that parents also agree to pay.

Third, a valid contract must be *supported by consideration,* which may be a promise to do or not to do a certain thing. Consideration must be reciprocal: both parties must give up something of value, and both must receive something of value in exchange.

> When Mrs. Linda Glenn came home from a particular shopping trip, she gingerly opened the large, flat carton in her husband's presence. The garment inside was stunning: a white, ranch-mink, fur coat—price $4,000. Her husband exploded in protest. "No mink-shmink rabbit coat is worth four grand!" he shouted. May the Glenns return the coat and obtain a refund on the grounds that the coat was inadequate consideration for $4,000?

No. Consideration need not be adequate; courts will not inquire into whether the bargain was absolutely fair to both parties or whether both received equal value. Suffice that something of value was given and

---

* In some states, a minor who misrepresents his age is liable in a civil action for the tort of deceit. California and other states say no, because this would indirectly give the adult seller the benefit of his invalid contract in the form of damages.

received. "One man's junk is another man's antique." The courts will not use "sensitive scales of gold" to measure the consideration. A store is not obliged to permit the return of goods that comply with the contract. Of course, to promote customer good will, some stores freely permit returns, either for similar goods or for credit, or sometimes for cash.

Fourth, a valid contract must be *legal in inception and execution.* One may not contract to commit a tort or a crime. An underworld "contract" to kill is a criminal conspiracy. Contracts for illegal drugs are void. Contracts to bribe public officials are crimes and also void.

Fifth, a contract that is valid is *made with genuine assent.* The agreement must not be clouded by fraud, or by certain types of mutual mistake, or by *duress* or *undue influence.* These occur when one party dominates another to the point that the latter's will or power of decision is not freely exercised. Duress may involve threats or actual physical harm; undue influence is a more subtle abuse of trustful reliance on another.

Sixth, a valid contract must be *in the form prescribed by law,* if relevant. Under the *statute of frauds,* for example, some contracts must be in writing and signed by the party to be held, for the agreement to be enforceable in court. Other contracts, such as insurance policies and installment sales, must include certain terms prescribed by law. Sometimes the law requires that terms be printed in type of at least a specified minimum size. Too often, in the past, "the small type" would take away benefits apparently provided by "the big type," as in certain insurance policies.

5. WHAT SPECIAL RULES OF LAW GOVERN SALES OF GOODS?

Under the Uniform Commercial Code adopted in some form by all states except Louisiana, certain special rules govern sales of goods. In every sales transaction, two critical questions arise: When does title or ownership pass to the buyer? When does the buyer assume the risk of loss or damage to the property, or enjoy the possibility of gain?

1. In *cash sales,* where the buyer takes immediate delivery, title passes and the goods belong to the buyer (along with the risk of loss) when he gets the goods (that is, upon receipt).
2. In *credit sales,* ownership and risk of loss may pass to the buyer even though payment and delivery are delayed. Often the seller will retain *legal title* under the law of secured transactions, as when goods are durable and of high value such as furniture and automobiles. Possession and *equitable title* go to the buyer, however, along with the risk of loss.
3. In *C.O.D.* (cash on delivery) sales, payment must be made before delivery of the goods. The buyer has both title and risk of loss.

If later inspection by him reveals some error or defect, he may demand relief from the seller.

4. In *sales on approval,* the buyer gets possession before he decides to buy. Title and risk of loss pass to him when he decides to buy. If he keeps the goods beyond the agreed time (or if no time is prescribed beyond a reasonable time) without notifying the seller, he is presumed to have approved and accepted the goods.

5. In *auction sales* the auctioneer may accept a bid, or offer, by the fall of his hammer or other signal. At that moment title passes, but risk of loss remains with the seller until delivery. Auction sales are generally made "with reserve," meaning that the auctioneer may withdraw the goods at any time and refuse to sell, unless he announces in advance that the sale is to be "without reserve."

Sample Case

At an auction sale of antique cars, Roland Royster was the highest bidder on a 1929 Rolls Royce sedan. He started the bidding with an offer of $500, but he was secretly willing to go as high as $15,000. No one else made a bid. The auctioneer said, "That's ridiculous!" and moved on to another car. Does Royster get the car for $500?

Royster is out of luck; the auctioneer withdrew the car from the auction in a sale with reserve.

6. WHAT CAN YOU DO IF A SELLER BREACHES A SALES CONTRACT?

In a sales contract, the seller may breach by failing to deliver as agreed, or by delivering unacceptable goods, or by simply repudiating the contract. As the aggrieved buyer, you may be able to negotiate an amicable adjustment or settlement, and this should usually be attempted. If this fails, the Uniform Commercial Code provides a variety of remedies of special interest to the commercial buyer, but also sometimes usable by the ordinary consumer and therefore worth knowing.

1. *Accept or reject the goods delivered,* or accept commercial units or parts of the total and reject the balance, paying for what is received. If any goods are accepted in ignorance of the breach, you as buyer may revoke your acceptance and return the goods, getting a proper refund. Note that *receipt* of goods means that the buyer takes physical possession or control of them; *acceptance* of goods means that the buyer agrees that the goods received are satisfactory.

2. *Cover.* In case of breach of contract by the seller, the buyer may cover by buying similar goods elsewhere. If he acts promptly and in good faith, he may then hold the seller liable for the difference in price.

3. *Sue for dollar damages* for the breach. The damages recoverable would include *incidental damages* (such as reasonable expenses to inspect, transport, and care for goods rightfully rejected) and *consequential damages* for losses resulting from the needs of the buyer which the seller knew of when the contract was made and which cannot be prevented by cover. Court costs would be recoverable, but not attorney's fees, unless agreed to in the contract.

4. *Cancel.* You may cancel the contract, returning to the original status, and still retain other rights against the seller, including suit for damages. In effect, the buyer revokes his acceptance. This remedy has sometimes been used by buyers of seriously and generally defective new automobiles, after dealers have failed to make necessary repairs within a reasonable time. They return the "lemon" and demand a refund. This is not always practicable because the dealer may deny that anything is seriously or fundamentally wrong with the car and refuse to take it back. Normally, the dealer is not obliged to replace a defective car with a new vehicle. He need only repair or replace the defective parts if within the warranty period (usually one year or 12,000 miles, whichever occurs first). Thus, a question of fact arises that may have to be resolved in court after some further lapse of time and added cost to the buyer for legal fees. Even if the buyer finally wins, he may be a loser in dollars, mental anguish, and physical strain. Such difficulties can be minimized by buying from an established dealer who has a reputation for fair dealing.

5. *Return* the obviously defective goods at the seller's expense. Here the buyer never accepts the goods as his own.

6. *Recover* the goods or their value if title has passed but the seller refuses to relinquish possession. This is called *replevin.*

7. *Demand specific performance* of the contract even though title remains with the seller. The buyer may insist on delivery of possession of goods and transfer of title under certain circumstances. This is done by court order when the subject matter of the sale is unique (for example, an original Rodin sculpture), and dollar damages would be an inadequate remedy; the buyer wants the goods, not money. If the seller refuses to deliver, he is in contempt of court and may be fined or jailed.

8. *Resell* the goods that the buyer has received and yet rightfully refused to accept as owner, or for which he has revoked his acceptance. If the goods are perishable or threaten to drop in price rapidly, and the seller has given no contrary instructions, the buyer must make reasonable efforts to resell them for the seller's account.

Sample Cases

Ronald Herron needed four dozen ornamental bushes of a particular variety to complete the landscaping of his yard before the rainy season. Northridge Nursery agreed to supply the bushes as described, but when delivered, they were the wrong kind and Herron rejected them. The Northridge manager could not assure delivery of proper goods for at least a month. Therefore, Herron bought replacement bushes of the proper variety at another nursery. Unfortunately, they cost 25 percent more. Is Northridge liable to Herron for the difference in price?

Yes. The seller has broken the contract, and the buyer may use the remedy of cover to buy similar goods from another supplier. Since Herron has acted promptly and in good faith, he may hold Northridge liable for the difference in cost.

Randolph Timmerman purchased a truck tank carload of propane fuel from the North Slope Petro-Chemical Corporation. He had the title. When the truck reached Denver, where Timmerman's retail gas company was located, North Slope refused to deliver. A gas shortage had developed in another area and they planned to divert the truck to a buyer there. Can Timmerman get the fuel?

Yes. Timmerman can use replevin to get his fuel, since the title has already passed to him and he needs only to force the seller to relinquish possession.

7. WHAT CAN A SELLER DO IF YOU BREACH A SALES CONTRACT?

If injured by a buyer who breaches the sales contract in an ordinary sale, the seller may withhold delivery; stop goods even if they are in transit to the buyer; resell the goods; sue for the purchase price or for damages; or cancel and sue for damages.

When a sale is made on credit, the seller simply enters the purchase on his books of accounts as an account receivable, showing that the buyer owes the purchase price. When the buyer pays for the goods, perhaps a month later, or in installments over a period of time, the debt is cleared. However, if the buyer *defaults* (that is, fails to pay, through no fault of the seller), the seller may sue him, get a judgment, and try to get execution against assets of the buyer. This takes time and money, and may be futile if the buyer proves to be *judgment-proof*: that is, he vanishes or goes bankrupt or simply has nothing that can be seized by the sheriff for the seller, under court order.

To avoid such a predicament, the seller may protect himself from the outset by insisting that the credit buyer sign a *security agreement*. This document is used to describe durable goods such as furniture or jewelry, which can become collateral—security for payment of the debt.* They can then be repossessed, or seized, under court order upon default by the buyer and retained or resold by the seller. However, under the Constitution (which guarantees that one's property may not be taken without due process of law), if the creditor seeks a court order or the use of law enforcement officers to retrieve goods after default, the buyer is legally entitled to formal notice of the seller's intention to repossess and to a hearing where he can state his side of the dispute.[2] The U.S. Supreme Court has, however, let stand lower court decisions that permit the seller himself (or his private agent or employee) to retake goods sold on credit if the buyer is in default. Thus, surreptitious "midnight" repossessions of automobiles, for example, without warning to the owners are legal if done privately and peacefully.

If the buyer has paid 60 percent or more of the cash price of the goods, the seller, after repossession, must resell them within ninety days, to comply with the Uniform Commercial Code (Sect. 9-505), unless the buyer gives up this right in a written statement. If less than 60 percent has been paid, the seller may notify the defaulting buyer of his intent to retain the goods in full satisfaction of his claim. If the buyer objects, a resale of the goods must take place within thirty days (UCC Sect. 9-505 (2)).

The proceeds of the resale go to pay first the costs of repossession, storage, and resale; then any balance due the seller; then the claims of other creditors (if any exist) against the goods. In the unlikely event that some surplus remains, the original buyer gets it. But if there is a deficit, he is still liable to the seller for such amount unless otherwise agreed. In most states (not California, which bars such *deficiency judgments,* except in motor vehicle sales), not only has the hapless buyer lost all he paid for the goods as well as the goods, but also he still owes a debt that could exceed the unpaid balance outstanding when he defaulted. Moral? Don't buy goods on time, especially in secured transactions. Or if you do succumb to "easy credit," be sure you can afford the payments.

8. WHAT IS MEANT BY AN "UNCONSCIONABLE CONTRACT" UNDER THE UNIFORM COMMERCIAL CODE?

The Uniform Commercial Code added to the consumer's arsenal the important concept of *unconscionability* (UCC Sect. 2-302). Few legal innovations have greater potential value for the protection of consumers.

---

* For obvious reasons food and rapidly worn-out clothing are not sold this way.

A court may now, as a matter of law, modify or void a contract clause or an entire agreement that it deems to be unconscionable at the time it was made. Although the code does not specifically define the term, the official comments attached to it state that the principle "is one of the prevention of oppression and unfair surprise." Abuses that could be so classified include:

1. buyer's disclaimer of warranty protection given to him by law
2. high pressure sales tactics
3. misrepresentation of quality
4. lengthy contracts, drawn up with legal assistance by the seller, duplicated in fine print with language that even lawyers have difficulty understanding
5. unequal bargaining power because of illiteracy (in English), ignorance, or poverty of the buyer
6. grossly inflated prices
7. misleading *referral sales schemes* (for example, a customer is told that his new, overpriced water softener will cost him nothing because he can easily get ten friends to sign up for the same item)
8. unfair penalty provisions in case of default
9. unreasonable repossession rights of the seller in case of default
10. costly credit insurance for which the seller gets a substantial rebate of the premium from the insurance company

> Mrs. Williams, poor and uneducated, was on welfare. She received $218 a month from the government to support herself and her seven children. Walker-Thomas Furniture Company knew this, and yet sold her a $514 stereo set on credit. She already had a balance outstanding of $165 for previous purchases. When she defaulted, the company repossessed the stereo and all the purchases on which she still owed money. The purchase contracts provided that title would remain with the seller until paid in full, and payments made would be credited pro rata on all outstanding bills. In effect, under this *"add-on-sale"* clause, the debt on each item was secured by the right to repossess all items. Was this unconscionable?

Yes. The contract terms were unreasonably favorable to the seller, and the buyer had no meaningful choice among alternatives because of the gross inequality of bargaining power.[3] Ordinarily, however, a person who signs an agreement—without fully understanding its terms—assumes the risk of dissatisfaction with a one-sided bargain. Read and understand the contract before you sign it.

Unfortunately, the victimized consumer must generally sue (or be sued) before he can get the benefit of the law. His own loss may not justify action on his part, even though many other consumers may have been similarly gypped. Few consumers have the courage, know-how, or re-sources to sue. Often they are unaware of the availability of a small claims court, or fear the imagined difficulties of using it. Some consumer advocates insist that justice will be achieved only through prosecution by government agencies such as the FTC and state attorney general offices, coupled with heavy penalties for wrongdoers. Others lament that government agencies are usually understaffed, underfinanced, and under-motivated, and may be captives of the industry they are supposed to regulate. Moreover, wealthy corporate defendants can delay final court decisions by legal maneuvering for years. If shut down by injunction, a swindler may start a new corporation and resume his corrupt practices.

Class actions, or lawsuits brought by one or a few on behalf of all (with all sharing in any recovery), may be the hope of the future, although they are no panacea. At the federal level, the class involved must be so numerous that conventional joinder (or combining of separate causes of action) is impracticable; the claims or defenses of the representative parties must be truly typical of the class; there must be a federal question and diversity of citizenship between plaintiff and defendant; absent mem-bers of the class must be notified (and this can be prohibitively expensive when many thousands are involved); basic questions of law and fact must be common to all plaintiff-consumers; the class action must appear to be superior to individual actions for the fair and efficient adjudication of the controversy; and, as noted earlier, since 1974 every plaintiff must have a claim of at least $10,000. The last requirement effectively blocks most federal class actions unless Congress acts to change the applicable law.

> Fifty named plaintiffs, as members of a class of 100,000 buyers of an electronic camera, sued the manufacturer. They alleged that false warranties had been made, and that there were breaches of express warranty and of implied warranty of merchantability. Is this an appropriate class action if the remedy sought by each plaintiff is damages amounting to several hundred dollars?

Yes, even though ultimately each member of the class would have to show his individual damages.[4] Because the remedy sought by each is less than $10,000, however, the action would have to be brought in a state court.

9. WHAT WARRANTY PROTECTION DO YOU HAVE AS A CONSUMER?

A *warranty* is the assurance given by the seller concerning the quality or performance of his product. Laymen often refer to warranties as guaranties. Some warranties are *implied* by law and exist even if nothing is said about them; other warranties are *express* and are usually stated in writing but may be oral.

Merchants, or professional sellers who deal in the goods, (as well as casual sellers such as ordinary laymen disposing of things owned) normally are held by law to make these three implied warranties when they sell a product:

1. *Warranty of title* (that the seller has the title he claims to have to the goods and the right to transfer or sell them)
2. *Warranty against encumbrances* (that the goods delivered will be free of liens or encumbrances—creditors' claims—of which the buyer is not aware at the time of contracting)
3. *Warranty of fitness for a particular purpose* (that when the buyer indicates the purpose for which he needs the goods and then relies on the seller's recommendation, the goods will be reasonably fit for the intended purpose)

> When Peggy Butler visited Mac's Sport Shack, she told the salesman that she was planning a backpack trip into the Great Smoky Mountains. Butler insisted on being outfitted with "Pathfinder" brand moccasin boots, and a "Kozy" brand sleeping bag. After several days in the wilderness, using this gear, she realized that neither product fit her needs. Her ankles were swollen and she caught pneumonia. Is Mac's Sport Shack liable on a breach of warranty of fitness for particular purpose?

No. The warranty is not given when the buyer insists on a particular brand, as here. Possibly Butler could hold the manufacturers if they had made express warranties as to the goods, and if these warranties were breached.

In addition to these three implied warranties, either a merchant or a casual seller may explicitly make the following express warranties:

1. *Warranty of conformity to description, sample, or model.* All goods supplied must conform to the sample or model shown at the time of the sale, or to the specifications provided.
2. *Warranty of conformity to seller's statement or promise.* If the seller openly states or writes some factual assertion about the goods, he is bound by his assertion.

Merchant sellers alone make two additional implied warranties:

1. *Warranty against infringement.* The goods sold are delivered free of any rightful claim of a third party under patent, copyright, or other legal protection.
2. *Warranty of merchantability.* This is an extremely important group of warranties, of which the most critical is that the goods are fit for the ordinary purposes for which such goods are used. Thus, a

rocking chair (or stereo or toaster or umbrella) should function as such and last a reasonable length of time (which might be many years) under ordinary use.

Normally no warranty of merchantability is implied in sales of second-hand or used goods. Similarly, a statement that the goods are sold "as is" or "with all faults" excludes all implied warranties of fitness.

> When Sam Fitz bought his new automobile, he reasonably looked forward to perhaps 100,000 miles of carefree motoring without breakdown of any basic parts if properly maintained and used. He received a written warranty from the dealer. It said, "This warranty is in lieu of and excludes all other warranties, express or implied, including the warranty of merchantability." The warranty covered defects in materials or workmanship "for one year or 12,000 miles, whichever occurs first." Did Fitz lose anything when he received this warranty?

Yes. Often manufacturers will provide express warranties that actually deprive the customer of some of the protection he would otherwise have under the implied warranty of merchantability. Without the express warranty and disclaimer, Fitz might have held the manufacturer liable under the implied warranty of merchantability for a reasonable time, well beyond a year, and 12,000 miles of use. How long would become a question of fact for a jury to decide.

10. MAY A SELLER DISCLAIM ALL WARRANTIES THAT OTHERWISE PROTECT THE CONSUMER?

Under the law, a seller may validly disclaim all warranties; fortunately, because of competitive pressure, this seldom happens. To exclude the implied warranty of merchantability, the seller must mention *merchantability* in his disclaimer or notice of exclusion.

Formerly, sellers were also often shielded from liability by legal requirements of *privity;* that is, the plaintiff would have to prove that he and the defendant were in privity, meaning that they were the contracting parties. Thus, a consumer might sue a retailer with whom he dealt, but not the much wealthier manufacturer who made the defective product. Most states have modified or rejected this archaic doctrine.

In *Henningsen* v. *Bloomfield Motors, Inc.* (32 N.J. 358, 161 A. 2d 69, 1960), the maker of a defective auto was held liable to the ultimate consumer under the implied warranty of merchantability since the maker's advertisements were directed to such consumers. The Uniform Commercial Code (Sect. 2-318) extends the warranty coverage to the consumer-buyer, his family, household members, and house guests. Innocent bystanders and others who are injured by a defective product must seek recovery on some other basis, such as strict product liability of manufacturers and middlemen in tort.

> While trying to persuade Marjorie Ayers to buy an expensive electric typewriter, Leon Cannon said that all parts were guaranteed and would be replaced without any charge if found defective within five years. The written purchase contract that Ayers later signed spoke of only a one-year warranty against defects in materials and workmanship. Moreover, it said that the customer would have to pay for one-half of the usual labor charge. Which terms really govern?

The one-year written warranty terms govern, unless the buyer can satisfy a judge that she was the victim of mistake, fraud, or illegality, or that the written contract was incomplete. This is the result of the *parol evidence rule,* which presumes that the contracting parties have included all previous desired oral or written understandings in the final, integrated written agreement. It is not good enough for a consumer to get all his important contracts in writing; he should make sure that the writing includes all desired terms stated correctly and completely.

11. WHAT STEPS CAN YOU TAKE TO PROTECT YOUR RIGHTS AS A CONSUMER?

In addition to an action for breach of contract or breach of warranty, you may use one or more of the following measures if you are an aggrieved consumer.

1. *Sue the retailer, wholesaler, or manufacturer for damages under the doctrine of strict product liability in tort,* if you have been injured because of some defect in the product. You need not prove intent to harm, nor negligence, nor breach of warranty; simply show that the product as manufactured was defective and thus caused the resulting personal injury or property damage. This extremely important protection for consumers is a recent judicial development. As of 1974, about forty states had followed California's lead in adopting the doctrine. Manufacturers can protect themselves by improving product designs, testing thoroughly before marketing, controlling quality in production, and finally by purchasing insurance against damage suits. Obviously, such measures cost money, and the added costs are passed on to all buyers of the particular product in the form of higher prices. Product liability cases have become a leading type of litigation, along with auto accidents and divorces. In 1971 an estimated half million such cases were on court dockets; by 1985, the figure is expected to more than double.
2. *Sue the manufacturer in tort for negligence*—that is, for his failure

to exercise due care in making the product, as a result of which you were injured. Negligence is difficult to prove in such cases, if only because of the lapse of time between manufacture of the product and injury of the plaintiff.

3. *Sue the seller for the intentional tort of fraud.* Here again, proof is difficult. To hold the defendant liable for fraud, you must prove that (a) the defendant lied or deliberately concealed a material, important fact (was not simply "puffing" or giving an exaggerated personal opinion); (b) he knew the statement was false, or he made it "with reckless indifference" as to whether it was true or false; (c) he intended to influence your decision; and (d) you were entitled to rely, and you did act reasonably in reliance, on his false statement.

4. *Complain to the local Better Business Bureau,* a voluntary private agency sponsored by the Chamber of Commerce. The BBB provides helpful information on fraudulent practices. Upon inquiry, it will say whether it has received any complaints about a given firm. However, its budget is limited; it does little investigative work; it has no legal staff to take action against wrongdoers; it has concerned itself primarily with flagrant cases of consumer fraud, but not with major issues such as truth in lending and product safety and limitation of exorbitant finance charges.

5. *Complain to the federal Office of Consumer Affairs* (Department of Health, Education and Welfare, 330 Independence Avenue, S.W., Washington, D.C., 20201), or to the appropriate consumer office in your state, or to both. If you do not know the address for the state agency, write to your governor, senator, or state legislative representative. Complaints about false advertising and unfair business practices may also be mailed to the Bureau of Consumer Protection (Federal Trade Commission, Washington, D.C., 20580). Often a letter to the president of the company that produced the defective product generates useful action. (If you do not know the company address, check it in *Thomas Register of Manufacturers* in your public library.)

6. *Complain to the district attorney of the county, or to the attorney general of the state.* In Sacramento County, California, for example, the D.A. has successfully cracked down on fraudulent used-car dealers (for setting mileage back on odometers); on massage parlors that are in fact facades for brothels; and on dishonest auto transmission shops that needlessly dismantle the automatic transmission and then confront the appalled owner with the parts and a proposed costly repair job.

Sample Case

"Honest Jon," a disreputable auto dealer, sold Harold Harrington a "new" car. In fact, the car was a demonstrator and had been driven 11,000 hard miles, but the odometer had been set back to show less than 100 miles. What can Harrington do?

He can rescind the contract (returning the car and getting his money back); retain the car and demand a refund of the difference in value between the car as represented and as delivered; or cancel the contract, return the car, and sue for the return of his money together with substantial punitive damages.

12. WHAT IS MEANT BY *CAVEAT EMPTOR* AND *CAVEAT VENDITOR?*

Until the consumer movement led to protective legislation and courts became more sympathetic to consumer needs, *caveat emptor* (Latin: Let the buyer beware) was the prevailing motto of the marketplace. It is still good advice because the law does not and probably cannot shield buyers from all hazards. The intelligent buyer studies the goods before buying and he understands comparative values. He knows that prices may be honest but misleading; neither the lowest nor the highest priced item is necessarily the best buy. Generally, however, value goes with price. For example, to pay a little more for a transistor battery or a pair of shoes or ballpoint pen may provide much longer life and superior performance well worth the added cost.

> Penelope Harris rushed into buying her new spring coat. Now she was very unhappy with it. The color did not blend with most of her dresses; the fabric was shoddy and soon showed signs of wear; the doubleknit weave was constantly getting snagged; it had to be dry-cleaned; the delicate color faded in the sun; she had paid an extra 18 percent in finance charges because she bought the coat on time. Worst of all, she never received a single compliment when she wore the garment. Does she have a valid cause of action against the seller?

No. All of her complaints are her responsibility; none is covered by customary warranties. Sellers are not required to guarantee personal satisfaction of buyers, and seldom do. In addition to the terms of any warranty, the buyer should investigate and evaluate other factors before buying: design, repairability, credit and delivery terms, availability of service facilities and replacement parts, trade-in privileges, and overall performance. Caveat emptor still makes sense. Investigate, understand, and compare—before you buy.

Nevertheless, because protective legislation has tipped the scales in favor of consumers, a new watchword in the marketplace is *caveat venditor* (Latin: Let the seller beware). The Uniform Commercial Code imposes a general obligation of *good faith* on both seller and buyer. Both are

expected to practice honesty in conduct and contract. For merchants, this also means observance of reasonable commercial standards of fair dealing.

13. WHAT FEDERAL LAWS ARE DESIGNED TO PROTECT YOU AS A CONSUMER?

Many laws have been enacted by Congress to protect consumers. More such laws are currently under consideration. Among the most important already in effect are the following:

1. *Federal Trade Commission Act of 1914.* Originally the Federal Trade Commission (FTC) was concerned almost exclusively with protecting business firms from monopolistic practices of competing firms. In 1938, the Wheeler-Lea Act gave the commission authority to prohibit "unfair trade practices," which are contrary to good morals and fair dealing. Enforcement was haphazard until 1969 when criticism by Ralph Nader and a special commission of the American Bar Association caused the FTC to change its strategy and tactics. In recent years it has used imagination and courage to help clean up advertising, credit and collection practices, and door-to-door sales.*

2. *Pure Food and Drug Act of 1906,* amended over the years, is now known as the federal Food, Drug, and Cosmetic Act. This law prohibits manufacture or sale in interstate commerce of any food, drug, cosmetic, or medical device that is adulterated or misbranded. Under its broad authority, the Food and Drug Administration (FDA) barred the sale in this country of thalidomide, the tranquilizer which was sold in Germany and which caused major congenital defects among thousands of unborn children.

3. *Product labeling acts* (Fur Products, Textile Fiber Products, Wool Products, Hazardous Substances) prescribe minimum standards for labeling the products covered. In 1966, the Hazardous Substances Act was amended to cover children's products that are hazardous either to the eyes or because of toxicity or flammability. Under the Child Protection and Toy Safety Act of 1969, the law was further extended to include electrical, thermal, and mechanical hazards for such goods.

4. *The Consumer Product Safety Act of 1972* created the Consumer Product Safety Commission with authority over the safety of design of almost every consumer product sold in this country. The only exceptions are selected products already regulated by other agen-

---

* Under FTC rules effective in 1974, a person who buys a consumer good or service costing $25 or more from a door-to-door salesman or telephone solicitor may cancel the order within three days after the sale without penalty.

cies: motor vehicles, guns, airplanes, boats, medical devices, drugs, bulk agricultural poisons, tobacco products, foods, and cosmetics. The commission is empowered to ban or recall hazardous products and to furnish comparative product safety information to consumers. It may set safety standards, require prominent warnings, order manufacturers to buy back defective items, or ban a product completely. If a product presents an "imminent and unreasonable risk of death, serious illness, or severe personal injury," the commission has emergency power to get a U.S. district court order to condemn and seize supplies of the product. The court can also order recalls and repairs or replacements of defective products, or price refunds. In time, the Consumer Products Act could prove to be one of the most important ever enacted for the protection of consumers. Much depends on how effectively it is enforced. As of this writing, it is too early to say. Annually, some thirty thousand fatalities and twenty million injuries are caused by unsafe consumer products, according to estimates, and so the commission will be busy.

5. *Mail fraud statutes* date back to 1890. They authorize postal officials to act against schemes or devices for obtaining money or property fraudulently through the mails.

   Under postal regulations (Section 3009 of the Postal Reorganization Act of 1969), any merchandise mailed to prospective buyers without their prior express request or consent is "unordered merchandise" and should be marked as such. If you receive such an item, you may treat it as a gift from the sender, and you have no duty to pay or respond. An exception is made to permit mailing of free samples, and also for merchandise mailed by a charitable organization soliciting contributions. Caveat: in general, if unordered goods are delivered by means other than the mail service, the recipient is not obliged to accept or return them. However, if he uses them, he is legally obligated to pay for them.

6. *Fair Packaging and Labeling Act* gives the FDA power to regulate labels of foods, drugs, and cosmetics. It gives the FTC power to do the same for other consumer commodities, defined as products used in the home that are rapidly disposed of or consumed. Net quantities must be shown in prescribed locations on the labels, along with other useful product information. The incredible variety of container sizes for various products has been reduced by means of voluntary industry programs of simplification and standardization.

7. *Radiation Control for Health and Safety Act of 1969.* The Secretary of Health, Education, and Welfare sets standards for radiation emission of consumer products, such as television sets.

8. *Flammable Fabrics Act of 1953,* as amended, is designed to keep

excessively flammable fabrics and products made from such fabrics out of interstate commerce. Originally aimed at clothing, it now also embraces household furnishings such as carpeting.

9. *National Traffic and Motor Vehicle Safety Act of 1966,* sparked by crusading efforts of Ralph Nader, has enabled the Secretary of Transportation to establish new safety standards for motor vehicles. It also requires notification of buyers by the manufacturer when defects are discovered.

10. *Consumer Credit Protection Act of 1968.* The most important section of this major act is known as the *Truth in Lending Act.* It requires a full disclosure of credit costs in installment sales and in loans. The creditor must disclose the total dollar finance charge and effective annual rate of interest or finance charge. No longer may sellers mislead gullible customers by quoting a credit cost of "only 1.5 percent a month"; they must disclose that the equivalent interest cost per year is 18 percent. The act also provides for a three-day "cooling off" period when a consumer agrees to borrow on the security of a second mortgage on his home. Under the law, he may still rescind and get back any money delivered to the creditor if he does so within the prescribed time. The act places no limit on the rate or amount of interest or carrying charge, although some consumer advocates think it should.

Traditionally, *garnishment* (attachment of the salary or wages of a defaulting debtor) has been a principal remedy for unpaid creditors. This means that the creditor gets a court order directing the debtor's employer to pay a certain portion of the employee's wages directly to the creditor until the judgment is paid in full. Sometimes employers used to fire workers who got into such financial trouble. Under the federal Consumer Credit Protection Act, normally the amount garnished may not exceed (a) 25 percent of the worker's weekly take-home pay, or (b) the amount by which the take-home pay exceeds thirty times the federal minimum wage ($2 an hour, or $80 a week, in 1974) or $60, whichever is less. Moreover, the employer may not discharge an employee simply because his wages have been garnished for any one indebtedness.

11. *Fair Credit Reporting Act of 1970* regulates consumer reporting agencies such as the Retailers Credit Association, and is designed to assure the confidentiality, accuracy, relevancy, and proper use of credit information. Whenever credit, insurance, or employment is denied, or charges are increased because of information in a credit report, the user of the report must so inform the consumer and supply the name and address of the consumer reporting agency that made the negative report. The consumer may then, in person or by telephone following a written request, contact the reporting agency, which must orally disclose (a) the nature and substance

of all information in its files on the consumer at the time (except medical information); (b) the sources of the information; and (c) the names of recipients of any report furnished for employment purposes within two years, and for other purposes within six months.

If the accuracy or completeness of the file is disputed, the agency must investigate, unless it has reasonable grounds to believe that the dispute by the consumer is "frivolous or irrelevant." If the information proves to be inaccurate or cannot be verified, the agency must delete it. At the consumer's request, the agency must notify any person designated by the consumer who has, within two years, received a report for employment purposes, or within six months for any other purposes. The agency must make the disclosure and reports without charge if the consumer acts within thirty days after getting notice of a denial of credit. Otherwise, reasonable charges may be made for notices of deletion of inaccurate information.

12. *Monroney Automobile Information Disclosure Act of 1958* requires that automobile manufacturers place the suggested retail price for new cars and accessories on the vehicle. Unfortunately, many consumers do not realize that these prices are overstated, in order to allow considerable room for dealer bargaining on the value of trade-ins or other items.

Sample Cases

Tasti-Treet Dietetic Foods, Inc., had $10,000,000 worth of canned fruits in inventory, all containing cyclamate, the artificial sweetener. Then the FDA barred future sales of products containing this chemical because of its suspected carcinogenic (cancer-causing) potential. Must the government indemnify (make good the loss of) Tasti-Treet and other manufacturers similarly affected?

No. The ban was a valid exercise of the government's police power, as stipulated in the Food, Drug, and Cosmetic Act. Any indemnity for loss would require special action and appropriation of needed money by Congress. In 1972, Congress refused to pass such legislation, which was estimated to cost over $500,000,000.

The Fun and Frolic Company supplied wholesalers with large quantities of a new rocket toy for the Christmas trade. The device would explode a small charge of powder and send a "rocket" into the sky at an initial speed of 90 mph. Federal inspectors examined the product and condemned it as hazardous. What can they do next?

In accordance with the Consumer Product Safety Act, hazardous or misbranded products may be seized and destroyed; injunctions may be issued against continued production and sale; and criminal penalties may be imposed. For individualized personal relief, however, the consumer—if injured—must still sue and obtain a judgment.

> Antonio Mendez bought a new house and as part of the purchase price, he signed a promissory note for $15,000 secured by a first mortgage on the property. The next day he decided he could not afford the high monthly payments. May he rescind?

No. The cooling-off rule of the Truth in Lending Act does not apply to first mortgages (or first trust deeds) on homes, because such credit has not been the basis for exploitation of ignorant homeowners in need of funds.

> Browning was denied credit by a large local department store because of unfavorable information in his credit report on file with the local credit agency. He visited the agency and insisted that he had a right to see his report. Is he correct?

No. Unfortunately, the consumer does not get to see or to duplicate the report on his credit; this is considered by many critics to be a serious shortcoming of the Fair Credit Reporting Act.

14. WHAT STATE AND LOCAL LAWS ARE DESIGNED TO PROTECT YOU AS CONSUMER?

A wide variety of consumer protection statutes and ordinances have been enacted at the state and local levels to protect consumers. Some provide for inspection and grading of meat, fish, and poultry products (matching federal laws that govern such goods when sold in interstate commerce); for standards of grains, fruits, and vegetables; for accurate weights and measures; for sanitary standards of restaurants and food factories; for licensing of professional persons and technicians; for the grading of milk and dairy products; for use of used materials in mattresses and furniture; for control of insecticides, such as D.D.T., used on farm products; for regulation of rates and levels or service by public utilities (gas, electricity, water, and telephone); for elimination of deficiency judgments in purchase money mortgages; and for elimination of fraudulent "diploma mill" schools.

California has been in the forefront with laws designed to protect consumers, but much remains to be done in this and other states. Some specific recent legislation enacted in California governs contracts for swimming pools (Civil Code 1725: they must be in writing and give a date certain for completion); sale of fine art prints (CC 1740: full disclosure is required to assure authenticity); mobile home warranties (CC 1797); contracts for dance studio lessons (CC 1812.50: maximum price of $2,500 and payments over no more than two years, with lessons for no more than seven years); contracts for health studio services (CC 1812.80: maximum price of $500 with payments over no more than two years).

California also has the following major protective laws for consumers:

1. *Song-Beverly Consumer Warranty Act of 1970 (CC 1790)* provides that the implied warranties of merchantability and of fitness[7] shall be co-extensive with any express warranty, provided the duration of the express warranty is reasonable.* In no event shall such implied warranty have a duration of less than sixty days nor more than one year following the sale of new consumer goods to the retail buyer. Thus, the consumer gets a small measure of protection against the seller who gives an express warranty that is more limited than the implied warranty. However, his rights under the implied warranties of merchantability and fitness are limited to just one year. Other states do not impose this time limit.

   Under the Song-Beverly Act, when a manufacturer of consumer goods sold in California makes an express warranty, he must provide sufficient service and repair facilities within the state to carry out the terms of that warranty. Normally the goods must be repaired or serviced within thirty days. If the goods cannot be made to conform to the express warranty, the manufacturer must either replace them with new goods, or pay the buyer an amount equal to his purchase price less a fair allowance for use before he discovered the nonconformity.

   What happens if the manufacturer does not provide service and repair facilities in this state? The buyer may return the goods to any retail seller for service, repair, or replacement under the warranty; otherwise the seller must return the purchase price, less an allowance for use by the buyer.

2. *Consumers Legal Remedies Act of 1970 (revised in 1973; CC 1750)* lists sixteen business practices that are illegal and permits a class action by one or more of the victims on behalf of all. Among the

---

*   The California Civil Code (1791.1) defines "implied warranty of merchantability" to mean that the consumer goods meet each of the following: (1) pass without objection in the trade under the contract description; (2) are fit for the ordinary purposes for which such goods are used; (3) are adequately contained, packaged, and labeled; (4) conform to the promises or affirmations of fact made on the container or label. "Implied warranty of fitness" means that when the retailer, distributor, or manufacturer has reason to know any particular purpose for which the consumer goods are required and, further, that the buyer is relying on the skill and judgment of the seller to select and furnish suitable goods, then there is an implied warranty that the goods shall be fit for such purpose.

outlawed practices are "advertising goods or services with intent not to sell them as advertised" and "representing that a part, replacement, or repair service is needed when it is not."

3. *Electronic Repair and Dealer Registration Law of 1963* (Business and Professions Code 9800) requires that radio and television repair dealers be licensed. They must provide written estimates of repair prices for labor and parts if requested, although they may charge for this. The price may not exceed the estimate without previous consent of the customer. Also replaced parts must be returned, unless they have to be shipped to the manufacturer under a warranty.

4. *Automotive Repair Act of 1972* requires all garages and service stations engaged in repair work to register with the state Department of Consumer Affairs. They are further required to post a sign in prominent view stating these major consumer benefits of the law: (a) written estimate for repair work; (b) detailed invoice of work done and parts supplied; (c) return of replaced parts if requested at the time the work order is placed; and (d) toll-free telephone service for complaints.

5. *Unruh Retail Credit Sales Act of 1959 (CC 1801)*—a landmark bill in the fight for consumer protection—requires that (a) an installment plan buyer of consumer goods or services be provided with a copy of the written agreement, with the printed portion in at least eight-point type; (b) delinquency charges not exceed 5 percent of the installment or $5, whichever is less (but a minimum charge of $1 may be made); (c) any assignee of the seller's rights is subject to all defenses the buyer has against the seller at the time of the assignment (meaning, for example, that you don't have to pay for defective goods simply because the bank or finance company holding the paper tells you to "pay us and complain to the merchant"); (d) the finance charge for a retail installment account or "revolving account" may not exceed 18 percent a year (or 1.5 percent on the outstanding balance from month to month) on a balance of up to $1000.*

In case of default and repossession by the seller, the buyer has a right to redeem the goods either within ten days after notice is given by the seller (by paying the amount of overdue payments owing under the contract), or anytime before resale by the seller (by paying the amount owing plus any repossession and repair or reconditioning expenses reasonably incurred). The seller may retain the goods in satisfaction of whatever balance is due, or resell them at public sale. The buyer gets any excess balance from the sale proceeds after

---

* If the outstanding balance is more than $1000, the finance charge may not exceed 12 percent a year on the excess over $1000 of the outstanding balance. A minimum charge of $1 a month is permitted if the computed charge is less than one dollar.

payment of expenses and balance due. However, if the proceeds of the sale are not sufficient, the seller may *not* recover a judgment for the deficiency from the buyer.

6. *Rees-Levering Act (CC 2981)* is similar to the Unruh Act, but governs retail sales and leases of motor vehicles to consumers. However, higher finance charges are permitted, which suggests that you should postpone your purchase, save your money, and later buy for cash, or arrange your financing with a credit union or bank, not with the dealer; you'll usually do better. The law permits a finance charge in any conditional or installment sales contract for sale of a motor vehicle to be as much as 1 percent of the unpaid balance, multiplied by the number of months elapsing between the date of the contract and the due date of the last installment (or $25, whichever is greater). Furthermore, upon default, repossession, and resale, if a deficiency remains the buyer is liable for this amount.

Sample Case

Jess Gariola bought a new compact foreign-made car from Sunset Motors, Eureka, California. He received a thirty-day express warranty, with no limit on mileage, but with a waiver of all other express or implied warranties. As luck would have it, his car developed major trouble in the transmission after thirty-five days of normal use. The dealer refused to repair it because he claimed the warranty had run out. What can Gariola do?

Under the Song-Beverly Act, Gariola can have the work done by another garage, and then sue Sunset Motors for three times the amount of his damages, plus reasonable attorney fees. Because of the willful violation, Sunset must pay in full.

15. ARE THERE LIMITS ON WHAT LENDERS OF MONEY MAY CHARGE?

Under California law, as in most states, lenders of money may not charge consumer-borrowers "whatever the traffic will bear." The basic limit on interest rates that may be charged by lenders is 10 percent a year. To charge more is *usury*. If more is charged, the borrower is still required to repay the principal, but he need not pay any interest. Indeed, he may sue and recover three times the interest paid within one year from the date of the action. Interestingly, the 10 percent limit does *not* apply to banks or savings and loan associations. They are licensed and regulated by other agencies. Loans against bank credit cards can cost 18 percent a year, but even this is less than the law allows to certain other lenders.

State legislatures have recognized that borrowers sometimes desperately need money, and yet their credit may be poor. Under such circumstances they could be highly vulnerable to criminal *loan sharks*, who charge interest of 100 percent and more a year, and who use strong-arm methods to enforce their illicit claims. To discourage loan sharking, and to allow for the added costs and risks in lending small amounts to poor people, states permit higher interest charges for small loans. California law permits certain charges as shown in table 8–1.

Many gullible people are persuaded by television and radio advertising (which need not state the true costs involved in borrowing) to borrow against the equity they own in their homes for money loans "to clean up all installment balances" or for other reasons. Here the legally permitted brokerage fees for arranging the loan add substantially to interest costs. Thus, in a second mortgage or trust deed, the charges can include 5 percent of the principal amount of the loan where the term of the loan is less than two years, 10 percent where the term is between two

TABLE 8–1

Monthly and Annual Interest Rates on Consumer Loans

Lender	Maximum Lawful Charge on Unpaid Balance per Month (%)	Annual Interest Rate on a Twelve-Month Contract (%)
Personal Property Broker (lending on security such as furniture*)	2.5 (to $200)	30
	2 ($201 to $500)	24
	1.5 ($501 to $1,500)	18
	1 ($1,501 and up)	12
Industrial Loan Company (Morris Plan)	2.5 (to $200)	30
	1.5 ($200 to $700)	18
	5/6 of 1 ($700 to $10,000)	10
Small Loan Company	2.5 (to $100)	30
	2 ($100 to $300)	24
Credit Union	1	12
Pawnbroker†	2.5 (to $100)	30
	2 ($100 to $500)	24
	5/6 of 1 (over $500)	10

* As an alternative to the charges listed here, the personal property broker may charge 1.5 percent a month (18 percent a year) on the unpaid principal balance.

† The pawnbroker may realize substantially more if the borrower does not redeem his pawned property, for which he may have received only a small fraction of true value in the amount of the loan.

and three years, and a shocking 15 percent where the term is three or more years, in addition to the customary maximum interest charge of up to 10 percent a year. Unscrupulous lenders give the impression that the loan is painless, especially since only interest is collected for perhaps three years; but then the full principal comes due in a "balloon payment." The borrower seldom has so large a sum and is compelled to refinance, paying a whole new set of costly charges. Borrowing on a second trust deed through a loan broker should be avoided if at all possible.

> Ruth Lang, a resident of Oshkosh, Wisconsin, bought some clothing and draperies from a local department store and added the full price to her revolving charge account. The finance charge was to be an additional 18 percent a year. The maximum interest permitted under the state's usury law was 12 percent a year. Must Lang pay the full 18 percent?

No. In a recent precedent-setting case, the attorney general of Wisconsin obtained an injunction against J.C. Penney to stop charging on revolving charge accounts.[5] The Wisconsin Supreme Court held that the 12 percent usury limit applied, although it did not strike down the higher charge for straight or closed-end installment sales. In revolving charge accounts, the unpaid balance is constantly changing and there is no clear difference between a cash price and a credit or time price. The court held that, in effect, it is a single price with a loan of the balance due at interest. Similar lawsuits are working their way up to the supreme courts of other states.

16. WHAT ARE YOUR RIGHTS AND DUTIES IF YOU USE A CREDIT CARD?

Credit cards have become a major factor in consumer finance. Banks issue them (for example, the all-purpose Bank Americard or Master Charge) as do also credit card companies (for example, the travel and recreation American Express card, Diner's Card, and Carte Blanche), independent oil companies, and stores.

Banks that provide credit cards collect a discount of from 3 to 5 percent from participating merchants, and in return handle the collections. Prices are not reduced for customers who pay cash, and this is not fair. In addition, the banks collect a carrying charge from customers who use the cards and do not pay promptly after billing. This added charge is generally 1.5 percent a month on the unpaid balance or 18 percent a year. Use of the card can be a great convenience as well as a temptation to overspend. Legally the debt may be extended at the buyer's option over many months; economically it should be paid before any carrying charge is assessed.

Under the federal Credit Card Act of 1970, the consumer must apply for credit cards. They may not be thrust upon him, as in the past, without his request or consent. Moreover, his liability for unauthorized use of his card by a thief or dishonest finder is limited to fifty dollars. This liability is imposed only if:

1. the cardholder requested and received the credit card, or signed or used it, or authorized another person to do so
2. the card issuer provided a self-addressed, prestamped notification to be mailed by the cardholder in the event of loss or theft of the card
3. the card issuer gave adequate notice of the fifty-dollar liability
4. the card issuer provided positive means of identification (for example, signature or photo of the cardholder on the card)
5. the unauthorized use took place before the cardholder notified the issuer that such use might take place

California's Song-Beverly Credit Card Act of 1971 provides some added protection. If you as a cardholder-buyer have some claim against the retailer in connection with a purchase made through the use of a credit card, that claim is also good against the card issuer. There are several preconditions:

1. The price of the product or service must exceed fifty dollars.
2. The purchase must have been made in California.
3. The cardholder must have made a written demand on the retailer with respect to the purchase, and attempted in good faith to obtain reasonable satisfaction from him.
4. The cardholder must give written notice to the card issuer specifying the name and address of the retailer, date of purchase, amount, goods or service bought, nature of defense or complaint, and what acts, if any, the cardholder has taken in attempting to obtain satisfaction from the retailer.

> John Smith had the brakes of his car relined and serviced by Speedy Brake Shop in San Diego. He paid $98 for the job, using his bank credit card. Shortly after his return to San Francisco, the brakes failed because of faulty installation. He made repeated efforts by phone and by mail to get the Speedy people to direct him to a local agency for correction of the job, or to pay for the extra work, which came to $65. They did nothing. Can he now refuse to pay this sum to the bank that issued the credit card?

Yes. The facts meet the first three conditions, and Smith can comply with the fourth when he refuses to pay.

17. WHAT CAN YOU DO IF YOU ARE SNOWED UNDER BY DEBTS?

Several alternatives are available to you as an individual consumer who is overwhelmed by debts and cannot make payments as they come due.

1. Contact your creditors and explain your predicament. Try to obtain a *voluntary extension of time.*
2. Allow selected secured creditors to repossess purchased items that you know you can get along without.
3. Obtain a *composition of creditors.* This may be done by a credit counselor who will collect a lump sum from you and distribute it to all your creditors under a plan whereby added time is allowed and sometimes the debts are voluntarily reduced in amount.
4. Apply for a *state wage earner receivership.* This is available in some states, such as Ohio. A court-appointed trustee collects all non-exempt wages of the debtor and distributes them pro-rata to all creditors. Repossessions and wage garnishments are prohibited while the plan is in effect.
5. Apply for a *federal wage earner receivership* under Chapter XIII of the Bankruptcy Act. The court normally approves a plan that calls for payments first to secured creditors (those with claims against particular assets) and then to those who are nonsecured. Repossessions are barred; creditors may not garnishee wages or seek to recover from the debtor's non-wage property; interest stops accumulating at the time the petition is filed in court. If the plan is not completed at the end of three years because of circumstances beyond the control of the debtor, the court may discharge him from whatever remains of his debts. The plan must be accepted by a majority of the unsecured creditors, both as to number and amount of claims, and by all secured creditors whose claims are included.
6. If all else fails, *go bankrupt.* Although most provable debts that you list are discharged, bankruptcy does not wipe the slate clean of all debts. You are still liable, after discharge, for such debts as unpaid alimony and child support; for taxes that became due within three years preceding the bankruptcy; for liabilities arising out of obtaining property by false pretenses or getting a loan or credit through a materially fraudulent statement of financial condition; or for debts resulting from willful or malicious injuries to the person or property of another.

Any property you own under secured transactions or installment sales backed by liens on the goods may be repossessed by specific creditors, as may your home if subject to a mortgage or trust deed. Other assets are turned over to the court and sold; the proceeds are used to pay your debts. But the debtor is not stripped naked. Much of his property is exempt from seizure by his creditors. California is unusually generous in this regard, exempting such varied assets as:

a. for any head of a family, or any person sixty-five years of age or older, an equity of up to $20,000 in a home, over and above all liens and encumbrances, or $10,000 for any other person; in the alternative, an equity of up to $5,000 in a house trailer in which the debtor or his family resides
b. household furnishings and appliances and wearing apparel, ordinarily and reasonably necessary to, and personally used by the debtor and his resident family, including a piano, radio, television receiver, shotgun, rifle, and provisions and fuel sufficient for three months
c. equity up to $300 in one motor vehicle over and above all liens and encumbrances, provided the vehicle is not worth more than $1,000
d. up to $1,000 of savings deposits in a savings and loan association
e. life insurance up to the amount obtainable with premiums of no more than $500 a year, as well as a policy of group life insurance
f. up to $2,500 actual cash value, over and above all liens and encumbrances, of tools and other property used by the debtor in his trade or profession, including a fishing boat and commercial motor vehicle

You may not repeat the process again for six years after discharge. This creates the paradoxical situation under which the credit of some debtors is better after bankruptcy than before.

Creditors—either in bankruptcy proceedings or in a simple enforcement of a judgment obtained in a lawsuit for money—may not take from the debtor any benefits arising out of disability or health insurance (if the premiums do not exceed $500 a year), workmen's compensation, unemployment compensation, public assistance or welfare payments, or social security payments. Moreover, in California, the exemption from garnishment or attachment of wages extends to all earnings of the debtor received for his personal services rendered at any time within thirty days immediately preceding the levy of execution if necessary for the use of the debtor's family in this state, unless the debts that are being collected were themselves incurred by the debtor, his wife, or his family for the common necessities of life (or were incurred for personal services rendered by an employee or a former employee of the debtor).

18. WHAT LEGAL REFORMS ARE UNDER CONSIDERATION TO HELP CONSUMERS IN THE FUTURE?

Many proposals are before legislative bodies to improve the status of consumers. Among the more significant are:

1. *Uniform Consumer Credit Code* (UCCC or U3C) has already been adopted in at least six states (Colorado, Idaho, Indiana, Oklahoma, Utah, and Wyoming). The law brings together a variety of consumer protection measures that have been enacted piecemeal in various states.

   a. The buyer in a door-to-door sale, who is so often high pressured into signing the contract, may avoid the agreement by paying a cancellation fee of 5 percent of the purchase price.
   b. Referral selling schemes ("Get ten friends to sign up and your siding job will cost you nothing!") are outlawed.
   c. Confession of judgment (a creditor gets a court judgment after default by the debtor but without a trial) and assignment of wages to a creditor are outlawed.
   d. If an installment debt is accelerated (that is, upon default of one payment, all payments come due), unearned credit charges must be refunded.
   e. If a balloon payment (under which all installment payments are low until the final one) is more than double the average of earlier scheduled payments, the debtor may require an extension on terms no less favorable than the first contract.
   f. When a buyer purchases a series of items on credit from a single seller and defaults, only those items that have not been covered by earlier payments may be repossessed.
   g. In credit sales under $1,000, the seller may either sue for the balance due or repossess the goods in case of default. He may not repossess, resell, and obtain a judgment against the defaulting buyer for the unpaid balance. (If the sales contract price is over $1,000, the seller may get a deficiency judgment. Similarly, if the debtor has borrowed money and given collateral, the creditor may sell the collateral in case of default and hold the borrower liable for the unpaid balance, if any.)

   The major objection of consumer advocates to this bill is the exorbitant scale of finance or carrying charges or interest it would permit: 36 percent on the unpaid balance up to $300; 21 percent between $300 and $1,000; and 15 percent on that part above $1,000. In the alternative, the creditor may charge 18 percent across the board. For revolving credit accounts, the ceilings are lower: 24 percent on balances of $500 or less and 18 percent on balances of more than $500.
2. *Federal Magnuson-Moss Consumer Product Warranty and Guaranty Act* would forbid warrantors to disclaim implied warranties, such as the comprehensive warranty of merchantability, and would authorize the FTC to make rules as to the terms of guaranties.
3. *Unit Pricing* by amendment to the Fair Packaging and Labeling

Act. To facilitate comparison of prices, consumer products used in and around the household and consumed during the first year of use would have to show the price per single unit of weight, measure, or volume. Some grocery chains are already voluntarily unit pricing many items on their shelves.

4. *Federal Consumer Protection Agency* would represent consumers before regulatory agencies that decide such matters as home heating costs (Federal Power Commission), interstate telephone bills (Federal Communications Commission), television program standards (Federal Communications Commission), airline ticket prices (Civil Aeronautics Board), and moving costs (Interstate Commerce Commission). Legislation to create this agency has been rejected by Congress thus far, opposition fearing "government harassment of business."

5. At the state level there are proposals to regulate funeral homes and undertaking practices; computer dating bureaus; child talent agencies; computer schools; debt collection practices; air charter flights; speculative land sales; endless-chain promotion plans; no-fault automobile insurance; telephone solicitation of sales; and credit insurance and title insurance rates and terms.

CASES, QUESTIONS, AND PROBLEMS

1. Greta Barbo knew she was allergic to most chemicals. While on vacation, she exhausted her supply of special facial cream and instead used the regular standard brand soap provided by the hotel. There had never been any complaints from other guests over the years. This time, Miss Barbo suffered a sudden painful and prolonged allergic reaction. Is the hotel liable to her for injuries suffered?

2. Joshua Burden, a high school senior, was generally considered Number One on his campus. He was a four-letter man, captain of the basketball team, star student, and varsity debater. One day, as the class entered the auditorium for an assembly, he whispered to Barby Dahl, "I'll see you at noon for Cokes® and burgers. Okay?" She smiled and nodded an eager acceptance. Was a contract formed?

3. Tom Fox took his portable color television into the Dandy-Handy Helper Shop in Los Angeles. They gave him a written estimate of $37.50 for labor and materials, maximum. When Fox returned to pick up his set, the charge was $81.90. Must he pay the excess $44.40?

4. Albert Loozer sold six hundred acres of prime grazing land in California's central valley to Bob Rockaman. Rockaman soon after drilled for oil on the land and struck it rich. This increased the value of the land by a fantastic amount. Loozer sued to rescind the sales contract, claiming a mistake. Who wins?

5. When Durell Donnelly bought his homeowners insurance policy, he was not pleased with many listed exclusions that limited the coverage and liability of the insurance company in case of fire. After a fire leveled his house, he asked a court to declare the exclusions unconscionable and not binding on him. Is it likely to do so?

6. Alfredo Reynoso and his wife spoke only Spanish. The installment contract for the shiny new refrigerator-freezer was written in English; they couldn't read it, nor was it translated for them. Reynoso told the salesman that they could nòt afford the machine, especially since he had only one week to go on his present job. Nevertheless, he and his wife signed the contract after the seller assured them that it would really cost them nothing because they would receive $25 credit toward the purchase price for each of the numerous similar sales they would arrange with friends and neighbors. The price was $900 plus $245.88 in financing charges; it cost the seller only $348. The Reynosos made one installment payment of $32 and defaulted. The seller sued for the full balance due, plus attorney's fees and court costs. Is he entitled to these sums?

7. Tom Perkins bought a used gasoline-powered machine for the express purpose of digging many hundreds of fence post holes on his ranch. He paid the seller, Bud Greenwall, $1750; nothing was said about warranties. Later he discovered that Greenwall's brother-in-law owned a 50 percent interest in the machine and did not want to sell it; that the Bank of Five Corners held a chattel mortgage on the machine for a balance due of $550; that the machine would not operate properly in that part of the state because of the hard-pan soil. Had any warranties been breached?

8. Dale Dave was a do-it-yourself hobbyist. His most prized Christmas gift was a multipurpose power-driven woodworking tool given him by an uncle. Joy turned into tragedy soon after when a defective bolt in the machine broke as he leaned over it while turning a desk leg at high speed. A fragment of metal struck and permanently blinded his left eye. Is the uncle liable for the injury?

9. Joan Betner was denied a credit card when she applied for one at a national bank credit card agency. Under the Fair Credit Reporting Act of 1970, she checked her credit record at the R.C.A. branch that

had been contacted by the bank, and she learned that the record erroneously listed her as divorced and jobless. In fact, she was widowed and employed as an office manager with a salary in five figures. When the bank was given the correct information, it still refused to issue the credit card. May it be compelled to do so?

10. Many banks and savings and loan associations collect monthly payments from hundreds of thousands of debtors who are buying their homes. The money is used to meet periodic payments of principal and interest on the loans, and also to pay taxes and insurance premiums when these come due. No interest is paid to the debtors, however, on their money while it accumulates before it is disbursed. Are these facts a suitable basis for a class action?

9

YOU
AS INSURED

1. WHAT IS INSURANCE?

In 1881 Jethro Hawkins received a homestead from
the U.S. government—a free grant of 160 acres on
the plains of western Kansas. After much sweat
and some blood and tears, he succeeded in cultivat-
ing most of it and in building a house for his family
and a barn for his cattle and hogs. His constant
concern was the weather: too much heat, cold,
wind, or rain, or not enough. The greatest threat
was fire, which could destroy in minutes the work
of years. All of his neighbors faced the same danger.
What could Jethro and his neighbors do to reduce
or share this risk?

Jethro could join with his neighbors in an insurance
company. At periodic intervals, each would pay a small
sum, or *premium,* into a common fund that would be used
to compensate a member of the group for any large loss
due to fire. By combining their individual small contributions, which each could well afford, the company could
pay off the occasional large loss, which would otherwise
be a crushing catastrophe for the victim.

2. HOW ARE INSURANCE COMPANIES ORGANIZED?

An insurance company can be organized as a *mutual company,* owned by the contributors. In exchange for the
premiums paid, each receives a contract of insurance called

a *policy,* which defines the rights and duties (or coverages and conditions) of insurer and insured. Expenses are shared and excess income (if losses are lower than expected) may be used to pay *dividends* (refunds of overpaid premiums).*

An insurance company may be organized as a conventional corporation, or *stock insurance company.* The shareholders own the firm and provide needed working capital by buying shares of stock. Policies of insurance are sold to the public. Income from premiums and from the investment of premiums is used to pay the fire losses, all expenses, and maybe also a return on the owners' invested capital.

Which Kind to Buy From?

Both mutual and stock insurance companies operate in the United States, selling fire, life, and other types of insurance. Their net premium rates are competitive. However, because of a host of variables—such as the selection of risks, loss experience, efficiency of operation, nature of coverage, and type of service—actual prices charged for comparable insurance policies differ from company to company. Here, as with most goods and services, it pays to shop before you buy.

The intelligent buyer of any kind of insurance will first satisfy himself that he is dealing with a reputable company. (Many mail order insurance firms are suspect; some have failed to pay contractual claims.) The buyer, called the *insured,* will then compare the rates in order to get full value for his money from the seller, called the *insurer.* This is often difficult to do, because terms vary widely and salesmen may have negligible or misleading information on comparative values.

If possible, you should get a copy of the proposed contract (the policy) and read it with understanding before you commit yourself. (It often happens, however, that the buyer sees the policy only after he has agreed to buy.) Read it carefully as soon as it is available to you. You are generally bound by its terms whether or not you read them.[1] If you need help in understanding the technical language, consult your insurance agent, your banker, a teacher or other knowledgeable friend, your accountant, or your attorney. In disputes over the interpretation of insurance contracts, courts tend to favor the insured because the insurer, with years of experience and expert legal help, drew up the contract.

The policy defines your rights and duties, and its detailed terms may surprise you; the coverage may be broader in some respects and narrower in others than you anticipated. You may sometimes request and obtain standard changes in the agreement, such as expanding the coverage (at a higher premium cost). You cannot, however, make changes in wording.

---

* This dividend is not the same as a dividend earned on corporate stock, and is not taxable as income when received.

If you are dissatisfied, and have no other recourse, you may stop premium payments and cause the policy to lapse. This withdrawal is not recommended unless you have already obtained protection from another company. If you terminate a property or casualty insurance contract before completion, you are generally entitled to a refund of premium for the portion not used.

Regulation of Insurance Companies

Policyholders receive considerable protection from state laws regulating the operation of insurance companies and the licensing of salesmen or agents. Most large companies operate in many states and could be subject to federal regulation as interstate commerce. However, the Congress in 1945 enacted the McCarran-Ferguson Act (Public Law 15, 15 USCA 1012), which assigned the task to the states. Unfortunately, not all states have acted with uniform effectiveness. You can help protect yourself by not believing exaggerated claims of bargain coverage, which may come to you in the mail or which you may see advertised in national journals and in newspapers. Also check on unknown companies in the annual insurance reviews published by the Alfred M. Best Company of Morristown, N.J., available in large public libraries.

3. HOW DOES BUYING INSURANCE DIFFER FROM GAMBLING?

A gambler by nature, Joe ("Lucky") Jorgen considered himself skilled and fortunate in cards and gaming of all sorts. He knew that insurance companies sometimes pay thousands of dollars after receiving premium payments of tens or hundreds of dollars. And so he surveyed the mid-Victorian mansions in his hometown and ordered fire insurance policies on each of them. Would the insurance companies sell him the policies and pay off in case of fire?

Not if they learned the stated facts, and they probably would. To buy insurance, one must have an *insurable interest* in the property or life of the insured. This means that he must benefit from the continued existence of the property or person and stand to suffer some direct financial loss if the property or life is destroyed. In fire insurance, for example, an owner or mortgage holder or even a tenant may have such an interest. This is sensible, for insurance is not intended to encourage calamities or arson! Nor is it meant to enrich the victim of a catastrophe; rather, it should *indemnify* him: make good his actual loss.[2] It is impossible to measure with precision the value of a human life. Hence, in life insurance the concept of indemnity is modified, and a person may buy any amount of coverage that one or more companies will sell him.

Health insurance and life insurance are unique in that theoretically there is no limit to the amount an insured may carry. What is your health or your life worth to you? In contrast, property insurance pays for a loss that can be more precisely and objectively defined. If you have $50,000 worth of fire insurance on a $25,000 house and it is totally destroyed, you still collect no more than $25,000.

In most states, the insurable interest in property covered by the policy must exist at the time the contract is made, as well as when the loss occurs.[3] With life insurance, it is sufficient that the insurable interest exists at the time the policy is purchased. Thus, a creditor who has a policy on a debtor's life may maintain it even after the debt is paid; a spouse may maintain a policy on the partner's life even after a divorce. A possible rationale for this rule is that a cash value may have been created for the policy owner through the savings element in life insurance policies, as explained later in this chapter.

Everyone has an insurable interest in his own life. Typically, he has an interest in the life of his spouse, dependents, or parents; he may have an interest in the life of a key employee or business associate. But to extend the list indefinitely would be to encourage gambling on the chances of when an insured will die or even to encourage hastening his death.[4]

Generally, no one profits when a policy "pays off." One should try to minimize or avoid risks (as by driving carefully and being health-conscious) even when covered by insurance.

4. MAY MINORS BUY INSURANCE?

Roderick Jackman, who was seventeen years old and a high school senior, bought a $1,000 policy of ordinary life insurance from his friend Vickie Doud, who had just been licensed to sell insurance. He also bought an automobile insurance policy from her. A month later they had an argument and Roderick decided to cancel or void the contracts and get his full premium payments back. May he do so?

Yes. In most states, general principles of contract law make a minor's contracts voidable at his option. However, in many states, including California, life insurance contracts of minors on their own lives or on the lives of dependents have been made nonvoidable by statute. Also, the minor may wisely choose not to void a contract for life or auto insurance, for example, because he wants and needs the protection.

5. WHAT KINDS OF INSURANCE ARE AVAILABLE?

Some people might say it was a day to be remembered. However, Marshall J. McSweeney, who owned a department store on Main

Street, would prefer to forget all the things that happened to him that day.

1. A shipment of portable television sets from Japan was lost when a cargo ship from Yokohama sank in a typhoon in the Pacific Ocean.
2. Lightning struck the company warehouse and the resulting fire leveled the building.
3. A fire broke out in the storage room of the store and the overhead sprinklers were activated. The water stopped the fire but ruined the merchandise.
4. The store cafeteria was shut down for the tenth day, because of a strike and walkout by the cooks and baker. Although other workers remained on their jobs, the strikers picketed the building and sympathizers threw plastic bags of red paint against the exterior walls.
5. McSweeney learned from his auditor that S.S. Suavve, his trusted treasurer, had embezzled at least $73,000 and had left for parts unknown.
6. Three armed robbers held up the cashier in the credit office and made off with $4,500.
7. Several years before, a customer had fallen into an open shaft that had been left unguarded. Today the state supreme court upheld the trial court's award of $125,000 in damages for injuries the customer suffered.
8. McSweeney's business partner died. To continue the business, McSweeney would have to somehow buy out his partner's interest. Where could he get the necessary cash?
9. A stock boy was injured when he fell from a ladder while changing a light bulb.
10. McSweeney learned that the title to the land acquired next door for parking space was defective.
11. McSweeney's bleeding stomach ulcer flared up and caused excruciating pain. He was rushed to the hospital for emergency treatment.

Could McSweeney, by buying appropriate insurance, have protected himself and his company against the losses listed?

Yes. In each case, insurance is available to cover the loss involved. Losses from many other perils can also be insured against: earthquakes, hail, frost damage, floods, forged checks, rain, bad debts, loss of a credit card, maternity, birth of twins, even breakdown during a closed circuit television broadcast of a championship fight. However, only four basic types of coverage are likely to concern the average person directly: life, health, auto, and property (fire or homeowners) insurance.

Life Insurance

Life insurance is really death insurance. It protects the beneficiaries of the insured against the risk of his premature death, which would deprive them of his earning power. Logically, the major reason for having life insurance (protection of earning power) also ends when the insured retires and stops working for salary or wages.

Life insurance protects against the risk of premature death from any cause. If the policy is limited to death by accident, the premiums are much lower because the probability of such an event is lower.

Health Insurance

Health insurance normally protects against the risk of incurring medical expenses caused by illness or accident. Some policies include preventive medicine, and pay for annual physical examinations. This type of comprehensive service is offered by health maintenance organizations (HMO), such as the Kaiser Permanente plan prominent in California. Disability income insurance is a variation that pays benefits if you are unable to work because of sickness or injury.

Automobile Insurance

There are several kinds of automobile insurance. *Bodily injury and property damage* insurance protects against the risk of incurring liability for injuring or killing someone or damaging his property, while you are driving a motor vehicle in a negligent manner. *Collision* insurance protects against the risk of damaging your own automobile in an accident or upset, regardless of fault. *Comprehensive* insurance protects against the risk of having your car stolen or damaged by other means listed on the policy such as fire, sandstorm, or vandalism. *Uninsured motorist* insurance protects against the risk of bodily injury suffered by the insured because of the negligence of an uninsured driver, or a hit-and-run driver.

Automobile insurance policies are commonly available with certain additional types of coverage, including notably *automobile medical payments* coverage. It pays the medical expenses of the insured and of any other occupants of the insured's auto if injured while occupying, entering, or leaving it, or if struck by another motor vehicle. If the auto is not owned by the insured, the policy covers medical payments only if the injury flows from the operation or occupancy by the insured or by a resident relative.

Homeowners Insurance

Homeowners insurance protects against many perils, notably the risk of loss to home and contents caused by fire or theft, as well as against the risk of liability for negligently injuring or killing someone or damaging his property, other than through the use of a motor vehicle. The policy never covers all risks—even though advertising sometimes gives the impression that it does.

6. WHAT TYPES OF LIFE INSURANCE ARE AVAILABLE?

All life insurance policies provide coverage for a definite term of years. Pure insurance simply *indemnifies* the insured or his beneficiary (that is, repays or compensates him for a loss) in accordance with the contract. If the insured dies during the term (or continuance) of the policy, the agreed benefit is paid. If he does not, no benefit is paid. This is similar to property or casualty insurance. If there is no fire loss, for example, during the year's term of a homeowners policy, no benefit is paid. Most popular types of life insurance policies include also a savings element, which is returned to the insured with interest if he cancels the policy.

Term Insurance Without Savings

The *level term policy* provides pure insurance. It is called level term since the benefit payable remains the same, or level, during the term of the policy. Such policies are usually sold for five-year periods. They can be renewed for additional five-year periods to age sixty-five, but each time at a higher premium because the risk of death rises as the insured gets older.

The *decreasing (or reducing) term policy* also provides pure insurance, but the benefit payable decreases gradually during the term of the policy. Thus, the $50,000 face value of a policy purchased at age twenty-five, for example, gradually decreases to zero at age sixty-five. The annual premium remains the same because the insured is buying less and less insurance—in spite of the rising risk of death with increased age. At the same time, however, he is probably acquiring other assets on his own that provide security. Also, his need to provide for dependents is declining as his children mature and establish families of their own.

Term Insurance with Savings

The *ordinary life policy* combines decreasing term insurance and increasing savings to the end of the term (usually age ninety-nine or one hundred). At this time, the accumulated savings (with interest) equal the face amount of the policy. Of course, long before then most such policies either mature because of the death of the insured, or are canceled. Upon the insured's death at any age before one hundred, the money paid by the insurance company includes both pure insurance and savings.

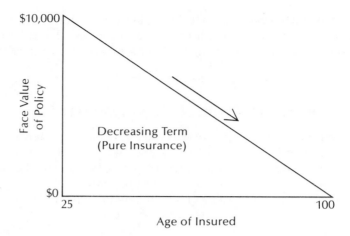

$10,000

Face Value
of Policy

Decreasing Term
(Pure Insurance)

$0

25

100

Age of Insured

Fig. 9–1.
Decreasing term
element in an
ordinary insurance
policy

Figure 9–1 shows how the amount of pure insurance gradually decreases until age one hundred. Figure 9–2 shows how the savings dollars the insured pays as part of his premiums gradually grow to cover the face amount of the policy at age one hundred. Superimposed, these two charts show that at any given time the benefit received is a combination of decreasing term (pure insurance) and increasing savings with interest. When a man, for example, buys a $10,000 ordinary life policy at age twenty-five, he obtains what is called an immediate testamentary estate; that is, if he were to die, his designated beneficiaries would get $10,000.

The insurance company collects a premium sufficient to cover the risk of the insured's dying, but also borrows money savings from him and agrees to pay them back at a later date, together with interest at a modest rate (usually 2.5 to 3.5 percent a year). Because the company contracts with the insured to repay a fixed sum, it invests the savings in fixed dollar media such as bonds and mortgages.

The insured can borrow against his policy or surrender it for a cash payment because the money he receives is his own accumulated savings with interest. The savings element constitutes the *loan value* or *cash surrender value* of his policy. During the first year of a policy, it offers neither of these values because most of the premium dollars go to pay the salesman's commission and other initial costs.

Sometimes insurance companies offer combination policies, such as the *family income policy,* or *family maintenance policy.* In each case, the basic policy is an ordinary life policy, supplemented by a term policy. The latter provides substantially more protection per dollar because it buys pure protection, perhaps for a limited term of years. A couple might need such protection when their children are growing up.

In a *limited payment policy,* the premiums are substantially higher than for an ordinary life policy, but the insured pays them for only a

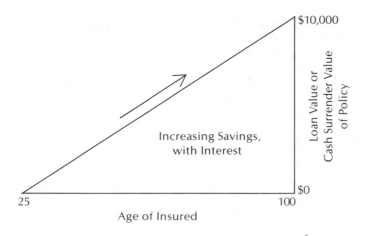

Increasing Savings,
with Interest

$10,000

Loan Value or
Cash Surrender Value
of Policy

$0

25

100

Age of Insured

Fig. 9-2.
Increasing savings
element in an
ordinary life
insurance policy

limited number of years, perhaps twenty or thirty. He is covered fully all the time, and the extra large payments (with interest) pay the cost of the insurance for the remainder of his life.

In an *endowment policy,* the premiums are still higher because the company agrees to repay the face amount to the insured when he reaches age sixty-five, typically. Were he to die before the stipulated age, the face amount would go to his designated beneficiary.

To their dismay, insureds may learn at their retirement that the endowment they saved for over the years buys much less than they expected. Life insurance with its fixed dollar values is especially vulnerable to the erosion in purchasing power caused by inflation. Some insurance companies now recognize this limitation of the fixed dollar savings component in their ordinary life insurance policies. They have therefore devised a new type of policy called *variable life insurance,* under which a prescribed minimum must be paid, but a higher return is possible. The company attempts to arrange this by investing some of the savings in variable dollar media.

cash surrender value   If an ordinary life policy is canceled, the insurance company pays back the savings and earnings on it as the cash surrender value. To the disadvantage of the insured, there is no cash surrender value payable during the first year or sometimes longer, because the company needs the initial premiums to pay the salesman's commission (about 50 percent of the first year's premium and 5 percent of the premiums paid for the next nine years) and other expenses.

The insured may borrow the loan value against his policy up to the full cash surrender value. The company charges him interest, but at a comparatively low true annual rate (5 to 7 percent) to compensate for investment earnings lost on the funds and to cover its expenses.

settlement options As owner of the policy, the insured may legally designate who the beneficiary or beneficiaries shall be and how the proceeds shall be paid. He may, for example, instruct the insurance company to hold the proceeds and pay the benefits gradually in order to prevent a beneficiary from dissipating them. If he fails to specify the method of distribution, after his death the beneficiary has the same settlement options to choose from. He may choose to receive:

1. the *face amount* of the policy in *one lump sum*. It is usually paid promptly. If payable to a named beneficiary, it need not go through a formal probate court procedure.
2. a *fixed amount,* broken into a series of payments that are made until the face amount (plus any added interest earned) is exhausted
3. a series of equal payments of a specified amount for a *fixed period* of time
4. *interest only* on the face amount of the policy, paid at specified intervals, to the primary beneficiary, sometimes with a limited or unlimited right to withdraw the principal. Any remainder of principal may then go to a designated person or persons when the primary beneficiary dies.
5. *fixed amount of lifetime income* for one or more named beneficiaries. Sometimes payments are guaranteed for five, ten, or twenty years. This is an annuity contract, and benefits will vary depending on an actuarial determination of how long the designated beneficiaries might live and collect.

tax status of life insurance benefits Life insurance benefits generally are not subject to state inheritance taxes (on the privilege of receiving) up to amounts specified by statute in the various states. In California, the total exemption for life insurance proceeds payable to beneficiaries is $50,000. Neither the insured nor the beneficiary pays income tax on the interest component of the policy proceeds as it accumulates while the insured lives. Nor are the proceeds taxable as income when received.

Life insurance benefits are included, however, in the estate of the insured for federal estate tax purposes (on the privilege of giving). This estate tax can be avoided by making the proceeds payable directly to named beneficiaries (instead of to the estate of the insured) and by having the insured also divest himself of most of the *incidents of ownership* of the policy. To do this, the insured, while alive, must formally and in writing give up the right to change beneficiaries, to collect the loan or cash surrender value, to pledge the policy as security for a loan, and to exercise any other rights with regard to the policy. He may continue to pay the premiums, but he may not retain any *reversionary interest* worth more than 5 percent of the value of the policy immediately before his death. Insurance agents can provide the necessary forms for the insured to complete to effect this divestment or relinquishment of control.

changing the beneficiary   The insured who retains the right to change the beneficiary named in his policy may exercise this right by simply notifying the insurer in writing. Forms are generally available from insurance companies for this purpose.

> Cameron Emrich bought a $100,000 policy of insurance on his life, in which he named his business partner, Benjamin Acosta, as beneficiary. After the partnership dissolved, Emrich kept the policy in force. Years later, he wrote his will, and in it he named his two children as beneficiaries under the insurance policy. Shortly thereafter he died. Who gets the $100,000?

Partner Acosta. The beneficiary in a life insurance policy may not be changed by will. Of course, if the proceeds of the policy were payable to the estate of Emrich, he could have changed the ultimate recipients by naming new donees in his will.

7. HOW DO THE COSTS OF THESE TWO TYPES OF LIFE INSURANCE COMPARE?

Insurance salesmen often try to dissuade prospects from buying term insurance by pointing out that the premiums for renewable level term policies rise shockingly in twenty, thirty, or forty years, whereas the premiums on ordinary life policies remain constant. What they fail to mention is that ordinary life policies include a decreasing term component, coupled with extra savings. Thus, the true or pure insurance in these policies decreases over the years. If the true insurance coverage remained the same, the premiums would also have to go up substantially, as with level term.

For a fair comparison of costs, the insured should contrast the ordinary or endowment policy with a decreasing term policy to age sixty-five or seventy (table 9–1). The latter would cost him perhaps one-fourth to one-sixth as much. If he faithfully invested the money thus saved on premiums over the years, he would always have a combination of term and personal savings equal to at least $10,000. At age sixty-five, however, he could have much more than $10,000, because he could probably earn more on his money than the insurance company pays (approximately 3.5 percent annual return) on the savings element in ordinary policies (fig. 9–3).

Life insurance companies are very much like banks or savings and loan associations in that both try to persuade customers to lend them money. Insurance companies, however, pay a lower rate of return than the insured could earn on his own. Of course, not all insureds have the self-discipline to save the difference in cost between the ordinary policy and the term policy and the skill to invest it at a profit. These people may be better advised to remain with the ordinary policy.

TABLE 9-1

Representative Premiums and Cash Surrender Values
for Five Types of Life Insurance Policies
(for a male, age 25, who buys
$25,000 face value of insurance)

Type of Insurance	Premiums			Cash Surrender Value at Age 65
	Monthly	Annual	Total to Age 65	
Ordinary life	$26.46	$303.00	$12,120	$14,250
20 payment life	$46.82	$525.25	$10,505	$17,250
Endowment at age 65	$40.47	$451.25	$18,050	$25,000
5-year renewable level term to age 65 (Coverage remains at $25,000.)	Varies with age	$105.50 at age 25, increasing every five years ($224.75 at age 45; $679 at age 60)	$10,873	None
Decreasing term to age 65 (Coverage starts at $25,000 and decreases by $625 a year.)	$6.60	$74.75	$2,990	None

8. IF A POLICYHOLDER FAILS TO PAY A LIFE INSURANCE PREMIUM ON SCHEDULE, IS HE STILL PROTECTED?

> At age twenty-one, Edmund Buchanan insured his life for $25,000 and paid the premiums annually for the next seventeen years. When the eighteenth premium came due, Buchanan was vacationing aboard a cruise ship in the Mediterranean. His mind was on other matters, and he simply forgot to pay the premium. The next day the ship ran aground in a storm and Buchanan was drowned. Does his insurance company have to pay off as agreed?

Yes. Technically the insurance contract lapses or terminates when an agreed-upon premium is not paid. However, as generally required by state statutes, insurers allow a grace period of thirty days after the due date,

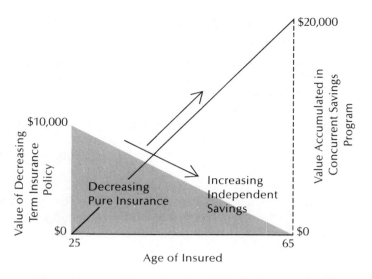

Fig. 9-3.
The projected value
of decreasing term
insurance combined
with independent
savings

while the policy remains in force. If the insured dies within that time, the unpaid premium is deducted from the face amount of the policy. Beyond that time, company regulations or statutes usually provide relief.

If Buchanan had not died and his policy has a cash surrender value, the *standard nonforfeiture law* would protect him against forfeiture by allowing him to:

1. demand the cash surrender value of his policy (approximately $5,000 in Buchanan's case) and let the policy lapse
2. use the cash surrender value to buy a fully paid-up policy of a reduced amount in ordinary life or endowment insurance (face value about $10,750 in Buchanan's case)
3. use the cash surrender value to buy a fully paid-up policy of level term insurance for the same face amount. (Buchanan's $25,000 coverage would last another twenty-eight years, when he would be sixty-six. He might obtain an even larger initial amount of reducing term insurance, if available, which would gradually decline to nothing when he reaches age sixty-five. Presumably his critical need for protection would then be over.)

If previously agreed to (at the time the policy was purchased or at least before default), Buchanan might get the benefit of an *automatic premium loan*. Thus, upon default, if there is sufficient loan value (which is the same amount as the cash surrender value), the company automatically pays the premium and charges it against such value. The amount of payment to be made in case of death is, of course, reduced by this or any other outstanding policy loan. The insured-borrower is under no compulsion to repay the loan.

9. DO INSURANCE COMPANIES PAY THE BENEFICIARIES OF SUICIDE VICTIMS?

> Percival Tresholi was despondent. When he married, he promised the world to his sweetheart—with condominiums and ocean cruises, servants and sweets. Years later he was still a very junior clerk in the city bank. After much troubled soul-searching, he bought $100,000 in life insurance, naming his wife as beneficiary. Three days later, after work, he jumped to his death from the tenth floor in the inside courtyard of the bank building. Will his widow collect?

No. Life insurance policies almost always exclude the risk of suicide when it is committed within two years of the purchase of the policy. In this situation, the insurer commonly refunds the premiums paid without interest—as is usually stipulated in the policy.

Under the *incontestable clause* generally required by law, the insurance company must pay the face amount of the policy if the insured commits suicide after two or more years from the date of issuance. (A would-be suicide seldom plans that far in advance.) After the incontestable period, the insurer cannot dispute or deny its liability on a policy by proving facts that formerly would have been a defense. The insurance company presumably has had ample time to determine whether a given policy should or should not be cancelled; thereafter the insured and his beneficiaries are spared the possibility of costly litigation in seeking to collect on the policy.[5]

In other words, after the incontestable period, the company may not avoid payment by claiming fraud, misrepresentation, or concealment by the insured in his policy application. For example, if the insured falsely states that he has never had a heart attack, and then dies of a heart seizure more than two years later, his beneficiaries are still entitled to the face value of the policy. If age were misstated, however, the face amount of the policy would be adjusted when the facts were disclosed, and the benefit paid would be the amount that could have been purchased with the original premium. (At an older age, premiums are higher because the probability of death is greater.)

The incontestable clause has been used to prevent the insurer from contesting even a policy where there was no insurable interest, but not all states go this far.[6] Most states properly permit the insurer expressly to exclude certain risks such as death caused by war or by the crash of a private airplane.[7]

10. SHOULD PARENTS BUY LIFE INSURANCE FOR THEIR CHILDREN?

> Manuel Torres has three children, ages two, four, and six. He wants them to have the opportunity to attend college, which

he never did, and so he welcomes the solution proposed by an insurance salesman to buy ordinary or endowment life insurance policies on each child. When each child is ready for college, Torres can borrow the loan value of that child's policy to cover his college costs. Should Torres buy the policies?

No. He is the family bread winner. If he buys any insurance, it should be on his life.

Insurance salesmen often try to persuade parents to buy life insurance policies on their children, saying, "The premiums will never be lower than now." But this merely reflects the fundamental fact that the risk of death is lower for a young person than for an old one, especially after the first year or so when the hazards of infancy are past. Rationally, such insurance does not make much sense, because life insurance should protect economic values. A child usually has no effective earning power to protect; no one is dependent on him for support. Indeed, he is typically a financial liability costing thousands of dollars until he matures. If the purpose of the insurance is to save money for his college education or marriage, the savings will probably accumulate faster and at a higher rate of return in many other savings or investment media.

It is possible that the minor will later become uninsurable because of accident or illness. This is unusual, but if it happens and he needs insurance, he can often get some protection as a member of a group (such as his fellow workers) under a plan that requires no physical examination.

11. WHAT ARE GROUP INSURANCE AND INDUSTRIAL INSURANCE POLICIES?

Group insurance policies are usually one-year renewable term, and the dollar amount is limited, frequently to $1,000 or $5,000. They are sold to employers for all employees, who may receive them as fringe benefits supplementing their regular income.

Industrial insurance policies are designed to be sold to industrial workers who cannot afford conventional policies. They are of declining importance but are still sold. The face amount is usually under $500, and premiums are collected in person by the salesman monthly or even weekly. The price may be only a few cents a week, but this nevertheless is much more expensive per dollar of protection than other policies because of the high labor costs involved, and because the mortality rate is higher for industrial workers. One common feature of such policies is the *facility-of-payment clause,* which permits the insurance company to pay the proceeds to the personal representative of the insured, or to any relative who appears to be entitled to them. Presumably the money will be used to pay funeral expenses. The insured may, however, name a beneficiary to collect if alive, provided that the claim is made within sixty days after death.

12. WHO NEEDS HEALTH INSURANCE?

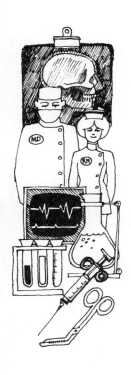

> G.M. Schiba did not have to be told about rising medical costs. A ten-day spell in a hospital cost him more than $100 a day; his family doctor charged him $200; a specialist surgeon asked $750; while the anesthetist charged $125. The experience drained him of all his ready cash and liquid savings, and he still had to borrow $500 from his credit union. What can he do to prevent a recurrence of such a financial burden?

Schiba can buy several types of health insurance, which permit him to budget for the medical costs of illnesses and accidents and do so at a price within his means, assuming he is employed and earning at least a modest income. If he is on welfare, or employed but poor enough to be considered medically indigent, society will probably provide needed medical care for him and his family. Likewise, if he is a man of wealth, he can take care of himself in case of emergency. But if he is among the large mass of Americans in the middle, he should consider buying health insurance.

13. WHAT TYPES OF HEALTH INSURANCE ARE THERE?

Health insurance is available to cover the various types of expenses that may be incurred: *hospital* expense insurance, *surgical* expense insurance, *regular medical* expense insurance (for routine services of physicians and nurses), and *major medical* insurance (which would take over in calamitous illnesses). If purchased alone, major medical would become effective after a prescribed deductible amount of medical expense had been incurred. The policy pays 80 percent of all added medical expenses in excess of the deductible amount, up to the agreed limit ($10,000 to $50,000, or more).

Since a serious illness may prevent a person from working for a prolonged period of time, the family breadwinner may want to purchase *disability income* insurance. This pays the agreed amount, usually on a monthly basis for a maximum of five years, while the insured is unable to work because of illness or injury. However, this is a comparatively expensive type of coverage. Since no one can be expected to acquire protection against all hazards because of costs that cut into other needed spending, it is usually advisable to dispense with disability income insurance altogether. Anyway, a qualifying illness must be quite extreme; most ailments do not totally disable a person for a prolonged time.

Legally, a person might qualify for payments from other sources while disabled. Depending on one's individual circumstances, these might include workmen's compensation (if injured on the job), disability insurance for employees (for off-the-job ailments, a coverage available in California, Hawaii, New Jersey, New York, and Rhode Island), social security (if totally disabled), sick leave or salary continuation plans provided by employers, and damages collected from another who is at fault in an accident (although there may be a long time lag before collection).

If one has life insurance, it makes sense to pay a little more in exchange for a *waiver of premium clause,* which suspends the payment of premiums after a prescribed period of time away from work because of disability.

14. WHAT SOURCES OF HEALTH INSURANCE ARE THERE?

Health insurance policies are written by many companies with a great variety of provisions as to what is covered and for how long. The leading programs available throughout the country are Blue Cross and Blue Shield. Blue Cross covers hospital expenses under approval of the American Hospital Association; Blue Shield covers surgical and regular medical expenses under approval of the American Medical Association. In a few areas, health maintenance organizations have been established under private auspices. These HMOs emphasize preventive medicine, while offering the full package of needed hospital-surgical-medical care. Examples would be the Kaiser Permanente and Ross-Loos plans in California and the Health Insurance Plan (HIP) in New York.

Rising expectations of the public for the best possible medical service as a basic right of every person, coupled with rising costs caused by inflation and higher priced talent using elaborate and expensive equipment, have led to demands for more government involvement in the medical care supply system. Most European countries have long had some form of socialized medicine. We already have Medicare, which provides mandatory hospital insurance, as well as optional voluntary medical insurance, to retired persons covered by social security. A federal program of comprehensive and compulsory health insurance is likely to be adopted in the foreseeable future.

15. WHAT TYPES OF AUTOMOBILE INSURANCE ARE AVAILABLE?

When Wally Wallace celebrated his eighteenth birthday, his father gave him his first car. "Remember," his father said, "you'll not be driving a horse, but three hundred of them. That can be worse than a stampede. So before you use these keys, let's see my insurance agent and make sure you're adequately covered." What sort of insurance coverage does Wally need?

Four basic types of automobile insurance are available to meet the hazards caused by motor vehicles and those who drive them.

Bodily Injury and Property Damage Insurance

Bodily injury insurance (also called personal liability or P.L. insurance) deals with claims resulting from injury or death to others, caused by the insured's negligence. Property damage liability insurance (also called P.D. insurance) deals with claims resulting from damage to the cars or other property of others, caused by the insured's negligence.

Collision Insurance

Collision insurance serves to indemnify (make good the loss for) damages to the insured driver's motor vehicle by collision or upset, whether or not the cause was his negligence. If the other party was at fault, the insurance company may pay the claim and then seek reimbursement from the wrongdoer by right of *subrogation:* the insurance company takes the place of the insured as creditor and succeeds to all of his rights to recover.

Comprehensive Insurance

Comprehensive insurance serves to indemnify the insured against any loss to his vehicle except by collision. It applies if his vehicle is stolen, vandalized, or otherwise damaged without a collision. The policy does not pay for loss caused by theft of personal effects (such as clothing, cameras, luggage) while left in the vehicle.

Uninsured Motorist Insurance

> Pedro Perez was at the wheel of his car, patiently waiting for the traffic light to turn green. Suddenly he heard and felt a horrendous crash from the rear. He was wearing a seat belt, and his head and chest were snapped in a violent whiplash. Although conscious, he was dazed and could not identify the hit-and-run car and driver that had rear-ended his car, U-turned, and roared off. What type of automobile insurance protects Perez in this situation.

Perez can recover his medical expenses, and in some states, his property damages, under uninsured motorist insurance. At relatively low cost, this type of policy normally pays up to $10,000 per person and $20,000 per accident (in California, the figures are $15,000 and $30,000) for bodily injury suffered by the insured as a result of being struck by an uninsured driver or a hit-and-run driver.

Automobile Medical Payments Insurance

Medical payments insurance covers medical and funeral expenses incurred by the named insured and relatives residing with him, as a result of bodily injury caused by accident while occupying, or being struck by, any motor vehicle. Sometimes this protection is extended to guests who are injured while occupying the insured automobile. Payments are made whether or not the insured was negligent or legally liable. If a person already has adequate health insurance, this additional coverage may be an unnecessary duplication. Of course, guests in the insured's car may not be so protected, and for their sake this comparatively cheap coverage may be justified.

> Alphonse Labordee found himself stranded in downtown Los Angeles after midnight. His wallet had apparently been stolen by a pickpocket, but he still had his airline ticket for the return flight to Chicago. In desperation, he "hot wired" the first idle car he found, and headed for the airport. He'd been drinking, and within a block he crashed into a telephone pole. Before it was all over, his medical payments totalled $6,548. Will the car owner's medical payments policy (limit $10,000) cover Labordee's loss?

No. The owner of the car must have given him permission to use the vehicle involved or he must believe the owner had given such permission. Here Labordee was a thief. His own medical payments coverage is inapplicable and so is the rest of his automobile insurance policy. If he also carried ordinary health insurance, his medical expenses would be covered.

16. ARE THERE WAYS TO SAVE ON AUTOMOBILE INSURANCE?

> K. Timothy Quinn is a graduate student, working at jobs on and off campus to support his wife and infant child. Every dollar is important in the family budget, and he is wondering whether he can economize on his automobile insurance. He knows that if he negligently injured (or killed) another while driving, he would be hard-pressed to pay a judgment, which could run into thousands of dollars. Even though he could clear himself of such a judgment by going bankrupt, he does not want to hurt others with no hope of making good their loss. Moreover, he would not like to have a discharge in bankruptcy on his credit record. What automobile insurance should he buy?

Quinn has limited freedom of choice if he is buying his car on time, as most people do. The seller, until paid in full, would undoubtedly insist that Quinn carry collision and comprehensive insurance. Because of his fear of incurring a huge debt in damages, Quinn decides to add bodily injury and property damage coverage to his automobile insurance "package." He finds that he can substantially increase the amount from a basic 10/20/5 (that is, in any one accident, the company pays up to $10,000 for injury or death to any one person or $20,000 to all persons, and $5,000 for property damage) up to 100/300/25 for only 40 percent higher premiums.

In two or three years, when the car is paid for, Quinn can prudently drop the expensive collision insurance, and also the expendable comprehensive coverage, because even total destruction of his car would not be a catastrophic loss. At least he should request the maximum *deductible.* Thus, he would pay the first $50 or $100 cost of any damage to his car, but his premiums would be substantially lower. Indeed, if a loss occurs, he might be wise to make no claim unless the damage far exceeds the deductible, because the company might cancel his policy after a series of small claims. If nothing else, the company would probably boost his premiums for the next year. In some states, however, statutes now limit the companies' cancellation right.

Quinn can also save on his automobile insurance by driving carefully and avoiding citations for moving violations; they too lead to rate increases and cancellations. An insurance company may legally refuse to insure an applicant for any reason logically related to the hazard insured against: he has a bad driving record because of accidents in which he was negligent, or moving traffic violations; he lives in a ghetto; he is under twenty-five or over sixty-five (hence more accident-prone); he is in a disfavored line of work (such as bartending, barbering, acting, or soldiering); he is physically or mentally handicapped; he is known to be a deadbeat (a slow-pay or no-pay on debts); or he drives a super-charged car. Such persons may still obtain coverage as *assigned risks* by paying what may seem to be inordinately high rates. The insurance companies in a given state rotate in accepting such risks.

Some companies give *discounts* to drivers who do not drink or smoke, or who travel very little and do not commute to work, or who drive compact cars. Young drivers may qualify for discounts if they are superior students who are on the scholastic honor roll or maintain a "B" average. Insurance companies believe that such persons have fewer accidents, and so the rate discrimination is legal.

17. MUST A PERSON BUY AUTOMOBILE INSURANCE?

In most states, no. In a few states (such as New York and Massachusetts) and in states that have adopted some type of no-fault automobile insurance, yes.

Most states have *financial responsibility laws.* In California, for example, if a driver is involved in an accident in which someone is injured or killed, or property damage exceeds $250, he is required to report the accident to the Department of Motor Vehicles within fifteen days, on a prescribed form (available from the department, from the police, or from insurance companies). If he is not covered by at least a minimum 15/30/5 policy, he must post cash or a bond for up to $35,000, or both his driver's license and vehicle registration may be suspended. Moreover, he must maintain this proof of financial responsibility for a period of three years following his involvement in the accident. These procedures and requirements apply even if he is not at fault. Most persons do carry at least minimum coverage. The practice is encouraged also by the fact that before a minor may drive, states usually require that his parent or guardian accept responsibility for injuries or property damage he may inflict on others. In California, for example, a 15/30/5 policy is required to satisfy this rule.

18. WHO IS COVERED BY AUTOMOBILE INSURANCE AND UNDER WHAT CIRCUMSTANCES?

> Sylvester McFarland has a wife and teen-aged daughter, Kim. All drive the family car. Are all covered by his automobile policy?

Yes, if the insurance company is notified that they all drive the family car. With respect to an owned automobile identified in a policy, the following persons are normally insured:

1. the named insured and his spouse, if residing in the same household
2. residents of the same household who use the vehicle with or without permission. (This applies even if the person is temporarily away from home. For example, if Kim goes to school in another state.)
3. any other person using the automobile with the permission of the named insured
4. any other person who might be liable because of negligence by the insured. (This could be the employer of the insured, if McFarland got into an accident while on company business.)

Under most policies, if you sell your car and buy another, your automobile coverage continues thirty days as a minimum or until the next policy anniversary date as a maximum. Thus, you are fully protected in case of accident during the transition period. However, the company should be notified promptly within the available time so that it can make necessary changes in your policy.

> While on vacation in Glacier National Park, Nelson Salbeck borrowed a four-wheel drive jeep from some friends and took off on a cross-country ride. Does his own automobile insurance policy cover him while he drives a borrowed vehicle?

Yes, Salbeck and resident relatives in his household are all covered when they drive non-owned passenger automobiles with the permission of the owner of the vehicle. A *non-owned automobile* is defined as an automobile or trailer not owned by, or furnished for, the regular use of the named insured or a resident relative.

> When Salbeck came home, he learned that his adult son, Jack, who still lived with his parents, had bought a new car with manual gearshift, and had insured it in his own name. Salbeck asked if he might try it out; Jack said yes, and the father took off. He had an accident in which the car was damaged, a pedestrian was injured, and so was Salbeck, all because of his negligence in shifting gears. Did Salbeck's insurance cover him?

No. Technically, the son's car is not non-owned since it is owned by a resident relative, the son. However, since Salbeck drove with his son's permission, the son's policy will cover the accident. Unfortunately, this might be much less than the more heavily insured Salbeck deems adequate for himself, and so he is vulnerable to a sizable claim for damages by the pedestrian. As a minor exception to the above rule, if Salbeck had borrowed his son's car while his own was being serviced or repaired, the son's car would be deemed a *temporary substitute automobile,* and both policies would cover the loss.

> Aaron Dittmar bought a trailer for camping trips, and hooked a light trail motorcycle to the rear of the trailer. Are these vehicles covered by Dittmar's automobile insurance policy?

The trailer is covered, without an added premium, for P.L. and P.D. (personal liability and property damage) only if designed for use with a private passenger automobile and if not used for business or commercial purpose. Courts are in conflict as to whether a motorcycle or motorscooter would be covered. Even when covered, the protection would extend only to the named insured and not to residents of the same household or others to whom he may have given permission for use. Prudence suggests that if you drive a motorcycle, confirm the insurance coverage with your insurance agent, preferably in writing. Of course, a policy may be written directly for a motorcycle.

A policy effective within the United States generally does not cover the insured beyond our borders unless specially endorsed in exchange for an extra premium. It is extremely important that you review your automobile liability and property damage coverage with your insurance agent before you leave to travel by car in foreign countries. If you do not and you have an accident while driving abroad, you may be incarcerated in a foreign jail because of inability to pay damages.

19. WHAT IS NO-FAULT INSURANCE?

Under no-fault, every driver is required to buy insurance. After an accident, each company pays the damages suffered by its insured, up to some prescribed limit, regardless of fault and without litigation. If there is a dispute as to the proper amount, an administrator decides after a hearing; there is no court trial. Each party collects from his own company for medical (or funeral) expenses and lost wages (for a limited time) both for himself and for other occupants of his car. Generally, one may not sue or recover any damages for pain and suffering or for disfigurement. However, if medical expenses exceed a certain minimum (perhaps $5,000 or $10,000), the victim may sue; if he can prove that the other party was negligent (with no contributory negligence on his part), he may recover a larger sum, including payment for pain and suffering.

Massachusetts has pioneered the idea; some twenty other states have followed suit and many more have the idea under consideration, probably waiting to see how well it works in practice. The experience with no-fault in Massachusetts thus far has been encouraging. Elimination of costly litigation and some economies in marketing of policies should reduce costs to drivers. Possible overall reduction of payments to injured persons would also reduce costs, but this cannot necessarily be considered good. Allowing litigation in aggravated cases may prove untenable. Possibly individuals who are not satisfied with recovery schedules under no-fault should be encouraged to buy additional accident and life and disability insurance coverage for themselves.

20. WHAT ARE SOME OF THE ARGUMENTS FOR AND AGAINST NO-FAULT INSURANCE?

Arguments For

Most Americans drive or ride in automobiles and thus repeatedly risk injury. Auto accidents are confused and confusing events: facts are elusive and subject to distortion because of faulty observations and fallible memories as well as "elastic consciences." Negligence is difficult to establish; even a little contributory negligence on the part of the plaintiff may bar any recovery in most states, even when the defendant was overwhelmingly at fault.

Courts in heavily populated areas are crowded with cases involving claims arising out of automobile accidents. Administrative delays may induce injured persons (perhaps hospitalized, out of work, and in desperate need of money) to accept less than a fair amount for their injuries from insurance company claim adjusters, and to waive their legal right to a trial. Juries are inconsistent in awarding damages and may be biased for or against plaintiff or defendant. Plaintiff lawyers are inclined to take only the cases that appear to promise victory, and yet they receive very substantial fees when victorious.

The costs of competitive selling of insurance are extremely high. Surveys have shown, however, that accident victims receive only about forty-five cents of every insurance premium dollar (the balance remaining with the insurer or going to lawyers who represent the plaintiff and the insurance company in the litigation). Many insurance companies have been unwilling to accept (unless on a high-price, assigned-risk basis) what they consider high-risk insureds, such as young people and members of minority groups. Recovery of benefits under policies is often uncertain and frequently involves much red tape and haggling as well as foot-dragging by insurers.

Arguments Against

Many trial lawyers and other concerned citizens, including some consumer advocates, object to the no-fault plan because it denies a plaintiff his right to his day in court, with the related opportunity for a full recovery. As in workmen's compensation insurance, the damages prescribed on the no-fault scale may be grossly inadequate for some plaintiffs. Indemnification for wages lost may also be inadequate, and nothing is paid for the pain and suffering and emotional distress caused by others' negligence. In less serious accidents many drivers are already covered by other health and accident insurance. For such insureds, no-fault could cause wasteful duplication. Disability insurance and workmen's compensation insurance cover many others who are involved in auto accidents. Moreover, anyone can already buy collision and comprehensive insurance, which are forms of no-fault insurance for property damage to one's own vehicle. Finally, many insurance companies favor no-fault because it removes decision making from juries composed of sympathetic peers of the injured and turns it over to paid professionals who act in the combined roles of judge, jury, and advocate.

21. WHAT IS FIRE INSURANCE?

For the typical adult, a private house is the costliest single asset he is likely ever to acquire. He usually makes a down payment from his own savings and borrows the balance under a long-term loan from a commercial lender, such as a savings and loan association. Then for perhaps thirty years he pays off the loan in monthly installments, which include interest and principal. As his equity or percentage of ownership of the house increases, the lender's interest in the house decreases. Meanwhile, the greatest hazard both he and the lender face is the possibility that a fire may break out and damage or completely destroy the building and contents. To protect their interests, both lender and buyer-borrower agree that the latter should purchase appropriate fire insurance or its equivalent.

By statute, most states now require that insurers use the *standard fire policy* prescribed by New York law, or some close variation. Structures built by man range from skyscrapers on Manhattan Island, New York, to lean-to feeding sheds for cattle in Manhattan, Kansas. Therefore, the standard policy must be supplemented by appropriate additional clauses, called *endorsements,* or by standardized printed *forms* that legally expand or reduce the scope of protection provided. Finally, the individual policy may be modified by additions or amendments called *riders* (usually typewritten and pasted to the policy).

The form in most common use is the *dwelling and contents form.* It provides coverage for:

a. the dwelling or house itself, together with equipment and fixtures, such as heating and air conditioning equipment
b. the contents, including furniture, clothing, and other household goods, but excluding motor vehicles, large boats, pets—all of which may be separately insured.

> When Jim Langley left for college, he took along most of his clothing, his stereo, typewriter, tennis racket, and some furniture. Soon after, a fire razed the fraternity house where he was staying and all of his belongings were destroyed. Is this loss covered by the fire insurance on his father's home?

That depends. The loss clearly would be covered by standard *off-premises extension* of coverage, but only up to 10 percent of the coverage of the contents of the home in his father's policy. Thus, if his father's policy gave $6,000 of contents coverage, Langley's belongings away from home would be covered for $600. Similar protection would extend to any property of the insured or of residents of his home, while such property is away from the premises but is still in the United States or Canada. Travel in Mexico and other countries requires that the traveler purchase local insurance, or first obtain an enlargement of the coverage of his American policy.

In addition to the off-premises extension noted above, five other extensions of the standard fire policy are available, always within defined limits:

1. appurtenant structures, such as an unattached garage
2. rental value (that is, the amount for which the structure could have been rented)
3. improvements, alterations, and additions made by the insured to a structure owned by someone else when the insured is only a tenant
4. property removal (to cover the value of contents moved to a new residence of the insured)

5. debris removal (to pay for removal of debris resulting from damage or destruction of insured property)

Whether one needs any of this extended coverage depends, of course, on his own circumstances. Remember you should not try to insure everything against all risks. It simply cannot be done, but in the process of trying you may become *"insurance poor,"* with so much costly coverage against a variety of hazards that you and your dependents literally suffer a serious reduction in your standard of living.

22. CAN THE STANDARD FIRE INSURANCE POLICY BE MODIFIED TO COVER OTHER NON-FIRE PERILS?

By payment of an additional premium, the basic contract may be modified with what is called the *extended coverage endorsement.* The amount of the policy remains unchanged but these nine additional perils are insured against:

1. windstorm (as when a tree is blown over by wind and crashes into the roof of a dwelling)
2. hail (as when hailstones smash windows and the rain spoils draperies)
3. explosion (originating within or outside the insured dwelling). Specific language excludes damage caused by sonic booms of jet aircraft, but damage from detonation of explosives in an ammunition train or from the demolition of old buildings would be included.
4. riot (a tumultuous disturbance of the peace by three or more persons assembled and joined together in an unlawful act of a violent type "to the terror of the people")
5. riot attending a strike
6. civil commotion (political disorders involving an uprising of a large group of people short of rebellion or civil war, but with a disturbance of peace and order). During the Great Depression of the early 1930s, action of groups of unemployed persons constituted civil commotions, as did some anti-war demonstrations during America's active involvement in the Vietnam War.
7. aircraft damage (caused by the crash of a plane or falling of any object from a plane)
8. vehicle damage (caused by vehicles other than aircraft, and which run on land or tracks). Specifically excluded is damage caused by vehicles owned or operated by the insured or by a tenant of the property covered. Also excluded are damages to the vehicles and their contents, as well as to fences, driveways, walks, trees, lawns, and shrubs.
9. smoke damage (when caused by a *hostile fire*—a fire burning where it is not intended to be). A blazing conflagration in a fireplace is "friendly" and no basis for recovery, even though paint on adjoining

walls blisters and nearby potted plants wilt from the heat. But if tiny burning twigs pop out onto the rug, the satellite fire is "hostile" and the resulting damage is covered. Smoke damage would be covered if caused by a friendly fire, provided the smoke results from the "sudden, unusual and faulty operation of a heating or cooking unit" while connected to a chimney by a smoke pipe or vent pipe. It does not include smoke from other sources, such as fireplaces.

> Sheila Womack was a physical culture faddist. She slept with windows wide open regardless of season or weather. During one especially violent storm, rain, hail, and snow were blown into her bedroom as she slept. Later she awoke to find her valuable Tibetan rug irreparably damaged, and the wallpaper in need of replacement. Were her losses covered by the extended coverage endorsement?

No. The losses resulted from Womack's initial action in opening the window. The result would have been different had the storm broken the window.

The *dwelling and contents form* of the standard fire insurance policy embraces an array of additional perils. All are quite unusual, but they can involve considerable loss for the insured in the absence of such coverage.

1. Steam and hot water system explosion
2. Vandalism and malicious mischief
3. Damage caused by burglars
4. Falling objects
5. Weight of ice, snow, and sleet
6. Collapse of the dwelling place
7. Leakage or overflow of plumbing, heating, or air conditioning systems
8. Breakage of glass constituting part of the dwelling house
9. Freezing of the plumbing
10. Injury to electric appliances and wiring by artificially generated currents

23. IN CASE OF LOSS, HOW MUCH DOES THE INSURER PAY?

> Duncan bought a lot in a new subdivision for $8,000 and had a house built on the lot for $30,000, its cost value. Thus, his total initial investment was $38,000. He occupied the house for ten years of its expected life of fifty years, and so has used 20 percent of its total original value. Applying what accountants call a simple straight-line depreciation, the building now has a

depreciated value of $24,000 ($30,000–$6,000). The lot and house together have a *market value* of $70,000 because of increased realty prices in the neighborhood. Building codes and methods and materials of construction have changed over the past ten years and prices are up; to erect a new building of like kind and quality would cost $50,000. This is the *replacement value*. Finally, insurance companies calculate what they call the *actual cash value* by deducting depreciation (based on the replacement value) from the replacement value ($50,000–$10,000). How much fire insurance coverage should Duncan buy? What would the company pay in the event of a total loss?

The land on which the house is built cannot be insured because it remains even after destruction of the building. Duncan would not want to build and could not build a depreciated replacement of his present home. Insurance companies now sell policies that pay the cost of replacement with no deduction for depreciation. He should probably therefore buy coverage for $50,000.

Since inflation and other forces are sending prices up, it behooves property owners to review their coverage from time to time to be sure that they are adequately protected. Most homeowners are reluctant, however, to spend the required premium to obtain 100 percent coverage. Moreover, they know that most fires do not cause total loss. If a homeowners policy is purchased for at least 80 percent of the replacement value, the insurance company will pay the full replacement cost up to the policy limit; many companies now require 90 percent. If the insured fails to carry the required percentage, the company will pay either the actual cash value (replacement cost minus depreciation) or the ratio of the amount of the policy to the amount of insurance he should have carried, whichever is greater. To avoid unreasonable claims, the company generally reserves the right to make repairs or replacements itself. Table 9–2 shows the varying amounts Duncan might collect depending on the amount of coverage he purchased and the extent of his loss.

There may be a serious problem of proof of loss as to personal belongings. It is a good idea to prepare a room-by-room list of all belongings, indicating the date and place of purchase as well as the price at that time. Antiques and items of high value should be photographed; this record may also help the police in their search in case of theft. Such inventories should be kept in a secure place away from the house, perhaps at the office or in a safe-deposit box.

In reading your policy you will find strict limits of liability for certain items such as furs, jewelry, antiques, and hobby collections of stamps and coins. A type of insurance called an *inland marine personal property floater* would protect such special items at a level closer to their true value. However, you may find the premiums prohibitively expensive. Your

TABLE 9–2

Amounts That Could Be Collected
on a House with a Replacement Value of $50,000
(if various policies were held and fire losses suffered)

Loss in a Fire	$20,000 Policy	$40,000 Policy	$50,000 Policy
10% ($5,000)	$ 2,500*	$ 5,000	$ 5,000
50% ($25,000)	12,500*	25,000	25,000
80% ($40,000)	20,000	40,000	40,000
100% ($50,000)	20,000	40,000	50,000

* If the insurance adjuster determines that the actual cash value is higher, the higher amount would be paid.

alternative is to assume the risk, taking whatever precautions you can to provide security in your home, or to move small valuables (including securities, notes, and cash) to a safe-deposit box in a bank.

The insurance company will, of course, pay nothing for fire damage to your property if it is determined that you intentionally set the fire. You would be guilty of the serious crime of arson. If someone else commits the arson and you are an innocent victim, you would be indemnified for losses suffered. Likewise, if you caused the loss through negligence or carelessness, you would still collect from the insurer. After all, it is negligence that causes most hostile fires, and this is precisely the hazard from which you seek protection.

24. WHAT IS HOMEOWNERS INSURANCE?

Even with the extended coverage endorsement added to the standard fire insurance policy, you as insured remain vulnerable to certain significant perils. To enlarge the umbrella of protection for the individual, and to do so at a price below the cost of a series of individual policies with equivalent coverage, the combined homeowners policy was developed. It is generally available in five variations or forms (called forms 1 through 5). Figure 9–4 indicates the coverage of the three basic forms.

Standard form 1 includes eleven listed perils. Broad form 2 adds eight more perils, none of which is likely to happen to you but which could be financially embarrassing or maybe devastating if it did occur. The comprehensive form 5 is referred to as an "all risks policy," but this is a misnomer. Actually the standard and broad forms list or identify specific perils you are insured against; the comprehensive form covers all pertinent perils but lists those that you are not insured against.

In all forms, personal liability insurance is also included to cover the risk, for example, of someone being injured on your premises, because of your negligence, or of someone's property being damaged through your

Forms	Perils	
STANDARD FORM (1)	1. fire and lightning 2. loss or damage to property removed from premises endangered by fire 3. windstorm or hail 4. explosion 5. riot, riot attending a strike, civil commotion 6. aircraft	7. vehicles, if not owned or operated by the insured 8. sudden and accidental damage from smoke 9. vandalism and malicious mischief 10. theft 11. breakage of glass constituting a part of the building
BROAD FORM (2)	12. falling objects 13. weight of ice, snow, sleet 14. collapse of building(s) or any part thereof 15. sudden and accidental tearing asunder, cracking, burning, or bulging of a steam or hot water heating system 16. accidental discharge, leakage or overflow of water or steam from a plumbing, heating or air-conditioning system	17. sudden and accidental tearing asunder, cracking, burning or bulging of appliances for heating water for domestic consumption 18. freezing of plumbing, heating and air-conditioning systems and domestic appliances 19. sudden and accidental injury to electrical appliances, devices, fixtures and wiring (TV and radio tubes not included)
COMPREHENSIVE FORM (5)	All perils **EXCEPT**: earthquake, landslide, flood, surface water, waves, tidal water or tidal wave, the backing up of sewers, seepage, war, and nuclear radiation.	

SOURCE: "A Family Guide to Property and Liability Insurance," 3d ed. (Insurance Information Institute: New York, n.d.)

Fig. 9-4. Perils against which properties are insured in a homeowners policy

negligence. In most cases, the insured receives the protection of his policy by settlement of claims without a lawsuit. The insurer is not liable, however, if the insured intentionally injures another or damages his property. Thus, an arsonist may not collect on his homeowners or fire insurance policy. Indeed, if his crime is detected, he can and should be prosecuted.[8]

The insurer has an implied obligation to act in good faith and to settle claims appropriately. If the insurance company fails to do so, and the insured is later required by judgment of court to pay more than a pretrial settlement offer, the company may be required to make good the loss in what is termed *excess liability,* beyond the limits of its policy.[9]

> After Ezilda Howell experienced a serious fire in her home, she decided to "get away from it all" for a while. She joined some friends on a ninety-day world cruise. Upon returning, she submitted a detailed claim to her insurance company. Must the company pay?

No. Ezilda failed to comply with the customary conditions of (1) giving written notice to the insurance company without unnecessary delay, and (2) providing—within sixty days after the loss—written proof of all losses, signed and sworn to by the claimant, listing all items and their cash values, all claims of others to the property (if any exist), and other relevant information.

25. WHAT IS SOCIAL INSURANCE?

> Thadeus Bibb's philosophy of life was to "eat, drink and be merry, for tomorrow you may die." He lived in rented furnished quarters all his life, used leased autos, and deliberately spent all he earned. At age sixty-five he lost his job because his employer required retirement at that age. He ruefully reflected on the many yesterdays that once were the tomorrows when he did not die, contrary to his youthful expectations. And so now he has no savings. Must he rely on private charity or public welfare to survive?

Not necessarily, even assuming that he cannot find another job. Over the years, his employers deducted a portion of his wages, matched the sum, and paid the total to the federal government. In effect, he has been saving under a compulsory program to provide insurance against certain risks as defined in the *Social Security Act of 1935,* which provides benefits to those who qualify because of old age, or as dependent survivors of insured persons, or disabled persons, or as persons over sixty-five in need of health services. Payments are generally related to the contributions made over the years by employer and employee, which in turn depend on income earned (table 9–3).

TABLE 9-3

Examples of Monthly Social Security Payments (Effective June 1974)

Benefits can be paid to:	Average yearly earnings after 1950*						
	$923 or less	$3,000	$4,000	$5,000	$6,000	$8,000	$10,000
You, the worker							
Retired at 65	93.80	194.10	228.50	264.90	299.40	372.20	412.40
Under 65 and disabled	93.80	194.10	228.50	264.90	299.40	372.20	412.40
Retired at 62	75.10	155.30	182.80	212.00	239.60	297.80	330.00
Your wife							
at 65	46.90	97.10	114.30	132.50	149.70	186.10	206.20
at 62, with no child	35.20	72.90	85.80	99.40	112.30	139.60	154.70
Under 65 and one child in her care	47.00	102.70	162.00	224.00	249.90	279.20	309.40
Your widow							
at 65 (if worker never received reduced retirement benefits)	93.80	194.10	228.50	264.90	229.40	372.20	412.40
at 60 (if sole survivor)	74.90	138.80	163.40	189.50	214.10	266.20	294.90
at 50 and disabled (if sole survivor)	56.80	97.10	114.30	132.60	149.80	186.20	206.30
Widowed mother and one child in her care	140.80	291.20	342.80	397.40	449.20	558.40	618.60
Maximum family payment	140.80	296.80	390.50	488.90	549.30	651.40	721.80

* Generally, average earnings covered by social security are figured from 1951 until the worker reaches retirement age, becomes disabled, or dies. The maximum benefit for a retired worker in 1974 (June or later) is $304.90, based on average yearly earnings of $6,132. The higher benefits shown in the chart, based on average earnings shown in the columns on the right, generally will not be payable until later years.

SOURCE: DHEW Publication No. (SSA) 74-10324

Despite much controversy over this comprehensive program since its inception, few persons suggest abolishing it or deny that it is a massive social response to a felt social need. As Winston Churchill once said, such social insurance brings "the magic of averages to the rescue of millions." Currently, more than 25 million Americans receive social security benefit checks every month.

Thadeus Bibb, as a retired man of sixty-five, now joins their ranks. The amount he receives will not be enough to maintain his former standard of living, but it should protect him from abject poverty. Under some circumstances, he might qualify for additional payments from the federal and state governments under the Supplemental Security Income program begun in 1974 and administered by the Social Security Adminis-

TABLE 9-4

Contribution Rate Schedules for Social Security

Year	Retirement, Survivors, and Disability Insurance	Hospital Insurance	Total
Employer-Employee, each			
1972	4.60%	0.60%	5.20%
1973–77*	4.85	1.00	5.85
1978–80	4.80	1.25	6.05
1981–85	4.80	1.35	6.15
1986–92	4.80	1.45	6.25
1993–97	4.80	1.45	6.25
1998–2010	4.80	1.45	6.25
2011+	5.85	1.45	7.30
Self-employed			
1972	6.90%	0.60%	7.50%
1973–77	7.00	1.00	8.00
1978–80	7.00	1.25	8.25
1981–85	7.00	1.35	8.35
1986–92	7.00	1.45	8.45
1993–97	7.00	1.45	8.45
1998–2010	7.00	1.45	8.45
2011+	7.00	1.45	8.45

* Under the law, the base was $12,000 in 1974 with automatic adjustments thereafter as earnings levels rise.

SOURCE: DHEW Publication No. (SSA) 73-10328

tration. A single needy aged person, or blind or disabled person in that year could receive up to $235 a month, and married couples could get up to $440 in California, which pays more than most states.

Social security benefits are designed to serve as a minimum or floor of economic support, not a maximum or ceiling. The prudent person will supplement anticipated social security benefits with his own private savings and investment program. In many cases, private employers, voluntarily or under union-management contracts, provide their own private pension or retirement plans.

Most American workers are now covered by social security, and through them their dependents are also covered. The contributions or taxes are geared to earnings up to a specified maximum, as indicated in table 9-4. The only significant excluded groups are federal, state, and local government employees who are covered under separate retirement programs, a few persons who work irregularly or earn very little, and older railroad workers who are covered by a separate program.

RETIREMENT

DISABILITY

SURVIVORS BENEFITS

HEALTH INSURANCE

26. IS SOCIAL SECURITY A PUBLIC RELIEF OR WELFARE PLAN?

No. Benefits are paid only to persons who have contributed to the program, or to dependents of such persons. The wealth of the individual is not the criterion; a millionaire may qualify for the benefits, and no doubt he would relish them in a special way because they are exempt from income taxes. Nevertheless, social security differs from private insurance in that persons of greater need (for example, those with more dependents, or with very low income) are favored with benefits that are disproportionate to the amounts contributed over the years. Also, when the program began, some persons were included even though they had not paid in as much as younger workers were required to. Social security is, after all, a social insurance program.

In addition to social insurance (Old Age, Retirement, Survivors Benefits, Disability, Health Insurance), the Social Security Act of 1935, as amended over the years, includes a number of important measures for extending true welfare assistance to persons in need, whether or not they have paid social security taxes. These programs have been administered in cooperation with the states, and benefits have varied depending on local legislation and financial support. Broadly speaking, welfare assistance is extended to (1) aged persons in need (as when they do not qualify for social security or the benefits paid are too low for minimal maintenance), (2) dependent children, (3) blind persons, and (4) persons in need of maternal and child welfare care, or public health or vocational rehabilitation assistance.

Space limitations preclude a detailed discussion of the benefits available under social security. If interested or concerned, get appropriate descriptive literature from your nearest Social Security Administration office. Certain highlights merit mention, however:

1. You must request benefits in order to receive them. The social security officials will not seek you out.
2. As a retired worker, you qualify for reduced benefits at age sixty-two or full benefits at age sixty-five. Your wife (or husband, if he depended on his working wife for support) also gets a benefit payment at age sixty-two, or even earlier if there are dependent unmarried children in the family.
3. Normally, dependency of children ends at age eighteen, unless they are physically or mentally disabled before reaching this age and their disability continues. Normal dependency continues until age twenty-two for full-time students.
4. If you, as a covered worker, are so disabled mentally or physically that you cannot engage in any substantial gainful activity, you and your dependents may be entitled to benefits.
5. Widows (or widowers who were dependent on their working wives) and unmarried children, as noted in (3) above, may receive survivor's

benefits if the worker dies. Dependent parents of a deceased worker may also qualify for benefits. Children may be eligible for benefits based on a grandparent's earnings if the natural parents are disabled or dead, and if the grandchildren are living with and supported by the grandparent.

6. Medicare provides hospitalization benefits, including nursing home care and home visits, for all eligible persons over sixty-five under what is called the compulsory Part A coverage. Part B coverage is optional and requires modest monthly payments ($6.70 in 1974) by the insured in exchange for coverage of doctors' fees and a variety of other medical costs. Neither is all-inclusive, and so supplemental private health insurance is advisable.

27. WHAT IS THE EMPLOYEE RETIREMENT INCOME SECURITY ACT?

In 1974 Congress enacted the Employee Retirement Income Security Act, which probably ranks in importance with the Social Security Act. Previously, a worker could faithfully perform his duties for many years, then be fired, or take sick, or change jobs, and lose all accumulated pension rights. There was no *vesting,* under which he became entitled to a share of the pension fund before retirement. Also, the employer's business might fail, or the funds provided might prove inadequate, or the pension funds might be mismanaged or even embezzled, and again the worker could be stranded without benefits.

An estimated thirty million workers are covered by private pension plans. The new law does not require employers to offer private pensions, but if they do, their plans must comply with stringent new regulations designed to protect these workers.

1. All employees must be permitted to participate if they are twenty-five years old and have worked for the employer for one year.
2. The employer must provide one of three vesting schedules: (1) 100 percent vesting at the end of ten years; or (2) 25 percent vesting in five years, 5 percent for each of the next five years, and 10 percent for each of the next five years; or (3) 50 percent vesting after ten years of service, with 10 percent additional vesting for each year of service thereafter. As an alternative, when the sum of an employee's age and service (at least five years) equals forty-five, he must be 50 percent vested.
3. The employer must adequately finance his pension plans. If it is underfunded and a deficiency develops, a 5 percent excise tax is imposed.
4. Unless a later date is agreed upon by employer and employee, benefit payments must start by the later of (1) normal retirement date or age sixty-five, whichever is lower, (2) ten years of participation, or (3) termination of service.

To help assure payment of benefits even when individual plans fail financially, a government corporation called the Pension Benefit Guaranty Corporation operates under the authority of the Labor Department. Financed by employers, the initial premium charge is $1 a year for each covered employee.

Any employee not covered by a company plan may take a federal income tax deduction of up to 10 percent of income, to a maximum of $1500 a year, and establish his own Individual Retirement Plan under prescribed rules. Also a self-employed person may take a federal income tax deduction of up to 15 percent of earnings, to a maximum of $7500 a year, to establish his own pension plan.

28. WHAT IS WORKMEN'S COMPENSATION INSURANCE?

Most workers in the employ of others are covered by *workmen's compensation* insurance. A worker who is injured on the job, or who becomes ill because of some job-caused hazard (such as coal dust causing silicosis in the lungs of miners), is entitled to medical care and other prescribed benefits for his support. If he is killed on the job, his dependents are entitled to benefits. In neither case are the benefits munificent. In California, for example, the maximum weekly benefit to an injured worker is $119; for a permanent disability the maximum payment is only $70 a week. The benefit payment in case of death is a modest $40,000 to a widow without children, or $45,000 if she has one or more dependent children.

The benefits are payable without a court case to prove the employer liable. His liability is absolute—unless the worker was voluntarily drunk on the job, or the injury was self-inflicted, or the worker was the aggressor in a fight. If a third party (other than a fellow worker) caused the injury, the worker may sue such third party directly and there is no limit on how much he may recover in the action.

Workmen's compensation is separate from disability insurance under social security, and so benefits may be collected under both programs. Generally, combined social security disability benefits and workmen's compensation benefits may total no more than 80 percent of the worker's average current earnings before he became disabled. Some disabled workers may get higher payments because (since 1973) the average current earnings may be based on the worker's highest earnings for any one year in the period starting five years before he became disabled.

A worker who is dissatisfied with an award of compensation may appeal his case to reviewing authorities within the administrative agency that handles workmen's compensation claims. He is entitled to the assistance of legal counsel for such appeals. Fortunately, no income tax is payable on workmen's compensation benefits, just as no tax is payable on pensions for personal injuries or sickness resulting from active service in the armed forces of any country. Disability payments paid to a worker by his employer may also qualify as tax-free sick pay, subject to certain limitations.

In a few states (California, Hawaii, New Jersey, New York and Rhode Island), employers are required to provide for their workers *temporary disability* insurance for disabilities that are not job-related.

29. WHAT IS UNEMPLOYMENT INSURANCE?

All covered employers of one or more persons are required to pay a federal tax of 3.2 percent on the first $4,200 of each employee's income to provide insurance benefits in the event the worker is dismissed and cannot find other employment. The tax rate is reduced when the state has its own qualified unemployment insurance plan, as is generally the case. Benefits vary widely among the states, although most require that the insured be unemployed for one week before any benefits are paid.

Benefits are paid for a maximum of twenty-six weeks. The period may be extended for as long as thirteen additional weeks when unemployment reaches a certain level in the given state. Benefits are usually related to earnings; maximum weekly benefits (including allowances for dependents) range from about $40 to $115, but these figures have been edging upward under the pressures of inflation and the reduced value of the dollar.

CASES, QUESTIONS, AND PROBLEMS

1. Would an insurable interest exist in each of the following situations?
   a. COMSAT, the commercial space satellite corporation, insures against the risk of a component malfunction that would prevent the launching of a new space satellite on schedule.
   b. The American Broadcasting Company (ABC), which has made elaborate plans to televise the event, insures against the possibility of a delay in launching.
   c. Members in physics I at a university insure against the hazard of a delay in the launching of the satellite because they plan to view the television broadcast.
   d. You insure the life of your best friend, naming his wife as beneficiary of the policy.
   e. You insure the life of a stranger after lending him $500 with interest at the maximum rate permitted by law.

2. Eric Garay bought a $100,000 life insurance policy on his own life. Three months later he killed his business partner during a heated argument, was tried for first degree murder, and was sentenced to

die in the electric chair. Must his insurance company pay the $100,000 to his designated beneficiary after the execution?

3. A thief burglarized Maria Fraticelli's house and stole some jewelry, including one of a pair of valuable earrings, which cost $3,500 and had appreciated in value. May Fraticelli recover the full value for the pair or set under her homeowners policy?

4. In June, Casimer Komski sold his summer cabin to Elroy Nichols, explaining that the fire insurance was paid in full to the end of the year. Three months later a fire destroyed the cabin.
a. Is Nichols entitled to recover on the policy?
b. Is Komski entitled to do so?

5. Nick Topodias thought the roof of his house was made of fireproof asbestos shingles, treated to look like wood. He said they were asbestos in his application for fire insurance. In fact, they were smooth-finished light cedar wood shingles. Soon after getting the policy, flaming embers from a neighbor's house fire landed on the Topodias roof and caused extensive damage.
a. Does the Topodias policy cover the loss?
b. Does the neighbor's fire or homeowners policy cover the loss?
c. Is the neighbor liable for the loss?

6. The Oliver Chandler home has a replacement value of $40,000. They buy $16,000 in fire insurance coverage. A fire later causes $25,000 in damages. How much will his insurance company pay?

7. In a no-fault insurance state, the statute permits suit when the amount of damages claimed exceeds $5,000 and provided medical expenses exceed $500. J.B. Moody is injured in an auto accident with Lamar X. Lennon and suffers the loss of one eye and serious facial disfigurement. His hospital bill alone exceeds $10,000. He sues Lennon for $300,000, including claims for medical expenses, property damage, loss of income, and pain and suffering.
a. May he bring such action?
b. Is he entitled to recovery in part or full?

8. After borrowing Brady's car with his permission, Dunning had an accident because of carelessness in making a U-turn. The driver of the other vehicle was faultless and his heavy-duty truck suffered no damage, nor did he. But Brady's car needed $750 worth of body work. Both Dunning and Brady have collision insurance coverage, each with a $100 deductible provision. Under which policy, if any, is Brady paid for his loss?

9. Jackie Knight, twenty-two years old, was insured by Metropolitan Life Insurance Company under a group policy for accidental death.

Jackie was an experienced swimmer and diver, and had made dives from upwards of seventy-five feet. One morning he and several friends were atop the Coolidge Dam, 139 feet above the water. After saying "What's the matter? Don't you think I can make it?" he jumped up on the ledge and took off in a graceful swan dive. Something went wrong. One witness said he misjudged the distance and landed on his back, called for help several times, and drowned. Metropolitan refused to pay, claiming the death was the natural and probable consequence of his own voluntary and foolhardy act, and not an accident. Decide.

10. Wenckus bought a life insurance policy in which he named his wife the beneficiary, and his mother the contingent beneficiary. He had also six minor children but made no will for the distribution of his estate among them. Later his wife killed him and was found guilty of manslaughter. Who gets the proceeds of the policy—the widow, the estate of the decedent (in effect, his children), or the decedent's mother?

11. Mrs. June Di Mare fell, up to her waist, through a defective tread in the staircase of Mrs. Rosina Crisci's apartment house. In addition to minor physical injuries, Di Mare developed a severe psychosis as a result of hanging some fifteen feet off the ground. There was no evidence of prior mental illness. Although psychiatrists called to testify did not agree that the accident caused her mental condition, all stated that a psychosis could be triggered by a sudden fear of falling to one's death.

Crisci has $10,000 of general liability insurance coverage under a policy issued by Security Insurance Company. The policy required Security to defend the suit for $400,000 brought by Di Mare and her husband. Security rejected an offer by Di Mare's attorney to settle for $10,000; it offered only $3,000. Security also rejected an offer to settle for $9,000, of which Crisci agreed to pay $2,500. In the trial that followed, the jury awarded Mrs. Di Mare $100,000 and her husband $1,000. Security paid $10,000, the limit of its policy. Then Crisci paid an additional $22,000, plus a 40 percent interest in some property, and an assignment of the Crisci's cause of action against Security. Mrs. Crisci, an immigrant widow of seventy, became indigent, her health declined, and she attempted suicide. She then sued Security for $91,000 for excess liability, and for her mental suffering caused by Security's alleged mishandling of the defense in the initial lawsuit. Decide.

12. The Lebanon Cemetery Association of Queens, Inc. bought a group life insurance policy for its employees from the Phoenix Mutual Life

Insurance Company. The master policy contained a provision that eligible employees for insurance coverage were all full-time employees working at least thirty hours a week. Simpson was an assistant secretary who worked only a few days each month for Lebanon. Nevertheless, he signed up for coverage and Lebanon paid the premiums as they came due. After the incontestable period of two years had passed, Simpson was killed during a robbery in the elevator of his apartment house. His widow sued to collect the insurance because Phoenix rejected her claim, saying her husband was not an eligible employee. If employment is a *condition* in the policy, Phoenix is liable; if it is a *limitation* (whereby the insurer simply refuses from the beginning to assume the particular risk) Phoenix is not liable. Decide.

13. Kreuger has never seen a doctor. He claims that he is healthy and does not need health insurance. He plans to let the government take care of him and his family if any of them gets sick or suffers an accident. Is he acting wisely?

14. Winger, age seventeen, gets permission from his father (the named insured on a family automobile policy) to take the family car out on a date with Krupa, also seventeen, and uninsured. Krupa, who does not have a driver's license, persuades Winger to let her drive. She negligently rams into a line of parked cars, two of them occupied. Claims of $125,000 in damages for personal injuries and property damage are filed by the victims, against Winger and Krupa and also the parents of each. Who is liable?

15. Anderson argues that he is quite willing and able to provide for his own needs after retirement and therefore should not be required to contribute to Social Security. Moreover, he claims the plan is a fraud because much of the money received in social security contributions or taxes is invested in U.S. government bonds. The proceeds are promptly spent on other current government needs. Later, when the social security payments must be made, the public—including maybe Anderson—will have to be taxed to pay off the bonds. Do you agree? Explain.

10

YOU
AS
HOMEOWNER

1. WHEN SHOULD YOU OWN A HOME?

Ideally a family (or an individual) should own a home
when the advantages of home ownership are meaningful
for them. There are disadvantages to home ownership, and
the decision to buy rather than rent should be made with
the care befitting a decision of major financial and personal
as well as legal consequence.

Advantages of Home Ownership

Typically, a house offers more spacious living accommodations in a more pleasant location than does an apartment. Consider the garage, storage space, number of rooms,
outside living areas, and appliance space. Of course, in some
areas houses with these features may be available to rent.

If well selected and properly maintained, a home is more
likely to appreciate in value than to depreciate, because
of limited available land, population growth, and rising
construction costs. Interest payments on the money borrowed to purchase a home are deductible (as are property
taxes) for income tax purposes. Because a home is a variable
dollar investment, it is the best hedge against inflation
available to most persons.

Buying a home offers the advantage of selecting a neighborhood with compatible people, away from congestion, street noise, and commotion. Ownership of a home may contribute to one's sense of security, employability, and status. It generally provides a better environment for bringing up children.

Disadvantages of Home Ownership

People tend to demand considerably more in housing accommodations when they buy than when they rent. Consequently, they pay more, even though they no longer contribute to the profits of a landlord. Thus, home ownership often involves near exhaustion of liquid savings for a down payment and closing costs. The balance of the purchase price, being borrowed money, involves a long-term commitment to payment of interest and repayment of principal. Sometimes, furnishing the house may involve credit purchases at inordinately high carrying charges. Location of the home in suburban areas usually boosts the costs of commuting, including automobile insurance. For example, a no-car or one-car family renting an apartment in the inner city may need to become a two-car family when they buy a home on the outskirts of town.

In addition to large outlays of money when the home is acquired, the monthly expenses may prove burdensome. Insurance premiums, utilities, property taxes, yard work and maintenance expenses must be paid. Most of these expenses are included in the rent of the apartment dweller and therefore are more easily budgeted for.

Home ownership involves many intangible aspects, which may be disadvantageous depending upon the people involved. In this category, consider yard work, neighbor relationships, commuting time, boredom with neighborhood routine, house and garden maintenance, and need or desire for mobility—the ability to move on short notice.

2. HOW DO YOU FIND AVAILABLE HOMES?

Three general categories of homes may be available: resale home, new subdivision home, and new custom-built home.

Owners of homes that are available for resale usually hire a real estate broker to find a buyer. The employment contract between a homeowner who wants to sell his home, and a real estate broker who is hired to find a buyer, is called a *listing agreement*. A person interested in buying a resale home usually reads the real estate want ads in local newspapers, drives through likely neighborhoods seeking properties with "for sale" signs, and contacts one or more real estate brokers in the community. Their services are normally free to the buyer; the seller pays any commission earned. Most brokers exchange information on available resale homes through *multiple listings*. A would-be buyer can learn about many homes for sale in an area by calling a broker who belongs to a multiple listing agency.

Many developers of subdivisions advertise in local newspapers. Prospects who visit a subdivision are usually given appropriate written data and shown furnished model homes. Typically, the subdivision developer has a real estate broker or salesman available at the premises to answer questions and handle sales.

A person who wants to build a custom home has to do the preliminary work of locating an available lot and obtaining the services of an architect or designer, a building contractor, and a lending institution. This can be accomplished by reading the real estate sections of newspapers, discussing the situation with real estate brokers, and meeting building contractors whose homes seem to fit the prospective buyer's desires and budget.

Three other types of home ownership are growing in importance and are available in either new or resale markets: the cooperative apartment, the condominium, and the mobile home. In the *cooperative apartment,* typically a corporation is formed to acquire land and erect a multi-unit apartment. Interested persons buy sufficient shares in the corporation to obtain the right to live in one of the units and to use the common areas (such as stairs, elevators, and gardens). The corporation arranges for a single mortgage on the property and pays taxes and other costs, allocating them to the shareholders. Unfortunately, if one owner defaults, the others may be obliged to carry a larger burden at least until the defaulter's unit can be resold to another buyer.

In contrast, in a *condominium,* each owner receives title to his own unit, and arranges necessary financing for it. Only the areas used in common are owned in common, typically by a corporation whose stock is owned by the unit owners. The corporation finances and maintains the common areas, and the owners of units share the related costs. Sometimes unscrupulous developers, especially in Florida, retain ownership of desirable commonly used facilities such as swimming pools, and charge unreasonably high fees for their use. The prudent buyer will carefully study and understand the contract of purchase before he signs—if need be, in consultation with his own lawyer.

Finally, the *mobile home* is available at prices starting below $10,000 and sometimes exceeding $50,000. Owners usually set down these homes in mobile home parks, with no expectation of moving them. Because the homes are compact and relatively economical, and include much built-in furniture, they have a special appeal for budget-minded couples, both young and old. Financing is typically for shorter terms (under seven years) with larger down payments (as much as one-third of the purchase price) than with standard homes.

3. WHAT FACTORS INFLUENCE THE SELECTION OF A PARTICULAR HOUSE?

Within a price range permitted by the buyer's budget, the most important factor in selecting a particular house from those available is probably its location. *General location* influences commuting time to work and shopping areas; the school and church districts within which a home is located; whether it is in the path of deterioration or growth; public transportation patterns; and proximity to medical care facilities and to recreation. *Specific location* indicates whether the neighborhood is declining; whether surrounding homes are of comparable value; whether local traffic, noise, or commotion is excessive; whether airplanes fly low patterns overhead; whether it is a poor television reception area; whether neighbors are likely to be compatible socially and economically; and so forth.

Another significant criterion for evaluating a house is the configuration of the house itself. Does the lot drain well? Is it located on a corner? Where does the sun shine in the morning and afternoon? Is there sufficient privacy? How old is the house? What is the condition of the electrical system? Of the plumbing? When was the roof redone? Are the rooms adequate for storage, furniture, and appliances? A myriad of other common sense questions should be considered. If you lack the necessary expertise to ask and answer such questions, let someone who knows help you.

> Bill and Hortense Dimm purchased a home soon after their marriage. Within six months, they discovered that the roof leaked profusely during heavy rainfalls; airplanes made landing approaches directly over their house; fumes and dust from the contiguous freeways settled around them; the ground was not suitable for vegetable gardening, their favorite hobby; and the lot failed to drain properly, leaving several inches of standing water in pools around the perimeter during the rainy season. In a rage they made an appointment with an attorney to see about "undoing" the purchase and getting their down payment back. What is he likely to say?

The Dimms' attorney will advise them that stupidity is not an acceptable legal basis for rescinding, or undoing the purchase. Everyone is responsible for his own decisions, and the law does not always guard the foolish or rescue them from the consequences of their mistakes. The Dimms can sell their house to some other gullible, uninquiring buyer. Generally speaking, they are not legally obliged to volunteer information about its disadvantages, but while dealing with prospective purchasers they must be careful not to misrepresent the facts as known to them.

This could be fraudulent and the basis for rescission as well as for a claim for damages. Also, they must not actively conceal known defects, as by boarding over termite-damaged woodwork.

4. HOW CAN A LAWYER HELP A PERSON WHO IS BUYING A HOUSE?

> Ted and Sally McIntosh were in the market for a home costing around $35,000. In attempting to decide whether to build a custom home or to buy a new or resale home, they contacted their attorney for advice about financing. What would his advice likely be?

Their attorney would probably advise the McIntoshes that financing is not a legal question. The most knowledgeable persons concerning the availability of loans and their terms are real estate brokers. Additional information can be obtained from local banks, FHA offices, and savings and loan institutions. Their attorney might also suggest that, after financing was arranged, he could review the sale documents, including the loan papers, from a legal standpoint and explain to them their rights and obligations arising from the transaction. The fee for this service would probably not exceed $100.

5. HOW CAN A BUYER FINANCE THE PURCHASE OF A HOME?

Most buyers do not have the cash to pay the entire purchase price of a home. Even if they did they may prefer to make a relatively low down payment with their cash, borrow the balance of the purchase price, and invest the rest of their available savings elsewhere. They assume that with continuing inflation and its rising prices and climbing wages, it will become progressively easier to pay off the fixed amount of the loan as time goes by.

Several different types of loans are available from private lenders.

1. A *conventional* loan is one in which the terms are not directly influenced by government regulations or subsidies.
2. A *Federal Housing Administration* (FHA) loan is one in which the repayment is insured by the U.S. government and so the lender cannot lose its money.
3. A *Veteran's Administration* (VA) loan is also one in which repayment is guaranteed by the U.S. government.

The principal lenders of these loans are savings and loan associations, commercial banks, and insurance companies. The terms of loans change from time to time. Thus, if one type of loan is not available with the desired terms, application for a different type may be made. Generally, borrowers seek the highest loan ratio (lowest down payment), longest loan repayment period, lowest interest rate, and lowest loan charges.

A person who is a California resident and a veteran may qualify for a *California Veteran* (Cal-Vet) loan, which is a direct loan from a California state government agency. Although the interest rate fluctuates with the cost of borrowing by the state, it is far below the private market rate because the government's credit is much better. Oregon and Wisconsin offer their veterans a benefit in the form of a loan repayment guarantee, but not a direct loan.

Some of the factors a borrower should consider in determining which loan is best for him are the repayment terms, interest rate, qualification requirements, and amount of the loan.

Repayment Terms

The longer the time span during which the loan must be repaid, the lower the monthly payment. For example, the monthly payment to amortize a 9.5 percent loan of $40,000 over twenty years is $372.86. The same loan repaid over a thirty-year period requires a monthly payment of $336.35—$36.51 a month less. These "savings" are offset by the increased amount of interest that must be paid because of the longer term. For example, the purchaser of a $45,000 home who borrows $40,000 of the purchase price will pay $89,486.40 ($372.86 x 12 x 20) over twenty years, whereas the total cost would be $121,086 ($336.35 x 12 x 30) if the term of the $40,000 loan is thirty years. This $31,599.60 difference goes to pay interest because of the longer term of repayment.

Nevertheless, there are distinct advantages in taking a loan with a longer term.

1. The longer repayment term gives the young buyer extra cash while he is young and needs it most as his family grows.
2. The young buyer's income is probably rising, and so he may be wise to postpone payments until later when they are easier to make.
3. Continuing inflation at 5 to 10 percent a year will help pay off the loan later with cheaper dollars.
4. A buyer might otherwise have to rely on costlier installment credit (18 percent or more a year) to buy needed goods and services if his extra cash goes into larger payments on his home.

Which type of loan allows the longest repayment term? Of the conventional loan sources, savings and loan associations and commercial banks can make a loan up to thirty years; insurance companies normally allow a maximum of twenty-five years; FHA and VA loans can be made for up to thirty years.

Interest Rate

Interest is the price of borrowing money. The higher the interest rate, the higher the monthly payment (which includes the principal and interest). For example, a real estate loan of $40,000 over twenty-five years at 9.5 percent interest requires a monthly payment of $349.48. If the interest is reduced to 7 percent, the monthly payment decreases to $282.72, a savings of $66.76 a month. Thus, the total payments are $104,844 ($349.48 x 12 x 25) for the 9.5 percent loan and only $84,816 ($282.72 x 12 x 25) for the 7 percent loan, a savings of $20,028. The person who cannot earn more than 9.5 percent on his savings elsewhere would probably be well advised to pay off such a home loan as fast as possible. Otherwise, if interest rates on real estate loans decline, he could refinance by getting a new loan at a lower rate and paying off the old. All costs should be carefully calculated before making such a change.

Interest rates vary from time to time. Those on FHA and VA loans are regulated by the federal government and tend to be among the lowest available. Interest rate should not be confused with loan charges, or *points,* which are "one shot" charges made by the lender at the time the loan is originated. A point is a percentage point. Thus, one and one-half points on a $40,000 loan is $600. It is designed to bring the effective or true cost of the loan into line with prevailing interest rates, and generally the seller pays the points to the lender in order to make the sale. When the seller can do so, he will boost the sales price of the house to cover this cost.

Qualification Requirements

To obtain a loan, a borrower must "qualify." The lender sets the qualifications, which may include a minimum monthly income on the part of the borrower. For example, a buyer has a good chance of qualifying for an FHA loan if his monthly income, less monthly loan payments, is 4.5 times the monthly installment required to service the loan. (The FHA may include a wife's income in the computation.) Thus, if the monthly loan payment is $250, the borrower's monthly income should be $1,375.

Amount of Loan

The greater the amount of money that can be borrowed to purchase a home, the lower the down payment that is required. Lenders will loan up to a certain percentage of the *appraised value* of the home. Conventional lenders can lend up to 90 percent of the appraised value. Thus, in order to purchase a home appraised at and selling for $30,000, a loan of $27,000 can be made, requiring a $3,000 down payment. FHA loans may equal 97 percent of the first $15,000 of appraised value, 90 percent on the next $10,000, and 80 percent on the remaining balance up to $33,000.

Promissory Note

The document that evidences the loan is called a *promissory note* (fig. 10–1). It is signed by the borrower, called the *maker*. (See chapter 11 for further information about notes.)

Collateral

The lender will not trust the borrower whose signature appears on the promissory note as the sole source for repayment of the loan. Usually too much money is involved. The lender will want *collateral,* or security, so that if the borrower *defaults* (fails to make the proper monthly payments in repayment of the loan), the lender may confiscate the security, sell it, and apply the proceeds of the sale to pay off the balance of the loan. This procedure is called *foreclosure.*

The customary collateral is the home that is being purchased by the borrower. The document that puts the home up as collateral is called

PROMISSORY NOTE

$_____ _____19__

I,_____(BORROWER)_____ PROMISE TO PAY TO_____

_____(LENDER)_____, OR ORDER, AT LINCOLN, NEBRASKA, THE

SUM OF $_____WITH INTEREST ON THE UNPAID BALANCE

AT_____%, IN MONTHLY INSTALLMENTS OF $_____

INCLUDING INTEREST COMMENCING ON THE_____DAY OF

_____19_____AND CONTINUING UNTIL PAID IN FULL.

_____
(Signed by BORROWER)

Fig. 10-1.   Example of a promissory note as used in mortgages

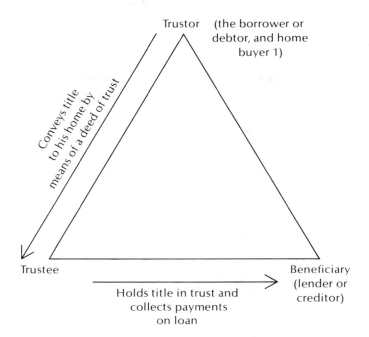

Trustor (the borrower or debtor, and home buyer 1)

Conveys title to his home by means of a deed of trust

Trustee

Holds title in trust and collects payments on loan

Beneficiary (lender or creditor)

Fig. 10-2. Relation among parties when a deed of trust is made

a *real mortgage.* The borrower or debtor is called the *mortgagor;* the lender or creditor is called the *mortgagee.* Very similar, but more common in California, is the *deed of trust* (fig. 10-2). It is signed by the borrower, who is called the *trustor.* The lender is called the *beneficiary.* The *trustee* (usually a title insurance company) holds title to the property solely for the purpose of either returning it to the borrower when the loan is paid off, or—in the event the borrower defaults—transferring the title to another purchaser so that the proceeds can be given to the lender.

6. HOW DOES A SELLER'S EQUITY IN A HOUSE AFFECT ITS SALE?

Equity is the excess of the market value of a property over loans outstanding against it. Frequently, the seller of a home will have only a small equity in his property. In such a situation, the purchaser may not need to borrow; rather he may *assume the loan of the seller.*

> Elbert Filbrick wanted to sell his home for $20,000. He owed $18,000 against it as represented by a promissory note payable to the bank in monthly installments of $141.37, including interest at 7 percent. The note was secured by a deed of trust on the home. Dorothy Evans wanted to buy the house by paying Elbert $2,000 for his equity and assuming his loan for the balance. Elbert contacted his attorney to find out what would happen to him if he sold his home in this manner and, if at some future time,

Dorothy failed to make her monthly payment. What would his attorney advise him?

Elbert's attorney would advise him that when Dorothy assumed the bank loan, she would become a debtor of the bank. The bank could either accept her as the sole debtor, and release Elbert from the loan, or keep both Elbert and Dorothy as debtors. In either case, if the bank is not paid each month on time, the trustee can sell the house at public auction and give the proceeds of the sale to the bank in satisfaction of the debt. This may not bother Elbert since he already received $2,000 for his equity; however, his credit rating could be affected negatively. In addition, if the loan was federally insured, and the sales price was less than the balance due, Elbert could be made to pay the bank any deficiency or unpaid balance on the loan remaining after the public auction.

In California and some other states, where the mortgage or trust deed was created as part of the original purchase (that is, a *purchase money mortgage* or *purchase money trust deed*), there can be no deficiency judgment. This law dates back to the Great Depression of 1929–1939 when many people lost their homes and substantial equities through foreclosures, and still would owe the lenders money.

7. HOW CAN A SELLER FINANCE PURCHASE OF THE HOME FOR THE BUYER?

The seller of a home that is "free and clear" of any loans may himself finance, or "carry," the buyer. In this situation, the buyer makes a down payment and signs a promissory note in favor of the seller. The seller, like a bank, will not be content with the mere promise of the buyer to pay the unpaid balance in monthly payments over a period of years: he will want the home put up as collateral and will, therefore, require the buyer to execute a deed of trust (or mortgage) in his favor. If the buyer fails to make payments when due, the trustee will sell the property (issuing a trustee's deed to the purchaser) and give the cash proceeds to the seller in satisfaction of the buyer's debt.

As an alternative method of financing the buyer, the seller may enter into a *land contract* with the buyer that will not require the seller to convey title to the buyer until after the property is paid for in full. This method is commonly used when a buyer cannot qualify for a loan and has no money for a down payment. In these circumstances, the buyer simply makes monthly payments to the seller for, say, thirty years. During this time, he is in possession of the property much as a rental tenant. After receiving the last payment, the seller conveys title to the buyer by *grant deed*.

From the buyer's standpoint, this is normally not a good method of purchasing a home, but he may not be able to arrange any other financing.

If he fails to make a monthly payment, he may be evicted and have nothing to show for his payments. However, if he has paid regularly for so long that it would be unfair to give him nothing, a court of equity may require the seller to recognize that the buyer has acquired some reasonable amount of equity in the property.

> J. Bartholomew owned a home free and clear, which he felt was worth $100,000. He ran an ad in the newspaper offering to sell for $125,000. Joe Slick wrote a letter in response to the ad offering to purchase the home for $125,000 with $1,000 down, the balance payable to Mr. Bartholomew over ten years at 10 percent interest. This would call for monthly payments of $1,639.28. Mr. Bartholomew was delighted; the deal was closed; Mr. Slick moved in on January 1, 1975, having paid $1,000 down. Joe immediately leased the premises to the Devil's Angels for a year for $4,000 cash in advance. Mr. Bartholomew contacted his attorney immediately to evict the Angels and to sue Joe. What advice will he likely receive?

Mr. Bartholomew's attorney would probably point out that Mr. Slick is the owner of the house and may rent it to whomever he chooses. If Joe fails to make the February 1 payment of $1,639.28, the only remedy Mr. Bartholomew has is to commence foreclosure. It would be possible, but legally very difficult, to evict the Angels immediately upon commencing foreclosure. Most likely they could not be evicted until the trustee sold the property. The Angels would have to look for Mr. Slick to obtain a refund of their rent.

Foreclosure could occur 120 days after recordation of the notice of default. If the house was misused during the 120 days, the loss could be Mr. Bartholomew's since his basic remedy is to apply the collateral, his former home, to Joe Slick's loan in full payment thereof. The buyer or anyone in possession with his permission may not impair the security by commiting *waste* (damaging the property through unreasonable use). Both the buyer and the tenants would be liable to the seller under such circumstances, but recovery could be difficult to obtain.

His attorney would very likely tell Mr. Bartholomew that all of this could have been prevented if he, as seller, had insisted either on a down payment sufficiently large to dissuade the buyer from walking away from the purchase, or on all cash, forcing the buyer to borrow the balance from a lending institution.

8. HOW IS AN OFFER TO PURCHASE A HOME MADE?

An offer to purchase real property, such as a home, must be made in writing, signed by both husband and wife in the case of community property. It must state essential terms, such as a description of the property, the purchase price, and financing terms. The offer is usually made on a document called a *deposit receipt* or an *agreement of sale and deposit receipt*. Normally, the real estate broker who has been hired by the sellers of the property to represent them assists the prospective buyer in completing the offer to purchase. Once it has been "accepted" by the seller (when he signs), a contract is created that is legally binding on both parties. Typically, if the buyer fails to complete the purchase after the agreement of purchase is made, the seller may retain the deposit made with the offer, as liquidated damages for the breach of contract. There is no legal requirement that a buyer include a deposit with his offer, but it is a sign of serious intent and ability to buy, and a seller would be most unlikely to accept an offer without one.

> Pete Bochamp made an offer to purchase Greenacre from Archibald Charter, who accepted in writing, complete with signature. Thereafter, Charter refused to complete the sale. Pete believed that Charter did this because he found out the property was worth more money. Pete contacted his attorney. What advice will he receive?

Pete's attorney will advise him that he has two remedies. He can sue in a proceeding in equity and request the court to order Charter to comply with the agreement, because every parcel of land is unique and one of a kind. This remedy is called *specific performance* and is available when dollar damages would be inadequate. In the alternative, Pete can sue at law and request the court to assess damages against Charter in an amount equal to his out-of-pocket expenses plus the *benefit of his bargain,* if any. This could be the difference between the price of Greenacre and of some comparable property.

In addition, and as a separate matter, if Charter had "listed" his property with a real estate broker, he would be obligated to pay the broker his commission, even though he failed to consummate the sale. This is so because the broker had found in Pete a "ready, willing, and able buyer" who had signed a written offer to buy on terms originally specified by the seller.

9. WHAT IS TITLE INSURANCE?

Standard title insurance is a policy of insurance whereby the owner of real property may insure against loss, up to the specified face amount of the policy, arising from a defect in the title to his property, as evident in the public records.

> Percy Fairchild bought Pancake Flat Ranch for $50,000 to grow rice. In connection with the purchase he acquired a standard

policy of title insurance. Thereafter, he began leveling the land and constructing ditches to provide for flooding as required in rice cultivation. He was served with a summons and complaint in which his neighbor, George Simplon, was plaintiff. George alleged that he has an easement across the middle of Pancake Flat for access of his cattle to his property, Sunnyview Estates. He requested the court to enjoin the land leveling, ditching, and future flooding and rice growing to protect his easement. Percy visited his lawyer for the purpose of suing the title insurance company for the apparent defect in his title. Will he win?

Percy will probably lose his case with George and will certainly lose his case against the title company. Among defects not covered by title insurance are *easements*—rights to use the land of another—that are not recorded. Many easements do not appear in the public records.

Title companies guarantee a property owner that they have accurately searched the public records. At the time the policy is issued, the owner is given a list of recorded documents. The accuracy of this list is guaranteed in a policy of title insurance. Loss arising from something in the public records that was not found by the title insurance company and therefore not placed on the list is insured. In addition, standard coverage title insurance covers some losses that may arise from matters not ascertainable from the official records—such as forgery, lack of capacity, or lack of delivery. Many lenders require extended coverage insurance against loss from any defect.

10. WHAT IS ESCROW?

In order to consummate the purchase of a house, many things need to be done simultaneously. At the moment title passes to the buyer, the buyer wants to be sure he has title insurance and fire insurance, the seller wants his money, the lender wants the promissory note and mortgage or deed of trust, the real estate broker wants his commission, and so forth. Since it would be impracticable for all these persons to meet and hand some things out with the left hand while simultaneously taking other things in with the right, the practice of hiring a third party, called *escrow*, developed.

Title companies and banks act as escrow agents. The escrow collects the required monies and documents from all the interested persons as necessary, and then, at the *close of escrow*, disburses and distributes them to the appropriate persons. Each party interested in a transaction "instructs" the escrow in writing as to what he will put into escrow and what he expects out of it upon its close. So long as the escrow complies with all of these instructions, it will not be liable for any losses suffered by any of the parties.

Closing Costs

> Carol Biller was buying Henry Foster's home for $30,000. She had arranged financing of $27,000 from an insurance company and anticipated putting down $3,000. Will she be required to pay more than $3,000 into escrow?

Yes. The seller will likely have prepaid real property taxes and fire insurance. He is entitled to be reimbursed so that he will have paid for these items only to the date of the sale. In addition, she will probably pay the cost of termite inspection, title insurance, and certain notary fees. All of these costs make up what are commonly called *closing costs*.

It is generally the responsibility of the seller, however, to pay for any corrective work that is revealed to be necessary because of damage by termites or dry rot. If Carol wants to have some preventive work done to avoid a recurrence of the problem, she would have to pay the bill.

The Legal Significance of Close of Escrow

Prior to close of escrow, the buyer has promised to buy, the seller has promised to sell, the lender has promised to lend, the broker has been promised his commission, and so forth. All of the promises are executory, still to be performed. At the close of escrow the buyer has received title to the home and is its owner; the seller has sold and no longer owns any interest in the property; the lender has made his loan, which the buyer has promised to repay; the seller has received his money, as has the broker. Most of the promises have been executed or performed. The buyer, as borrower, must of course continue to make payments as promised.

11. HOW IS A HOME TAXED?

A home may be located within the boundaries of both a county and a city as well as within various districts—school, college, flood control, mosquito abatement, air pollution control, park, water, sewer, and so forth. All of these units of government need money to perform their services. Each year these needs are expressed in a budget, which reflects the total money local government must obtain from its residents in order to function.

Taxation of property, including homes, is the principal method by which local government obtains these funds. All properties are taxed in proportion to their value, whether they are residential, commercial, industrial, or whatever. The county assessor appraises each property at its fair market value (called *full cash value*) and divides this value by four (in California) in order to arrive at its *assessed* value. (These values are listed on the *assessment roll*.) The entire budget is then divided by the total assessed value of all property to arrive at the *tax rate:* the percentage that must be applied to the value of each parcel of property in the county to determine how much its share of the entire budget should be.

In this way property owners are taxed in proportion to the value of the property they own. A property worth 30 percent more than another property will be liable for 30 percent more in taxes, if both are within the same districts. Also, a home worth $75,000 will be liable for exactly the same amount of tax as a service station worth $75,000, if both are within the same districts.

If government expenditures (budgets) increase, taxes increase. If government expenditures are constant, total tax revenues are constant regardless of whether assessed values increase or decrease. Of course, an individual's property may be reappraised and if his assessed value goes up, his specific tax bill will rise. Conversely, a person whose property goes down in assessed value will pay a lower tax. Increases or decreases in assessed values or tax rates have nothing to do with increased total taxes, which can occur only when government expenditures increase.

Property taxes are paid twice a year, in December and April. Some lenders require a borrower to pay taxes monthly to the lender, who in turn remits them to the tax collector twice a year. The lender is thus assured that the homeowner has set aside enough money to pay the taxes when due.

> Frank McBece owned a home with fair market value of $20,000. Its assessed value is $5,000. The combined tax rate is $13 for each $100 of assessed value. How much must Frank pay in property tax?

Frank must pay a total of $650 ($5,000 ÷ 100 × $13).

12. WHAT IF THE SELLER LIED ABOUT THE HOUSE?

> C. J. Thomas and his wife, Joan, decided to sell their home. Each Sunday they had an open house when their real estate broker arranged to have prospective purchasers inspect the home. One such person, Art Shab, asked C. J. whether the neighbors ever made unusually loud noises or otherwise caused problems, and whether the home was insulated. C. J. answered that the neighbors "were beautiful" and "Yes, the building was well insulated." In truth, and as known to C. J., the neighbors were extremely boisterous and noisy, often screaming profanities in the early hours, and their children were known to break windows, empty garbage cans over neighbor's fences, and race motorcycles up and

down the street. Likewise, as known by C. J., the house was not insulated. Art purchased the home and shortly thereafter learned about the neighbors and the insulation. He contacted his attorney seeking to undo the purchase. Will he succeed?

Yes. Art will succeed if the seller (1) made a representation (2) of a material fact, (3) knowing the statement to be false, (4) which asserted fact was reasonably relied upon by the buyer, and (5) thereby induced the buyer to consummate the purchase. The falsehood concerning the "beautiful" neighbors is irrelevant because it is only personal opinion. What is admirable to some is anathema to others. However, the presence or absence of insulation is a question of fact. If the lack of insulation was obvious to an ordinary layman, Art would again be out of luck. But since it is not readily ascertainable, Art may obtain either of two remedies. If it would cost $1,000 to cure the defect, he may recover that sum as compensatory damages. He could also seek, and might receive, an additional sum as exemplary or punitive damages because of the intentional deception or fraud by C. J. Alternatively, he may rescind the purchase, giving the house back to C. J. and receiving his down payment and other monies expended in the purchase.

Here are some examples of statements of personal opinion—often exaggerated—that a seller may make, without fear of a rescission.

"This house is really worth much more."

"This is the finest home in the area."

"This is the best constructed home you will ever live in."

"Taxes will never go up in this neighborhood."

"The value of this house will increase 5 percent a year."

If false, statements such as the following may justify a rescission or action for damages.

"A new roof was installed on this house two years ago."

"All excess surface water drains off during the rainy season."

"There are no termites."

"The septic tank was emptied last month."

As a general proposition, the seller has no obligation to say anything. After all, no one knows everything, and the law cannot specify in meaningful detail what should be known by the seller and disclosed by him. The buyer, moreover, is free to investigate and to inquire—and then answers of the seller must be truthful, to the best of his knowledge.

However, if the seller knows that the house began sliding toward a cliff as the result of a recent earth tremor, he would probably have a duty to reveal that fact to a prospective purchaser who had no reason to suspect the presence of such a serious problem. He would have a similar affirmative duty of disclosure as a matter of elemental honesty if he knows of a serious termite infestation that is not evident to the ordinary reasonable prospective buyer. Also, if he speaks, he must tell the whole truth. In describing a lot intended for building construction, he may not say that one section is filled ground and fail to mention others with similar soil.

13. WHAT HAPPENS IF A HOMEOWNER FAILS TO MAKE THE AGREED UPON MONTHLY LOAN PAYMENT?

Upon default by the buyer, the beneficiary of the deed of trust (the lender) may simply do nothing for a while, giving the homeowner extra time to pay, or he may start proceedings to sell the property. The trustee, at the request of the beneficiary, begins the sale arrangements when he records a notice of default with the county recorder. At any time within the following ninety days, the homeowner (trustor) may *reinstate* his loan by paying up all delinquent monthly payments and, in addition, by paying the trustee's fees and costs. After ninety days from the date of recordation of the notice of default, the borrower can retain his property only by paying off the entire unpaid balance of the loan. If the borrower does this, the trustee will give the borrower a *deed of reconveyance,* in effect canceling the deed of trust.

If the borrower does not reinstate the loan within the ninety days or pay off the entire unpaid balance, the trustee will conduct a public sale, usually about thirty days after the end of the reinstatement period, and sell the property to the highest cash bidder. In order to convey ownership to the successful bidder, the trustee will issue a *trustee's deed.* The steps involved in this transfer of money and property are shown in figure 10–3.

In states where real mortgages are involved instead of trust deeds, only two parties are involved in the transaction: the mortgagor (borrower or debtor) and the mortgagee (lender or creditor). A promissory note for the amount of the loan is signed by the mortgagor, and it is secured by a mortgage which constitutes a lien or claim against the real property. If the loan is defaulted, the mortgage is enforced by judicial foreclosure, which also involves a public auction of the property under court approval. However, the mortgagor typically has a full year after the foreclosure sale during which to redeem his property by paying the balance due on his debt plus added costs and fees. No such right of redemption exists after a sale under a trust deed. Obviously the trust deed arrangement is more attractive to the lender.

If the homeowner has not vacated the premises by the date of sale, the new owner can bring an unlawful detainer action to evict the former owner. The trustee will take the proceeds of the sale and deliver them to the beneficiary in satisfaction of the unpaid balance of the original loan. Any surplus is given to the borrower (trustor).

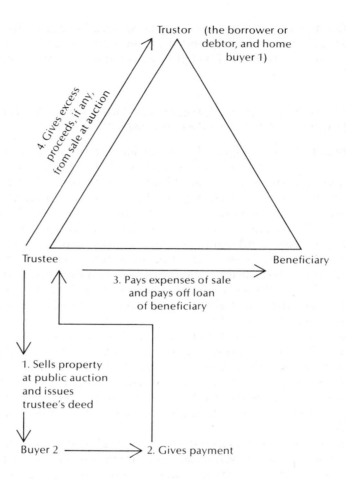

Trustor (the borrower or debtor, and home buyer 1)

4. Gives excess proceeds, if any, from sale at auction

Trustee

Beneficiary

3. Pays expenses of sale and pays off loan of beneficiary

1. Sells property at public auction and issues trustee's deed

Buyer 2 ⟶ 2. Gives payment

Fig. 10-3.
Steps taken after default in a deed of trust

Ed and Mary Marchant married soon after college. Anticipating a large family, they bought a four-bedroom, two-bath tract home for $32,500. They both worked and, because of their combined incomes, had little difficulty meeting their budgeted monthly obligations: payments on the promissory note (real mortgage or deed of trust), $215; property taxes, $35; furniture, $80; auto, $150; yard equipment, $20; yard maintenance, $20; telephone, $35; other utilities, $50; life insurance, $30; food, $150; clothes, $40; income taxes, $500; and recreation, $20. Mary's mother loaned the Marchants the down payment for an unspecified period of time. When Mary became pregnant and therefore quit working, Ed's income alone was not sufficient to meet all expenses and "keep the ship afloat." They contacted an attorney and inquired about letting the house go back to the seller or lender and getting a refund of their down payment. What would their attorney advise them?

Their attorney would advise them that the home purchase cannot be undone or rescinded because of their financial miscalculation. If they "let the house go back," they will lose their down payment and may suffer considerable intangible loss of credit standing. They can attempt to salvage something by selling the house; but the law affords no relief for unrealized financial expectations, whether they arise from pregnancy, job loss, disability, the draft, or some other cause. On resale, a commission of perhaps 6 percent to a real estate broker could be nearly $2,000, and this would consume the original down payment.

Prospective buyers should anticipate such difficulties before agreeing to buy. The Marchants should have lowered their sights and purchased a less costly property that Ed's income alone could sustain. Or they should have remained in rented quarters until their savings and his income increased substantially.

14. HOW DOES A HOMEOWNER RESELL?

The owner of a home that is for sale usually lists the property with a real estate broker.

> Rupert and Eunice Wallace purchased their home in 1965 for $30,000 and have put about $5,000 into improvements, including a swimming pool. Theirs is the most attractive home in the neighborhood, and they want to sell for $38,500, even though no other nearby home has sold for more than $31,500. The unpaid balance on their loan from Acme Savings and Loan Association is $26,000. Although one of Rupert's business associates, Archie Manning, has expressed an interest in purchasing the home, the Wallaces decide to secure the services of a licensed real estate broker, Sam Saltzman.
>
> On January 15, 1975, Sam has the Wallaces sign a customary six-month listing agreement, which provides for a price of $38,500 and a commission to Sam of 6 percent of the sales price. On March 15, Archie Manning offered to buy the Wallace home for $35,000, which they accepted because there had been no buyer interest at any price above $30,000. Rupert telephoned Sam to cancel the listing, because they had found a buyer themselves at the price of $35,000. Sam replied, "Fine, you may mail me a check for the $2,100 you owe." Does Rupert owe a commission equal to 6 percent of $35,000 even though Sam did not find the buyer and the listing called for a 6 percent commission on $38,500?

The Wallaces owe the commission unless the listing specifically authorized them, as owners, to sell without paying a commission. Such a listing is called an *exclusive agency listing.* Most listings are *exclusive listings,* which require payment of a commission regardless of who sells the home, including the owner. A real estate broker is the agent of the property owner. The employment contract is simply referred to as a listing. The employment agreement may contain whatever terms the owner and broker agree upon, such as whether or not the owner may sell the property himself without payment of a commission. The basic promises made by the property owner in a listing, or employment contract, are (1) to authorize the broker to solicit purchasers by advertising, multiple listing, posting signs, and so forth, and (2) to pay a specified commission if the broker finds a purchaser who is ready, willing, and able to purchase at the listed price. The basic promise made by the broker in the listing is to use his best efforts and diligence in finding a purchaser.

If the broker finds a purchaser willing to buy at a price lower than the listed price and the owner accepts the offer, he may not then refuse to pay a commission because the broker failed to find a buyer ready, willing, and able to buy at the listed price. Acceptance of the lower price effectively amends the listing, or employment contract, to provide for a commission based on the actual sales price. Therefore, the commission that the Wallaces would owe Sam would be based on $35,000 rather than on $38,500.

15. WHAT IS A LEASE?

A *lease* is a document that transfers the exclusive possession of property from the owner, called a landlord, to a tenant for a fixed period of time, commonly one year. *Rent* is the price paid by the tenant for the possession during the term.

> Marie Jones and Diane Dressler desired to share the rent of an apartment during the fall semester at California State University, Sacramento. They signed an agreement to pay a total of $130 on the first day of each month, and to give thirty days' notice of any intention to vacate. They paid one full month's rent in advance. Did Marie and Diane sign a lease?

No. A lease calls for a fixed period of time for a total sum of money, which may be paid in monthly installments. An agreement to rent on a monthly basis is simply a *rental agreement.* The basic difference is that in a lease, obligations extend for the duration of the lease period, whereas in a month-to-month rental all obligations of the parties may terminate in thirty days at the decision of either the landlord or the tenant. If the rental agreement so provides, a month-to-month rental may be terminated on as little as seven days' notice, or three days' notice if the tenant is in default as by failing to pay rent when due under California law.

16. WHAT ARE THE LEGAL OBLIGATIONS OF A LANDLORD AND TENANT?

A tenant, whether of a house or an apartment, is obligated to do whatever he agreed to do in the lease. Typical obligations of a tenant are (1) to pay rent, (2) to take reasonable care of the premises, and (3) to use the premises in a reasonable manner—all for the entire term of the lease or while he is in possession. The basic obligation of a landlord is to provide facilities fit for human habitation for the term of the lease or tenancy. These obligations are stated in general terms by the law, but should be specified as precisely as possible in the lease to avoid misunderstandings and possible litigation.

> Tyson Wadd leased apartment 8A for the period of January 15 to September 15, 1975, for the total rent of $1,200 payable at the rate of $150 on the 15th of January and each month thereafter except that the August 15 payment was made in advance.
> Ty failed to make his June 15 payment and informed his landlord that he would "use up the last month's rent" and vacate on July 14. Is this legal?

No. Prepaid rent belongs to the landlord upon abandonment of the lease. Ty is therefore in default in his rent on June 15 although he has already paid for the month August 15 to September 15. Since Ty is in default, the landlord may evict his tenant by bringing an action in unlawful detainer. If Ty simply leaves the premises on June 15, no eviction is necessary; however, if Ty stays on, an *unlawful detainer action* will be in order. The landlord would institute unlawful detainer by giving Ty a notice either to pay the due rent within three days or to give up possession. After the three days, a summons and complaint for unlawful detainer may be served and, in due course, Ty could be removed from possession by the sheriff pursuant to court order. The landlord thus may be entitled to the prepaid rent, damages for loss of rental income (if greater than the prepaid rent), and attorney fees (if provided for in the lease). In addition, in California, the court may award the landlord treble damages. The landlord would have substantially the same remedies if the basis for evicting Ty were other than nonpayment of rent, such as causing waste of the premises, continually having loud and boisterous parties, or otherwise breaching some important term in the lease contract.

> Upon receiving a notice to pay rent within three days or give up possession, Ty consulted his attorney. He complained that the landlord had failed to repair the dishwasher and also that the heating was inadequate. What remedy does Ty have for these problems?

Ty could pay the rent due June 15, thereby automatically terminating the unlawful detainer remedy of the landlord. Then he could pursue his remedies as tenant for the failure of his landlord to repair. The law generally provides that if a landlord fails to maintain proper weather protection, plumbing, hot water, heating, lighting, garbage disposal facilities, and safe floors and stairs, he has allowed the premises to become untenantable. The tenant's remedy is to complain and then wait a reasonable time. If the conditions are not corrected, the tenant in California may then spend up to one month's rent in making repairs and deduct that sum from his monthly rent. Ty could probably not assert this "repair and deduct" remedy against his landlord in the unlawful detainer action because he has neither given notice orally or in writing nor waited a reasonable time.

Misunderstandings frequently arise concerning refund of cleaning deposits paid in advance by tenants. The landlord must refund any portion of the cleaning deposit not actually used to clean the premises so that they are comparable to their condition at the beginning of the lease.

Damage deposits may be retained by the landlord only if necessary to restore the premises to their condition at the beginning of the term except for normal wear and tear, which is an expense of the landlord.

Caution! Landlord and tenant rights and obligations are dependent in part upon the terms included in a lease or rental agreement and in part upon the general law *regardless of what provisions are contained in the lease.* For example, a provision whereby the tenant waives (gives up) his right to "repair and deduct" is void as being against public policy. The legal obligation of the landlord to maintain the premises, however, can be transferred to the tenant by agreement.

17. HOW MAY TITLE TO YOUR HOME BE HELD?

Title may be held (1) by one person in severalty, (2) by two or more persons (co-owners) as tenants in common, (3) by two or more persons (co-owners) as joint tenants with right of survivorship, or (4) by two or more persons (co-owners) as partnership property. Twenty-seven states also permit a variation of joint tenancy between husband and wife called tenancy by the entireties. Eight states, including populous California and Texas, permit community property, a variation of co-ownership by a married couple.

> Jake Lewiston owned 1000 bushels of grain. Mary Maitland also owned 1000 bushels of identical grain. In order to reduce storage charges, they combined their grain into one large heap in one storage barn. What is the nature of Jake's and Mary's ownership interests?

Jake and Mary are co-owners of undivided equal interests as tenants in common. Tenants in common could have unequal interests in a property: one could own one-third and the other two-thirds, for example, or ten people could each own a one-tenth interest. Tenancy in common is the way strangers or friends who are not close relatives generally hold common ownership of property. If one dies, his heirs get his share.

If Jake and Mary were married and lived in a community property state, they would be co-owners of undivided interests held as community property. If they were business partners in the grain-selling business, they would be co-owners of undivided interests held as partnership property. If they agreed that upon one's death, the survivor would become the owner of all the grain, regardless of the will of the first to die, they would be co-owners of undivided interests held in joint tenancy. All of the foregoing would be true if the grain were real property—that is, if Jake and Mary each owned 50 percent of a farm, for example.

Co-ownership exists where two or more persons own undivided interests. An interest in property is undivided when no one co-owner is entitled to any particular part of the property.

If Jake and Mary decided not to mingle their grain and kept it physically separate, they would be sole owners of *divided* interests. Jake would be the owner, in severalty, of his grain and Mary would be the owner, in severalty, of her grain. This would be true if instead of the grain, they held real property—for example, Harvey owned the north forty acres and Mary owned the south forty acres of a farm. Since the grain is a *fungible* good (meaning that any unit is essentially the same as any other unit), Jake and Mary can mix their grain together. They can even add grain of the same grade owned by others. Nevertheless, Jake and Mary could remain owners of the grain in severalty. Either could withdraw his or her proportionate share of the total. It makes no difference whether each gets his or her original grain back; all units are the same.

> Mr. and Mrs. Colton Gradd decided to purchase their first home. During escrow they were advised by the real estate broker to take title in joint tenancy. Should they do so? What alternatives should they consider?

As a general proposition, owning a home in joint tenancy is the preferable form of ownership. Upon the death of one joint tenant, transfer of ownership to the survivor is quicker and costs less because the property need not go through probate. (See chapter 14.) Joint tenancy property cannot, however, be affected by a will, and may be vulnerable to death tax problems. In some states, Mr. and Mrs. Gradd would probably take title as tenants by the entireties, with essentially the same effect as if they were joint tenants. In eight states, they might consider taking title as community property. Then either may will his (or her) 50 percent share; and the property obtains a new tax basis, or valuation, at the level prevailing upon death, instead of at the time of purchase. If resold, there would be no capital gain.

> John Boles and Jerry Calnay, unrelated, owned Sky-High Ranch as joint tenants. Upon learning that their respective interests would go to the survivor regardless of any will, they decided to change their ownership form. May they do so?

Yes. John and Jerry can simply deed the property to themselves as tenants in common. Now both may will their respective shares or 50 percent interests; if either dies without a will, the decedent's share goes to his surviving heirs. Typically, a *quitclaim deed* is used for this purpose. It is a deed by which the *grantor,* or transferor, of land, merely gives up any claim he may have to the property. He makes no promises or warranties to the grantee, or transferee, about the condition of the property or his title. The quitclaim deed is appropriate when land is transferred by gift or to clear some possible "cloud on title," which might otherwise be the basis for a later lawsuit.

More frequently, when real property is sold, the grantor uses a *warranty deed.* In it he makes certain covenants or promises:

1. seizin (the grantor has full ownership of the exact estate he is conveying)
2. against encumbrances (the property is free of liens or claims of third persons except as noted)
3. quiet enjoyment (the title will not be challenged successfully by third parties)
4. further assurances (he will execute any further documents that may be required to perfect the grantee's title)

In California and states where title insurance policies provide considerable assurance of clear title, the simple *grant deed* is commonly used: "I, Mr. A, grant to Mr. B certain real property described as _____. Signed A." It is notarized to permit recording in the County Recorder's Office. By use of the word *grant* the grantor impliedly warrants that (a) he has not previously conveyed the property to someone else, and (b) the estate conveyed is free from encumbrances done or suffered by the grantor or those under him, unless noted.

Married persons can change the form of ownership of property held as community property to tenancy in common or joint tenancy, or vice versa, by deed. Under some circumstances, courts have held that even though held in joint tenancy, the husband and wife actually intended to and did hold the property as community property.

Paul Gerb made an appointment with his attorney, Sid Lifkin, to discuss an estate plan. Among other things, Paul desired that, should his wife survive him, the family residence (which was his separate property owned in severalty) would be available for her use as long as she lived. But he did not want his daughter, Melody, to get the house upon his wife's death. He felt that if he simply left the home to his wife, Melody would ultimately receive the property. Will Sid be able to solve Paul's problem?

Yes. Sid can advise Paul that the house may be left to his wife for her use only so long as she lives; thereafter it would be automatically transferred to someone else designated by Paul in his will. A person whose interest in property lasts only as long as he lives is said to be a *life tenant,* the owner of a *life estate.* After Paul dies, his wife would be powerless to prevent the home from going to the person already named in his will. The person who will ultimately receive the property is called a *remainderman.* It is possible to have successive life tenancies, and tax advantages may be obtained with this type of ownership. The life tenant has all rights and duties incident to exclusive possession of the property. However, he may not injure the interest of the remainderman by committing waste.

Jeanette Wilkins, a widow, was the life tenant of a beautiful home in Carmichael. She decided to paint the house with purple and black stripes, to install strobe lights in the front yard, and to grow organic vegetables instead of a lawn. Saul, her son, was remainderman in severalty, and sought a court order enjoining waste of the life estate. Will Saul succeed?

No. Damage of a permanent nature has not been threatened nor has it occurred. If Jeanette decided to remodel the house or to fill a room with two feet of water in order to raise organic gold fish, Saul would succeed in his action.

1. What legal form of ownership of real property would be most appropriate in each of the following cases:
   a. Three middle-aged sisters, active in professional careers and never married, decide to buy and occupy a townhouse. They have lived together harmoniously in an apartment for many years and are very concerned about each other's well-being.
   b. Twenty-five alumni decide to buy a summer home for use by students and student clubs of their university.

CASES, QUESTIONS, AND PROBLEMS

c. Two neighbors, good friends, buy an old abandoned warehouse as a speculation.

d. Husband and wife buy a home.

e. After graduation from college, five classmates become partners in a business to conduct drag races. They buy a parcel of empty land along a freeway on the outskirts of town.

2. A friend tells you: "As a kid, I remember the sacrifice we made just so that our parents could pay off the mortgage on our house as fast as possible. I'm never going to buy a house and get into that rat race!" Is he right or wrong? Explain.

3. "Rising costs have effectively priced most Americans out of the housing market." True or false? Explain.

4. Do income tax laws indirectly subsidize the private home owner?

5. a. In general, a home seller (or his agent) is not required to volunteer unfavorable information about a property. If asked a specific question calling for a factual answer, he is not obliged to say anything. But if he answers, he is legally obliged to tell the truth to the best of his knowledge. What questions should you ask the seller or his agent, and yourself, before you buy a house to live in?

   b. What special advantages and disadvantages, or assets and liabilities, do you recognize in your present housing? Could the disadvantages have been avoided or rectified by proper inquiry and action at the time of purchase?

6. "The law generally does not protect the stupid against their own folly."

   a. Give some examples of when the law does not provide such protection.

   b. Give some examples of laws that do provide this protection.

7. At a local stationery store, buy copies of a short-form and a long-form real property residential lease. If possible, get samples of commercial leases from a local law library or from attorney friends. What terms or provisions do you think should be included in a lease and why? Would your answer be different if you were the landlord instead of the tenant? How are such conflicts of interest resolved?

8. The amount that may be borrowed on a home loan is affected by the appraisal value. How does an appraiser determine the value to be placed on a house?

9. Ian McTavish had fond memories of his youth in Scotland. Years later when he prepared the subdivision plans for development of a summer resort community around a small lake he owned in upper

New York, he decided to convert it into a wee bit of Scotland. All buildings would have to conform to prescribed Scottish country village styling and be limited in size. Only persons of Scottish ancestry would be permitted to own property in the community. All would have to belong to the Church of Scotland (Presbyterian). McTavish included the above provisions as restrictions in deeds, which grantees agreed to when they purchased lots in his subdivision. Are the deed restrictions enforceable in court?

10. Concern over pollution (of air, water, and soil, especially), congestion (in urban areas), and exhaustion (of natural resources) has resulted in a growing body of laws designed to protect the environment. As a consequence, what sorts of laws restrict the freedom of a landowner in the use and enjoyment of his land? What is the legal basis for such legislation?

11

YOU AS SAVER, INVESTOR, AND USER OF COMMERCIAL PAPER

1. WHAT IS THE DIFFERENCE BETWEEN SAVING AND HOARDING? BETWEEN SAVING AND INVESTING?

> It was payday, Alger Horatio's first. Under his employment contract, he received a check for $125.76, after deduction of legally imposed federal and state income taxes and the FICA (Federal Insurance Contributions Act). What basic options are legally open to him for using his earnings?

Horatio may spend what he earned as he sees fit. Whatever, if anything, is left over, he may give away, hoard, save, or invest.*

Giving

The law encourages giving to charities, by permitting donors to include charitable donations among deductions

---

* Horatio could even destroy all or part of what he earned. Human behavior is not always rational.

in calculating annual income taxes. The law also encourages giving to relatives and friends who do not qualify as charities, by taxing gifts made while the donor is alive at a lower rate than gifts made from his estate after he is dead.

Hoarding

Horatio could simply keep his money, preferably in a secure or carefully guarded place such as a safe-deposit box in a bank. Some people who hoard money prefer to stuff it in a mattress, the back of a drawer, or a can in the ground. People who have obtained money illegally or criminally, or who have failed to report the income for tax purposes, may hoard it in order to keep its existence secret.

Hoarding is legal, even if a person hoards gold. For more than forty years after 1934, when the United States ended the convertibility of paper currency into gold coins or bars, private American citizens were not permitted to keep gold coins or even paper certificates specifically exchangeable into gold, unless the items were of special numismatic value to collectors, or the gold was used for decorative or industrial purposes. Although paper currency is still not convertible into gold in this country, the legal ban on private ownership of gold was lifted in 1975. Some persons regard gold as a durable store of value in times of social and economic turmoil and uncertainty. The metal presents special problems of safe storage, and it is unproductive, earning no interest or other return. Of course, it can increase in value; but like any commodity, its value can also decline.

Economically, hoarding is usually considered foolish. The hoarded money may be stolen, forgotten, or destroyed by fire or other hazard.* Moreover, it is not being used productively in commerce to help produce goods or services, and thus to earn more money.

Saving

Horatio may save his money by *lending* it to a savings institution such as a commercial bank, or to a savings and loan company, or to a life insurance company (by buying an ordinary life or endowment policy, for example), or to a government or business corporation (by buying bonds), or possibly to an individual. In each case, the borrowing institution

---

* If currency is burned, but there are legible pieces in the ashes, preserve the remains carefully and write to the Currency Redemption Division, U.S. Treasury Department, Washington, D.C., for further instructions on how to proceed. If the currency can be identified, new currency will be issued. A certified statement of the claimant may be required explaining the circumstances of the loss, especially if less than half of a given note can be identified. Fraudulent claims may lead to criminal prosecution.

or individual legally contracts to return the *principal* (the number of dollars received as a loan) plus a specified rate of *interest* (payment for the use of the money) at some agreed-upon date in the future or on demand.* If the interest or principal on the loan is not repaid as agreed, there is a breach of contract. The lender may take legal steps to force a court-ordered sale of assets pledged by the borrower as security, if the loan was *secured* (as by a first mortgage on a factory building). If the debt is *unsecured,* the lender may sue the borrower, get a judgment, and then get a court order to seize and sell any available nonexempt assets of the borrower.

A fixed amount of dollars is given and received, regardless of the possible change in their value or *purchasing power* during the life of the loan. Because of *inflation* (which essentially means rising prices), a dollar might buy two loaves of bread in 1975 when it was loaned, but only one loaf in 1985 when it was repaid. Interest earned over the ten years would offset some of this loss, or erosion, of purchasing power. But as long as inflation continues, as most economists believe it will, the borrower pays off his loan in "cheaper" dollars than those he originally received.†

Lawyers, economists, and politicians have not been able to devise a practical solution to this obvious injustice, which deprives millions of people of billions of dollars. Hurt especially hard by inflation are elderly retired persons who live on relatively fixed incomes. The burden is lighter on wage and salary earners, and others whose incomes may rise as fast or faster than prices generally. The prudent person recognizes the harsh reality of inflation and takes steps to protect himself by keeping a minimum of his excess funds in fixed dollar savings except for short periods of time.

Investing

Horatio can avoid losing money value through inflation by investing in variable dollar media (fig. 11–1). Legally, he becomes owner or co-owner of an asset, which is likely to increase in value as the value of the dollar decreases and prices go up, as growth in population increases the demand for assets, and as the asset itself is maintained and expanded.

During the unprecedented recession of the mid 1970s, interest rates on fixed dollar investments rose to 10 percent a year and more, and

---

* On loans between friends or relatives, sometimes interest is not charged. On business loans, sometimes the interest is deducted in advance as a *discount,* and the face amount of the loan is then paid at maturity. For example, I might lend you $1,000 but give you only $925, with the understanding that you will repay me $1,000 in one year. The effective rate of interest is just over 8 percent ($75 ÷ $925).

† From 1929, when the stock market crashed, until about 1932, the country and the world experienced the Great Depression. Such gross *deflation* is not likely to be repeated, if only because governments have learned how to use tools to prevent it—and are willing to use them.

FIXED DOLLAR	VARIABLE DOLLAR
Checking account (bank)	Common stock
Savings account (bank)	Mutual funds (that buy common stocks)
Deposit account (savings and loan association)	Your own business
Credit union shares	Your own home
Bonds (Series E, H, Treasury, municipal, state, corporate)	Real estate (improved and unimproved)
Note secured by mortgage or trust deed	Real estate investment trusts
Savings element in ordinary life insurance policy	Social security benefits (pegged to the cost of living)
Preferred stock	Tangible personal property (paintings and other art objects, diamonds, rare coins, rare stamps, and the like)*
Mutual funds (that buy bonds)	

COMBINATION MEDIA (FIXED AND VARIABLE)

Balanced mutual funds (which buy stocks and bonds)

Variable annuities

Convertible preferred stock (convertible into common stock)

Convertible bonds (convertible into common stock)

*Most personal property wears out or becomes obsolete.

Fig. 11-1. Examples of savings and investment media

bonds could be bought at substantial discounts. If held until the price rose (as effective interest rates declined) or until maturity in some cases, they would provide generous capital gains and in effect serve as variable dollar media.

For example, a $1,000 bond is sold by XYZ Company at par for $1,000, with interest at 5 percent a year ($1,000 × 5% = $50). Later issues pay higher rates of interst. Persons who want to sell their XYZ bonds have to reduce the price to, say, $750. The $50 still paid in interest is now an effective rate of more than 6 percent on the amount paid ($50 ÷ $750). Moreover, if the new owner holds a bond until it matures and is paid off by XYZ Company some years in the future, he will receive the additional capital gain of $250 ($1,000 face value − $750 price).

As bonds increased in value, stock prices dropped dramatically, and dividends generally failed to keep pace with rising prices. Nothing is certain, but many observers see this situation as grossly abnormal and predict a gradual reversal of the prevailing pattern of price and yield (return on investment) for bonds and stocks.

common stock Suppose you buy some shares of common stock in a progressive, growth-oriented business that produces goods for the market-place. If the business prospers, perhaps partly by charging higher prices for the goods it sells, some or all of its profits may be distributed to you and the other stockholders in the form of a cash dividend. Usually at least some of the profits are retained by the managers of the corporation for reinvestment in the business. This reinvestment should be reflected in a higher market price for your shares of stock.

If you want to get your investment back, together with this *capital gain* (that is, the increase in the value of your capital or principal), you simply sell your shares to someone else. The amount of income received, together with capital gains over a period of time from such variable dollar media, should be higher than the income obtainable from fixed dollar media—but not necessarily. There is no contractual agreement that the amount invested will be paid back at some agreed-upon time, with some agreed-upon return. However, this uncertainty about results may be justified by the potentially higher return on your investment.

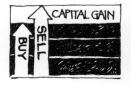

preferred stock Some corporations offer an investment medium that has both fixed dollar and variable dollar qualities: *preferred stock*. A contractually agreed-upon dividend must be paid on it before any pay-ment is made on common stock. Often it is *cumulative*: if a dividend is passed (not paid) in one year, it must be paid in the future before any dividend is paid on the common. It may also be *participating*: if the agreed dividend of, say, $6 is paid on the preferred, $6 may then be paid on the common, and any additional dividends of, say, up to $2 a share must be paid to both preferred and common. Any excess would go exclusively to holders of common stock. Also, if the corporation goes out of business, creditors (notably bond holders) are first paid off, then preferred stockholders. In many cases of bankruptcy, little or nothing remains for the common stockholders.

> Gwen O'Quinn bought 100 shares of noncumulative preferred stock in the Valley-Hi Corporation at $100 a share *par value* (the face value printed on the certificate). They were to pay a dividend of $7 a year before any dividends were paid to common stockholders. For two years, Valley-Hi Corporation lost money, and the directors paid no dividend. Then for two years it made good profits that more than offset the losses. Nevertheless, the directors decided to pay no dividends because they feared another setback and needed to buy additional equipment and supplies. In the fifth year, business boomed. They decided to pay a dividend on common. They could afford to pay all of the dividends on preferred that had been passed over. What dividend is Gwen O'Quinn legally entitled to?

If a dividend of $7 were paid for each of the five years, she would get $35 a share, or $3,500 for her 100 shares. But her stock is noncumulative, and so she gets only $7 a share for the current year, or $700 in total. Common stockholders get the rest.[1]

2. WHO RUNS THE CORPORATION?

> Manfred Heidleberger owned 500 shares of common stock in General Motors Corporation. Does he have a legal right to say how the corporation shall be run?

Theoretically, yes; practically, no. General Motors, the largest American industrial corporation, is owned by more than a million stockholders who hold more than 285 million shares of common stock (as well as some preferred stock). Each common share entitles its owner to one vote. On most questions decided at the annual meeting of shareholders, a majority vote is decisive. There is no hall large enough to hold all of the shareholders. Most would not attend even if they could. They are interested in the return on their investment, but must rely on professional managers to run the company. *Proxy* forms are sent to all shareholders. When they sign and return these forms, they authorize the designated directors to vote their shares.

The principal business conducted at the legally required annual meeting of shareholders is the election of directors for the coming year. Under the Model Business Corporation Act, there must be at least three directors, whose duty it is to manage the business and affairs of the corporation.

Since its welfare depends on their deliberative judgment, they may not vote by proxy.* Not uncommonly, they vote themselves back into office and the election becomes a formality.

The directors may meet as infrequently as once a year, and so they select officers to manage the day-to-day corporate business. In most states, the principal officers required by law are a president, vice-president, secretary, and treasurer.[2]

The same persons often serve as directors and officers, especially in a small, closely held corporation, where they may also be the principal stockholders. In a large corporation, where votes are obtained by proxy from perhaps thousands of shareholders, a self-perpetuating board of directors would have ample opportunity to abuse their power. One legal device to give minority stockholders some voice in management is *cumulative* voting. When it is available under the *by-laws* of the corporation (that is, the private rules for its internal government), each stockholder may concentrate all his votes on one candidate for office. Thus, if he has 100 shares and five directors are to be elected, he may give all 500 votes to one candidate for just one of the five positions. If other minority shareholders join him, it is more than likely that they can get at least one person of their choice on the board.

3. WHAT ARE MUTUAL FUNDS?

> Victor Hayden had heard that you should investigate before you invest. When he started to read the annual reports of corporations and check their records of performance in Moody's publications, he was overwhelmed by the mass of data. He became thoroughly confused, frustrated, and annoyed. Should he choose a company at random, or drop the whole project and simply put his money in a bank savings account?

Neither. Another alternative is to solicit the advice and recommendation of a broker, who will charge nothing for this service since he earns his profit through commissions on purchases and sales of securities for customers. If Hayden has a substantial sum to invest, say $50,000 or more, he can retain a professional investment counsellor, who will make the decisions for him and manage his *portfolio,* or securities owned —for a fee.

As another possibility, he can study a few *investment companies,* or *mutual funds,* as they are popularly known. These are open-ended trusts,

---

* *Greenbur, Trustee* v. *Harrison,* 143 Conn. 519, 1956. Generally a majority vote of the directors present at a meeting where a quorum is present decides all questions. Typically a majority of the authorized number of directors constitutes a *quorum* for the transaction of business. See, for example, California Corporations Code, Sect. 816, 817.

in which investors buy shares. The money received is invested in securities of many active corporations in keeping with the objective of the investment company: income, growth (capital gains), or security, or a combination of these three. Some specialize in certain fields such as electronics, chemicals, or foreign securities. Under the Investment Company Act of 1940, the Federal Securities Exchange Commission closely regulates the operations of investment companies.

The investor pays a sales charge, or *load,* of approximately 9 percent of the *net asset value* (assets of the fund minus liabilities divided by the number of shares outstanding) of his shares when he buys. He usually pays no charge when he sells, except perhaps a nominal service fee. Because of the sizable load, one should not buy such fund shares unless he intends to keep them for a long time, in order to spread out this acquisition cost. Better still, he might select a *no-load fund,* which he buys by mail, and for which he pays no sales charge.

In any event, he will pay an annual management fee of one-half of 1 percent (or less) of the average assets of the fund for the period. This charge is reasonable in exchange for the services and advantages provided: knowledgeable selection and disposal of securities; diversification of the investment because of the variety of shares owned by the fund; convenience of acquisition (it can be done by mail with a modest sum); safekeeping of shares, if requested; accurate bookkeeping and periodic accounting; clear and simplified income tax records; possible accumulation through automatic reinvestment of earnings, if requested; and convenience of disposal or liquidation under a planned schedule or as a lump sum.

4. SHOULD EVERYONE INVEST?

Arno Smith is twenty-five years old and unmarried, and has no accumulated savings or investments and no significant debts. After carefully budgeting his anticipated income and expenses for the year ahead (including income taxes and property taxes), he concluded that he would have excess earnings of $125 a month. Friends and business associates give him conflicting advice as to what to do with this money. What should he do? Eat, drink, and be merry—for tomorrow may never come?

Smith is very much alive after a quarter of a very tumultuous century. He decides that he, the nation, and the world will probably survive at least fifty more years. It makes sense to plan ahead. In the light of his personal life style, he reviews his short- and long-range plans. Much depends on whether and when he expects to get married, and whether he is contemplating any major purchases in the near future (such as a new car or a boat, a down payment on a house, furniture, or appliances).

Many personal finance authorities make the following recommendations to a person considering embarking on an investment program.

1. Enjoy a *reasonably comfortable standard of living.* It is folly to make great sacrifices in the real present to save for satisfaction of wants in an uncertain future. Remember that social security, often coupled with private pension plans provided by employers, serves as at least some assurance of minimal support in retirement.
2. Meet *all major capital equipment needs* (notably an automobile and furniture) without resorting to costly installment purchases or credit financing. It is seldom sensible to buy goods or services at a heavy service charge of 18 percent or more a year when your savings may be earning 5 percent and your investments 10 percent.
3. Have *adequate life, health, automobile, and homeowners insurance.*
4. Have from *one to three months' take-home pay in readily available fixed dollar media* for possible emergencies (such as illness or lay-off) as well as opportunities (such as a good buy on a car, jewelry, or encyclopedia).
5. Have *enough saved in a fixed dollar medium* (such as a savings and loan account) *for a down payment on a house,* if purchase of one is planned. This could amount to as much as 10 to 20 percent of the anticipated purchase price.

Typical *short-range objectives* (realizable within three to five years), for which fixed dollar savings media are most appropriate, include major household items, an annual vacation, holiday gifts, anniversaries, and birthday celebrations. Typical *long-range objectives* (requiring five to forty or more years), for which variable dollar media are more appropriate, include higher education for children and adults, extensive foreign travel, ownership of a business, comfortable retirement, and an estate after death to be given to heirs or to charity.

5. WHAT IS COMMERCIAL PAPER?

Andy Brandwine lives in San Francisco and has a friend, Armando Lopez, who lives in Miami, to whom he wants to send a wedding gift of $500. How can he do this at minimum expense and with maximum safety?

Brandwine would probably use a bank check for $500, drawn on his bank in San Francisco, and made payable to the order (and only to the order) of his friend Lopez.* Brandwine would mail the check (using

---

* He could also send the money via Western Union Telegraph, or he could purchase five $100 postal money orders (at 40¢ each) and mail them. In each alternative, the cost is higher than with checks.

ordinary mail, because the check without Lopez's "order to pay" in the form of an endorsement is valueless to anyone else, and Lopez would deposit it in his checking account in a bank in Miami. The Florida bank would return the check to San Francisco, through banking channels, for collection. When honored by payment, Brandwine's bank would deduct the amount from his account and eventually send him the cancelled check (along with any others and a routine, usually monthly, statement of all transactions in his account).

Such simple transfers of funds, as well as many ordinary business purchases and savings and investment transactions, are usually accomplished through one or more types of *commercial paper* (sometimes called negotiable instruments). National and international economies could not function without these credit instruments. To regulate the legal rights and duties of the parties involved, rules have developed over the hundreds of years during which these documents have been used.

Commercial paper can be prepared for precise amounts of money as required for particular transactions. It is fairly safe. A person may, for example, keep a large sum of money in a bank checking account and carry a checkbook, which gives him ready access to his funds and yet is useless to a thief. When properly prepared, commercial paper can also be safely sent through the mails.

Only the named payee can legitimately collect the specified amount. To permit someone else to collect, the payee must *endorse* (that is, sign the back of) the instrument, thus giving his order to pay. Sometimes commercial paper is made payable to "bearer." Since anyone can be a bearer, it is normally unwise to make instruments so payable unless one is personally depositing the paper in a bank or is exchanging it for value in a purchase.

The prudent person makes sure he knows and can trust the person who transfers commercial paper to him. He asks that such person endorse the instrument in his presence. If there is any doubt about identity, he asks to see appropriate identification, such as a driver's license, club membership card, or credit card. Later, if the instrument is *dishonored* (that is, not paid when due), the holder can go back to his endorser (or endorsers) and collect.

Four basic types of commercial paper are recognized by the Uniform Commercial Code and are in common use. Two are called "two party paper" because only two parties are initially involved (other parties may join in later): *one person promises to pay money to another.* The other two types are called "three party paper" because initially three parties are involved: *one person orders a second person to pay money to a third person.*

Two Party Paper

In a *promissory note* (fig. 11-2) or a *certificate of deposit* (fig. 11-3),

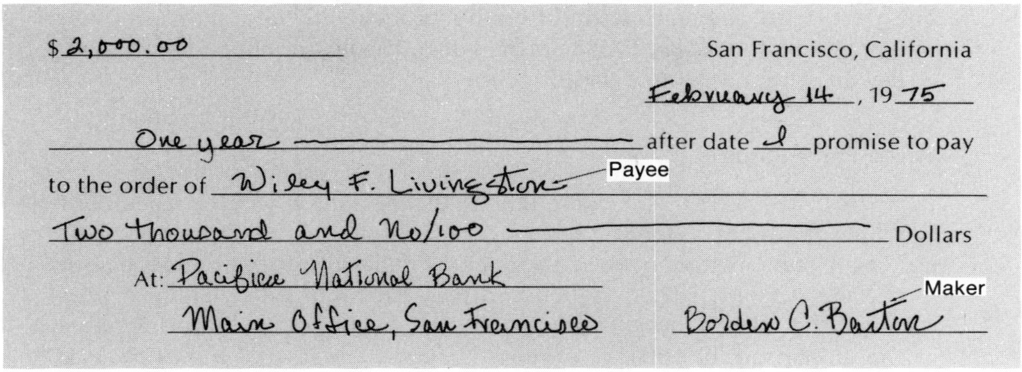

$2,000.00   San Francisco, California

February 14, 19 75

One year ——————————— after date I promise to pay

to the order of Wiley F. Livingston ——— Payee

Two thousand and no/100 ———————— Dollars

At: Pacifica National Bank

Main Office, San Francisco   Borden C. Barton ——— Maker

Fig. 11-2. Sample promissory note

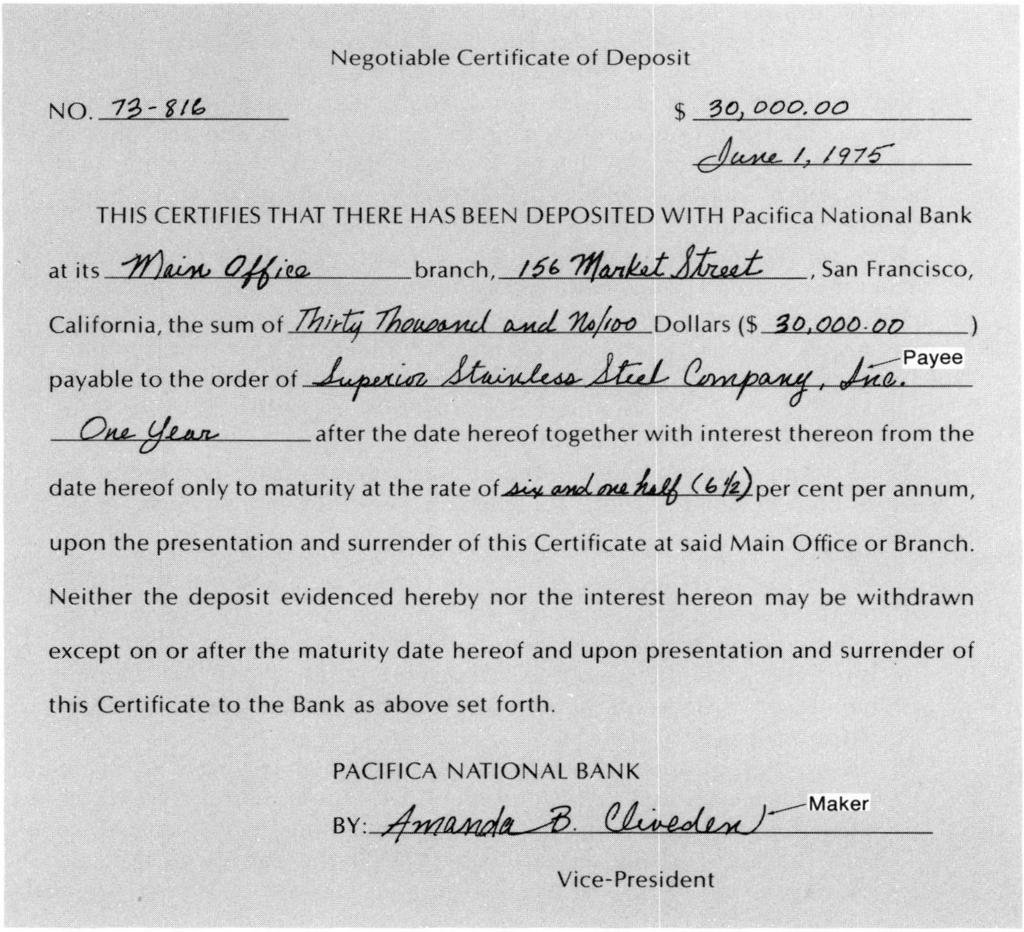

Negotiable Certificate of Deposit

NO. 73-816 $ 30,000.00

June 1, 1975

THIS CERTIFIES THAT THERE HAS BEEN DEPOSITED WITH Pacifica National Bank

at its Main Office   branch, 156 Market Street   , San Francisco,

California, the sum of Thirty Thousand and No/100 Dollars ($ 30,000.00   )

payable to the order of Superior Stainless Steel Company, Inc. ——— Payee

One Year   after the date hereof together with interest thereon from the

date hereof only to maturity at the rate of six and one half (6½) per cent per annum,

upon the presentation and surrender of this Certificate at said Main Office or Branch.

Neither the deposit evidenced hereby nor the interest hereon may be withdrawn

except on or after the maturity date hereof and upon presentation and surrender of

this Certificate to the Bank as above set forth.

PACIFICA NATIONAL BANK

BY: Amanda B. Cliveden ——— Maker

Vice-President

Fig. 11-3. Sample certificate of deposit

one party (the *maker*) unconditionally promises to pay a certain sum of money to a second party (the *payee*) or to the bearer of the instrument, either on demand or at a definite time.

Three Party Paper

In a *draft* (fig. 11–4), one party (the *drawer*) signs a written document in which he unconditionally orders a second party (the *drawee*) to pay a certain sum of money to a third party (the *payee*) or to the bearer of the instrument, either on demand (sight draft) or at a definite time (time draft). If the drawee agrees to pay, he indicates his acceptance of the obligation by writing "accepted" across the face of the draft, and signing and dating it. As *acceptor,* he is primarily liable to pay the amount of the draft.

If the drawee is a bank and the instrument is payable on demand, it is a *check* (fig. 11–5)—by far the most common type of commercial paper. Billions of checks, worth trillions of dollars, are used annually. Even with the aid of data-processing equipment, which can read the magnetic identification numbers (for the bank, branch, and account) in the lower left corners on checks, thus speeding up their sorting and distribution to banks involved, the sheer volume threatens to inundate the American banking system.

New approaches are being devised to cut down on the need for many checks. For example, some employers now cooperate with banks in crediting their employees' bank checking accounts directly for wages and salaries earned. Electronic data-processing equipment is thus programmed to take the place of payroll checks. Employees, in turn, can instruct their banks to make routine payments (such as for utility services) from their accounts, also electronically.

Since forgers can sometimes take advantage of errors on checks, be sure to observe the following guidelines when filling out a check:

1. Date it the day you write it—month, day, and year.
2. Write the payee's name. Checks may also be made out to "cash" or to "bearer"; but, as noted earlier, this is usually a dangerous practice since anyone can then become the payee.
3. Write the amount close to the dollar sign so that other figures cannot be added. Write cents figures smaller than dollar figures, and underline them.
4. Spell out the amount, beginning at the far left to leave no room for someone to make an addition. Write the amount of cents as a fraction, and draw a line through any remaining blank space. Make sure that the written amount agrees with the figures on the line above.

$ 4,250 00/xx   *Milwaukee* Wisconsin   *November 8*, 19 75

Ninety days (90) after date   PAY TO THE

ORDER OF *Humming Toy Products Company* —Payee

Four Thousand two hundred fifty and no/100   Dollars

VALUE RECEIVED AND CHARGE THE SAME TO ACCOUNT OF

TO: *Harlow Hogan* —Drawee

      8 Broadway, Milwaukee   *Martha B. Pitkin* —Drawer

NO._____

NOTE: To accept this draft, Hogan would write the word *accepted* across its face, date it, and sign it.

Fig. 11-4. Sample draft

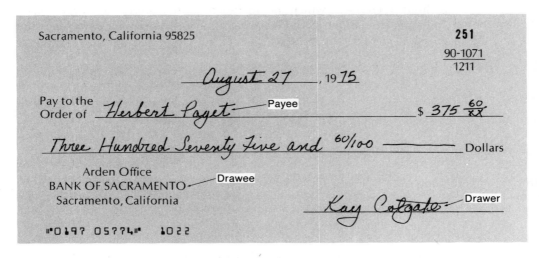

Sacramento, California 95825   **251**

                                                90-1071

                                                 1211

                August 27, 19 75

Pay to the
Order of *Herbert Paget* —Payee $ 375 60/xx

Three Hundred Seventy Five and 60/100 ——— Dollars

      Arden Office
BANK OF SACRAMENTO —Drawee
  Sacramento, California

                            Kay Colgate —Drawer

⑈0197 05774⑈ 1022

Fig. 11-5. Sample check

5. Sign your name exactly as it appears on the signature card you signed when opening your account. Do not vary your use of initials or names.

If you make an error in writing a check, void the check and discard it. However, if it is a minor error—as in an Arabic numeral—you may insert the correct figure, circle it, and initial it. After you have written a check, be sure to record the number (which appears in the upper right corner of prenumbered checks), date, payee, and amount in a separate register of checks, so that you can easily review the canceled checks the bank returns to you.*

6. WHAT TYPES OF ENDORSEMENT ARE USED IN TRANSFERRING COMMERCIAL PAPER?

Oliver Allingworth owed Joseph Billgrey $3,000. He could not pay immediately and so he gave Billgrey a promissory note for that amount, payable to the order of Billgrey in one year with interest at 7 percent (fig. 11–6). Billgrey needed cash immediately, and so he promptly transferred the note to Sean Collins who paid him $2,250. Billgrey endorsed the instrument on its back (fig. 11–7). On the due date, when Collins tried to collect, Allingworth said he was sorry but could not pay. Shortly after, he went bankrupt. Could Collins collect from Billgrey, the endorser?

No. Billgrey disclaimed liability on the instrument with the words "without recourse," which he included in his *qualified endorsement*. (Collins is the holder of the instrument, even though his name does not

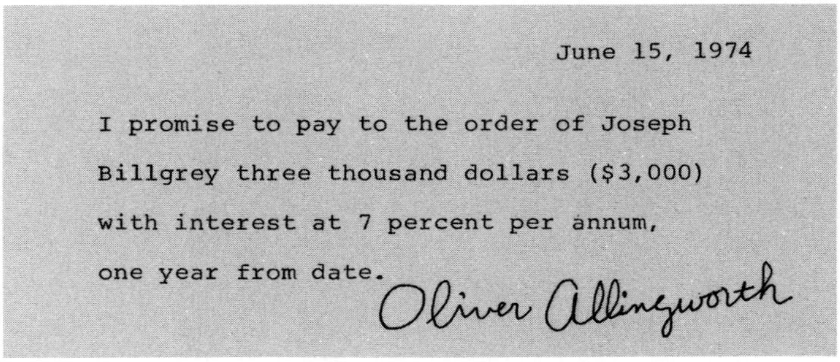

Fig. 11-6.
Allingworth's
promissory note to
Billgrey

June 15, 1974

I promise to pay to the order of Joseph
Billgrey three thousand dollars ($3,000)
with interest at 7 percent per annum,
one year from date.

Oliver Allingworth

---

* Checks are now generally photographed on microfilm by the drawee bank when honored (paid), and so even if you lose a canceled check that you have written, you can obtain a photographic copy from your bank. This copy is acceptable as legal evidence, for example, to prove that you have paid the related debt. The bank usually makes a small charge of about a dollar for this service.

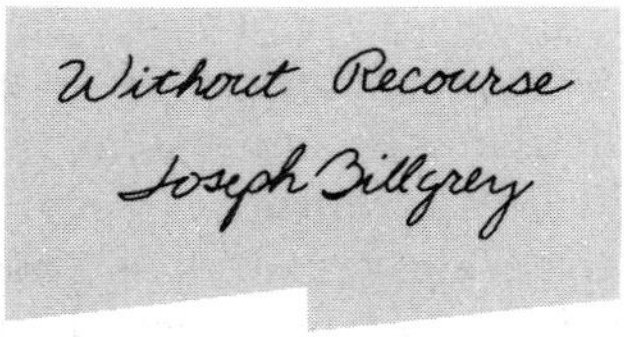

Fig. 11–7. Billgrey's endorsement of the note, transferring it to Collins

appear on it nor has he signed it.) Collins was evidently aware of the added risk involved because he was willing to take the instrument only at a 25 percent discount ($3,000 − $750 = $2,250) from its face value.

Under certain unusual circumstances, Billgrey might still be liable to Collins for breach of certain *warranties* or assurances implied by law.* Any person who transfers an instrument, and receives consideration, makes several warranties to his transferee and to any subsequent holder who takes the instrument in good faith.

a. He had good title to the instrument, or is authorized to act for one who has good title, and the transfer is otherwise rightful. For example, Billgrey warrants that he did not defraud Allingworth to get the note.

b. All signatures are genuine or authorized. Thus, Billgrey impliedly assures Collins that Allingworth's signature is not a forgery.

c. The instrument has not been materially (that is, importantly) altered. For example, the interest clause was not added or changed after Allingworth signed.

d. He has no knowledge of any *insolvency proceeding* (for example, petition for bankruptcy or other situation where the debtor cannot pay his debts as they come due) instituted with respect to the maker or acceptor of the instrument, or against the drawer of an unaccepted draft or bill of exchange. Thus, to Billgrey's knowledge, Allingworth has not filed a petition to go bankrupt.

e. He has no knowledge of any defense of any party that is good against him.† For example, to Billgrey's knowledge, Allingworth is not a minor who could refuse to pay because of incompetency.

To avoid these *warranty liabilities,* Billgrey would have to add the words "without warranty" to his endorsement. Such liability-limiting qualifications to endorsements are seldom used because transferees do not want to pay value for instruments when the transferor is not willing

---

* The warranties made by one who transfers commercial paper by delivery without endorsement (and this is possible with bearer paper) are the same as those made by an unqualified endorser, but they run only to the *immediate transferee* and then only if he has given some consideration for the instrument.

† If the endorser does not use the words "without recourse," he gives all the listed warranties to transferees; but as to item (e) he warrants that no defense of any party is good against him. This is stronger than saying that he has no knowledge of any defense.

to stand behind them. Perhaps, if Billgrey was working for Collins and merely served as a middleman, the endorsement "without recourse and without warranty" would be appropriate.

The most commonly used endorsement is the *blank endorsement,* a simple signature (fig. 11–8). It is the shortest and therefore easiest to use but is not recommended unless the holder gets immediate value in exchange for his instrument, or unless he is at a bank or savings institution and is using the instrument to make a deposit. Otherwise, a thief might steal the instrument with its blank endorsement, or it might be lost before transfer or deposit, and a finder with wrongful intent might pick it up and transfer it for value. The blank endorsement changes the order instrument into a bearer instrument, which anyone can transfer for value. Much preferred is the *special endorsement,* which gives only the named endorsee the right to collect the face value when due, or to negotiate the instrument to a subsequent holder (fig. 11–8).

A final category is the *restrictive endorsement,* which states the use to be made of the instrument, or may impose a condition on payment (fig. 11–8). Other examples of restrictive endorsements are "Pay to Sutter Savings and Loan Association for deposit only," "Pay to any Bank for collection only," "Pay to Tom Collins only," "Pay to Al Kazar as agent on account of Oscar Tremain, principal" or "Pay to Acme Construction Company upon completion of garage at 867 Fifth Avenue, Springvale." The restrictive endorsement does not prohibit further negotiation even when it clearly tries to do so. However, with some technical exceptions for banks, all transferees must recognize the restrictive terms by applying the value involved in accordance with the endorsement.*

7. WHAT IS A HOLDER IN DUE COURSE?

In general, when you receive commercial paper, it is to your advantage to qualify as a *holder in due course* (HIDC). As such, you merit a preferred status in the eyes of the law, and certain defenses that bar payment of the instrument and that are good against ordinary holders of commercial

Fig. 11–8.
Types of
endorsement

Blank Endorsement — Joseph Billgrey

Special Endorsement — Pay to the Order of Sean Collins Joseph Billgrey

Restrictive Endorsement — For deposit only Joseph Billgrey

---

* A bank is not affected by the restrictive endorsement of any person except the holder who transfers the instrument to the bank, or who presents it to the bank for payment.

paper are not good against you as a HIDC. It is a long-established public policy to encourage people to use and to freely accept checks and other commercial paper in their business dealings. Hence, the special protection of the HIDC, as well as any subsequent holder, who is known as a *holder through a holder in due course*. Their unique standing helps explain why checks are used much more extensively than cash in settling accounts today.

To qualify as a holder in due course, you must:

1. Be in possession of bearer paper, or of order paper, either originally issued to you or properly endorsed to you by a prior holder.
2. Give value for the instrument (for example, by delivering goods or services or by lending money).
3. Take the instrument in good faith; that is, you must act honestly in getting the paper. For example, there is not a gross difference in your favor between what you give in value and what you get.
4. Take the instrument before it is overdue, and with no knowledge that it has been previously dishonored, or that it has been outstanding and unpaid for more than a reasonable time if it is *demand paper* (that is, an instrument payable at any time at the option or on the demand of the holder). For example, if a note is due on September 1, 1974, and you buy it on October 15, 1974, you may have a good collectible contract right, but you are not a holder in due course.
5. Take the instrument without notice or knowledge that any party to the instrument may have a defense against its payment, or that some other party also claims to own it.

> Waldemar Amer owed Bruce Cameron some money. To help settle the debt, Amer drew a ninety-day time draft (that is, a draft payable ninety days from the date of acceptance) for $10,000 on Malcolm Beatty, payable to Cameron (fig. 11–9). The draft was for a shipment of canned pineapple chunks from Amer's Hawaiian plantation to Beatty. When Cameron presented the draft to Beatty, Beatty accepted it but shortly after complained because a large percentage of the shipment was spoiled. A month later Cameron explained the difficulty to you, claiming Beatty was trying to "pull a fast one." He said the draft should be worth face value when due, but he needed cash immediately, and so he offered to transfer it to you for ten cents on the dollar. You agreed, gave him $1,000, and he endorsed it to you in a special, qualified endorsement (fig. 11–10). Are you a holder in due course?

No. Although you are a holder of order paper properly endorsed to you, and although you have given value for an instrument that is not overdue or previously dishonored, there are clouds over your status. You

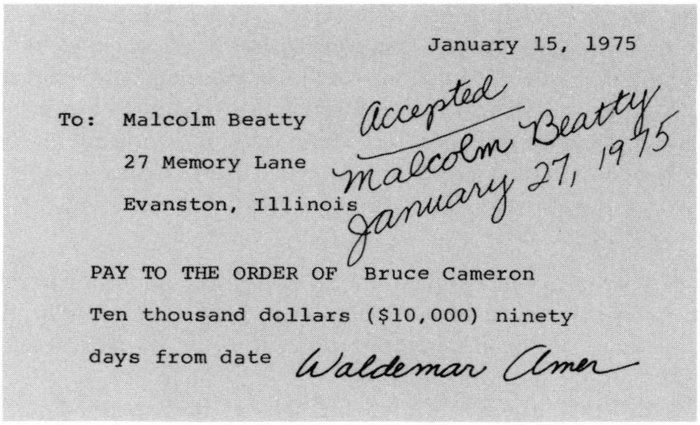

January 15, 1975

To: Malcolm Beatty

27 Memory Lane

Evanston, Illinois

accepted
malcolm Beatty
january 27, 1975

PAY TO THE ORDER OF Bruce Cameron

Ten thousand dollars ($10,000) ninety

days from date *Waldemar Amer*

Fig. 11-9.
Amer's draft to settle
a debt to Cameron

knew Beatty had complained and may have a defense, and although you gave value, it was a fraction of the face value. Moreover, Cameron used a qualified endorsement, which, under these circumstances, is further evidence that he doubted the validity of his claim for $10,000 against Beatty. If Beatty told the truth about the condition of the shipment, he has a defense against paying Cameron or order on the draft (as well as against Amer on the underlying debt for the pineapple). Since the endorsement was qualified, you have no claim against Cameron.

When you receive commercial paper, carefully examine it. Be sure there is no evidence of erasures or changes; the instrument could have been altered, in which case—as a holder in due course—you could collect no more than its original value even if it is genuine. Thus, if a properly prepared note for $100 has been illegally raised by some wrongdoer to $1,000 before you received it, the maker who is primarily liable to pay is obliged to give you only $100. You must collect the remaining $900 from the crook—if you can catch him, and if he still has the money when you do.

As the case may be, strive to know the maker (of notes), drawer (of checks), acceptor (of drafts), endorser (of any paper) before you take commercial paper. If any one of them proves to be a forger and yet obtained value from you, the loss is yours. It is extremely difficult to catch "paper hangers," as forgers are known.

Be sure the instrument you receive is not overdue. A promissory note may have a specified due date. If you are the holder, present it to the maker for payment on the due date.

8. WHAT SHOULD YOU DO IF YOU RECEIVE A CHECK OR A PROMISSORY NOTE?

You became the holder and rightful owner of a check for $500, drawn by Dan Dalton against his checking account at the Bank

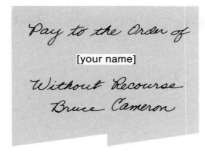

Fig. 11-10.
Cameron's qualified
endorsement of the
draft to you as
holder

of Americus Vespucci, and made payable to Paul Parker (fig. 11–11). Using the special endorsement form, Parker properly negotiated the instrument to you on the day it was drawn (fig. 11–12). In exchange, you gave Parker your used motorcycle. You promptly presented the check for payment at the Bank of Americus Vespucci, but the bank clerk said Dalton's account had insufficient funds to cover it. You immediately phoned Dalton; he apologized profusely and solemnly promised enough money would be deposited as soon as he made some overdue collections. "Hold the check and send it through next week," he said. You waited a week and redeposited the check, and again it was returned, stamped "insufficient funds." Frustrated and annoyed, you phoned Parker, your endorser, and demanded payment from him. Was he liable?

No. Parker was discharged from liability to pay, even though he had been *secondarily liable* on the check originally because of his endorsement. Although you correctly presented the instrument for payment without unreasonable delay, you failed to give prompt and proper notice of dishonor when the check was first dishonored.

Michael Burski is the holder of a promissory note signed by Maria Olivetti and due on February 24, which happens to be a Saturday. Must he present it for payment on that day?

No. If the due date is not a full business day, such as a Saturday or legal holiday, presentment must be made on the next full business day. If the maker fails to pay, he has dishonored the note. He is primarily liable, and the holder has the full period prescribed by the applicable statute of limitations (four years in California) in which to sue for the money due. But this may be costly for the holder, even if the note provides (as is often the case) for payment of court costs and reasonable attorney fees by the defaulter. The maker, after all, may have left for parts unknown, or he may be judgment-proof and without adequate cash or other assets for payment.

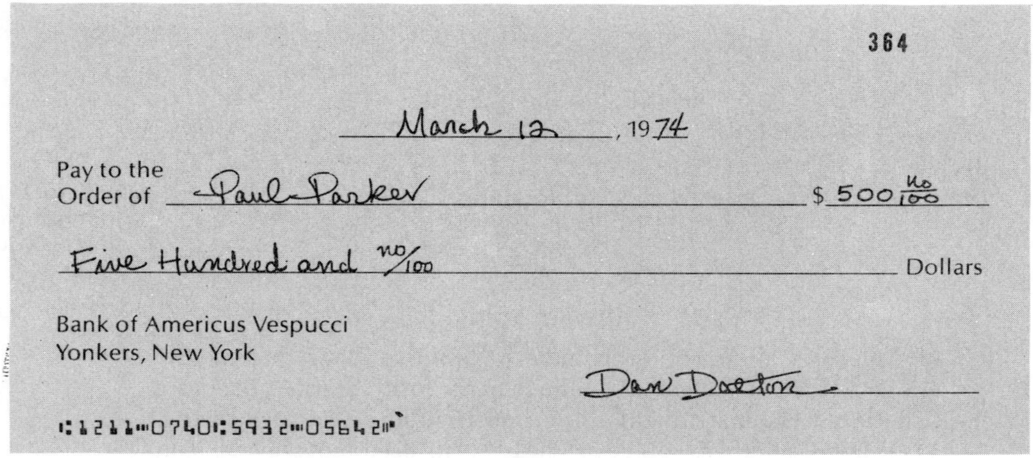

March 12, 1974

Pay to the
Order of _Paul Parker_ $ 500 no/100

Five Hundred and no/100 _____ Dollars

Bank of Americus Vespucci
Yonkers, New York

Dan Dalton

⑆1211⑉0740⑆5932⑉05642⑈

Fig. 11-11.   Dan Dalton's $500 check to Paul Parker

The situation is vastly improved for the holder, if a financially responsible endorser has also signed the instrument. If you are the holder of a promissory note, for example, and an endorser has signed the instrument, be sure to notify him no later than midnight of the third business day following dishonor or failure to pay by the maker. The law is a stickler on this; time is of the essence and precisely measured. Therefore, present all instruments promptly and properly for payment when due; if not paid, give prompt *notice of dishonor* to endorsers, who are secondarily or contingently liable. After such notice, the endorser is bound to pay you. If he does pay, by *right of subrogation* he takes over your claim against the maker who was primarily liable.

Presentment for payment (which is a prerequisite to holding secondary parties liable) may be excused under some circumstances—as when a diligent effort is made but the person who is supposed to pay cannot be found at the place where payment is to be made. The place (for example, a bank) is usually specified in the instrument; if not, then the place to go is the debtor's business during business hours or his residence before normal time of retiring.

In the case of a check received directly from a drawer, present the instrument for payment within a reasonable time at the bank on which it was drawn. Obviously, in most cases the check will be deposited in the holder's bank and must go through banking channels to the bank on which drawn. What is "reasonable time" is determined by the nature of the instrument, banking or trade usage or custom, and the facts of the particular case. The Uniform Commercial Code (Sect. 3-503-2) specifies reasonable periods for ordinary checks drawn and payable within the United States.

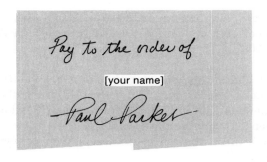

Fig. 11–12.
Paul Parker's
endorsement of the
check to you

a. With respect to the liability of the drawer, thirty days after date of the check or date it was issued, whichever is later*
b. With respect to the liability of an endorser, only seven days after his endorsement

Prompt cashing of checks received is a matter of common sense and good business practice. If there is any default, do not rest on your rights; press for payment.

To sum up: present all commercial paper promptly and properly for acceptance (when needed), and for payment. If dishonored, give proper and prompt notice of dishonor to parties who are secondarily liable, if any such names appear on the instrument as endorsers. If an endorsed check is dishonored by nonpayment, be sure to notify your endorser no later than midnight on the third business day following dishonor. Failure to do so releases him from all liability. Sometimes there are two or more endorsers. In such a case, an endorser may hold a prior endorser liable, but must give notice of dishonor before midnight of the third business day after he himself received notice.

9. WHAT MIGHT YOU DO IF A SELLER OR A LENDER REFUSES TO TAKE YOUR PERSONAL CHECK IN LIEU OF MONEY?

Under federal law, *legal tender* must be accepted by a creditor when offered in payment of a debt. It includes paper currency and coins, but not checks ("bank money"), even though most payments in total amount are made by check. The check is accepted, but only if the bank on which it is drawn later "honors" it, is the debt deemed paid.

Because of a physical disability, Carol Buffom cannot obtain a driver's license. She belongs to no widely recognized clubs or trade

---

* This would take care of the rare situation where the bank failed during the time between proper deadline for presentment, and the actual delayed date of presentment. If the depositor-drawer had enough money on deposit to cover the check, and now that money is gone, the loss is imposed on the tardy holder. If the depositor-drawer suffers no loss because of the delay, he is normally still liable on the underlying debt for which the check was originally issued.

associations, and has no credit cards. When seeking to cash personal checks, she is commonly asked for some identification. What can she do?

Buffom might join an organization that provides identification cards. She might use her Social Security card. In California, she might apply to the Department of Motor Vehicles for an identification card similar to a driver's license (available for a small fee).

The seller (or lender) who refuses to accept your personal check may fear several possibilities.

a. Because of carelessness or a mistake (as when husband and wife both write checks against one account), you may have insufficient funds on deposit, and so the check will not be paid when it reaches your bank.

b. Motivated by criminal intent, you have either opened no checking account or established a dummy account. In the latter case, you might have deposited $150 and then written a series of checks for different payees, in each case keeping the face amount below the $150, should the payee call your bank for confirmation of a sufficient balance.

c. You may be a forger wrongfully using the name of a reputable person who has an established checking account, or using any name that sounds credible.

You can normally reassure the seller by providing proof of your identity as by displaying your driver's license, credit cards, membership cards in clubs, employee identification card, or a special check credit card that the seller has issued after a careful investigation. Unfortunately, such cards may be stolen, or forged, and used illicitly. The seller may be anxious to accommodate you; after all, you probably are honest. Therefore, he takes the check, but perhaps only if it is your personal check, and only if it is for less than a certain limited amount, and only if the cash change required does not exceed a nominal sum. Goods are not as desirable to criminals as cash; they have to be disposed of and usually bring only a fraction of their price. Sometimes, especially if a substantial sum is involved, the seller (or lender) may ask you to persuade a third party, known to him to be trustworthy, to sign the instrument as a co-maker or endorser. This person is called an *accommodation party*. If you fail to pay, the holder may look to him for payment.

10. WHAT CAN YOU DO IF A CREDITOR REFUSES TO ACCEPT YOUR CHECK?

An advertisement in *Playboy* magazine offers leather jackets at the attractive price of $59.50. The ad says: "No credit. Send no cash or personal checks. Only cashier's checks or certified checks will be accepted." Why does the seller impose such restrictions?

The seller is afraid that cash may be lost, stolen, or misdirected if sent through the mails. He fears personal checks for reasons noted earlier. But he knows he is effectively protected if he gets a cashier's check or certified check. A *cashier's check* is drawn by a bank official (usually the cashier or his representative) against the bank's own reserves, payable to the order of the person you designate. You pay the face amount plus a small fee (twenty-five to fifty cents is typical) when you buy the check. Alternatively, you could write a personal check payable to the order of the seller, and ask your banker to certify on the face of it that sufficient funds are on deposit and will be available to pay the check when presented. The check is stamped *certified check,* and for a modest fee the bank sets aside from your account the specified amount for the purpose of honoring the check when it returns for payment.

Do not agree to serve as co-maker or accommodation party on any negotiable instrument unless you are willing and able to honor the instrument by payment if the party primarily liable defaults. In the opinion of the sober-headed seller or lender, there is such a possibility—if not a probability. When a person asks you to help him in such a manner, his credit may be so poor that experts on credits and collections have doubts about his ability or willingness to pay later. Frankly, they don't trust him. Should you?

11. IS A PERSON WHO IS PRIMARILY LIABLE ON COMMERCIAL PAPER ALWAYS LEGALLY BOUND TO PAY WHEN THE INSTRUMENT IS PROPERLY PRESENTED FOR PAYMENT?

> Johnny Gordon, a minor, signed a promissory note payable to Alexander Magnus, an adult. Magnus endorsed the instrument to Clifford Montgomery, another adult, who paid value and took the instrument as a holder in due course. When the note came due, Gordon refused to pay, claiming the absolute universal defense of infancy. Must Gordon pay Montgomery? If not, must Magnus pay Montgomery?

No, Gordon need not pay; infancy is an absolute or universal defense and it is good against even holders in due course who are themselves quite blameless. However, Magnus would be liable to Montgomery under the stated facts. Magnus should have confirmed Gordon's minority status, and then refused to deal with him unless his parents or some other adult co-signed.

Normally, the maker of a promissory note or certificate of deposit, the acceptor of a draft, and any person who in writing guarantees payment of an instrument, are all liable to pay the instrument when properly presented for payment. When a check is presented for payment, the drawee bank normally pays if sufficient funds are on deposit in the drawer's account. If the bank refuses to pay, proper notice of dishonor must be given to the drawer of the check, or he may be discharged from liability like the drawer of an ordinary draft. However, if there is a valid underlying debt for which the check was given, the drawer remains liable.

Persons asked to pay an instrument may deny liability because of some legally recognized defense that excuses them from making payment. Defenses are classified as *limited defenses,* which are good against any holder except a holder in due course, and *universal defenses,* which are good against the world, including a HIDC. If you are called upon to pay and can prove any of the universal defenses, you simply are not obliged to pay any amount to anyone.

Limited Defenses

1. *Ordinary contract defenses.* For example, you give a check for goods that are never delivered. You can stop payment on your check by telling your bank not to honor the check when presented and refuse to pay the seller. But if the instrument has been transferred to a HIDC, you are obliged to pay him, even though the bank may have stopped payment at your request. Your remedy then would be to pursue the seller.

2. *Fraud in the inducement.* For example, the seller induces you to buy a used car by saying that the engine has been overhauled when in fact he knows it has merely received a routine tuneup. You need not pay the seller; you must pay a HIDC.

3. *Prior payment or cancellation.* For example, you pay a note but neglect to pick it up and either destroy it or stamp it "paid." If the instrument gets back into commercial circulation and a HIDC obtains it, he could collect on it from you. This means that you would have to pay twice. The effect is similar if the instrument is cancelled, but not so stamped or marked. Your recourse is against the person who sold it to a HIDC.

4. *Incapacity of the defendant.* For example, a note is signed by the defendant maker acting under the undue influence of another person. The undue influence deprives him of the free exercise of his own will.

5. *Simple duress.* For example, you sign a check because the payee threatens to sue you, or to prosecute a relative for some alleged crime, if you refuse. You may legally and effectively stop payment on the check as to the payee, but not as to a HIDC. After all, if you and your relative are innocent, you could have called the payee's bluff.

6. *Nondelivery of the instrument.* For example, you complete a negotiable instrument and carelessly leave it on your desk. It has not been delivered to the payee, a normal requisite. That night a thief steals it and negotiates it. He cannot collect, but a HIDC who becomes the owner may.
7. *Conditional delivery of the instrument.* For example, you give a real estate broker a check for $1,000 as a down payment on a house. The check is to be delivered to a seller who is aware that certain conditions are to be met (such as repairing leaks in the roof before any payment is made). The broker delivers the check before the conditions are met. You need not pay the seller if he tries to collect, but you are obliged to pay a HIDC who seeks payment.
8. *Theft.* For example, a thief steals from a holder an instrument that has been made payable to bearer or endorsed in blank. He cannot collect, but an innocent HIDC to whom he sells the instrument can.
9. *Unauthorized completion.* For example, you sign a check and let the payee insert the amount payable, and he inserts a figure in excess of the amount you authorized.

Universal Defenses

1. *Forgery or lack of authority.* For example, someone forges your name as the drawer of a check, or an alleged agent signs your name without any authorization by you. Under the Uniform Commercial Code, you have an affirmative duty to exercise reasonable care and promptness in examining your bank statement and all cancelled checks.[3] Promptly notify the bank of alterations or errors discovered; if you are not to blame because of carelessness in preparing the checks, the bank must take the loss unless it can recover from the party who deposited the check. Your signature is on file in the bank records, and they can compare it with those on checks that are honored. The bank should (and normally does) require an endorsement of the depositor, whom it knows (or should know).
2. *Fraud as to the nature of the instrument.* For example, a baseball star, without negligence, signs what is fraudulently represented to be an autograph book but is in fact a promissory note. Or an immigrant, illiterate in English, acting reasonably, is persuaded to sign a note under the false impression that it is a lease contract for an apartment.
3. *Illegality.* For example, a note signed by a California resident to settle a Las Vegas gambling debt is not collectible in California, where most gambling is illegal.
4. *Duress depriving control.* For example, a wrongdoer beats you mercilessly, or waves a gun and threatens to kill you, demanding that

you sign a note. You finally sign. Any resulting contract would be null and void, not merely voidable.

5. *Incapacity as a minor.* For example, a sixteen-year-old gives her personal note for $750 for a series of ballet lessons, then changes her mind, and refuses to pay.

6. *Alteration.* For example, a holder materially and fraudulently increases the face amount of a note from $500 to $1,500. The subsequent HIDC can collect no more than $500 on the instrument from the primary party.

12. IF YOU PLACE YOUR MONEY IN A BANK CHECKING ACCOUNT OR BANK SAVINGS ACCOUNT, ARE YOU PROTECTED AGAINST LOSS IF THE BANK FAILS?

Joan Barnes received $50,000 from the estate of her recently deceased uncle Leighton Noble. While debating what to do with the money, she deposited the full amount in a savings account in the Local Lender Bank. To her dismay, the bank closed its doors shortly thereafter when auditors discovered that Mr. Eleazer Hookayew, a cashier with thirty years of apparently faithful service, had embezzled more than $4 million. Will Barnes get her money back?

Perhaps, but not necessarily. If the Local Lender Bank was a participating member of the Federal Deposit Insurance Corporation (FDIC), as most banks are, every individual depositor and saver is insured against loss up to $40,000. If during the liquidation or reorganization of the bank, the assets prove sufficient to pay more on claims of savers and depositors, Barnes may receive part or all of the remaining $10,000 and even accrued interest earned.

To protect herself beyond the limit of $40,000, she should have deposited some of her funds in one or more additional banks with FDIC insurance. She might have achieved the same result by opening a separate account (up to $40,000) in the Local Lender Bank in the name of her spouse, if married, and another account in the name of her husband and herself as joint tenants. If she has children, she could also have opened insured accounts in their names, with herself as trustee.

Similar insurance protection is available in savings and loan associations, and also in credit unions. Investors who leave cash and securities with licensed security brokers are now protected up to $20,000 for the cash and $50,000 for the securities, under the Securities Investor Protection Corporation (SIPC). This coverage is limited to losses caused by the bankruptcy or other financial difficulty of the broker; the customer suffers his own losses and enjoys his own gains on the fluctuations in the market price of the securities he owns and in their earning power.

The federal Securities Exchange Commission (SEC) regulates the organized securities exchanges or markets (such as the New York Stock Exchange and the American Stock Exchange), and also requires disclosure of facts about proposed business ventures before substantial amounts of stocks or bonds are sold to the public in interstate commerce. However, the SEC in no way guarantees success of your investments. Individual states regulate the organization of corporations and their issuance of securities in intrastate commerce. The controls are varied and differ widely in scope and effectiveness.

CASES, QUESTIONS, AND PROBLEMS

1. A check is drawn on the Occidental National Bank by Umberto Amoya and his business partner, Andrew Dixon. They both sign it and make it payable to Claire Debussy. Debussy endorses it with a special endorsement to Max Maxwell. Maxwell endorses it in blank and gives it to C. D. Ensign. Identify the parties involved as drawer, drawee, payee, endorser, endorsee, transferee, and holder.

2. Sam Kwong sent a properly prepared check for $129.50 to his landlord, Wing Moy, in payment of a month's rent. Moy says he never received the check.
   a. What should Kwong do?
   b. Could a finder or thief cash the check and thus defraud Kwong of $129.50?

3. Carl Conant owed you $250. To settle the claim, he offered to transfer to you a $250 (face value) promissory note that he owned. It was made by Roger Dykstra payable to Norman Kemper, was due in six months, and carried interest at 6 percent. Kemper had endorsed it in blank, transforming it into a bearer instrument, when he negotiated it to Conant. Now Conant offers to transfer it to you by simple delivery. What should you do?

4. a. You are a sales agent for Lifetime Books, and receive several notes and checks from customers, payable to you, for company goods sold. What endorsement should you use if you do not want to be liable on the papers when you transfer them to your employer?
   b. You are in your bank, depositing several checks made payable to you. What endorsement would be adequate and proper?
   c. You are sending several checks payable to you, to your bank by mail. What endorsement should you use?
   d. Someone pays you with his payroll check. What endorsement should you have him use? What if he simply signs his name?

5. Gerold C. Lynx obtained a promissory note from Bernard Schlock by fraudulently promising to deliver some goods. Lynx never performed, but realizing that Schlock had a defense against him, he negotiated the instrument to an innocent HIDC, Thomas Mitsui. As a gift, Mitsui later turned the note over to the local Buddhist Church for its building fund. When the church presented the instrument for payment, Schlock refused to pay, saying that (a) he had been defrauded by Lynx and (b) the church was not a HIDC and could not collect. Decide.

6. In a discussion with John Demott Jones concerning commercial paper, Leslie Laughlin said that, in a promissory note, the presence of certain provisions and lack of certain others would destroy its negotiable character. The note would be an ordinary contract at best, transferable by assignment, with the assignee subject to all defenses. Jones insisted that the negotiability of the note would not be affected and that some of the variations might make the paper more readily acceptable in trade. Who is right on each of the following points?
   a. The date is omitted.
   b. The note is postdated (that is, dated with a date later than that of execution) or antedated (that is, dated earlier than the actual date of the document).
   c. There is no seal.
   d. The note calls for payment in foreign currency (such as German marks or British pounds).
   e. The note fails to state that value is given or received.
   f. The note calls for collateral (security for payment), and permits sale of the collateral upon default.
   g. The note permits acceleration of the due date if an installment of interest or principal is not paid.
   h. The note calls for payment of collection costs and reasonable attorney fees in case of default.
   i. The note was signed by the maker with a rubber stamp of his name.
   j. The name of the payee is misspelled in the note.
   k. The note says IOU instead of "I promise to pay to the order of
   _____."

7. Clifford A. Foxboro was a busy physician. When he received checks from patients, he often slipped them into his desk drawer, where they might sit for months. This happened to Ben Berg's check for $200: the doctor presented it for payment three and one-half months after it was issued.
   a. The bank has failed in the interim, and Berg has lost 75 percent of his deposit as a result. Is he still liable to Foxboro for the full amount of the check?

b. If Berg had closed his account and moved, and the bank returned the check to Foxboro marked "account closed," would Berg be a criminal? Is he still liable to pay the debt?

c. If the check had an endorser, would he be bound to pay if Berg failed to pay when the check bounced?

8. Sylvia Glore says that she does not need a checking account because she can buy individual cashier's checks when she needs a check. Do you agree with her?

9. After winning $1,700 while playing the gambling game of "21" at Reno, Harold Hadly's luck changed and he lost all his winnings plus the $300 stake he had when he began. He asked the club for credit and received an extension of $500 in credit after signing a promissory note for that amount, payable in thirty days. As luck would have it, he also lost the $500, whereupon the club put him on a bus for a free trip back to his home in San Francisco. Must he pay the note when it comes due?

10. Wilbert Walczak makes a promissory note that is conventional in all respects except that it promises payment in one hundred ounces of silver of a designated purity. Is it a negotiable instrument?

11. An economist and a lawyer were discussing the requirement under the Uniform Commercial Code that commercial paper must call for the payment of a certain sum in money. The economist insisted that the true value or purchasing power of money is changing constantly and that therefore no promises or orders to pay money could qualify under the U.C.C. What answer could the lawyer give?

12. Draw up a balance sheet listing as assets all the things of value you (or your parents) own. On the liabilities side, list what you owe to others, including any balance due on the purchase price of an asset. The difference between the assets and the liabilities is your net worth. (If the liabilities exceed assets, you are in a deficit situation.) Identify each asset as a fixed, variable, or mixed dollar medium.

13. Identify your short- and long-term savings and investment goals. How are they likely to change as you get older? How should this affect the amount and placement of your savings?

12

YOU AS EMPLOYEE

1. DOES EVERYONE HAVE THE RIGHT TO WORK FOR PAY?

No. The U.S. constitution does not specifically recognize the right to work for pay. In 1946, however, Congress enacted the Employment Act, which committed the federal government to achieving full employment through "all practical means" for those able, willing, and seeking to work. These means include a job-finding program under the leadership of the U.S. Training and Employment Service; gathering and interpreting economic data and advising the President and Congress through the Council of Economic Advisers; regulating the flow of money and credit; and government taxing and spending. We have never achieved 100 percent employment—if only because of seasonal changes in demand for help, and job hunting and changing to improve one's situation. In 1973, out of a population of 210 million, more than 88 million Americans were gainfully employed in civilian pursuits, and 2.3 million in the armed forces. As many as 4.3 million persons (4.9 percent) in the labor market, however, were without jobs; and the figure went beyond 5 percent in 1974 and even higher in certain depressed areas.

Wayne Duda cheered when he was honorably discharged from the army, but now he needed a job and couldn't find one. He heard that his state had enacted a "right to work" law, and so he went to a state employment office, described his skills as a truck driver, and demanded a job as his legal right. Must he be employed?

No. Right to work laws, which have been enacted in eighteen states, in no way guarantee every able and willing person a job. The term was coined to gain voter support for legislation that outlaws union shops. In states with such laws, a worker is not obligated to join a union or pay dues to keep his job. Many workers believe such laws are designed to weaken unions rather than to protect jobs or the true "right to work."

2. ARE SOME PERSONS BARRED FROM GAINFUL EMPLOYMENT BY LAW?

Yes. Under the federal *Fair Labor Standards Act,* minors may not be employed in "oppressive" labor—occupations that are particularly hazardous for them or detrimental to their health and well-being, as determined by the U.S. Secretary of Labor. For persons between sixteen and eighteen, such jobs include logging, slaughtering and meat packing, roofing, and building demolition. For persons between fourteen and sixteen, employment in occupations (other than mining or manufacturing) may be permitted, provided it does not interfere with their schooling or health and well-being. Permitted categories include office and clerical work, retailing, price marking and shelving, deliveries by foot or bicycle or public transportation, garden work (without power tools), and gasoline station work (without the use of pits and racks).

Farm child labor is generally permitted, even when children are not working for their parents on a family farm. In 1971, 800,000 children made up a fourth of the nation's paid farm-labor force. Most states regulate such work. Oregon, for example, bars employment of children under age ten in fields and orchards. New Jersey permits children over age twelve to work as long as sixty hours a week, but not over ten hours a day. The American Friends Service Committee (Quakers) has decried this practice as reminiscent of industrial child labor, which was outlawed in 1938. The problem has not been resolved to date by federal or state legislation.

States have enacted various laws regulating the employment of women. Many of these were generally designed to protect them from oppression, as by limiting hours and night employment, forbidding duties that require lifting heavy weights, and requiring rest periods and rest rooms. Their effect, however, has often been to bar women from certain jobs. Because of the women's liberation movement and the federal Civil Rights Act of 1964, many states have repealed laws governing the employment of women.

The federal *Equal Pay Act of 1963* prohibits wage discrimination on the basis of sex for equal work on jobs that require equal skill, effort, and responsibility and that are performed under similar working conditions. Unfortunately, years of discrimination have placed most women employees in positions of less responsibility and lower wages than men. In 1973, in a bellwether out-of-court settlement, American Telephone and Telegraph Company paid $15 million in back wages to persons who allegedly had been victims of past discrimination by the company on the bases of sex and race. Other companies have made similar retroactive payments; many have adopted new employment and promotion policies to comply with the law.

3. WHAT SORT OF DISCRIMINATION IS BARRED BY LAW?

Employees in G. R. Coleman's machine shop in a small New England town accurately reflected the social makeup of the community. All were white, Anglo-American, Protestant, male, and highly skilled. Coleman was proud of his business and its products, and he ascribed much of its success to the homogeneity of the work force. He therefore refused to hire Samara Fuguady when she applied for work. She was not only a woman, but also a native of southern Egypt, dark black, and a Muslim. "It's not that I'm prejudiced," Coleman said, "but your presence would be disruptive and no one would be happy—least of all you." Is Coleman within his legal rights in refusing to hire Samara?

No. Under the *Fair Employment Practices Law* (better known as the *Civil Rights Act of 1964*), it is unlawful for an employer "to fail or refuse to hire or to discharge any individual, or otherwise to discriminate against any individual with respect to his compensation, terms, conditions, or privileges of employment because of such individual's race, color, religion, sex, or national origin."[1] A similar proscription applies to employment agencies and to labor unions.[2]

Under the act, however, discrimination in pay and other employment practices are permitted if in conformance with a bona fide (good faith) (a) seniority system; (b) merit system; (c) system that measures earnings by quantity or quality of production; (d) system that distinguishes among employees who work in different locations; or (e) system that is based on the results of a professionally developed ability test (not designed or intended to discriminate on any of the barred bases), provided the test is job-related in that persons who do well on the test do well on the job, and vice versa.

Important amendments to the Civil Rights Act of 1964 were made by Congress in the *Equal Employment Opportunity Act of 1972.* For the first time, the Federal Equal Employment Opportunity Commission (EEOC) was given power to institute civil actions in court to eliminate violations of the law. Formerly, it had to rely on informal methods such as conferences and conciliation, which an employer could ignore. The individual victim seldom was willing or financially able to take his grievance to court. Now the EEOC may do this for him.

Employers may be found in violation of the law, for example, unless they can prove that business necessity or successful performance of the job requires such practices as tests for hiring or promotion, minimum educational requirements, disqualification because of prior arrest records, word-of-mouth referral systems, and discharge because wages have been garnished.

> Sharon Rockwell lost her job with the Majestic Admiral Products Corporation when she was forty-five years old. A friend told her about a similar job that had just become available in the Crescent Moon Company because of the death of the incumbent. When Rockwell applied, the personnel manager said, "You are eminently qualified for the assignment, except that you're too old. We're looking for a bright college graduate with maybe five years of experience. We want her to grow with the company." Does Sharon have any legal recourse?

Yes. Three years after the Civil Rights Act became law, Congress passed the *Age Discrimination in Employment Act of 1967,* which applies to persons between forty and sixty-five years of age. It makes it unlawful for an employer in interstate commerce to fail or refuse to hire, or to discharge any individual, or otherwise discriminate against him with respect to his compensation, terms, conditions, or privileges of employment, because of his age. This law also applies to employment agencies and unions. It permits discrimination when age is a bona fide occupational qualification, and it recognizes the propriety of disciplining or even discharging a person for good cause. Enforcement of this law has been difficult and unsatisfactory. Employers find other bases for refusal to employ the more mature worker—including "over-qualification" for the available job.

4. WHAT IS MEANT BY "AFFIRMATIVE ACTION" IN EMPLOYMENT PRACTICES?

> After preliminary screening for the job of computer programmer at the Acme Electronics Company, Jack Wellington (black), Alfredo Ramirez (Chicano), and Richard Ellis (white) were the remaining contenders for the job. All appeared to be qualified or qualifiable with a minimal amount of training. Ellis, however, was also a graduate of the University of Arizona, had five years of experience, and came highly recommended by his previous employer. Most of Acme's contracts are with the federal govern-

ment and almost all of its employees are white males. Who should Acme hire?

To keep its federal supply contracts, Acme should hire Wellington or Ramirez. Because of many years of discrimination in employment against women and minorities, the federal government has decided that heroic efforts are needed to provide them with more opportunities for gainful employment. Accordingly, by threatening to terminate lucrative supply and research contracts, the federal government (such as the Department of Health, Education, and Welfare) has pressured employers to take steps to hire and to promote minorities and women, in percentages roughly equal to their representation in the neighboring community. This has sometimes led to reverse discrimination against qualified male employees and male applicants. Presumably, such persons can take adequate care of themselves; they can look for and find jobs where federal contracts do not give the government this corrective weapon.

Some legal experts question the constitutionality of affirmative action. Efficiency experts insist that employment and promotion should be based on merit. Opponents of affirmative action say the Civil Rights Act of 1964 calls for neutrality, with no discrimination for or against anyone. Proponents argue that with neutrality, corrective action might take a generation or longer, and that's too long. Thus far, the U.S. Supreme Court has not been called upon to face the affirmative action issue directly. However, in a 1971 decision, the Court unanimously held that it is a violation of the Civil Rights Act of 1964 for an employer to require a high school diploma and a passing score on a general intelligence test for employment or promotion, when neither can be demonstrably related to job performance.[3] Moreover, the Court held that employment and personnel management "practices, procedures, or tests neutral on their face and even neutral in terms of intent, cannot be maintained if they operate to 'freeze' the status quo of prior discriminatory employment practices."

The Court did not say that present employees must be fired to make way for women and minorities. Nor did it say that such victims of prior discrimination must be given preferential treatment in hiring. But it may so rule in the future, as a logical extension of its past decisions. Someday maybe Congress will legislate or the Supreme Court will adjudicate that all employers must adopt a meaningful affirmative action program.

5. MUST YOUR CONTRACT OF EMPLOYMENT BE IN WRITING?

No. Usually the contract of employment is oral, although the employee may be asked to complete a formal application, and may receive a handbook telling about the company, its policies and rules. However, if the job calls for a long-term commitment and cannot be completed within a year, the contract must be in writing and signed by the party to be held. That is, to bind the employer, the employee must get the employer to sign; reciprocally to bind the employee, the employer must get the employee to sign. The business-like solution is for both to sign, and for each to get and keep a copy of the contract.

The law that mandates such written evidence is called the *Statute of Frauds and Perjuries,* an English innovation dating back to 1677. It assumes that persons of poor memory or elastic character may forget or even *perjure* themselves (lie under oath) in testifying about so important an agreement if it suits their needs. In addition to agreements that cannot be performed within one year, the Statute of Frauds applies to certain other contracts, including those for a transfer of an interest in real property (as well as leases for more than one year, in California), and for the sale of goods worth $500 or more.

If there is no written memo, properly signed, the agreement is not illegal; it is simply not enforceable in a court of law. Obviously, if the parties are willing, they may perform without reference to any writing, complying with all the terms of their oral agreement. But this is not recommended. Indeed, even when the agreement does not have to be in writing under the Statute of Frauds—and most do not—it is good preventive law to put it in writing and to have at least the other party sign if much money, time, or detail is involved.

> Ben Lockhart and Hal Heinz were classmates and buddies while in college, and their friendship endured after graduation. After both were well established financially, they entered into a complicated oral contract under which Lockhart agreed to employ Heinz as a consultant for five years, and Heinz agreed to sell Lockhart his 6000-acre ranch along with $200,000 worth of farming equipment. They shook hands and agreed that the word of each was his "bond." Was either legally bound?

No. The employment contract, the sale of the real estate, and the sale of the goods worth well over $500 were governed by the Statute of Frauds. Of course, both Lockhart and Heinz may say "my word is my bond," shake hands, and then perform as orally agreed; but neither can be legally compelled to do so.

If a union is involved in employment relations, the contract is almost always in writing and quite detailed. It is negotiated by union officials with the employer or his management representatives through *collective bargaining.* One or a few of these officials represent all workers in the *bargaining unit*—an employee group that, on the basis of common interests or related skills and duties, is deemed an appropriate unit for collective bargaining. If necessary, the Federal National Labor Relations Board decides who belongs in a given bargaining unit, and then conducts an election to determine whether the majority of workers want to be represented by a union and, if so, which union.* In large companies, there may be many bargaining units and many different unions.

Historically, a major division has existed in the labor movement between unions that seek to include all workers in a given industry (such as all steel workers or all auto workers, skilled and unskilled) as represented by the *Congress of Industrial Organizations* (CIO) and unions that seek to represent a specialized craft (such as all plumbers, or all tool and die makers) as represented by the American Federation of Labor (AFL). The two have been united since 1955 in a single organization, but certain large blocks of unionized workers have not allied themselves with this combined AFL-CIO (such as the Teamsters and the United Mine Workers).

6. WHAT ARE YOUR BASIC DUTIES AS AN EMPLOYEE?

> Two weeks after being employed as a deckhand on Plato Parnasis's 180-foot yacht, the *Invincible,* Jake Morgan refused to obey an order of the Chief Mate Ben Blight, to swing over the side and scrape and repaint a section of the hull. Morgan argued that nothing had been said about such dirty and potentially dangerous duties when he was hired. Moreover, he said he was too tired. May he be fired?

Yes. Scraping and painting are customary duties of deckhands. This was reasonably implied, if not explicitly expressed, in their employment agreement. Also, being too tired during working hours is no excuse for refusal to do a job. An employee is duty bound to obey reasonable orders and to comply with reasonable rules. He cannot be required to do anything that is illegal, immoral, or contrary to public policy. Nor can he be compelled to do work not covered by his contract. Thus, if Morgan had been hired as a steward or engineroom mechanic, he could properly refuse to do the scraping and painting of the hull.

An employee is not a slave nor an indentured servant bound to remain for a prescribed time. He can quit at any time, but he has no legal right to quit in breach of his contract. If he quits without good cause before his contract ends, he is liable in damages. However, employers seldom sue their employees. The contract term is usually short (a week or a

---

* It is not essential that all or even a majority of all eligible workers vote. However, the NLRB will not certify a union as bargaining agent for all, even if it received a majority of the votes cast, unless a substantial or representative number of eligible employees did participate in the election.

month, for example) even though it may be extended by informal renewal for a lifetime. Moreover, a lawsuit would be resented by other employees, and any sizable judgment obtained would be uncollectible.

If the defaulting employee is highly valued, and has quit during his contract term to take a better paying job elsewhere, his first employer cannot compel him to return. But a court of equity might grant the employer a *negative injunction* barring the employee from working for anyone else during the contract term. To defy the court order could mean citation for contempt and a possible fine or jail sentence, or both.

Every employee is duty bound to use reasonable skill in performing assigned work, to perform it conscientiously (that is, to do "an honest day's work for an honest day's wages"), and to do nothing contrary to the interests of his employer. For example, he may not sabotage equipment, steal supplies, or sell company secrets to competitors.

> Ed Block was a stationary engineer in charge of a battery of boilers at the Metropole Chemical Works. Safety valves would prevent a major explosion, but the equipment could be seriously damaged even if the fail-safe devices worked perfectly. All controls had to be closely monitored and regulated.
>
> One day Block's wife left him after a prolonged argument over their son, who had been arrested on a narcotics possession charge. The son had been found in the apartment of his older sister, who had eloped the week before with a thrice-divorced carnival roustabout twenty years her senior. Understandably but not excusably, Block had "killed off" a large bottle of bourbon before he went to work on the swing shift. Within an hour he was sound asleep at his control panel. The boilers soon overheated and shut down automatically. Repairs would cost at least $5,000, to say nothing of the cost of disrupted production and spoiled goods in process, worth perhaps another $30,000. Is Block liable for the loss?

Yes. Theoretically, an employee may be charged with the cost of his employer's products he spoils or the value of equipment he damages either intentionally or through negligence. Practically, most employers absorb such spoilage costs as part of the price of doing business, and they pass them along in higher prices for the finished product. They seldom go beyond dismissing the errant employee. Insurance sometimes helps cover the costs.

7. WHAT ARE YOUR BASIC RIGHTS AS AN EMPLOYEE?

Every employee is entitled to *compensation* for his services as agreed upon. If no figure was specified, it is the prevailing or customary wage, or whatever would be reasonable under the circumstances. Sometimes (as in many sales jobs) pay in the form of commissions is contingent upon particular performance, such as a specified percentage of all sales made. State laws commonly require payment every two weeks or sometimes weekly.

The employee does not receive all he earns. Legally, the employer withholds federal income taxes (and, in some states, state income taxes) and social security taxes, and pays them directly to appropriate government agencies. By agreement with the employee, deductions are also common for such purposes as buying insurance, government savings bonds, or company stock; paying off company credit union loans; paying union dues (called the *"check off"*); or putting money into savings.

If wages are not paid, an employee has the usual rights to sue for money owed. Special legislation in most states and under federal bankruptcy laws gives him a preference or priority over other creditors of the employer.

> David Gorski was employed as a sales engineer by the Apogee Corporation at a salary of $400 a month plus a commission of 5 percent of all net sales made. The company supplied him with a car and agreed to pay all expenses of its operation and maintenance. (Apogee had so many agents on the road that it set aside the equivalent of premiums on automobile insurance, and thus self-insured.) At the end of the first month, Gorski submitted an itemized bill of $109 for gas and oil and $375 to cover the cost of replacing the wheels and tires that had been stolen. Were the items claimed by Gorski collectible as part of his compensation?

No. Although Gorski was entitled to both sums, technically the $109 was *reimbursement* for expenses properly incurred, and the $375 was *indemnification* for a loss suffered. Neither is compensation; neither is includable in his taxable income.

Every employee is entitled to reasonably safe working conditions. The federal *Occupational Safety and Health Act of 1971* broadly requires the employer in interstate commerce to "furnish to each of his employees employment and a place of employment which are free from recognized hazards that are causing or are likely to cause death or serious physical harm to his employees."[4] The law extends to such diverse items as equipment, protective clothing, vapor and noise levels, and in-plant health facilities. It provides for inspections, investigations, issuance of citations, judicial review, and penalties for violations. All states have a variety of local regulations governing production in intrastate commerce in the interests of worker health and safety.

An employee has no legal right to *fringe benefits,* but competition and union pressure have made them an integral part of most employment contracts. Such benefits are provided in addition to the regular wage or salary. They may include life insurance, medical and dental insurance, legal aid plans, vacations and holidays with pay, regular coffee breaks, tuition assistance, social and recreational programs, sick leave, sabbatical leave with pay, profit sharing, stock purchase plans, bonus payments, and private pension plans to supplement social security.

8. HAVE WORKERS ALWAYS HAD THE RIGHT TO JOIN WITH FELLOW WORKERS IN UNIONS?

No. The history of relations between labor and capital (or between workers and professional management hired by the owners of capital) is long and stormy. In 1806, a group of Philadelphia boot and shoemakers (called cordwainers) who joined together were found guilty of common law criminal *conspiracy* and fined. About thirty-five years later, the Supreme Court of Massachusetts in another classic case, *Commonwealth* v. *Hunt,* rejected the idea that a combination of workers was criminal simply because of their concerted action. The proper test, the court said, was the purpose of the combination; if intended "to induce all those engaged in the same occupation to become members," it is not unlawful. "Such an association might be used to afford each other assistance in time of poverty, sickness, or distress; or to raise their intellectual, moral, and social condition, or to make improvement in their art; or for other proper purposes."[5]

Nevertheless, unions continued to be harassed by court action instituted by employers who resisted any invasion of their decision-making power. For example, the federal *Sherman Antitrust Act of 1890* was enacted to protect trade and commerce against unlawful restraints and monopolies of business firms, but was zealously applied by courts to unions. Also, injunctions were often used to restrain concerted labor activity such as *picketing* (patrolling outside a business location to encourage workers to join the union, or to gain recognition from the employer, or to gain sympathy and support from third parties). But the pendulum eventually did swing in the opposite direction to favor labor and union organization.

> To get a job at the Champion Hereford Company packing plant, Orlando Ortez was required to sign a contract in which he agreed never to join a union while employed by Champion. Was the agreement binding?

Yes, before 1932; no, ever since then. In that year, the United States and most other nations were mired in the greatest economic depression man had ever known. Under the leadership of President Franklin D. Roosevelt, many new socioeconomic laws were enacted as part of the

New Deal. In the labor field, two important laws have survived challenges to their constitutionality and endured to this day.

1. The *Anti-Injunction Act of 1932 (popularly known as the Norris-LaGuardia Act,* after its prime movers) regulates the issuance of injunctions by the federal courts in labor disputes. Together with the Clayton Act, it effectively exempts unions from prosecution as monopolistic trusts or conspiracies in restraint of trade. It also outlaws *yellow dog contracts,* under which an employee agrees never to join a union, as a condition of employment.

2. The *National Labor Relations Act of 1935 (the Wagner Act),* recognizes the right of employees to form, join, or assist unions and to bargain collectively with employers through representatives of their own choosing. The act listed and outlawed five unfair labor practices of employers.

> Antonio Mondalli and Jack Smith were the two youngest and toughest workers at the Iceberg Cold Storage and Ice Company. When their request for a wage boost to match community levels was denied, they started to persuade other workers in the plant to join them in forming a local union or to affiliate with the Teamsters' union. When Artemus Finley, owner-manager of Iceberg, heard of the talk, he promptly fired Mondalli and Smith. Do they have any recourse under the law?

Yes. They can file a complaint with the nearest office of the National Labor Relations Board. For intrastate businesses, in some states they could apply to a comparable state board. In either case, the board could order their reinstatement with back pay.

In applying the Wagner Act, the National Labor Relations Board sometimes favored the revitalized unions unfairly. And so the pendulum eventually swung back with two new laws that restrained unions, but did not deprive them of their basic rights. The *Labor Management Relations Act of 1947 (Taft-Hartley Act)* amends the Wagner Act and adds a list of unfair labor practices of unions. It outlawed the *closed shop,* in which one must belong to the union before getting a job. It banned *secondary boycotts,* in which pressure is brought by striking workers against neutral third parties who supply or buy from the struck employer. For example, workers on strike at a furniture factory may not picket the independent retail stores that sell the furniture.

Farm workers are not covered by this act. In the late 1960s and early 1970s Cesar Chavez and his striking United Farm Workers were therefore able to picket stores that handled grapes and lettuce from non-unionized farms. This apparent advantage of farm workers is more than offset by the fact that employers are not legally obliged to recognize farm worker unions or to bargain collectively with them. Some observers predict that Congress will soon amend the law to include farm labor.

The Taft-Hartley Act reintroduced the injunction against strikes, but made it available only at the request of the National Labor Relations Board or of the President, in case of disputes that endanger the national health and welfare. After an eighty-day "cooling off" period in such cases, during which time the issues are investigated and reported upon by a public board, the strike may resume—to be ended possibly by government seizure and operation under an act of Congress.

> Loren Hillton was a rugged individualist and opposed joining any mutual help organization as a matter of principle. He was also a highly skilled toolmaker. Some time after he was hired by Advanced Avionics Corporation, the company signed an agreement with the toolmakers union that called for a union shop. Must Hillton now join the union or lose his job?

Yes. In a *union shop* an employee must join the union within thirty days after being hired. It is legal under the Taft-Hartley Act, although some states have enacted *"right-to-work" laws,* which outlaw this limited approach to union security and stability. Employers who accept the union shop reason that if they have to deal with a union, it may as well include all workers in the bargaining unit. There is likely to be less internal discord; the union leaders feel more secure and are less likely to make outrageous demands or promises to justify their existence. Also, since the union provides benefits, the members understandably believe all workers should share the costs; those who do not join are regarded contemptuously as "freeloaders."

A variation of the union shop is the *agency shop,* in which all employees in the bargaining unit (non-members as well as members) support the union by paying union dues as a condition of employment.

The *Labor Management Reporting and Disclosure Act of 1959 (Landrum-Griffen Act)* is sometimes called the bill of rights of union members because it guarantees their rights to participate in union affairs, protects their freedom to speak up in union meetings, and requires that they be kept informed about the union's financial condition.

> Raul Keroupian had joined the union at his plant shortly before the day of the meeting at which officers were to be selected. When nominations were made from the floor, someone moved to elect the entire incumbent slate by acclamation. Keroupian swallowed nervously, then stood up, and said "I don't think we can do that; it would be illegal." There were hoots and cat calls from the back of the room and he sat down. Was he correct?

Yes. Among other things, the Landrum-Griffen act prescribes that every local labor organization must elect its officers not less often than once every three years by secret ballot among the members in good standing.

9. DO MOST WORKERS BELONG TO UNIONS?

No. In our nation's civilian work force of more than 88 million persons, fewer than 20 million are union members. Comparatively few professional workers, government employees, and white collar workers belong to unions. Moreover, many union members are employed in *open shops,* where union membership is not required as a condition of getting or keeping a job, or in firms where no union is recognized as the representative of all employees.

> Although a union had been selected by a majority of the workers in his department, Virgil Redman refused to join. There was no union shop agreement, and he insisted on making his own "deal with the boss." "After all," he said, "I've been doing it that way for more than thirty years of mutually satisfactory service. And I don't intend to stop now." May Redman make his own contract with his employer governing his compensation and other terms of employment?

No. When a union is designated as the bargaining representative for workers in a given unit, it represents all workers in that unit, nonmembers included. This is true even when only a bare majority of eligible workers who participated in the representation election belong. They could constitute a minority of all workers in the bargaining unit.

Thus, simple numerical totals of union membership are misleading; they underestimate the true scope of union control. Unions are very strong in certain key industries: steel, coal mining, transportation, and printing and construction trades. Moreover, the wages and conditions set forth in union contracts tend to become the model for all other labor contracts. Unions exert more pressure on legislatures through lobbying efforts made possible by their unity and access to large sums of money from dues of many members.

Unionized workers, as a class, tend to enjoy an economic advantage over others. In 1966, for example, according to the U.S. Bureau of the Census, union members earned a median income of $6,824, 20 percent more than the $5,705 received by non-union workers. Almost two-thirds of all union members were employed full-time year round, compared with about half of non-union workers.[6] Union members also often enjoy more fringe benefits than others, including longer paid vacations, more holidays, health and life insurance programs, and private pension plans, as well as greater job security and protection from arbitrary or capricious action by supervisors.

10. WHAT ARE UNFAIR LABOR PRACTICES OF EMPLOYERS?

Gerard Gunness was a brilliant inventor who had built up his company to its present leading position in its field. To do it, he had worked as many as eighty hours a week for thirty-five years. When an international union sent professional organizers to his plant to sign up his 500 production workers, he was upset and enraged. Quickly calling a general assembly on company time, he reviewed the history of the business and reminded his employees that he had always paid union-scale wages or better. He said he wouldn't have "any union troublemakers from Chicago taking over now. We'll all be sorry if it happens, I'll see to that!" He refused rebuttal time when requested by union spokesmen. When the National Labor Relations Board ordered a representation election to decide whether the workers wanted a union, and if so, which one, Gunness had his supervisors distribute "Vote no" buttons to all. Nevertheless, the union won with a comfortable majority. Gunness was surprised, offended, and embittered. He then sent a letter to the homes of all workers announcing that since the union won, there would be no more 5 percent Christmas bonus payments as in the past twelve years. Was Gunness guilty of any unfair labor practices?

Yes. In different cases, several of the actions of Gunness have been found to be unfair employer labor practices by the NLRB: the "Vote no" buttons;[7] the making of an anti-union speech while denying the union request for equal time to reply;[8] withholding a long-established bonus.[9]

The National Labor Relations Act provides that it is an unfair labor practice for an employer to do any of the following.

1. Interfere with, restrain, or coerce employees in the exercise of their rights to form, join, or assist unions, or to bargain collectively, or to act in any concerted fashion for their mutual aid or protection; or to interfere, restrain, or coerce employees who choose to refrain from any such union activities.
2. Dominate or interfere with the formation or administration of any labor organization or to contribute financial or other support to it.
3. Discriminate in regard to hire or tenure or other conditions of employment in order to encourage or discourage membership in a union. (An exception here permits the union shop).
4. Fire or otherwise discriminate against an employee because he has filed charges or given testimony under the act.

5. Refuse to bargain with a labor organization that represents a majority of his employees in the bargaining unit.[10]

11. WHAT ARE UNFAIR LABOR PRACTICES OF UNIONS?

In a small one-company town in the Pacific Northwest, an outside union was trying to organize the lumber mill workers. Emotions had been aroused; the atmosphere was tense. There were strong pro- and anti-union elements both in the community and in the mill. Finally the union leaders called a strike, and workers who had already signed up (a minority of the total) joined the picket line. They massed at the main gate and tried to prevent non-union, non-striking employees from entering. Strong language soon degenerated into violent action. Blows were struck; rocks were thrown; an employee's car was overturned and burned; some non-strikers were followed home by a large group of heckling, chanting strikers. Were these legitimate means of gaining union recognition?

No. The violent and coercive behavior was illegal. Decisions of the NLRB and of appellate courts have outlawed physical violence, mass picketing at plant gates, and a large group of strikers following a small group of non-strikers away from the picket line.[11]

The list of union unfair labor practices that are illegal under the National Labor Relations Act includes the following:

1. To restrain or coerce employees in their right to join or to refuse to join a union.
2. To restrain or coerce an employer in his selection of his representative to engage in collective bargaining or adjustment of grievances.
3. To cause or to try to cause an employer to discriminate against an employee in violation of the rule that the employer shall not discriminate in order to encourage or discourage union membership.
4. To refuse to bargain collectively in good faith with an employer.
5. To engage in *secondary boycotts* (that is, a refusal by strikers or sympathizers to deal with a neutral party in a labor dispute, such as a supplier or customer of the struck company).
6. To engage in *jurisdictional disputes or strikes* (for example, where two unions claim the right to represent the same workers, or the exclusive right to do certain work).
7. To require payment of excessive or discriminatory initiation fees for joining a union.
8. To cause or attempt to cause an employer to pay for services that are not performed or are not to be performed. This rule against *featherbedding* actually has been interpreted by the U.S. Supreme

Court to permit the employer and union to agree "what, if any work, including bona-fide make-work shall be included as compensated service." Thus, a printers' union is not guilty of featherbedding if it insists on setting anew all type for pages that come from outside the plant already set in the form of mat—even if the newly set "bogus type" is then destroyed and the original mat is used in the actual printing.[12] However, it would be illegal to require two workers to be employed for a job that requires just one, with the second doing nothing.

9. To engage in unreasonable recognition picketing (for example, where a valid representation election has already taken place within the preceding twelve months).

10. To strike or terminate a contract without giving notice to the employer and to the *Federal Mediation and Conciliation Service.* Normally, each party is bound to serve a written notice upon the other at least sixty days before the expiration date. The Mediation and Conciliation Service has no authority to prescribe terms or to impose a settlement, but its experts seek to assist the disputants in reaching an acceptable settlement.

11. To enter into *"hot cargo" agreements,* which permit employees to refuse to handle or work on goods shipped from a plant where the workers are on strike, or to refuse to perform any services that may benefit an employer included on a union "unfair" list. Exceptions are made and restrictions of the outlawed type are permitted in the building construction industry and in the apparel and clothing manufacturing industry.[13]

12. DO MOST WORKERS ENGAGE IN STRIKES?

No. Most workers are not unionized, and strikes are normally called by unions. A *strike* is a concerted refusal by employees to perform the services for which they were hired. The strikers do not quit permanently; they consider themselves employees and plan to return to their old job when the strike ends. By then, they hope that their employer will have acceded to all or some of their demands. The strike is the ultimate weapon of unions, even as the ultimate weapon of employers is the *lockout*—a shutdown of operations in response to union activity or demands. Neither is used casually nor frequently, although the strike is much more common.

According to the U.S. Bureau of Labor Statistics, from 1961 through 1970, the number of work stoppages caused by strikes and lockouts ranged from a low of 3,362 in 1963 to a high of 5,715 in 1970; the number of workers directly involved ranged from 940,000 in 1963 to 3,300,000 in 1970—not a shocking number in a work force of approximately 80 million at that time. The percentage of estimated working time lost during these periods was less than half of one percent in both years (.11 percent in 1963 and .37 percent in 1970).

These figures do not reflect the full impact of a labor strike, however. They do not show the indirect or secondary effect on other companies that are forced to cut back or even shut down because their markets or sources of needed supplies are cut off. Nor do they reflect the inconvenience and added cost or deprivation imposed on the disputants as well as on innocent third parties. A strike of elevator operators in a large skyscraper, for example, can immobilize the business of most of the thousands of tenants.

Society accepts these costs, even as it accepts the costs of competition that sometimes force business firms to close at great loss to investors and other dependent parties. *Compulsory arbitration* of labor disputes might eliminate strikes, but most persons reject the idea of having a third party (or panel) make decisions on the issues, which will then be binding as a matter of law. Some disputants are not even eager to utilize government or private conciliation and mediation services, in which the third party uses reason, advice, and persuasion to bring labor and management together in a voluntary settlement.

Once labor and management agree on the terms of an employment contract, it is common practice to include a clause requiring arbitration of disputes that may arise over the interpretation and operation of the contract. For example, a worker may claim that his duties qualify him for a higher-paying wage classification; or a worker may charge a foreman with unfair discrimination against him in the assignment of dangerous or unpleasant jobs.

13. WHAT KINDS OF STRIKES ARE THERE?

Pat McGillicuddy was unhappy with the wages, hours, work schedule, plant rules, heating and lighting of the work room, fringe benefits (there were none), and supervision at his place of employment. After weeks of grumbling and complaining to his fellow workers, one day he got up from his work bench, put on his coat and hat, and shouted so that all in the large room could hear: "I strike!" Then he walked out the door and started to picket in front of the building. Was he on strike?

No. McGillicuddy's employer can take his action to mean that he has quit and can replace him. If there is a union and it orders a strike in which all members walk out in an *economic strike* (over wages, hours, or conditions of employment), the employer may legally hire strike-breakers as permanent replacements. If, after the strike is over, the jobs again become available, the employer must hire the economic strikers provided they have not taken substantially equivalent permanent jobs elsewhere. If the strike was an *unfair labor practice strike* prompted by one or more unfair labor practices of the employer, the striking workers retain full rights to their jobs and must be restored to them when the strike ends. Moreover, the offending employer must pay back wages to the striker.

> The Snug Fit Shoe Corporation had a three-year contract with its production workers under a collective bargaining agreement. The union vote approving the contract had been very close and initial dissatisfaction had gradually turned into outspoken protest. After sixteen months, the workers defied their leaders and announced through a spokesman: "We're on strike. To prevent strikebreakers from taking our jobs, we're going to stay right here in the plant." A sitdown had begun. Friends and relatives brought them sleeping bags and food for a long stay. Was the strike legal?

No. *Sitdown strikes* in which workers retain possession of the employer's property are illegal.[14] Moreover, this was a *wildcat strike* in violation of the contract and without consent of the union. As such, it constituted an unfair labor practice and the employer could hire permanent replacements for the strikers, who would be evicted by the police and would be subject to punishment. Sometimes workers of one employer walk out when workers of another employer go on strike or are locked out. This is a *sympathy strike* and obviously is more serious than the common union labor practice of refusing to cross a picket line. It is a variation of an economic strike and the employer may treat it as such.

14. MAY AN EMPLOYER REQUIRE HIS EMPLOYEES TO WORK MORE THAN FORTY HOURS A WEEK?

If an employer is engaged in interstate commerce covered by the *Fair Labor Standards Act of 1938* as amended *(Wage and Hour Law)*—and most employers are—he may ask his employees to work more than forty hours a week but must pay them for the overtime at a rate not less than one and one-half times the regular rate. Certain limited exceptions are provided, as for seasonal industries (where the maximum at regular rates is fifty hours a week) and for companies processing agricultural products (limit, forty-eight hours a week).

The same act as amended provides a minimum hourly wage of $2.10 for most covered employees until January 1, 1976, when it goes up to $2.30. For employees of certain retail firms, the $2.30 wage is to be reached in January, 1977; for agricultural employees it is to be reached in January, 1978. These minima apply to old and young alike.

> Leslie Rockwell was delighted when, fresh out of college in 1950, he was hired as a management trainee by the Majestic Admiral

Products Corporation. His beginning salary was $500 a month. Now he is a division sales manager earning five times as much, but consistently working fifty to sixty hours a week. When he travels, his work week is even longer and he is on the road half of the time. Recently Majestic was absorbed in a merger with General Products Company, and Rockwell has been informed that his services will not be needed after three months. His wife is urging him to claim overtime pay for all the extra hours he has given to the corporation. Is he entitled to this pay?

No. The maximum hour provisions of the Wage and Hour Law do not apply to certain occupations, including (a) executive, administrative, and professional employees as well as teachers in elementary and secondary schools; (b) outside salesmen; (c) employees of retail or service establishments with annual sales under $250,000; and (d) an employee in agriculture who is the parent, spouse, child, or other member of the employer's family.

California's Industrial Welfare Commission in 1974 issued new regulations that permit a ten-hour working day for many employees before overtime wages apply. Overtime must still be paid in most cases after forty hours of work in one week. The eight-hour working day remains in the food canning, freezing, and preserving industry; but ten-hour workdays are permitted in the manufacturing, personal service, mercantile, transportation, amusement, recreation, and broadcasting fields. This rule could encourage adoption of the four-day, forty-hour work week.

The National Labor Relations Act distinguishes between management and other employees. Although the act states that nothing in it shall prohibit a supervisor from becoming a member of a labor organization, no employer is obliged to bargain collectively with his supervisors.[15] Therefore, unions of supervisors are seldom seen. The question of which employees are managerial is determined by actual job responsibilities, authority, and relationship to management (the process of getting things done through other people's efforts).

15. WHAT HAPPENS IF YOU ARE INJURED ON THE JOB?

It was a glorious spring day as Willie Jon Fisher climbed to his work station 125 feet above the bay. A steel worker, he was paid premium wages for assuming the risk of his hazardous job on the new Silver Door Bridge. In a burst of youthful exuberance, he took off his hard hat; waved to his pal, Don Jones, twenty feet above; and danced a quick jig on the beam where he stood. Jones shouted, "Simmer down and get to work!" and then tossed a short section of cable at Fisher. The cable struck his head and he fell, striking a cross beam before the safety net caught his unconscious body. Fisher suffered permanent injuries and never returned to the job. Is his employer liable in any way?

Yes. Any covered employee injured on the job is entitled to benefits under *workmen's compensation laws,* which are found in all states.* In most employment situations, if a worker is killed on the job, his dependents are entitled to benefits. These payments are far from lavish, but they are reasonably certain.

Under the old common law, the employer might escape all liability if he could prove that the worker knew the hazards involved and assumed the risk, or that he was guilty of contributory negligence, or that some fellow employee was at fault and caused the accident. In Fisher's case, all three defenses might have been raised at common law. Now, however, such defenses are not admissible. The injured worker is generally paid benefits, with very few exceptions: for example, if the injury was self-inflicted, or was the result of voluntary intoxication, or was the result of a fight in which he was the aggressor.

California is one of the few states that also cover workers (but not their dependents) for disability resulting from off-the-job accidents or diseases. Employees pay the cost of this coverage through payroll deductions of premiums.

Because of the penurious payments made under state plans for injuries or death, and because some workers are excluded from coverage, a strong effort is being made as of this writing to provide federal coverage in states that fail to meet minimum standards.

16. IF YOU INVENT SOMETHING, DOES YOUR EMPLOYER OWN THE PATENT RIGHTS?

It depends on your employment contract. If you were hired to do research and development work, your employer probably has exclusive rights to your brainchild. When Frank Dorian, an engineer in the Boston research lab of the Gillette Company, devised the "Trac II" two-bladed safety razor, it was touted as the "most significant shaving discovery since King C. Gillette invented the safety razor seventy-five years ago." The company proceeded to invest millions of dollars in the perfection and production and marketing of the new product. According to a news magazine report, "the triumph seems likely to go to his [Dorian's] pocketbook as little as it has gone to his head—at least for a while. Gillette, a paternalistic company with no unions, no bonuses and no inventor's royalties, has done little but shake Dorian's hand."[16]

---

* In California these laws have recently been renamed worker compensation.

Patent rights are usually covered by written contract with employees hired to do such creative work. The company may sometimes retain rights to discoveries for a period of time after the inventors leave its employ. But then, they simply did what they were hired to do and agreed to do; and few such workers in a team approach laboratory become Frank Dorians.

If there is no expressed or implied contract covering inventions, the employee owns the patent rights to his inventions. This is true even if he used company time and materials in his research and discovery. However, if an invention was made on company time, the employer has a *shop right* to use it in the operation of his own plant without payment of royalties or other charges.

17. WHAT IS A MECHANIC'S LIEN?

> When Raymond Brockett and his wife Yvonne built their dream house overlooking the river in the valley town where they lived, they exhausted their savings and all the credit they could muster to pay the general contractor. Within a few days after they took possession, they were appalled to receive claims from seven employees of the general contractor and several employees of subcontractors for a total of $15,000 unpaid wages. Must they pay?

Yes. In many cases when a worker (or a contractor-employer) does a job on property belonging to another, such as a car or house, he is entitled to a *lien,* or claim against the improved property, if not paid promptly. To enforce his lien, he can normally arrange a court-ordered sale of the property to recover money due.

In a sense, the reverse is also true. If a worker fails to pay bills that he owes, his creditors may *garnish* (or attach) his wages, generally after obtaining a judgment from a court. Under the *Federal Consumer Credit Protection Act (the Truth in Lending Law),* only a limited portion of his wages may be taken, however. The amount garnished may not exceed (a) 25 percent of his weekly take-home pay, or (b) the amount by which the weekly take-home pay exceeds thirty times the federal minimum wage, whichever is less. The federal law also prohibits an employer from firing a worker because his wages have been garnished for any single indebtedness.

1. Some members of a union in New York City worked in local factories that made electrical equipment. Other members of the same union installed such equipment on construction jobs. To help protect the factory jobs of its members, the union persuaded contractors to buy their electrical equipment only from the local manufacturers who were unionized. Moreover, the local equipment manufacturers agreed to confine their New York sales to contractors who employed members of the union. Manufacturers of electrical equipment from outside New York complained, claiming the agreements referred to violated federal antitrust laws. The union defended, claiming it was no longer subject to antitrust laws. Was the union guilty of antitrust law violation?

2. For good cause, Shamrock Properties fired Barney Barker, an employee. Barker then got a job with the union that was bargaining agent for all shop employees of the corporation. Barker was vindictive and told several persons, including the corporation's personnel director, that he hoped Shamrock would "go broke—they deserve it!" Later the union selected Barker as one of its bargaining representatives to negotiate a new contract with Shamrock, but company officials refused to attend any meeting so long as he was included at the table. Is Shamrock guilty of the unfair practice of refusing to bargain collectively?

3. After a strike was called, Phil Thornbush joined fellow workers on the picket line at the Brown Derby Brewery. There was no violence, and only two picket posts of six to eight men each marched around the plant twenty-four hours a day. Thornbush was arrested and convicted under a state statute that made loitering and picketing a misdemeanor. He appealed, claiming the statute violated his constitutional right to free speech. Should the conviction be reversed?

4. The technicians at television station KTVE went out on strike in a dispute over terms of a proposed contract. The strike dragged on for weeks. Ordinary picketing seemed to be ineffective, and so some of the strikers prepared and distributed 5,000 handbills, which in sharp language disparaged the quality of KTVE programs. Thereupon, the employer fired those responsible for the printing and distribution. Was KTVE guilty of an employer unfair labor practice?

5. Douglas Corcoran was young, strong, and ambitious. On his first job he consistently exceeded the production rates agreed upon informally between the employer and the union. Some union members tried to persuade him to change, but he laughed at them and said he was aiming at a foremanship. He did expect to be promoted, but instead he was fired. This happened after the union threatened a strike if

he stayed on. Was either union or employer guilty of an unfair labor practice?

6. After an early April flash flood washed out a bridge on an important highway, Calcoa Construction Company got the contract to make emergency repairs, and Chuck Snyder was one of the experienced workers hastily employed to do the job. It was midnight, and bitter cold. During a coffee break, Snyder drank more whiskey than coffee— "to stay warm." After he returned to work, he finished off a bottle and was warm and mellow, but intoxicated. Unsteady on his feet, he slipped on the muddy bank, fell into the swirling waters and was drowned. Are his widow and orphaned children entitled to death benefits under the workmen's compensation law?

7. Although employed by Supreme Scientific Instrument Company as an ordinary heavy machine maintenance man, Emanuel Mayer spent many hours in the company research laboratory. He did this before and after work and sometimes, when his services were not needed elsewhere, even during his regular work shift. During his lab time, he devised an ingenious fitting to prevent backflow in pumps and had the device patented in his own name. Then he told the company employment manager about his achievement and asked for transfer to the lab as a technician on a permanent basis. Refused, Mayer sought and got a job with Supreme's arch-rival, A-OK-Atomics, which bought his patent. Now Supreme claims it is entitled to the patent. Is it?

8. For years, Pacific Electrophonics employed almost no blacks and no Chicanos, and it had only a few female managers. After passage of the Civil Rights Act of 1964, Pacific began to send representatives into schools to recruit women and minority persons as employees. The board of directors of the corporation also ordered top management to arrange the promotion of more women and minority persons to positions of management responsibility. Paul Worthington, a white male Anglo-Saxon Protestant, could not get a job with Pacific. He claims the corporation's new hiring and promotion practices are an illegal and unconstitutional type of "reverse discrimination." Is he right?

9. In a series of annual contracts, production workers of the Basic Stereo Component Company received substantial wage boosts and fringe benefits. If they worked overtime, many skilled union members earned more than their own foremen. This annoyed the foremen, and so they organized a union of their own. They insisted that their employer bargain collectively with them over their demands for equivalent or superior benefits. Is Basic legally obligated to do so?

10. During his last semester before his graduation from CSUS, Lawrence LaPorte met with a representative of the Pleistocene Petroleum Products Company at the university placement office. In their discussions, the company rep indicated that an employment offer would undoubtedly be made. Ten days later, LaPorte received a telegram offering him an excellent job in Kuwait for an initial term of three years, with possibility of renewal. He immediately sent a telegram accepting the offer. There was no formal written contract of employment. Is Pleistocene legally bound? Is LaPorte legally bound?

11. Victor Fusee was employed by a small daily newspaper with a circulation of about 10,000. All of the papers were sold locally except for less than 2 percent, which were regularly sold out of the state. Fusee claimed he was protected by the federal Fair Labor Standards Act (Wage and Hour Law) and was therefore entitled to time and a half wages for all overtime he worked. The publisher insisted he was engaged in intrastate commerce, not interstate commerce, and so could not be bound by the federal law. Who is right?

12. Should Congress abolish the right to strike and the right to lockout workers, and substitute a program of compulsory arbitration of all labor-management disputes that cannot be settled by the parties themselves?

13. Many employers require retirement of their employees upon reaching age sixty-five. Is this a good policy? Is so, should the age be lowered to sixty? To fifty-five? Should different ages apply to different occupations? Social Security retirement benefits are reduced if more than a certain sum is earned after retirement. Should this rule be abolished to encourage continued employment?

14. Unions and employer groups are sometimes organized to include most workers and companies in a given industry. Bargaining may be conducted for the entire industry; a shut-down affects all and tends to be felt more acutely by the public. Should industry-wide bargaining be banned by law?

15. Should state right-to-work laws be extended nationally? or should such laws be abolished?

16. If the employment rights of women, blacks, Chicanos, American Indians, and Asian-Americans are recognized and upheld through affirmative action programs, may other definable minority groups in the nation legitimately demand similar preferential treatment? Who, for example? With what possible effect on the program? With what possible effect on American efficiency and productivity?

13

YOU
IN BUSINESS
FOR YOURSELF

1. MAY ANYONE START ANY BUSINESS OF HIS OWN?

Theoretically, yes. Practically, no. Licenses and financial qualifications are required for certain business ventures. Under the law, exclusive licenses are given in fields where unlimited competition would be impracticable or wasteful—for example, radio and television, public utilities, and transportation. Typically, in such cases, to get and keep the necessary license (which may ensure a virtual monopoly), the business firm must provide a certain level of service and charge legally prescribed rates or prices. This can be a costly limitation on freedom of action, as many owners of stocks and bonds issued by railroads can attest. Independent administrative agencies such as the federal Interstate Commerce Commission (ICC) regulate interstate service, and comparable state bodies govern intrastate service. As a consequence, railroad lines are kept open even though they lose money and should probably be abandoned to trucks and other transporters. Paradoxically, one fear of legislators is that giant railroads, if given freedom to charge what they please, could cut rates selectively, thus forcing truckers out of business.

To protect the public, the law requires business firms in certain fields to demonstrate minimum financial responsibility before they open. Banks, savings and loan associations, insurance companies must first obtain prescribed,

substantial amounts of capital. In still other occupational fields, the entrepreneur must attain technical or professional competence through formal schooling and then demonstrate it through formal examination. This is true of lawyers, doctors, dentists, barbers, cosmetologists, morticians, real estate salesmen and brokers, building contractors, insurance salesmen, and many others.

In general, however, in our free enterprise system, all fields are open to all persons. Anyone may attempt to enter even those fields that require certain qualifications. Usually the principal problem or obstacle to going into business for oneself is not legal, but economic and psychological. An entrepreneur needs capital—funds to buy supplies and equipment, to rent or buy quarters, to hire help, to finance production and sales, and to extend credit to customers. Among the personal qualities needed for success in business are intelligence, energy, ambition, initiative, courage, foresight, and industriousness—qualities that do not often come together in one person.

Another economic deterrent to going into business for oneself is the likelihood of failure. Most new business ventures do not survive. Failure may entail not only loss of one's own time and money (and often that of others), but also an embarrassing retreat and disposal of the business piecemeal or as a unit, perhaps just barely breaking even.

Succeeding in a business of one's own is difficult. *Profits*—the excess of revenues (or receipts) over costs (or expenses)—do not flow in automatically. They entail bringing labor, materials, machines, and manpower together; combining and coordinating them efficiently to produce a marketable commodity or service; pricing it competitively; advertising and selling it; and billing and getting paid (perhaps after a delay because of credit extension). Then the government takes as much as 50 percent or more in income taxes. (Presumably prices were adjusted to absorb this tax. The consumer who gets the primary benefit of the goods thus indirectly pays the tax just as he pays other costs involved in the production of goods and services.)

The entrepreneur would like to "maximize" his profits—an elusive concept probably meaning he'd like "more." But practically he is happy to settle for a reasonable return on his invested capital, together with a reasonable salary for his services.

2. WHAT LEGAL FORMS OF BUSINESS ORGANIZATION ARE AVAILABLE?

Alexander Gadsden had saved almost $10,000; he knew where he could borrow again as much for as long as five years. He had several trustworthy and competent friends who might be interested in joining him in a business venture if he asked for their help. He had been employed for several years as a tennis instructor at the largest private club in town and had done most of the chores in the sport shop on the premises, as well as in the front office. Now he considered starting a private tennis club of his own. What form of business organization should he use?

Alexander could use any of a number of possible forms of business organization recognized by law. The most important in terms of popularity and volume of business are sole proprietorship, partnership, and corporation.

Sole Proprietorship

Alexander could be the sole owner of his business. As such, he would own all assets, be liable without limit for all liabilities or debts, be entitled to all profits, and suffer all losses. Unless he delegated his authority to hired help, he would have the privilege and burden of making all decisions. In all likelihood, his hours would be very long and he would carry the problems of the business "under his hat" wherever he went. His income from the business would be regarded as ordinary personal income and would be taxed as such (up to 50 percent at the federal level).

Partnership

Alexander could join with one or more other persons in an association to carry on as co-owners the business for profit.[1] Although the partners may contribute unequal amounts of capital, and spend unequal amounts of time at work, they share the profits and losses equally unless they agree to some other plan of distribution.

If Alexander puts up most of the capital, he may insist on getting most of the profits and his partners may go along with his demand. Third party creditors, however, are not bound by internal agreements of the partners. Thus, Alexander could be liable without limit for debts of the firm and might not be able to collect from the other partners their share of a loss. When a partner retires from the business (with or without good cause), goes insane, or dies, the partnership is *dissolved*. Unless arrangements are quickly made to carry on the business, it must be sold in some haste (as a unit or, even worse, piecemeal). After this *winding-up* period, the partnership is *terminated*. With a little sensible advance planning, however, the losses inevitable in such forced sales can be avoided. Arrangements can be made to form a new business and to carry on.

For example, two partners might enter into a *buy and sell agreement*, funded by life insurance. Partner *A* buys a policy of life insurance on partner *B*'s life, and agrees to buy out *B*'s interest in the firm over a prescribed period of time if *B* dies first. The insurance proceeds would help pay the bill. Reciprocally, Partner *B* buys a life insurance policy on *A*'s life and agrees to buy *A*'s interest if *A* dies first.

In a partnership, each partner is an agent of the other partner or partners; each may enter into contracts for the firm with third parties, and all partners are bound. Because of this great power and its related potential for abuse, no partner may join the firm unless unanimously approved by existing partners. Likewise, all partners must agree on modifications in their partnership agreement and on fundamental changes in company objectives and operations. Ordinary business decisions (such as setting policies on purchasing, pricing, or warranties) are made by a majority. If there are disagreements, a majority vote resolves them. Individual partners may make decisions for the firm, acting within the policies established by the majority. If there is a deadlock, which can easily happen with an even number of partners, not infrequently the firm falters and must be dissolved.

income taxes Income taxes are not levied on partnership income, although the firm must file an information return. Each partner's share of income, whether distributed or not, is taxable as part of that person's individual income. This could be disadvantageous if the partner already enjoys a sizable income from other sources. He might prefer to have the money remain in the business, as is possible in a corporation.

limited partnership In this cross between a partnership and a corporation, at least one partner must be a *general partner* with unlimited responsibility for firm debts.[2] However, if the business fails, the *limited partner,* like a corporate shareholder, stands to lose no more than he invested plus his share of any earnings retained by the firm. He is not individually liable for firm debts. To preserve this privileged status, however, the limited partner may not assist in the management of the firm.

Corporation

In a corporation, the stockholders elect three or more *directors* who are legally responsible for managing the business. The directors select *officers* (president, vice-president, secretary, and treasurer), who actively handle the routine affairs of the company, usually with the assistance of hired workers. (See figure 13–1).

Alexander could form a small, *close or closely-held corporation,* in which he might be the sole stockholder and dominant director, as well as president.[3] As owner of all the stock, he could find two or more cooperative directors and necessary officers. In most states, three incorpo-

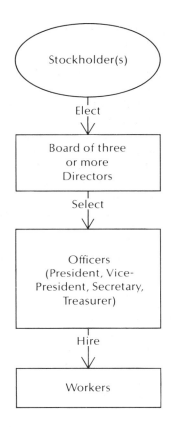

Fig. 13-1.
Organization of a
corporation

rators may obtain a *charter,* or permit to do business, from the state. Sometimes this entails simply getting approval for the *articles of incorporation,* which tell the purposes of the firm, identify its managing directors, describe its capital structure (that is, what sort of shares of stock are to be sold), and give its principal address.

Although the corporation is a legal entity and as such is liable without limit for its debts, the shareholders are investors who can lose no more than they paid for their shares, plus any amount the company reinvested for them out of retained earnings.* This *limited liability* feature of the corporate form of organization appeals to many persons, and so corporations are able to raise large amounts of captial for the mass production and mass distribution of goods, so critical in our mass consumption

---

* In rare cases, shareholders buy stock at a discount, or below the par value (printed on the face of the share). If the corporation later fails financially, creditors may insist that the shareholders pay the balance of the value. In California, the directors may avoid this embarrassing possibility by declaring at the time of sale that the full value is the reduced selling price or stated value.

society. Paradoxically, a banker may refuse to lend money to a close corporation unless its officers guarantee the loan, agreeing to be personally liable in full. Thus, the advantage of limited liability may be lost in the small corporation owned by just one or a few individuals.

Unlike the partnership, a corporation lives on when stockholders die, or when its shares are bought and sold or transferred by gift in life or by inheritance upon death. The corporation is an artificial person in the eyes of the law, and so it may be chartered to last indefinitely, into perpetuity. Practically, it may fail and "die" (be dissolved) if it is seriously mismanaged, or if a key official (possibly the sole stockholder and president) dies. Generally, however, the fact that it is an *entity,* separate from its owners and officers, permits it to endure, and facilitates the easy transferability of shares of stock. This appeals to investors, but again most persons are understandably reluctant to buy shares in closely held corporations. They properly fear failure of the business, or the possibility that dominant owners who are also officers will pay high salaries to themselves and declare low or no dividends.

income taxes   The corporation pays a 22 percent federal income tax on net taxable income up to $25,000 and a total tax of 48 percent on any excess.* If the earnings are distributed in dividends, the receipts—after a $100 exclusion per person—are subject to a second, even larger (up to 70 percent) federal tax on the personal income of each shareholder. To avoid this second levy, corporate directors may decide to declare no dividends, retain the earnings, and reinvest them in the business.†

stock splits and stock dividends   To keep stockholders happy when no cash dividends are declared, the directors may *split* the existing stock—giving, for example, two shares for each one owned. Since there is no cash distribution, the new shares are not taxable. Because the earnings were retained to be used in the business, the company should be earning more and the aggregate of shares should be worth more than before. If a shareholder wants to take his portion of the profits in cash, he can sell one or more of his shares of stock. For federal tax purposes, he will pay a capital gains tax of 25 percent on the first $50,000 and a maximum of 35 percent on the excess, which may still be substantially less than he would have paid in ordinary income tax if he had received a cash dividend. The split may also be designed to bring the stock price

---

*   In California, as in many states, a state income tax is also imposed on corporate income (7.6 percent on most corporations) as well as on personal income (at a rate up to 10 percent) received as dividends. In some states, the government takes more than half of all the earnings of a corporation, plus more than three-fourths of certain earnings of individuals.

†   However, if the earnings are retained and not reinvested, the Internal Revenue Service imposes a special penalty tax of 27.5 percent on the first $100,000 of any such accumulations in excess of $100,000, and 38.5 percent on the remainder.

within *trading range,* a lower level that is more appealing to investors and speculators. As a result, a share that sold for $100 before it split four for one might now be worth $26 to $30 times four ($104 to $120).

As an alternative, the corporation's directors could declare a *stock dividend* by issuing, for example, one new share for each share owned. The net effect is essentially the same as in a stock split, but technically the stock dividend involves a bookkeeping transfer from the retained earnings account to the capital stock account. Thus legally, such transferred and permanently capitalized earnings are no longer available for the payment of cash dividends.

3. IS A CORPORATION EVER REGARDED AS A PARTNERSHIP?

Max Rogarous started his mobile home construction business as a sole proprietorship. He built the first unit in his garage. As the business prospered, he added a partner and later incorporated the company in order to raise more capital by selling stock to seven wealthy friends. All nine owners are now in the upper tax brackets and quite unhappy with their tax status. The firm pays the 48 percent federal corporation income tax and when cash dividends are declared, each owner has to pay a whopping personal income tax on money received. Can they end this double taxation and still get the profits?

Yes. They could change the firm back to a partnership, but none wants the burdens of sharing in management with Rogarous and his hired assistants, and all fear the hazard of unlimited liability for firm debts. They are also fearful of the inevitable dissolution when a partner withdraws or dies, even though arrangements could be made to carry on.

Therefore, they elect to be treated as a *sub-chapter S corporation,* as permitted by the Internal Revenue Service.[4] The company retains its corporate status but is considered a partnership for federal income tax purposes. No federal corporate income tax is paid; all income is shared by the stockholders according to their equity in common stock. As in a partnership, the income is regarded as earned whether or not distributed to the owners. They pay only their personal income taxes.

To qualify as a sub-chapter S corporation, certain conditions must be met.

1. It may have no more than ten shareholders.
2. It may have outstanding only one class of stock, normally common.
3. It may not include any nonresident shareholders.
4. At least 80 percent of its income must come from active operations (no more than 20 percent may be "passive" investment income such as rents, dividends, and interest).

4. WHAT HAPPENS IF THE CORPORATE FORM IS USED TO PERPETRATE A FRAUD ON CREDITORS?

> With minimal capital of his own, Irving Tuttle went heavily into debt to organize a corporation so that he could use the assets to pay himself a high salary, and then file for bankruptcy for the corporation. When he organized a second corporation and went through the same routine, some of his corporate creditors sued him and sought payment from his personal assets. Will they succeed?

Yes, in all likelihood. A court "tears aside the corporate veil" and holds the owner (or owners) liable without limit as sole proprietor or partners when the corporation has been organized to perpetrate a fraud on creditors, as here. There is, of course, nothing illegal or immoral about incorporating to obtain the advantage of limited liability for shareholders. Prospective creditors can request financial statements from the corporation, or indirectly through a report by a credit rating agency. Then they can refuse to extend credit if the corporate assets appear to be inadequate to meet all debts as they come due.

Sometimes a sole proprietor or partner, before starting a risky business venture, will transfer certain assets to a spouse or relatives. If the transfer is made before the risky business begins and debts or liabilities are incurred, creditors of the business (sole proprietorship or partnership) cannot reach the transferred assets to get paid. Before extending credit, they should check on the assets and liabilities of the prospective debtor, and possibly require special security. To meet this requirement, the proprietor or partner may need to persuade his relative(s) to return the assets or to co-sign promissory notes.

5. WHAT ARE THE COMPARATIVE ADVANTAGES AND DISADVANTAGES OF THE LEADING FORMS OF BUSINESS ORGANIZATION?

In table 13-1 the three principal forms of business organization are rated from 1 (best) to 3 (worst)—from the owner's standpoint—in regard to several basic characteristics.

Limited partnerships have gained in popularity in recent years, since they can be made somewhat permanent and may be used as tax shelters. In a corporation, losses, if any, are suffered by the corporation, a legal entity. Only indirectly, through changes in the value of stock, is the shareholder affected. In a limited partnership, losses immediately pass to the partners and they can charge them off against other income. For example, a doctor in the highest income bracket invests in a limited partnership, which buys an apartment house. The apartment house shows

TABLE 13-1

Legal Forms of Business Organization Compared

Characteristics	Sole Proprietorship	Partnership	Corporation
1. Ease of starting	1	2	3
2. Cost of starting	1	2	3
3. Ease of transferring interest	2	3	1

4. Independence
   Sole control
   Receipt of all profits
	1
	1
	1
		2
		2
		2
			3
			3
			3 } (1 if sole owner of stock)

5. Privacy	1	2	3
6. Duration	3	2	1 (3 if sole owner of stock)
7. Liability for debts	2	3‡	1 (3 if owner guarantees debts)
8. Income tax status	1	1	2 (1 if corporation retains earnings)
9. Credit rating	2	1	3 (1 if owners guarantee debts)
10. Potential for growth	3	2	1
11. Division of labor and access to specialists	3	2	1
12. Availability of incentive plans and fringe benefits (pensions, profit-sharing plans, group life insurance, health insurance)	2*	2*	1†

Note: 1—normally most favorable to owner; 3—normally least favorable to owner.

* May utilize Keogh Plan for tax-free accumulation of retirement benefits.

† May be expense to corporation and not taxable income to recipient, or deferred until retirement when total personal income is down and therefore applicable tax rate is lower.

‡ 1 for limited partner if limited partnership.

a large bookkeeping loss because of high depreciation expense. This is a "paper loss" because it is based on a bookkeeping entry for depreciation of the structure, and does not reflect any out-of-pocket cash disbursement. Nevertheless, it is recognized as a real loss by the IRS, and the doctor may use it to offset some of his cash income, which he therefore may retain and enjoy.

6. DOES THE LAW AFFECT THE INTERNAL OPERATIONS OF YOUR BUSINESS?

> When Mrs. Polly Gerber started making canned fruit and jam preserves in her kitchen, she never dreamed that neighbors would beg her to sell them some of her output. But they did and she did. Within three years she rented a factory building and started producing in quantity, employing fifty-seven persons and selling in three western states. She was a sole proprietor and a rugged individualist. She insisted that as long as she paid her property tax and income tax, Uncle Sam and all "government snoopers" would have to "keep their cotton pickin' hands off her business." Is she right?

No. If she hasn't already discovered the truth, she soon will. The long arm of government regulation will reach into many corners of her operation, telling her what she must do or not do.

1. Obtain a local business license.
2. Comply with local, state, and federal health and food purity regulations governing the sanitary conditions in the factory and the quality of the output.
3. Comply with federal laws regulating the packages used and the disclosure of contents on the labels.
4. Comply with safety requirements for the benefit of her employees under state and federal occupational safety laws.
5. Pay minimum wages and limit work to maximum prescribed hours, or pay premium wages for overtime.
6. Recognize the right of the workers to organize into a union or unions of their own choosing. If a majority join, bargain in good faith with them over wages, hours, and conditions of employment.
7. Pay Workmen's Compensation Insurance premiums to compensate any workers who may be hurt on the job.
8. Do not discriminate in hiring or promoting workers on the basis of race, sex, color, religion, national origin, or advanced age.
9. Contribute FICA taxes to provide unemployment, disability, retirement and survivors' benefits for the workers and their families. Withhold and transmit to state and federal taxing authorities income taxes due from employees.
10. Do not violate antitrust laws, engage in unfair trade practices, or discriminate among customers in pricing (in violation of the Robinson-Patman Act).
11. Comply with the corporation code of the state and with state (and possibly federal) regulations governing the issuance of securities (if she decides to incorporate).

12. Stand behind the implied warranties on the products. (She may be liable to anyone who is injured if a product sold proves to be defective.)
13. Comply with regulations on fuel use to reduce pollution of the air, and with regulations on waste disposal to reduce pollution of the water.
14. Be careful not to make false or misleading statements in any advertisements.
15. Comply with the law of contracts, of agency, of commercial paper, of bailment, of torts and of all other fields when applicable.

7. HOW DOES GOVERNMENT REGULATE THE GROWTH AND SIZE OF A BUSINESS?

Under such statutes as the federal Sherman Anti-Trust Act of 1890, and the Clayton Act and Federal Trade Commission Act of 1914, the law forbids attempts to monopolize by illegal means, to fix prices, or to engage in unfair trade practices. It does not outlaw aggressive but honest competition even when the effect is to drive competitors out of business. It does not proscribe growth from within, by doing a better job at a lower price. For example, Henry Ford became the leading manufacturer of cars and dozens of his competitors went "belly up" as his company survived and prospered. He cut prices, improved quality, and boosted both wages and profits. Were he, at that time, or were his successors today, to try to grow by merging with competitors, the federal government would say no because unacceptable combinations tend to reduce competition.

8. CAN YOU LEARN A BUSINESS IN ANOTHER'S EMPLOY AND THEN COMPETE WITH HIM IN A BUSINESS OF YOUR OWN?

During three summers of full-time work and four school years of part-time work while in college, and four years of full-time employment after graduation, Jonathan Bock learned practically all that could be known about Zuball's men's wear retail business. Then he quit, and using savings and borrowed funds, plus the know-how he'd acquired from Zuball, he opened his own men's wear shop in the same town. He was more progressive, kept inventories low but with fresh merchandise and latest styles, and advertised imaginatively. Zuball's volume declined as Bock's increased. Finally Zuball, exasperated, sued Bock for damages and asked the court to enjoin (stop) him from continuing to do business of that type in the same town. "He learned the business in my shop; now he's ruining me," Zuball complained. "It's unfair." Decision?

For Bock. In general, in our free enterprise society anyone is free to go into business and to compete as vigorously as he can, so long as it is honest competition. When Zuball hired Bock, he might have persuaded him to sign a contract under which Bock would agree to give Zuball the patent rights to any inventions he devised while in Zuball's employ, or within a reasonable time thereafter. He might have required Bock to agree not to use any of Zuball's trade secrets (such as price lists, customer lists, cost figures, and production techniques) in competition with him, although the law provides this protection anyway. He might have persuaded Bock to agree not to compete with him for a reasonable period of time and within a reasonable geographical area after leaving his employ. Courts frown on such contracts because they do tend to restrain free trade and enterprise, but the agreements will be upheld if carefully drafted and if reasonable in terms.

Here Zuball failed to make any such provisions. Bock is free to compete. He could open a store next door if he so desired. He may not steal any of Zuball's trade secrets, but to learn "the ropes" in the employ of a going concern is a time-tested, acceptable, and prudent prelude to going into business for oneself. A mutually beneficial variation is to buy an interest in your employer's firm, either in stock (if it is a corporation) or as a partner (if it is a partnership or sole proprietorship). Frequently, the sole owner needs and wants a responsible buyer to purchase his interest when he retires or dies, and employees may be the best prospects.

9. WHAT IS FRANCHISING?

As Don Powers and Janet Zinda drove down the main street of Hometown, U.S.A., Don said: "Count the retail stores that are locally owned and run and those that belong to national corporations based in New York, Chicago, or other large business centers." The casual survey disclosed that most were owned by out-of-town corporations: Sears, Ward's, Gimbel's, Kinney Shoes, See's Candies, Richman Bros, Walden Book Store, Joseph Magnin, Liberty House, J.C. Penney. A few were local. But a fairly large number were hard to classify because Don and Janet had seen them in other cities they had visited around the country, and yet they knew the stores were owned by local businessmen: MacDonald's Hamburgers, Colonel Sanders' Kentucky Fried Chicken, A & W, Denny's Restaurant, Pancake House, Abbey's Carpets, Chevron (Standard) Gasoline, Howard Johnson's, Motel 6, TraveLodge. What are these business firms?

Franchises. Under a contract with a corporation headquartered elsewhere, a local person obtains the right to use the name of the national firm and to enjoy its established goodwill. The national corporation, as *franchisor,* typically provides assistance in selecting a location; in building, furnishing, and stocking the place; in bookkeeping; and in other details of operation. In exchange, the *franchisee* pays an initial fee and an annual percentage of its gross (total) or net revenues. It may also agree to buy supplies from the headquarters and to comply with established standards of operation.

The carefully chosen franchise is one way to minimize the risks involved in going into business for oneself, especially since the most common cause of business failure is mismanagement and the franchisor helps to anticipate and meet this problem.

Because some franchisors are unscrupulous and dishonest, they have been subjected to special legal controls. In California, for example, under the Franchise Investment Law, full disclosure of terms is required and the offeree must be given a copy of the prospectus at least forty-eight hours before the contract is signed.

10. WHO CAN YOU CALL UPON FOR ASSISTANCE AND ADVICE IF YOU GO INTO BUSINESS FOR YOURSELF?

The individual enterpreneur need not stand alone when he confronts the countless problems of finance, production, marketing, personnel, and information systems in transforming his dream business into a profit-making concern. At the outset, and as legal problems arise, he should consult a qualified attorney at law. He will need a banker. For assistance in setting up his books of accounts and in preparing necessary tax returns, a qualified accountant (preferably a certified public accountant) is a must. He would do well to consult the nearest office of the federal Small Business Administration, an agency created to help persons such as himself with valuable advice, and sometimes with financial assistance. He will need a reliable realtor when he buys or rents real estate, and a good insurance agent to help him select appropriate coverage. If he advertises extensively, he'll need an advertising agent. Sometimes a business management consultant can prove useful. Most lines of business have trade associations, and their publications, conventions, and seminars are an invaluable source of useful information. Always ready and eager to provide assistance are suppliers and would-be-suppliers of inventory and equipment.

In the final analysis, however, these expert specialists can do no more than advise and assist him. He must decide and do. He must manage the business, plan ahead, set up a suitable internal organization, staff it with qualified help, direct them in their activities, and exercise adequate follow-up and control to make sure that things get done according to plan. Overall, he must coordinate the work of those who assist him in accomplishing the mission of the firm, be it production or distribution of goods or services at the retail or wholesale level, or some combination of the listed components. He will probably find that there is a direct correlation between rewards received and effort expended.

1. Can you name a product or service that is sold in this country under monopolistic conditions?

2. Since a limited partner may not share in the management of the firm, why not simply lend money to a general partnership?

3. Alan Goldspun invested close to $50,000 of his family's money in his retail delicatessen and snack bar. He netted an average of $15,000 during the past three years. The volume levelled off, and he was able to handle it comfortably by working six days a week from ten in the morning to seven in the evening. Only during rush hours (about twenty hours a week) did his wife, Marcie, have to help out. He used to earn about $12,000 annually as manager of the restaurant in Grant's Department store, although the hours were shorter (five days, eight-hour shift). He now has an opportunity to sell out for $45,000 to Zack Saul, a promoter who intends to start a franchise chain of such shops. Should he sell?

4. Harold Hitachi has an uncanny talent for identifying land on the outskirts of town that is ripe for development. He has made a fortune building shopping centers and apartment houses, but is too busy to do more than invest $100,000 as a limited partner in Sam Subishi's limited partnership, which operates supermarkets featuring fresh fruits and vegetables. After much pleading by Subishi, Harold agreed to review the plans for ten new locations. He approved seven and gave convincing reasons for dropping three. Is Hitachi a limited partner?

5. Is any one form of business organization most advantageous for minimizing income taxes?

6. A group of college seniors were discussing the problem of making money. One insisted that current income tax laws make it impossible for anyone to become a millionaire today in the United States. The only millionaires, he said, inherited their wealth or married into it. Is he right?

7. Is the purpose of every business to earn maximum profits?

8. What important forms of organization are used in various fields of business other than sole proprietorship, partnership, and corporation?

9. It is sometimes said that accounting is the language of business and that everyone should know how to read a balance sheet and income statement. What are these documents?

10. What qualities should a good business partner possess?

14

YOU AS ESTATE PLANNER

1. WHAT IS ESTATE PLANNING?

Dave and Dorinne Decker are a young married couple, with a daughter, aged two, named Dorinne after her mother. Dave is twenty-eight years old; the senior Dorinne, twenty-six. He is a program analyst and earns $13,500 gross salary annually. Although Dorinne worked as a teacher for several years after their marriage six years ago, she quit shortly before the baby arrived and has since concentrated on being a mother and a homemaker, occasionally serving as a substitute teacher. One day Dorinne said, "We should have an estate plan. In fact we should have worked one out two years ago." Dave replied: "Sure, sure. Let's make one when I retire at sixty-five, if we're loaded with dough by then!" Who is right?

Neither, but Mrs. Decker is closer to the truth. The Deckers should have made an estate plan at the time of their marriage. Although it is probably true that most estate plans are prepared for elderly couples in the upper income tax brackets, the reasons for such action arise much earlier in life. Penalties for procrastination may be substantial, regardless of economic status. In fact, estate planning may be more valuable for persons of modest means, because each dollar in the estate has to stretch further. Needless to say, single persons can also benefit from systematic estate planning.

Estate planning refers to the *systematic analysis of the financial assets and liabilities of an individual* (or a married couple); it serves basically to maximize beneficial use of assets while alive, and to make appropriate arrangements for the disposition of these assets after death. There are several major objectives for this type of planning.

1. To provide for, or recognize, and respect the economic needs of the planner while alive. (If a spouse is involved, his or her living needs are also a primary concern, as well as those of other dependents.)
2. To provide for heirs and other beneficiaries as generously as possible.
3. To minimize or eliminate income taxes while alive, and estate and inheritance taxes after death.
4. To avoid the delays, costs, and publicity of *probate* (the process of proving the validity of a will in court, coupled with administering the decedent's estate).

Even in its simplest form, estate planning is complex and therefore should be done with the aid of a qualified lawyer. In handling large estates (worth, perhaps, more than $150,000), the lawyer is likely to confer with a tax consultant, who may also be an accountant, as well as with the client's insurance agent. Although a well-drafted estate plan may properly remain untouched for years until the client dies, a review and possible revision may be in order whenever a major event may influence the plan. Such events include a significant change in the client's financial status, place of residence, or dispositive (giving) intentions; the birth or death of a beneficiary, or a major change in his or her circumstances (such as marriage, divorce, or serious illness); or a significant change in applicable state or federal laws. Even a so-called "last will" can be amended by a *codicil,* or revoked completely, or replaced with a more appropriate document, so long as the maker is still alive.

2. WHAT ARE THE PRINCIPAL ELEMENTS OF ESTATE PLANNING?

After some cajoling and diplomatic nagging by Dorinne, and especially after a very narrow escape from death in a serious automobile accident, David Decker finally said: "Okay, Okay. Relax. I'll buy a $10,000 life insurance policy and I'll write a will. Now how about a kiss, and let's talk about more cheerful things. Dorinne teasingly said: "No kiss. First do what you promised." The next day Dave went to a local stationery store, bought a printed form for a will, filled in the blanks (leaving all of his estate to Dorinne), signed and dated it, put it in a shoe box with their other valuable papers, and carefully returned the box to its hiding place on the closet shelf. The next week he bought a policy of endowment life insurance maturing at age sixty-five naming Dorinne beneficiary. Should Dorinne now kiss Dave because he has acted lovingly and wisely?

No. The will is useless because it fails to comply with strictly construed statutes on the subject. Moreover, he should not keep valuable papers in a box at home where they are subject to loss by theft or error, and to destruction by fire. They belong in a safe-deposit box or in his lawyer's vault. Not only is the endowment insurance policy the most expensive type he can buy, but also the amount is grossly inadequate for his family's needs.

A common rule of thumb for determining how much life insurance to buy is five times the principal breadwinner's annual take-home pay. For Dave Decker, this amount is around $60,000, which should be adjusted upward if inflation further reduces the value of the dollar. He can afford to buy this much insurance if he buys a reducing term policy (chapter 9). After his daughter matures and leaves home, the need for insurance will drop—unless other children are born in the meantime. Much less insurance may be required for the support of a wife alone, depending on her life style, employability, age, health, likelihood of remarriage, and other sources of support.

Another approach is to project the earnings of the breadwinner until retirement and to calculate their present value. If we assume that Dave will work until age sixty-five (thirty-seven years from now) and that his income will average $20,000 a year, he should earn $740,000 by the time he retires. Supplying a comparable amount of life insurance appears to be prohibitively expensive. Of course, his family would not need that much money in one lump sum if he were to die right now. His beneficiary should probably plan to invest some of the insurance proceeds so that they will continue to help meet the family's financial needs. Nevertheless, a person should not beggar himself with exorbitant life insurance premiums. Better to assume some of the risk of premature death and use available funds as they are needed now for food, clothing, shelter, recreation, and education.

A third approach is to add all annual expenses, including payments on a home mortgage. Determine how much will be available from social security, private pensions, and other sources. Then buy enough life insurance to cover the balance and select a settlement option that provides an annuity to cover expenses monthly for five to ten years, or until death if the dependent spouse is of advanced age. (See the discussion of settlement options in chapter 9.)

Working together and with the help of a qualified lawyer, Dave and Dorinne could customize one or more elements of estate planning to fit their needs and to comply with applicable statutes.

1. Draw up a *personal balance sheet* to show their assets (things of value owned, including a home) and liabilities (debts owed to others). It is also advisable to prepare a *budget,* to monitor their earning, spending, saving, and investing on a monthly and an annual basis.
2. Buy *life insurance* (possibly on both of their lives) in an amount appropriate for the needs of their beneficiaries. Select a suitable settlement option for each policy.
3. Write a *will* for each spouse, specifying the recipients of all possessions.
4. Write a *letter of last instructions,* explaining where important records are located.
5. Maybe transfer certain assets into *joint tenancy,* so that they will pass to the surviving joint tenant without going through probate.* (In a community property state, maybe transfer separate property into community property.)
6. Maybe use, in common law states, the marital deduction (in community property states, for separate property only) to reduce the size of the taxable estate.
7. Make *inter vivos* (Latin: among the living) *gifts* as needed, perhaps to reduce the size of their estate.
8. Set up *trusts* (inter vivos or testamentary, or both), and specify whether the beneficiary is to have the power to decide who shall have what after his own death *(power of appointment).*
9. Review *pension plans* (both social security and private) to see how much retirement income they can expect from these sources.
10. Maybe invest in *annuities* to supplement the fixed income expected from pensions.
11. If a major asset is a sole proprietorship or partnership, set up a suitable buy-sell agreement, coupled with a Keogh Plan tax-free pension plan.
12. If a major asset is stock in a closely held corporation, set up buy-sell agreements, coupled with qualified plans for deferred compensation through profit sharing or company pension plans.[1]

Buy-Sell Agreements

When a principal asset in the estate is a business—be it a sole proprietorship, partnership, or closely held corporation—a special estate planning

---

* Nevertheless, death taxes may be imposed on the value of the assets unless the survivor contributed to their cost, or unless they were a valid lifetime gift and the survivor treated his equity in the joint tenancy as his own and paid applicable property and income taxes. Also, the saving on probate costs may be lost later in added capital gains tax if the property has increased substantially in value; only half of it gets the new basis of value as of the date of death of the first joint-tenant. When the survivor sells, he pays a full capital gains tax on his half.

problem arises. If nothing is done in advance, and the business person dies, the surviving spouse may face a financial crisis and suffer heavy avoidable losses.

No family business runs itself. The key to its success is the ability and effort of the owner-manager. Because he (or she) will not live forever, the possibility should be faced that death may occur before retirement and before an orderly disposal of the business can be arranged by the executive himself. Therefore, while still alive, he should anticipate the inevitable. If he is a sole proprietor, he might contract with a trustworthy employee to have the latter buy the business when he dies. He might also provide at least part of the necessary funds by buying an insurance policy on his life, naming the employee as beneficiary—the proceeds to be used to buy the business. Employer and employee can share the cost of the premiums. Under this buy-sell agreement between employer and employee, any unpaid balance of the purchase price might be paid to designated heirs of the employer over five or more years.

A similar buy-sell arrangement can be made between partners. While still alive, the business man might take one or more employees into the firm as partners. The partners then buy life insurance policies on each other and use the proceeds to buy out the decedent's interest upon death. The business, which is worth much more as a going concern in active operation, continues to function (although technically the old partnership is dissolved by death of any partner).

In a closely held corporation, other stockholders or employees may be persuaded to enter into reciprocal agreements to buy or sell stock upon the death of any member. Again, funding can be arranged through life insurance, along with agreements to pay any balance over a period of years.

The Keogh Plan

To help equalize pension benefits between employees of large corporations and self-employed persons, including professional people, Congress in 1962 enacted the Smathers-Keogh Act, making possible what are known as Keogh Plans. Formerly, the self-employed individual had to pay income taxes on all of his net earnings, including the money he invested in various media for his retirement. Under the Keogh Act, as amended in 1974, the qualified person may contribute up to 15 percent of his earned income (up to $7,500 annually) to an approved agency such as a mutual fund, savings and loan association, bank, or insurance company. This income with any earnings on it remains tax-free until the individual retires and withdraws the money in a lump sum or in installments. By then his regular income has dropped sharply and presumably his tax burden will therefore be less. A self-employed person who has some full-time employees must include them in an approved pension plan if he takes advantage of the act for himself.

RETIREMENT PLANS FOR THE SELF-EMPLOYED

3. WHAT TAXES IS THE ESTATE PLANNER TRYING TO REDUCE OR TO AVOID?

Arthur Wright, a well-paid middle management executive, and his wife, Corita, have been married for thirty-two years. Both are approaching age sixty-five. Their estate is worth more than $200,000, mostly in stock, corporate bonds, and long-term savings and loan association savings accounts. They have three married children, all with families of their own. Arthur expects to work until he reaches sixty-five and then retire on a company pension, which will be more than ample for himself and Corita when combined with social security benefits. They expect to leave their estate to their children eventually and wonder whether they can save any taxes by acting now. Can they?

Undoubtedly. Arthur is at the peak of his earning power, and the government therefore takes more from every dollar he and Corita earn on their investments than it would if the investments were held by the children, who are in much lower tax brackets. By giving the children at least part of the $200,000 estate, they would substantially reduce their income taxes, both federal and state.

If they do nothing, the estate may pass to the surviving spouse after one of them dies. When the survivor dies, what is left of the estate goes to the children. Both the surviving spouse and the children will thus have to pay *death taxes* (estate and inheritance). These levies, however, can be legitimately minimized.

Every person is allowed an exemption of $60,000 in the calculation of the federal estate tax on the privilege of giving. If the total property in the estate (called the gross estate) is under $60,000, no tax is due. From the gross estate, certain deductions are allowed: funeral and probate expenses, all personal debts outstanding, contributions to charity, and the marital deduction. After these deductions, the estate tax rates (table 14–1) are applied. These rates go up as the base increases, making the estate tax a progressive tax. Rates for the federal gift tax are 75 percent of the estate tax rates, but otherwise follow the schedule presented in table 14–1.

Most states impose a death tax: either an estate tax (on the estate as a whole) on the privilege of giving, or an inheritance tax (on the distributive share) on the privilege of receiving. A handful of states have no death tax.* Nine states impose an estate tax.† All but twelve states

---

* States with no death tax: Alabama, Arkansas, Florida, Georgia, and Nevada. The first four do levy a modest tax designed to equal the credit allowed against the federal estate tax for the death taxes paid to other jurisdictions.

† States with an estate tax: Arizona, Mississippi, New York, North Dakota, Oklahoma, Oregon, Rhode Island, South Carolina, and Utah.

impose an inheritance tax.* Finally, all but seven states impose a modest additional estate tax to absorb the maximum credit allowed against the federal estate tax for death taxes paid to other jurisdictions.†

4. WHAT ARE THE TAX CONSEQUENCES OF GIVING AWAY PARTS OF ONE'S ESTATE WHILE ALIVE?

Federal

The tax "bite" can be reduced by making gifts while one is alive. Up to $30,000 may be given to one or more *donees* (receivers) at any time, in any amounts, free of federal tax. If gifts exceed the specified amounts, the applicable gift tax rate is 25 percent lower than the estate tax that would be imposed if they were made after death. Moreover, the property given is thus removed from the costs, publicity, and delays of probate. Skirting these costs may result in substantial savings, as suggested by the sample fee structures in table 14–2.

Arthur and Corita could give $30,000 each (or $60,000) plus $3,000 each (or $6,000) times three, the number of their children—a total initial transfer of $78,000, tax free. In each of the following years they could make additional gifts of $18,000, tax free. The donee never has to pay a tax on gifts received. He may, of course, later be subject to a property tax on what he owns or to an income tax on what he earns with the gift. However, he may be in a lower income tax bracket than the donor, and the donor has moved into lower income tax and estate tax brackets.

Arthur and Corita said they would think about the gift idea but did nothing. Two years later Arthur, a heavy smoker, was stricken with lung cancer. His doctors told him he probably had six months to live. The news gave Corita a heart attack, and her doctor said she would probably predecease Arthur. These tragic developments persuaded them to make gifts of the full $78,000. Both died within a year. Now the IRS tax collector claims that the gifts should be included in their estates for tax purposes. Is he correct?

Yes. There is a presumption that any gift made within three years of the date of death was a *gift made in contemplation of death*. This presumption can be rebutted if the executor of the estate can prove that the donors acted because of other, living motives. For example, they recently had medical examinations, were found to be in good health,

---

* States that have no inheritance tax: Alabama, Arizona, Arkansas, Florida, Georgia, Mississippi, Nevada, New York, North Dakota, Oklahoma, South Carolina, and Utah.

† States that do not impose the additional estate tax for federal credit: Mississippi, Nevada, North Dakota, Oregon, South Dakota, Utah, and West Virginia.

TABLE 14-1

The Federal Estate Tax

Dollar Amount of Tax on Estate (third column)	Bracket Rate on Excess (over amount in third column) (%)	Taxable Estate
$ 0	3	Up to $5,000
150	7	5,000
500	11	10,000
1,600	14	20,000
3,000	18	30,000
4,800	22	40,000
7,000	25	50,000
9,500	28	60,000
20,700	30	100,000
65,700	32	250,000
145,700	35	500,000
233,200	37	750,000
325,700	39	1,000,000
423,200	42	1,250,000
528,200	45	1,500,000
753,200	49	2,000,000
998,200	53	2,500,000
1,263,200	56	3,000,000
1,543,200	59	3,500,000
1,838,200	63	4,000,000
2,468,200	67	5,000,000
3,138,200	70	6,000,000
3,838,200	73	7,000,000
4,568,200	76	8,000,000
6,088,200	77	10,000,000

NOTE: The federal estate tax is imposed only after the $60,000 exemption is deducted from the gross estate.

and so did not expect to die soon; or the gifts were clearly made to help their children buy homes, or as part of a long-range financial program that began when the children were married; or the gifts were made to reduce the parents' income taxes. Here, however, the Wrights clearly expected to die very soon, and so they made the gifts.

In making gifts, it is generally wise to give property that has not increased much in value since the donor bought it. This is because the market value at the time the property is given determines the gift tax. But the basis (or "cost") to the donee is the cost to the donor (plus any gift tax paid). Thus, if Arthur and Corita give their children stock that has increased in value from $10,000 to $40,000, and the children sell the stock, they will have to pay a capital gains tax of 25 percent

TABLE 14-2

Probate Fees in California and New York

Amount of Estate		Fee Percentage of Estate (%)	Cumulative Total Estate	Cumulative Total Fee
California				
First	$ 1,000	7	$ 1,000	$ 70
Next	9,000	4	10,000	430
Next	40,000	3	50,000	1,630
Next	100,000	2	150,000	3,630
Next	350,000	1.5	500,000	8,880
All above	500,000	1		
New York				
First	10,000	4	10,000	400
Next	290,000	2.5	300,000	7,650
All above	300,000	2		

on the $30,000 gain. The estate tax could be less. When the property goes through probate, it is given a new cost-basis (generally the market value at date of death). Obviously, some calculations are in order.

Regardless of the tax consequences, the well-being of the donors and donees should determine whether and when gifts are appropriate.

State

Tax laws are in constant flux, but as of 1974, twelve states have gift taxes.* The rates are generally low in comparison with federal levies, especially when close relatives are involved.

Table 14–3 gives the California schedule of gift taxes. (The same rates are used also with inheritance taxes.) There is an annual exclusion of $3,000 for each of an unlimited number of donees. The lifetime exemptions apply to gifts made while the donor is alive, and identical exemptions are available for gifts made after his death by will or by intestate distribution without a will.

5. WHAT IS THE MARITAL DEDUCTION?

Arthur and Corita Wright were residents of a common law state. Can Arthur, who has been the sole income producer in the Wright family, improve the property status of himself and his wife for tax purposes?

---

* States with gift taxes: California, Colorado, Louisiana, Minnesota, North Carolina, Oklahoma, Oregon, Rhode Island, Tennessee, Virginia, Washington, and Wisconsin.

TABLE 14-3

California Gift Tax

Amount of Gift (or Bequest)	Tax By Classes of Donees (%)		
	A	B	C
	Wife, husband, lineal ancestor, lineal issue, certain mutually acknowledged or adopted children, minor child	Brother, sister, and their descendants; wives or husbands; widows or widowers	All other persons (such as distant relatives and friends)
On excess after deducting the applicable exemption from $25,000	3	6	10
On next $25,000 to $50,000	4	10	14
On next $50,000 to $100,000	6	12	16
On next $100,000 to $200,000	8	14	18
On next $200,000 to $300,000	10	16	20
On next $300,000 to $400,000	12	18	22
Over $400,000	14	20	24
Lifetime Exemption	$5,000*	$2,000	$300

*Applies to all members of class A except minor children, who are entitled to a $12,000 exemption.

Yes. He can take advantage of the marital deduction both for gifts in life[2] and for gifts made in a will.[3]

Since 1948, married persons in noncommunity property states have enjoyed the same estate-splitting advantage as people in community property states long possessed. In California and the other seven community property states (Arizona, Idaho, Louisiana, Nevada, New Mexico, Texas, and Washington), basically all property acquired during marriage by the labor, skill, or efforts of either spouse is deemed to belong to both equally. This automatic joint ownership reduces not only the estate of either upon death, but also the taxes.

In noncommunity property states, a spouse may use the marital deduction to deduct up to one-half of the total value of the gift made to the other spouse, free of any gift tax. Thus, a wife may give her husband, or a husband may give his wife, $6,000 in any given year, free of gift tax. Half is excluded as a regular annual exclusion available to anyone. The other half is the marital deduction.

In community property states, the conversion of the separate property of one spouse into community property represents a gift of only one-half of the property (from the husband or wife whose separate property makes up the gift). In addition, and more significantly, one spouse may give the other up to 50 percent of the value of his (or her) adjusted gross estate by will. The full amount thus given is then excluded from his estate for tax purposes. In a community property state, a spouse who owns separate property, may give 50 percent of it to his (or her) survivor, free of estate tax. Failure to take advantage of the marital deduction is usually folly of a very high order.

6. WHAT IS A WILL AND HOW DOES IT FIT INTO AN ESTATE PLAN?

A will is the legal expression of a person's wishes as to the disposition of his property, to take effect after his death. The author of a will is called a *testator* or *testatrix*.

A well-drafted will can provide many advantages.

a. Property is distributed as the testator wishes. Some beneficiaries get more, some less; specific assets, such as heirloom jewelry, go to specified donees.

b. Gifts may be made to charity, to distant relatives, to friends, or to faithful employees—people who would get nothing if there were no will.

c. Taxes may be avoided, as by taking the marital deduction and by creating testamentary trusts.

d. Confusion is avoided, as to what the assets are and who the heirs are. Also avoided are possible lawsuits among contending claimants, a lawyer-enriching drain of estate assets and a costly effort for the claimants.

e. The testator may nominate whomever he pleases as guardian(s) for his minor children and their estates. Otherwise, the court must make the decision.

f. A personal representative (*executor* or *executrix*) may be named to handle the estate (for a statutory fee). Otherwise, the probate court must name an *administrator,* someone perhaps the decedent would not have chosen.

g. If a will does not waive fidelity bonds (an expense to the estate), they may be required to assure faithful performance of duty by the personal representative and the guardian.

h. Provision may be made to avoid successive probate proceedings if the testator and the principal beneficiary die at the same time, or close together (as could happen because of an accident).

i. The will may direct the executor to pay from the estate inheritance taxes as well as estate taxes. Therefore, gifts to named beneficiaries will not be reduced by these levies.

j. The will can give funeral instructions (although this can also be done in a letter of last instructions outside the will).

A personal balance sheet, listing assets and liabilities, should accompany a will and be updated periodically—such as when the testator completes his annual income tax statement. A letter of instructions may also be prepared. It is not binding on the executor but can be helpful in telling the location of assets and liabilities and suggesting how to deal with them. Funeral directions may be included here or in the will.

7. WHAT TYPES OF WILLS ARE VALID?

> After Dave Decker learned that his form will was worthless, he decided to make a will entirely in his own handwriting, signed and dated by himself. He knew that a person could validly make such a will, and so he carefully wrote the following words on a blank sheet of paper: "I give all I own to Dorinne." He signed and dated the paper. Is it a valid will?

Although a person can prepare a valid will without witnesses, in his own handwriting, signed and dated by himself, Dave has probably failed in his attempt. Why? Because no one can be certain whether he intended to leave his property to his wife or to his daughter, both named Dorinne.

Even if it could be established that he intended his wife, the will would be defective because he then would have failed to mention his daughter. In California, under the *pretermitted heir statute,* a testator must either make some settlement on or give equal share of his property to the child (or grandchild, if the child is dead and there is a grandchild) by way of advancement while the testator still lives, or name the child as a beneficiary in the will, or make it clear in the will that the omission of the child was intentional.[4] Thus, a parent may give a child little or nothing, but he must do so expressly; if he overlooks the child, the assumption is that the omission was inadvertent and not intended.

Three types of wills are recognized as valid in California and in most other states: formal or witnessed written will, informal or holographic unwitnessed written will, and nuncupative or oral will.

Formal Will

The formal will is usually prepared by a lawyer; it is generally typewritten. It must be signed at the end *(subscribed)* by the testator. The subscription must be made in the presence of two witnesses, or in their presence the testator must acknowledge it to have been made by him or under his direction.* The testator must intentionally declare to the witnesses when he subscribes (or acknowledges) that it is his will, and

---

* Seven states require three witnesses: Connecticut, Louisiana, Maine, Massachusetts, New Hampshire, South Carolina, and Vermont.

ask them to serve as witnesses. Finally, the witnesses must sign in his presence. California and some other states also require that they sign in the presence of each other.

The formalities are strictly enforced by the courts and provide added assurance of validity. After all, the testator will be dead when the will "speaks," and he will not be able to challenge possible fraudulent claimants. If the witnesses are also dead at that time, their handwriting must simply be authenticated. In most states, the testator must be an adult, and must be mentally competent. This means he must understand the nature of a will; the nature and extent of his property at least in general terms; the nature of his relationship to relatives and friends who are "the natural objects of his bounty." He must not be insane at the time; but illiteracy or physical or mental infirmity caused by old age (such as senility) will not prevent him from making a valid will.

Holographic Unwitnessed Will

The second type of will must be handwitten entirely by the testator, and signed and dated by him. It is a legally acceptable form but is not recommended for most persons because, not knowing the law, they may fail to express their intentions properly or to take advantage of readily available techniques to minimize costs, including taxes.

Oral or Nuncupative Will

The third type of will may be made only when the testator is in fear of imminent death (for example, a soldier about to go into battle or an accident victim with fatal injuries). Two persons must hear his expressed intentions; one or the other must have been asked by the testator at the time to bear witness that such was his will; one witness must reduce those intentions to writing within thirty days after they were spoken; such writing must be offered in court within six months after the words were spoken. By this means, the testator may dispose of personal property worth no more than $1,000, but he may not dispose of any interest in real property. Because of the limitations and special requirements, nuncupative wills are very uncommon in California.

8. WHAT HAPPENS TO A PERSON'S ESTATE IF HE DIES WITHOUT LEAVING A WILL?

If there is no will, or if a will is rejected because defective, the estate is distributed under the state's law of *intestacy* (that is, without a testament or last will). In many cases, this procedure probably accomplishes what the decedent would have wanted done. Table 14–4 shows the pattern of intestate distribution of noncommunity property under California law. Community property goes to the surviving spouse if there is no will.

TABLE 14-4

Intestate Distribution of Noncommunity Property
under California Law

Deceased	Survived by	Estate Goes as Indicated to Surviving				
		Spouse	Parent(s)	Child (or Children)	Brothers or Sisters	Next of Kin
Husband or wife	No descendants, parents, brothers, sisters, or their descendants	All property				
	One child	1/2		1/2*		
	Two or more children	1/3		2/3 (divided among them)*		
	Parents only	1/2	1/4 to each (or 1/2 if only one surviving)			
	Brothers and sisters only	1/2			1/2 (divided among them)†	

TABLE 14-4
(continued)

Deceased	Survived by	Estate Goes as Indicated to Surviving				
		Spouse	Parent(s)	Child (or Children)	Brothers or Sisters	Next of Kin
Widow or widower or single person	Parents only		1/2 to each (or all if only one surviving)			
	Brothers and sisters only				All property†	
	No descendants, parents, brothers, sisters, or their descendants					All property
Widow or widower	Child or children			All property (divided equally among them)*		

*Descendants of a deceased child take his share.
†Descendants of a deceased brother or sister take his or her share.

9. CAN LIFE INSURANCE PROVIDE SPECIAL ASSISTANCE IN ESTATE PLANNING?

> Karen Kendrick is an heiress who has never married. She appreciates works of art and over the years has converted most of her inheritance into personal jewelry, and a magnificent Palm Beach residence with a collection of very valuable paintings and sculpture. When she discussed her estate plan with her lawyer, he pointed out the special liquidity problem she faces. Most of her assets cannot be readily disposed of, and yet their high value means that her executor will need considerable cash to pay the estate and inheritance taxes. Can life insurance help her out?

Yes. Because life insurance is payable in cash shortly after death, it is often relied on to provide liquidity for payment of death taxes. Then heirlooms need not be sold or, if sold, they need not be sacrificed at forced-sale prices.

Life insurance can be useful to persons of more moderate means as well. For comparatively low premium payments, a person may immediately acquire, in effect, a much larger estate because his designated beneficiaries will receive the face value of his policy when he dies. It is usually best to have the face value made payable directly to them. If the proceeds are paid to the decedent's estate (from which bequests are made under his will), they enlarge his estate and subject it to higher attorney's fees, executor's allowances, and death taxes.

If the insured retains any *incidents of ownership* (such as the right to change the beneficiaries or to borrow the loan value of the policy), the face amount of the policy will be included in his estate for death tax purposes. Many states, however, exempt insurance proceeds from inheritance taxes—at least up to a designated figure ($50,000 in California).[5]

To be relieved completely of federal estate taxes, the insured policyholder must give up the incidents of ownership. Technically, any *reversionary interest* (that is, something of value that the policyowner retains) worth more than 5 percent of the value of the policy immediately before the death of the insured is considered an incident of ownership. The policyowner may continue to pay the premiums. If he stops, the beneficiary can continue to pay them.

10. WHAT ARE TRUSTS AND HOW DO THEY FIT INTO AN ESTATE PLAN?

> Charles Waldmann, II, and his wife, Johanna, are quite wealthy. They are also quite concerned that if either of their two children, Charles III or Anna Jo, inherit the family fortune, it will be dissipated within a short time. The children have never worked

and, in the opinion of their parents, neither knows the value of a dollar. They belong to a young jet set and are considered to be spendthrifts even by their own friends. What can the parents do to protect their children against squandering the inheritance?

A likely solution is the creation of a *trust*. Essentially, a trust is a property interest held by one person (called the *trustee*) for the benefit of another person (called the *beneficiary*). Commonly, a third person (called the *trustor* or *donor*) gives the trustee the legal title to property to manage for the benefit of the beneficiary, who is said to have the equitable title.

Inter Vivos Trusts and Irrevocable Trusts

As trustors, the Waldmans can create one or more trusts while still alive. These would be inter vivos trusts. The effect would be to keep the property out of the trustors' estates at their deaths, and thus avoid the costs and delays of probate. If made *irrevocable* (that is, the property transfer is permanent and cannot be called back or rescinded) either permanently or for at least ten years, the income from the trust would be taxable to the trust as an entity, or to the beneficiaries, if they receive the income. This type of trust could be very helpful to the Waldmans, especially if they are in a high income tax bracket.

The Waldmans could direct the trustee to enforce certain provisions.

1. The children shall receive the income from the trust.
2. The children may not give away or sell their rights in the trust.
3. Creditors of the children cannot reach the trust.
4. The trustee may spend part of the principal of the trust, if necessary, for the welfare of the children (discretionary power to "invade the corpus").
5. The trustee shall pay the living expenses of the children rather than giving them cash from the trust.
6. The trustee shall transfer 25 percent of the trust to each child when he or she attains age thirty, and the balance at age forty. (Presumably, they would have settled down by then and could be entrusted with the assets as their own.) Or the parents could direct that the principal remain intact and go to the grandchildren. This would eliminate a possible levy of estate taxes upon the trust assets when their children die (assuming that they still have these assets).

Testamentary Trusts

The Waldmans, if typical, would be reluctant to make the trust irrevocable because they themselves may need the money before they die. Therefore, they might create *revocable inter vivos trusts,* which they could terminate at any time, thus regaining full control over the assets. The trust income would be taxable to them, and the principal would be included in their estates. In the alternative, they might create *testamentary trusts* in their wills. Such trusts are revocable so long as the testator lives and can change his will, but become irrevocable upon his death.

The Rule Against Perpetuities

The rule against perpetuities that applies to private trusts says that title must *vest* (that is, some beneficiary must get full and unrestricted possession and control over the property) no later than a life or lives of persons in being, plus twenty-one years, plus (in case of a posthumous child) the applicable period of gestation. This rule prevents a trust from accumulating and compounding income for perhaps ten generations, by which time a small sum may have grown to a prodigious amount.

11. WHAT ARE SOME OTHER USES OF TRUSTS?

> H. Arnold Amesbury dearly loves his wife, who is fifteen years his junior. He is afraid that if he dies first, as is likely, she will not be able to manage the family estate alone. She might let herself be talked into foolish investments or, worse, into remarriage to someone interested mostly in her money. What can Amesbury do to protect his wife against such developments?

He can create a testamentary trust for her, specifying that she gets the income and that the trustee may invade the principal if necessary for her welfare. When she dies, the property will not appear in her estate, where it would boost her estate tax. Instead, it can be distributed to the children, for example, or even held for the grandchildren. As an alternative, it can be distributed to charities or to other beneficiaries selected by H. Arnold himself, or designated by his wife if she is given power of appointment. This useful estate planning tool enables the trustor to postpone deciding which child or children or other ultimate beneficiaries shall receive what. In these ways, a trust can be used to frustrate would-be fortune hunters who prey on wealthy and unsophisticated widows.

Sometimes trusts make sense when the beneficiary is ill, mentally retarded, or very old. The trustor may even set up a trust naming himself as beneficiary when he reaches a certain advanced age, or earlier if he wants to be spared the burden of managing his estate. He may also create a trust and name it as beneficiary of one or more insurance policies on his life. This is often preferable to letting the insurance proceeds go as a lump sum to a beneficiary who does not know how to handle such a sum—or to leaving the money with the insurance company under a settlement option whereby the company keeps the money and disperses it as directed, meanwhile paying a modest 2 to 3.5 percent interest on the principal. Not infrequently, this option involves creating an annuity, under which the insurance company guarantees payment of a fixed sum to a designated beneficiary until he (or she) dies, or to two persons (until the death of the second). Generally, a person can earn a higher return on his money than the annuity provides, by either investing the money himself or having a trust company handle it for him. In addition to higher returns, he may benefit from capital gains and the flexibility not available with annuities.

A *discretionary sprinkling and accumulation trust* may sometimes be appropriate, especially when flexibility is vital to meet the changing needs of family members who are beneficiaries. The trustee is authorized to decide who among the designated beneficiaries shall receive payments of income or principal or both. Beneficiaries who need more can get more; those who need less, get less. To help the trustee distribute the trust funds, the trustor specifies guidelines, which might include maintaining a stated standard of living or comfort and general welfare for beneficiaries, and allowing special payment for educational or medical fees. Income not paid out is accumulated and ultimately distributed as part of the principal, according to plan.

12. WHO MAY BE A TRUSTEE AND WHAT DOES A TRUST COST?

The testator may choose as trustee a competent and trustworthy relative or friend, or a commercial trust company with its staff of experts.

Fees must be paid to trustees, but the benefits may be well worth the expense. In a testamentary trust, the probate court fixes the trustee's fees. In California, for example, an annual fee of three-fourths of 1 percent of the fair market value of the trust estate is commonly specified. To determine whether a fee is reasonable, the court considers the size of the estate, time required, services performed, and results achieved. In inter vivos trusts, the fees are negotiated. Common percentages charged are three-fourths of 1 percent of the fair market value of real estate and obligations secured by real estate, and three-fifths of 1 percent of the fair market value of other assets in the trust estate.

The percentage may be less for a very large trust (say, one in excess of $500,000). Corporate trustees frequently charge one-tenth of 1 percent as an acceptance fee when the trust takes effect, and a 1 percent distribution fee for all amounts they distribute. Trustees, like attorneys and personal representatives in probate proceedings, are also entitled to extra compensation for special services and expenses (such as defending a lawsuit).

13. WHAT ARE CONSERVATORSHIPS AND GUARDIANSHIPS?

Peter Whidbey, aged seventy-two, is a millionaire who periodically engages in behavior his family considers eccentric. His son Ed has been particularly disturbed since Peter bought a large sailboat and announced his intention to sail to the South Pacific with an all-female crew. Ed contacted an attorney about how to stop his father from squandering the family fortune. Can Ed tie up his father's money?

Not unless there is more to the story. Peter appears to be capable of handling his own affairs, including his money. However, if he were physically or mentally unable to do so, his son could petition the court to declare a *conservatorship*. A responsible person would be named the *conservator,* who would manage the *conservatee's* assets and personal affairs. He must make periodic reports to the court, showing the business and personal transactions that have occurred. Although the conservatee is without authority to handle his own affairs, he can still make, or modify, a last will. A conservatorship will not, however, be declared simply to stop an eccentric person from overspending and thereby dissipating his estate.

In some states, an alternative procedure (called *guardianship*) is available for those who, for any reason, are unable to care for themselves. Usually, a guardianship is created to provide for a minor whose parents are dead. An adult who is infirm may be judicially declared incompetent, and he is then called a *ward.* The person in charge of the ward's personal and financial affairs is called the *guardian.*

Conservatorships and guardianships are created without the consent of the infirm or incompetent person. In each situation, the court monitors the activities of the person in charge, and the infirm person is without legal capacity to act for himself.

CASES, QUESTIONS AND PROBLEMS

1. Joe Mariano never made a will. Now he is flat on his back in a hospital bed, after being in the crash of his private sports plane. Both arms are in casts, and he has extensive internal injuries. But his mind is alert and he can talk. Realizing that the prognosis is negative, he calls for his lawyer. Can they prepare a formal, witnessed will even though Mariano cannot write his name?

2. Much of the emphasis in estate planning is on how to reduce or completely avoid income taxes, gift taxes, and death taxes (estate and inheritance). Are such tax-dodging techniques legal and ethical?

3. What happens if a decedent leaves no will and no heirs?

4. Mr. and Mrs. John Burke are in the 50 percent tax bracket and would like to reduce their income tax. They are considering transferring $50,000 worth of corporate bonds (earning 8 percent per annum) to their son, Kermit, when he gets married, to help him with the major expenses of the first few years of married life. However, the bonds are part of their retirement income program, and so they would like to have them back in ten years. What should they do?

5. Plans for the transfer of an estate often take effect many years after they have been drafted. How is a decedent's will affected when it has not been revised but certain circumstances have changed?
   a. A beneficiary named in a will has died before the testator.
   b. A witness to a will has died before the testator.
   c. An executor named in a will has died before the testator, or is alive but refuses to serve as executor.
   d. A trustee dies.
   e. Property given away by specific legacy (for example, "I give my friend Jackson Kohler my two-carat diamond ring") has been disposed of before the testator dies.
   f. There are not enough assets to cover all legacies made. (For example, a testator gives $5,000 to each of thirty named nephews and nieces, for a total of $150,000; but after all available assets are converted into cash, only $60,000 remains.)

6. "Estate planning is preventive law at its best." Do you agree? Explain.

7. When Pauline Puffington died, she left her entire estate of $3 million to a trust for the care of her twelve pet chihuahua dogs and fourteen cats. After they died, the principal was to be paid to a designated society for the prevention of cruelty to animals. Relatives challenged the will, proving not only that she was eccentric and senile when she made it, but also that she was insane when she died. Can the will be enforced?

8. Brian Dorsett was convinced that making a will was tantamount to writing one's own death warrant. Even after he married and the twins arrived, he did nothing to assure the economical transfer of his estate to his family after his death. He was a hard-driving individual, and had acquired an estate of close to $150,000 by age thirty. Then he suddenly died of a heart attack. Under the state's laws of intestacy, his wife received one-third of his separate property and the twins, aged five, shared the balance equally. What avoidable expenses and burdens has he imposed on his widow?

9. Of the various elements of estate planning, which is most useful?

10. a. To make a will and to leave property to others is considered a privilege, not a fundamental right, by many experts on taxation. Do you agree? Why or why not?

b. Should death taxes be increased to the point where all property of value (or perhaps in excess of a certain sum, say $25,000) in a decedent's estate is collected by the government when he dies? Should gift taxes be similarly increased? Would such changes affect the way people spend and save their money? How? Would the effects, overall, be good or bad? Are present death tax rates (federal and in your state) too high or too low?

c. If death taxes were made confiscatory, would there be any need for estate planning?

NOTES
SUGGESTED READINGS
GLOSSARY

NOTES

1 You and the Constitution

1. *Marbury* v. *Madison,* 2 L. Ed. 60, 1803
2. *United States* v. *Nixon, Nixon* v. *United States,* 94 Sup. Ct. Rep. 3090, 1974
3. *People* v. *Rodriguez,* 35 C.A. 3d 900, 1973
4. *Communist Party of the United States* v. *Subversive Activities Control Board,* 367 U.S. 1, 1961
5. *Schenck* v. *United States,* 249 U.S. 47, 1919
6. *Dennis* v. *United States,* 341 U.S. 494, 1951
7. *Terminiello* v. *Chicago,* 337 U.S. 1, 1949
8. *New York Times Company* v. *Sullivan,* 376 U.S. 254, 1964
9. *Curtis Publishing Co.* v. *Butts; Associated Press* v. *Walker,* 388 U.S. 130, 1967
10. *Roth* v. *United States* and *Alberts* v. *California,* 354 U.S. 476, 1957
11. *Stanley* v. *Georgia,* 394 U.S. 557, 1969
12. *Miller* v. *California,* 413 U.S. 15, 1973
13. *New York Times* v. *United States,* 403 U.S. 713, 1971
14. *Brown* v. *Board of Education,* 347 U.S. 483, 1954
15. *Mitchell* v. *United States,* 313 U.S. 80, 1941
16. *Harper* v. *Virginia Board of Elections,* 383 U.S. 663, 1966
17. *Shelley* v. *Kraemer,* 334 U.S. 1, 1948
18. *Mapp* v. *Ohio,* 367 U.S. 643, 1961
19. *Gideon* v. *Wainwright,* 372 U.S. 335, 1963
20. *Miranda* v. *Arizona,* 384 U.S. 436, 1966; *Escobedo* v. *Illinois,* 378 U.S. 478, 1964
21. *Katz* v. *United States,* 389 U.S. 347, 1967
22. "Justice Douglas Salutes His Old 'Super Chief' (Warren)," *Los Angeles Times,* Aug. 6, 1974
23. *Reynolds* v. *Sims,* 377 U.S. 533, 1964
24. *People* v. *Miller,* 7 C. 3d 219, 1972
25. *Apodaca* v. *Oregon,* 406 U.S. 404, 1972
26. *Johnson* v. *Louisiana,* 32 L. Ed 2d 152, 1972
27. *People* v. *Anderson,* 6 C. 3d 628, 1972
28. *Furman* v. *Georgia,* 408 U.S. 238, 1972
29. *In re Antazo,* 3 C. 3d 100, 1970
30. *Sailer Inn, Inc.* v. *Kirby,* 5 C. 3d 1, 1971
31. *Dunn* v. *Blumstein,* 92 S. Ct. 995, 1972

2 You, Law, and the Courts

1. *Plessey* v. *Ferguson,* 163 U.S. 537, 1896
2. *Brown* v. *Board of Education,* 74 S. Ct 686, 1954
3. *Parr* v. *Municipal Court,* 3 C. 3d 861, 1971
4. *People* v. *Crowe,* 8 C. 3d 815, 1973

3 You as Victim or Accused of Crime

1. *People* v. *Penny,* 44 C. 2d 861, 1955; *Collum* v. *State,* 65 Ga. App. 740, 1941; *People* v. *Chavez,* 77 C.A. 2d 621, 1944
2. *People* v. *Alday,* 10 C. 3d 392, 1973
3. *People* v. *Lathus,* 35 C.A. 3d 466, 1973
4. *Cohen* v. *California,* 403 U.S. 15, 1971
5. *People* v. *Kelly,* 10 C. 3d 565, 1973
6. *People* v. *Sirhan,* 7 C. 3d 710, 1972
7. *Restatement of Torts,* Second, P. 76, comments e, f, 1965
8. *U.S.* v. *Russell,* 93 S. Ct. 1637, 1973
9. *People* v. *Superior Court,* 35 C.A. 3d 621, 1973
10. California Penal Code, Sect. 26
11. *Apodaca* v. *Oregon,* 32 L. Ed. 2d 184, 1972
12. *Johnson* v. *Louisiana,* 406 U.S. 356, 1972
13. *Pettit* v. *State Board of Education,* 10 C. 3d 29, 1973
14. *Watson* v. *State Board of Education,* 22 C.A. 3d 559, 1973; *Governing Board* v. *Brennan,* 18 C.A. 3d 396, 1971; *Board of Trustees* v. *Stubblefield,* 16 C.A. 3d 820, 1969; *Morrison* v. *State Board of Education,* 1 C. 3d 214, 1969
15. *In re Gault,* 387 U.S. 1, 1966

4 You as Tortfeasor or Victim

1. *McCormick* v. *Haley,* 37 Ohio App. 2d 73, 1973
2. *Contento* v. *Mitchell,* 28 C.A. 3d 356, 1972
3. *Hollman* v. *Brady,* 16 Alaska 308, 1956; *Schessler* v. *Keck,* 125 C.A. 2d 827, 1954; *White* v. *Valenta,* 234 C.A. 2d 243, 1965; *Larive* v. *Willitt,* 154 C.A. 2d 140, 1957; *Cepeda* v. *Cowles Magazines,* 328 F. 2d 869, 1964; *MacLeod* v. *Tribune Pub. Co.,* 52 C. 2d 536, 1959; *Myers* v. *Berg,* 212 C. 415, 1931
4. *Werner* v. *Southern California Newspapers,* 35 C. 2d 121, 1950
5. *Kuhns* v. *Brugger,* 390 Pa. 331, 1957
6. Restatement of Torts, Sect. 283 B
7. *Roller* v. *Roller,* 37 Wash. 242, 1905
8. *Goller* v. *White,* 20 Wis. 2d 402, 1963
9. *Gibson* v. *Gibson,* 3 C. 3d 914, 1971

5 You as Student

1. U.S. Constitution, Preamble
2. Ibid. Article I, Section 8(12) and (13)
3. Ibid. Article I, Section 8(1)
4. *Brown* v. *Board of Education,* 349 U.S. 294, 1955
5. *Green* v. *County School Board of New Kent County, Virginia,* 391 U.S. 430, 1968
6. *Griffin* v. *County School Board of Prince Edward County,* 377 U.S. 218, 1964. See also *Poindexter* v. *Louisiana Financial Assistance Commission,* 36 USLW 2150, 5th circuit, 1967.
7. *Serrano* v. *Priest,* 487 P 2d 1421, 1971. The case was sent back to the trial court on a procedural question, and will no doubt return again to be decided on the substantive issue.

8. *San Antonio Independent School Districts, et al.* v. *Rodriguez,* 93 S. Ct. 1278, 1973
9. *Milliken* v. *Bradley,* 41 L. Ed. 2d 1069, 1974
10. *Meredith* v. *Fair,* 371 U.S. 828, 1962
11. *De Funis* v. *Washington,* 507 P 20 1169, 1973
12. *De Funis* v. *Odegaard,* 94 S. Ct. 1704, 1974
13. California Education Code 12101
14. Ibid. 12154 et seq.
15. Ibid. 12157
16. Ibid. 5950
17. "Report of National Commission on Reform of Secondary Education," Kettering Foundation, Dayton, Ohio, 1973
18. *Pierce* v. *Society of the Sisters of the Holy Names,* 268 U.S. 510, 1925
19. *Wisconsin* v. *Yoder,* 92 S. Ct. 1526, 1972
20. *In re Shinn,* 195 C.A. 2d 683, 1961
21. *Everson* v. *Board of Education of Ewing Tp.,* 330 U.S. 1, 1947
22. *Visser* v. *Noonsack Valley District No. 506,* 33 Wash. 2d 198, 1949
23. *Lemon* v. *Kurtzman,* 480 U.S. 602, 1971
24. *Committee for Public Education and Religious Liberty, et al.* v. *Nyquist, etc.* 93 S. Ct. 2955, 1973
25. *Engel* v. *Vitale,* 370 U.S. 421, 1962
26. *School District of Abington Tp.* v. *Schempp,* and *Murray* v. *Curlett,* 374 U.S. 203, 1963
27. California Education Code 1086
28. Ibid. 8533
29. Ibid. 8503 and 8753
30. Ibid. 9031
31. Ibid. 8506
32. *Griswold* v. *Connecticut,* 381 U.S. 479, 1968
33. *Medeiros* v. *Kiyosaki,* 52 Hawaii 436, 1970
34. *Leonard* v. *School Committee of Attleboro, Massachusetts,* 349 Mass. 704, 1965
35. *Richards* v. *Thurston,* 424 F. 2d 1281, 1970
36. *Breen* v. *Kahl,* 419 F. 2d 1034, 1969
37. *Jackson* v. *Dorrier,* 424 F. 2d 213, 1970
38. *McLeod* v. *State,* 154 Miss. 468, 1929
39. *State* v. *Marion County Board of Education,* 202 Tenn. 29, 1957
40. *State ex. rel. Idle* v. *Chamberlain,* 39 Ohio Ap 2d 262, 1961
41. *Ordway* v. *Hargraves,* 323 F. Supp. 1155, 1971
42. California Education Code 10602
43. *Robinson* v. *Sacramento City Unified School District,* 245, C.A. 2d 278, 1966
44. *Waugh* v. *Board of Trustees of the University of Mississippi,* 237 U.S. 589, 1915
45. California Education Code 10606
46. California Civil Code 1714.1
47. *Elfbrandt* v. *Russell,* 384 U.S. 11, 1966. See also *Aptheker* v. *Secretary of State,* 378 U.S. 500, 1964
48. *Sweezey* v. *New Hampshire,* 354 U.S. 234, 1957
49. *Whitney* v. *California,* 274 U.S. 357, 1927

50. *Bridges* v. *California,* 314 U.S. 252, 1941
51. *Esteban* v. *Central Missouri State College,* 415 F. 2d 1077, 1969
52. *Stacy* v. *Williams,* 306 F. Supp. 963, 1969
53. *Dickey* v. *Alabama State Board of Education,* 273, F. Supp. 613, 1967
54. *Dixon* v. *Alabama State Board of Education,* 294 F. 2d 150, 1961
55. *Esteban* v. *Central Missouri State College,* 415 F. 2d 1077, 1969
56. *Soglin* v. *Kauffman,* 418 F. 2d 163, 1969
57. AAUP Bulletin, No. 53, 1967
58. *Ziegler* v. *Santa Cruz City High School District,* 168, C.A. 2d, 277, 1959
59. *People* v. *Cohen,* 292 N.Y.S. 2d 706, 1968
60. *Piazzola* v. *Watkins,* 442 F. 2d 284, 1971
61. *Moore* v. *Student Affairs Committee of Troy State University,* 284 F. Supp. 725, 1968

6 You as Owner or Driver of a Motor Vehicle

1. *Shimoda* v. *Bundy,* 24 Cal App. 675, 1914
2. *Shmatovich* v. *New Sonoma Creamery,* 187 C.A. 2d 342, 1960
3. *McNear* v. *Pacific Greyhound Lines,* 63 C.A. 2d 11, 1944
4. *Lovett* v. *Hitchcock,* 192 C.A. 2d 806, 1961
5. *Lozano* v. *Pacific Gas and Electric Co.,* 70 C.A. 2d 415, 1945, and *Wurl* v. *Watson,* 67 C.A. 625, 1924
6. *Taylor* v. *Pacific Container Company,* 148 C.A. 2d 505, 1957
7. *Parker* v. *Auschwitz,* 7 C.A. 2d 693, 1935
8. *Martin* v. *Helson,* 82 C.A. 2d 733, 1947
9. California Vehicle Code 17150
10. *Richards* v. *Stanley,* 43 C. 2d 60, 1954
11. *Munson* v. *Friedman,* 154 C.A. 2d 73, 1957
12. *Martinez* v. *Southern Pacific Company,* 45 C. 2d 244, 1955
13. *Druzanich* v. *Criley,* 19 C. 2d 439, 1942
14. *Huebotter* v. *Follett,* 27 C. 2d 765, 1946
15. Vehicle Code 16000 et seq. as amended in 1974
16. Business and Professions Code 25602
17. *Vesely* v. *Sager,* 5 C. 3d 153, 1971
18. *Guyton* v. *City of Los Angeles,* 174 C.A. 2d 354, 1959
19. *Hughes* v. *MacDonald,* 133 C.A. 2d 74, 1955
20. *Jones* v. *Brown,* 176 C.A. 2d 184, 1959
21. See, for example, California Vehicle Code 23109
22. Ibid. 21703
23. *Rath* v. *Bankston,* 191 C.A. 274, 1929

7 You as Family Member

1. *Earley* v. *Commonwealth Dept. of Welfare,* 317 A. 2d 677, 1974
2. *Roe* v. *Wade,* 410 U.S. 113, 1973; *Doe* v. *Bolton,* 410 U.S. 179, 1973
3. *Bilsky* v. *Bilsky,* 309 N.E. 2d 697, 1974
4. *Rhoad* v. *Rhoad,* 318 A. 2d 551, 1974
5. *Gerhardt* v. *Gerhardt,* 310 N.E. 2d 224, 1974

6. *Whetstone* v. *Whetstone,* 169 Ill. App. 171, 1925
7. *Wertlake* v. *Wertlake,* 318 A. 2nd 446, 1974

8 You as Consumer

1. 3 C.C.H. Trade Regulations Rep. Par. 19,681—FTC, 1971
2. *Fuentes* v. *Shevin,* 32 L. Ed. 2d 556, 1972
3. *Williams* v. *Walker-Thomas Furniture Co.,* 350 F. 2d 445, USCA, District of Columbia, 1965
4. *Metowski* v. *Traid* Corporation, 28 C.A. 3rd 332, 1972
5. *Wisconsin* v. *J.C. Penney Co.,* 48 Wis. 2d 125, 1970

9 You as Insured

1. *Scaslon* v. *Western Fire Insurance Co.,* 4 Mich. App. 234, 1966
2. *Osborne* v. *Security Insurance Co.,* 155 C.A. 2d 201, 1957
3. *Gillis* v. *Sun Insurance Office, Ltd.,* 238 C.A. 2d 408, 1965
4. *Riggs* v. *Commercial Mutual Insurance Co.,* 125 N.Y. 7, 1890
5. *Prudential Insurance Company of America* v. *Prescott,* 130 Fla. 11, 1937
6. *Bogacki* v. *Great Western Life Insurance Co.,* 253 Mich. 253, 1931
7. *Metropolitan Life Insurance Co.* v. *Conway,* 252 N.Y. 449, 1930
8. *Fedele* v. *National Liberty Insurance Co.,* 184 Va. 528, 1945
9. *Communale* v. *Traders and General Insurance Co.,* 50 C. 2d 654, 1958

11 You as Saver, Investor, and User of Commercial Paper

1. *Guttman* v. *Illinois Central R. Co.,* 189 F. 2d 927, 1951
2. California Corporations Code, Sect. 821
3. Uniform Commercial Code, Sect. 4-406

12 You as Employee

1. Fair Employment Practices Law (Civil Rights Act of 1964), Sect. 703(a) (1)
2. Ibid. Sect. 703(b) and (c)
3. *Griggs* v. *Duke Power Co.,* 401 U.S. 424, 1971
4. Occupational Safety and Health Act of 1971, Sect. 654(a)
5. *Commonwealth* v. *Hunt,* 54 Mass 4, 1842
6. "Labor Union Membership in 1966," p-20, No. 216, U.S. Department of Commerce, Bureau of the Census
7. *Charles* v. *Weise Company,* 133 NLRB 765, 1961
8. The May Company, 136 NLRB 797, 1962
9. Peyton Packing Company, 129 NLRB 1275, 1961
10. National Labor Relations Act, Sect. 8(a) (1–5)
11. *NLRB* v. *National Maritime Union,* 175 F. 2d 686, 1949; Cory Corporation, 84 NLRB 972, 1949; Sunset Line & Twine Co., 79 NLRB 1487, 1948
12. *American Newspaper Publishers Association* v. *NLRB* 345 U.S. 100, 1953
13. National Labor Relations Act, Sect. 8(b) (1–7)
14. *NLRB* v. *Fansteel Metallurgical Corporation,* 306 U.S. 240, 1939
15. National Labor Relations Act, Sect. 14(a)
16. *Newsweek,* October 11, 1972

13 You in Business for Yourself

1. Uniform Partnership Act, Sect. 6
2. See Uniform Limited Partnership Act
3. See Model Business Corporation Act
4. Internal Revenue Code, Sect. 1371–1379

14 You as Estate Planner

1. Internal Revenue Code, Sect. 401
2. Internal Revenue Code, Sect. 2523
3. Internal Revenue Code, Sect. 2056
4. California Probate Code, Sect. 50
5. California Inheritance Tax Law, Sect. 13724

SUGGESTIONS FOR FURTHER READING

1 You and the Constitution

The Constitution of the United States of America: Analysis and Interpretation.
Prepared by the Legislative Reference Service of the Library of Congress. Senate
Document No. 232. Washington, D.C.: Government Printing Office, 1964.
> The most comprehensive presentation of the U.S. Constitution with annotations of
> related cases decided by the U.S. Supreme Court to June 22, 1964.

Konvitz, Milton R., ed. *Bill of Rights Reader.* Ithaca: Cornell University Press,
1973.
> A collection of essays on the most important and most fascinating section of the
> Constitution—the amendments known as the Bill of Rights.

Tresolini, Rocco J., and Shapiro, Martin. *American Constitutional Law.* New
York: Macmillan, 1970.
> A college text that examines important constitutional issues in depth.

2 You, Law, and the Courts

Black, Henry Campbell, and the publisher's editorial staff. *Black's Law Dictionary.* 4th ed. St. Paul: West Publishing Co., 1968.
> This outstanding law dictionary can serve as a one-volume encyclopedia of highlights
> of the law for the layman. Generous references to cases, statutes, and other sources
> can be used as leads for detailed research.

Busch, Francis X. *Trial Procedure Materials.* New York: Bobbs-Merrill, 1961.
> Provides an excellent opportunity for gaining insight into the actual operation of
> courts.

Glaser, William A. *Pretrial Discovery and the Adversary System.* New York:
Russell Sage, 1968.
> Reviews the history of discovery and its contribution to the quest for truth and
> justice.

Lineberry, William P., ed. *Justice in America: Law, Order and the Courts.* New
York: H.W. Wilson, 1972.
> A provocative collection of essays under broad headings such as "Crisis in the Courts,"
> "Thumbs on the Scales of Justice: Why the Defense Can't Rest," and "Overhauling
> the System: What Can Be Done?"

3 You as Victim or Accused of Crime

Clegg, Reed K. *Probation and Parole, Principles and Practices.* Springfield,
Ill.: Charles C. Thomas, 1964.
> Presents practical aspects of the two major techniques used by society to help
> rehabilitate convicted criminals.

Inbau, Fred E., and Aspen, Marvin E. *Criminal Law for the Layman: A Guide
for Citizen and Student.* Philadelphia: Chilton, 1970.
> A succinct and informative description of basics, with many hypothetical cases.

Perkins, Rollin M. *Cases and Materials on Criminal Law and Procedure.* Mineola, N.Y.: Foundation Press, 1972.
> An authoritative study of substantive and procedural criminal law by the leading
> authority in the field. Intended for law school students.

Sussman, Frederick B., and Baum, Frederic S. *Law of Juvenile Delinquency*. Dobbs Ferry, N.Y.: Oceana Publications, 1968.

A study of the critical area where most criminal activity has its beginnings.

Weston, Paul B., and Wells, Kenneth M. *The Administration of Justice*. Englewood Cliffs, N.J.: Prentice-Hall, 1967.

A comprehensive manual for the serious student of criminal law.

4 You as Tortfeasor or Victim

Belli, Melvin. *Ready for the Plaintiff*. New York: Popular Library, 1965.

A personal account of experiences by the trial lawyer who is known as the "king of torts."

Prosser, William L. *Handbook of Torts*. St. Paul: West Publishing Co., 1971.

The outstanding reference for authoritative information on torts in all their variety.

Restatement of Torts. 5 vols. Philadelphia: American Law Institute, 1965–66.

A group of experts in the field analyze, synthesize, and systematically restate the law of torts. Based on actual practice but also pointing the way for future development. Contains many practical examples and hypothetical cases to illustrate principles and rules expounded.

5 You as Student

Nolte, Mervin. *School Law in Action*. West Nyack, N.Y.: Parker Publishing Co., 1971.

Discusses a number of key decisions and offers guidelines for school administrators.

Nussbaum, Michael. *Student Legal Rights, What They Are and How to Protect Them*. New York: Harper & Row, 1970.

Emphasizes the student's legal situation while attending a college or university. Popular style.

Reutter, E. Edmund, Jr., and Hamilton, Robert R. *The Law of Public Education*. Mineola, N.Y.: Foundation Press, 1970.

A textbook-casebook on the law directly affecting public education. Offers an excellent survey of the law as it relates to such topics as the operation of school boards, duties of teachers, and treatment of students.

6 You as Owner or Driver of a Motor Vehicle

Gray, Cornelius R. *Digest of Motor Laws*. Falls Church, Va.: American Automobile Association, 1974.

A comprehensive compilation of automobile and traffic control regulations in all states.

Keeton, Robert E., and O'Connell, Jeffrey. *After Cars Crash: The Need for Legal and Insurance Reform*. Homewood, Ill.: Dow-Jones and Richard D. Irwin, 1967.

This book started the drive for no-fault automobile insurance.

Rubin, Charles G. *A Former Prosecutor Tells How to Win Your Case in Traffic Court*. Beverly Hills: McGil Publishing Co., 1971.

This book could prove useful to some readers even when they are represented by counsel.

7 You as Family Member

Donelson, Kenneth, and Donelson, Irene. *Married Today, Single Tomorrow.* New York: Doubleday, 1969.

> A nontechnical study of divorce and its legal and psychological implications.

Goldstein, Joseph, and Katz, Jay. *The Family and the Law.* Riverside, N.J.: Free Press, 1965.

> A lawyer and a psychoanalyst join to present a very comprehensive technical review of the field, with extensive quotations from actual cases. Good for the serious student.

Harper, Fowler V., and Skolnick, Jerome H. *Problems of the Family.* New York: Bobbs-Merrill, 1962.

> Integrates various disciplines that deal with family affairs, including the social sciences and the law.

Pilpel, Harriet F., and Zavin, Theodora S. *Your Marriage and the Law.* New York: Collier Books, 1964.

> A popular guide to the legal rights and obligations of family members.

8 You as Consumer

McClellan, Grant S. *The Consuming Public.* New York: H.W. Wilson, 1968.

> A collection of essays arranged under such broad topics as "Citizen as Consumer," "The Role of Government as Protector," and "Business and Consumer Protection."

Nader, Ralph, ed. *The Consumer and Corporate Accountability.* New York: Harcourt Brace Jovanovich, 1973.

> A leading critic presents his view of the problem. (Read along with *Things Ralph Nader Never Told You* (New York: Harper & Row, 1973), essays from *Fortune Magazine* that provide a contrary view.)

Sanford, David, ed. *Hot War on the Consumer.* New York: Pitman, 1969.

> Aptly described by the publisher as a "provocative exposé of the outrageous exploitation of the American public." Contains crusading essays from the *New Republic,* which help to show that legislation has not corrected all evils in this field.

Several popular, consumer-oriented magazines provide information about consumer problems as well as solutions and suggestions on how to improve one's status as a consumer:

> *Changing Times—The Kiplinger Magazine* (1729 H St., N.W., Washington, D.C. 20006)
>
> *Consumer Reports* (published by Consumers Union of U.S. Inc., 256 Washington St., Mt. Vernon, N.Y. 10550)
>
> *Consumers Digest* (6316 N. Lincoln, Chicago, Illinois 60659)
>
> *Money* (published by Time, Inc., Time & Life Bldg., Rockefeller Ctr., New York 10020)

9 You as Insured

Appleman, John Alan, and Appleman, Jean. *Insurance Law and Practice.* St. Paul: West Publishing Co., 1969.

> Daughter joins distinguished father in the revision of this definitive treatise. Well-indexed, and kept current with pocket supplements. A good source of authoritative information on detailed points of interest.

Greider, Janice E., and Beadels, William T. *Law and the Life Insurance Contract*. Homewood, Ill.: Irwin, 1968.
>A successful translation of technical legal principles of life insurance into layman's language.

Heins, Richard M. *Fundamentals of Property and Casualty Insurance*. Bryn Mawr, Pa.: American College of Life Underwriters, 1960.
>A handbook on property and casualty coverage addressed primarily to life insurance agents, but useful for any reader.

10 You as Homeowner

Friedman, Milton R. *Contracts and Conveyances of Real Property*. New York: Practicing Law Institute, 1974.
>A definitive treatment of real estate transactions. Explains what should be done, and why, in drafting contracts and conducting negotiations.

Kratovil, Robert. *Real Estate Law*. Englewood Cliffs, N.Y.: Prentice-Hall, 1969.
>A popular leading text used in university business schools.

Rose, Jerome G. *The Legal Adviser on Home Ownership*. Boston: Little, Brown & Co., 1967.
>Offers useful suggestions for the first-time home buyer.

11 You as Saver, Investor, and User of Commercial Paper

Bailard, Thomas; Biehl, David L.; and Kaiser, Ronald W. *Personal Money Management*. Chicago: Science Research Associates, 1973.
>The fourth unit in this textbook offers several chapters on various aspects of investing.

Engel, Louis. *How to Buy Stocks: A Guide to Successful Investing*. New York, Bantam, 1972.
>A comprehensive survey in simple language.

Forbes (60 Fifth Ave., New York 10011)
>Each year the August fifteenth issue includes a survey of mutual funds and their performance.

Hastings, Paul, and Mietus, Norbert. *Personal Finance*. New York: McGraw-Hill, 1972.
>Logically traces the problem of personal finance through five views of property: its acquisition, enjoyment, increase, conservation/protection, and ultimate disposition in retirement and after death.

Investment Companies. New York: Wiesenberger Services. Published annually.
>Provides authoritative background information and analyzes the performance of leading load and no-load funds.

12 You as Employee

Chruden, Herbert, and Sherman, Arthur. *Personnel Management*. Cincinnati: South-Western, 1974.
>Discusses labor relations as viewed by a manager (a perspective that an employee should understand).

Cox, Archibald, and Bok, Derek C. *Labor Law*. Mineola, N.Y.: Foundation Press, 1969.
> An authoritative law school textbook.

Labor Law Course. New York: Commerce Clearing House. Published annually.
> An excellent one-volume summary of federal labor law. Kept up-to-date through periodic revisions.

13 You in Business for Yourself

Heyel, Carl, ed. *The Encyclopedia of Management.* New York: Van Nostrand Reinhold, 1973.
> Nearly two hundred leaders in their fields of specialization wrote articles for this one-volume compendium of information that should be known to every manager of a business of his own.

Kelley, Pearce C.; Lawyer, Kenneth; and Baumback, Clifford M. *How to Organize and Operate a Small Business*. Englewood Cliffs, N.J.: Prentice-Hall, 1968.
> A college textbook that presents a practical approach. Legal aspects are not emphasized.

Small Business Administration (Public Information Office, SBA, 1441 L Street, N.W., Washington, D.C. 20416)
> Many very useful pamphlets on aspects of small business operation may be obtained from this source—some for a nominal charge and some for free.

14 You as Estate Planner

Wren, Harold G. *Creative Estate Planning*. New York: Practicing Law Institute, 1970.
> Comprehensive presentation includes wills, life insurance, future interests, pensions, and trusts. Written for lawyers but useful for the serious layman.

Farr, James F. *A Trustee's Handbook*. Boston: Little, Brown & Co., 1962.
> Difficult reading, but an authoritative survey of this highly technical field.

GLOSSARY

abet To help or assist another in committing a crime.

abortion, illegal The unlawful termination of a human pregnancy by any means. Also called "procuring miscarriage."

abortion, legal The lawful termination of a human pregnancy (as, for example, by a licensed physician with the consent of the mother during the first trimester—three months from conception).

acceptance a) Assent by one party to an offer, thus creating a contract. b) The process by which a drawee agrees to pay a draft by writing his signature on its face and usually also the date and the word *accepted*.

acceptance of goods When the buyer acknowledges that the goods received are satisfactory. (See also "receipt of goods.")

accession Addition to or natural increase in property already owned (as when a dog has puppies).

accessories after the fact Persons who harbor, conceal, or otherwise voluntarily and intentionally aid a known perpetrator of a crime to escape arrest or punishment. They are guilty of criminal conduct, but not of the crime of the known perpetrator.

accessories before the fact Persons who encourage or assist a perpetrator of a crime—as by planning, advising, standing guard, or driving a get-away car. They are guilty as principals, but in some states to a second degree with lesser punishment.

accommodation party A person who gives the strength of his credit to another person, by signing commercial paper as a co-maker or endorser.

accomplice A person who, in voluntary and intentional cooperation with the principal offender, is associated in a crime before, during, or after its commission.

accusation Formal commencement of a criminal case, made by a district attorney or a grand jury.

accusatory pleading A document specifying the crime committed and accusing the defendant of its commission. (See also "indictment" and "information.")

acquitted Found not guilty of a crime by judgment of the court.

actual cash value The value of property as calculated by insurance companies, by deducting depreciation from the replacement value.

add-on sale A clause (sometimes illegal) in some credit sales contracts whereby every item of a series sold to a given buyer becomes part of the collateral for repayment of the entire debt. Thus, default in one payment may result in repossession of items paid for in full.

adjudicate   To hear and decide in a judicial action (court proceeding).

administrative agencies   Units of federal, state, and local government that may possess legislative, executive, and judicial powers in specialized technical areas where intelligent regulation requires action by experts.

administrator, administratrix   A person appointed by a court to dispose of the estate of a decedent who dies without leaving a valid will (intestate).

adultery   Open and notorious sexual intercourse by a married person with someone other than the offender's wife or husband.

adversary system   The system in which the parties to a legal dispute are opponents, each producing in the trial evidence that supports his own position.

affirmative action   Positive policies and practices designed to assure employment of women and of minorities until their percentages in the work force approximate their percentages in the community.

agency shop   A company or department where all employees in the bargaining unit must pay union dues whether members or not.

aid and abet   To assist the perpetrator of a crime indirectly, while present at the time and place, as by serving as a lookout or driver.

allegations of fact   Plaintiff's statement of facts, contained in his complaint.

alien   A person born outside the jurisdiction of the United States and who has not become a citizen through naturalization.

amnesty   Action by a legislature or chief executive to abolish and forget a specified offense, generally of a political nature such as treason or rebellion by a large group. Contrasted to pardon, which remits or abates punishment imposed on an individual, generally for a breach of the peace.

annulment (of marriage)   The legal proceeding to cancel or abolish a marriage relationship because of some defect that existed when the contract was entered. The court decrees that no valid marriage ever existed, whereas a divorce or dissolution terminates a valid marriage.

answer   A document filed by a defendant on receipt of a summons and complaint. Prepared by the defendant's attorney, it is filed with the clerk of the court and a copy is given to the plaintiff.

appellant   The party in a trial who appeals to a higher court for review of the decision.

appellate courts   Tribunals that review the results reached in prior trials conducted in lower, or subordinate, courts.

appellee   The party in a trial who defends the judgment of the trial court on appeal.

arbitration   A method of settling disputes by having a third party(ies) decide them. If mandated by law, it is compulsory arbitration; if agreed to by the parties, it is voluntary arbitration.

arraign   A criminal court proceeding prior to trial during which the charge (indictment or information) is read to the accused and the trial date is set if he pleads not guilty. If he pleads guilty, the judge may sentence him immediately, but may wait for a probation report.

arrest   To take a person into custody in order to charge him with commission of a crime. May be done with or without a warrant.

articles of incorporation   A document by which a corporation is formed and organized under law for indicated purposes.

assault, criminal   The crime of unlawful attempt, coupled with present ability, to commit a battery. There is no touching.

assault, civil   The tort of creating apprehension in the mind of the victim of some harmful or offensive touching. There is no requirement of present ability of the actor to inflict actual harm.

asset   Any thing of value owned.

assumption of risk   The plaintiff voluntarily enters a situation where risk of his injury is recognized and accepted by him. Therefore, he has no claim for any injuries suffered.

attachment   See "garnishment."

attempt   A crime in itself when the accused intends to commit a crime and takes a substantial step toward its commission. Evil thought and even simple preparation are not enough to constitute attempt.

attractive nuisance doctrine   The doctrine under which trespassing minors may collect damages if attracted onto the defendant's premises by a man-made instrumentality that has special appeal to children and may cause injury (such as a railroad turntable).

auction sale   Public sale where an auctioneer solicits offers, or bids; normally the goods are sold to the highest bidder.

automatic premium loan   Upon failure to pay a premium for a life insurance policy, if there is a sufficient cash surrender value, the company automatically pays the premium and charges it against such value as a loan.

automobile insurance   Insurance against hazards flowing directly from the ownership and operation of motor vehicles.

automobile medical payments coverage   Automobile insurance that pays the medical expenses of the insured and of other occupants of the insured's vehicle injured in an accident.

bail Security posted with the court to assure that the accused, if released, will voluntarily return for further criminal proceedings.

balance sheet Written list of assets of a business (or individual) with stated dollar values; offset or balanced by a list of liabilities and by the equity of the firm (or individual), called the net worth.

balloon payment A lump sum due at the end of a period of time during which payments on a loan have consisted of interest but little or no principal.

bankruptcy Proceedings under federal law whereby all assets of a debtor (excluding certain exempt property) are distributed to his creditors. He is then discharged or excused from the legal obligation to pay most of his debts.

bargaining unit The department of a company or other employee group that is deemed appropriate for collective bargaining purposes, based on common interests or related skills and duties.

battery Any harmful or offensive touching of another human being without excuse or his consent; usually involves violent infliction of injury.

bearer Any person in possession of commercial paper that is made payable to bearer or is endorsed in blank.

beneficiary a) The person designated by the insured to receive the proceeds of an insurance policy. b) The person designated by the trustor to get the benefit of the property in a trust. c) A person who receives the benefit of a contract between two other persons.

benefit of his bargain The respective consideration to which each party is entitled in a contractual agreement.

Better Business Bureau A voluntary private agency sponsored by the Chamber of Commerce to help inform consumers of fraudulent sales schemes.

bill of exchange See "draft."

Bill of Rights The first ten amendments to the U.S. Constitution.

blank endorsement Endorsement of commercial paper by signature alone.

board of directors A group of usually three or more persons elected by the stockholders to manage a business corporation.

bodily injury and property damage insurance Automobile insurance that protects against the risk of incurring liability for injuring or killing someone else in a negligent manner, or for damaging his property.

bond Written promise by a borrower to pay a lender a fixed dollar sum of interest for a prescribed time, and to repay the principal on a stated date. (If payable within a year, it may be referred to as a note.)

booking   Police practice of fingerprinting, photographing, blood testing for alcohol, and subjecting an accused person to similar actions after arrest.

breach of contract   A party fails to fulfill his part of a legally binding agreement.

breach of legal duty   To ignore the responsibility to act as an ordinary prudent man under law.

briefs   Written arguments addressed to the appellate court by counsel for appellant and for appellee, including points of law and authoritative case support for their respective positions.

burden of proof   The duty to produce evidence as a trial progresses. In a civil case, facts are proved by a preponderance of the evidence. In a criminal case, the measure is proof beyond a reasonable doubt and to a moral certainty.

burglary   At common law, the crime committed by breaking and entering the dwelling house of another in the night with intent to steal. Expanded generally by statute to include other buildings, tents, railroad cars, and vessels, and embracing any felonious intent whether or not the felony is committed.

business invitee   A person invited onto the premises by the occupier of land for business purposes designed to produce a profit.

buy and sell agreement   A contract under which business partners (or stockholders in a closely held corporation) reciprocally agree to buy and sell their interests in the firm to each other upon the death of either.

by-laws   Private rules for the internal government of a business corporation. Normally adopted by the board of directors.

cancel (contract)   After breach by seller, to return parties to their original status. Buyer may still sue for damages.

capital   a) Money and credit needed to start and continue a business. b) Total assets of a business. c) Shares of stock representing ownership of a corporation.

capital gain   An increase in the value of a capital asset, such as a house or share of stock.

case citation   Reference that identifies a legal case and tells where it may be found in a reporter system that publishes opinions of appellate cases. For example: *Hochgertel* v. *Canada Dry Corporation,* 25 Conn. Supp. 109, 197 A 2d 342.

case-in-chief Calling witnesses and introducing into evidence documents, photographs, or whatever else bears upon the issue in a trial.

cashier's check A check drawn by the cashier in his official capacity on his own bank, payable to the order of a person designated by a customer.

cash sale transaction The buyer gets possession and title to goods in exchange for concurrent payment of money as the price.

cash surrender value The sum a life insurance company refunds if an ordinary policy is cancelled.

cause of action a) Exists when a court would grant plaintiff a judgment if plaintiff's allegations in a complaint were true. b) The right to bring suit against another.

Caveat emptor (Latin: Let the buyer beware.) The buyer should investigate and rely on his own judgment regarding the shortcomings of goods before purchase.

Caveat venditor (Latin: Let the seller beware.) The seller should exercise appropriate care to assure that goods sold are of fair value and suitable for human use, or be subjected to possible legal sanctions.

certificate of deposit An acknowledgment in writing of receipt of a certain sum of money by a bank, with an unconditional promise, signed by the maker bank, to repay the money (generally with interest) to the order of a named payee, or to any bearer, at a definite time.

certificate of incorporation See "charter."

certificate of ownership A legal document issued by a state government showing who owns a vehicle (that is, has title to it).

certificate of registration A legal document issued by a state government permitting operation of a motor vehicle on the highways of the state.

certified check A check drawn by a depositor but stamped and signed by a bank official to indicate that sufficient funds are on deposit and set aside to pay the check when presented.

certiorari (Latin: to be informed of) Process by which the U.S. Supreme Court may consider an appeal from the highest court of the state, when a federal consitutional question is presented.

challenge (of juror, for cause) To exclude any prospective juror when his bias or prejudice is established.

challenge (of juror, peremptory) To exclude a prospective juror without specifying a reason. The number of such challenges is limited.

charter (of corporation) Permit to do business as a corporation, issued by government. Also known as certificate of incorporation, approving articles of incorporation submitted by incorporators of the business.

check (negotiable) An unconditional order in writing to a drawee bank, signed by a drawer depositor, to pay on demand a certain sum of money to the order of a named payee, or to any bearer.

check off Arrangement under a union contract whereby the employer deducts union dues from wages of members and pays them directly to the union.

civil law a) The branch of law dealing with civil rights, civil duties, and their enforcement. b) The total system of law embracing civil and criminal matters, used in the ancient Roman Empire and copied on the continent of Europe in modern times. The law was defined by experts and imposed from above by the Emperor. Contrasted to English common law.

civil rights Rights that a man has as a person and by virtue of his citizenship, with special reliance on the Thirteenth and Fourteenth Amendments to the U.S. Constitution.

class action A representative suit in which one or a limited number of parties sue on behalf of a larger group to which they belong.

close corporation A corporation whose stock is owned by one person or very few persons. Also known as closely held corporation.

close of escrow The time when all required monies and documents from all interested persons are distributed by the escrow agent to appropriate persons in connection with the sale of real property.

closed shop A company or department where only union members may be hired or remain employed. Generally prohibited by federal Taft-Hartley Act.

codicil A document prepared to change a will that has already been made.

cohabitation Living together as husband and wife without first observing legal marriage procedures.

collateral Goods or other things of value (such as stocks and bonds) that serve as security for payment of a debt.

collaterals Relatives who are brother, sister, uncle, aunt, cousin, and so forth. (See also "lineals.")

collective bargaining Negotiation of an employment contract between representative(s) of the union, and representative(s) of the employer.

collision insurance Automobile insurance that protects against the risk of damaging your own automobile in a collision or upset regardless of who is at fault.

commercial paper All negotiable instruments—such as checks, drafts, promissory notes, and certificates of deposit—whose creation, transfer, and discharge are governed by the Uniform Commercial Code.

commercial property   Property used in trade or commerce, contrasted to residential or industrial.

common law   The total system of law that originated in medieval England, and was adopted by the United States at the time of the Revolution. Expressed originally in opinions and judgments of the courts, it is judge-made law that reflects the customs and usages of the people. Contrasted to Roman civil law, it is found throughout the English-speaking world. Also called unwritten law.

common law marriage   The bond formed when a man and a woman live together as husband and wife without civil or religious formalities. A legal form of marriage in some states.

common stock   Shares representing ownership in a business corporation. They have no contractual rate or amount of dividend payment, but do usually have voting power.

community property   All property acquired (in a community property state) by the husband or the wife during marriage other than by gift or inheritance, or as profits or income from separate property. (See also "separate property.")

commutation   Reduction of punishment for a crime by the chief executive—for example, death sentence to life imprisonment.

compensation   a) Payment by an employer to an employee for services rendered. b) Payment for losses incurred, as from an accident on the job.

compensatory damages   Money awarded by a court to the victim of a tort to pay for injuries suffered, or to a victim of a breach of contract to place him where he would have been had the contract been performed. (See also "special damages.")

competent parties   Persons qualified to make contracts. Minors and insane persons are generally regarded as incompetent and their contractual agreements may be void or voidable rather than valid.

comprehensive insurance   Automobile insurance that protects against losses from having your car stolen or damaged by other listed means such as vandalism.

complaint, civil   A document filed by the plaintiff with the court and served on the defendant to inform him of the facts constituting the cause of action. (See also "summons.")

complaint, criminal   a) A written statement filed by complainant containing facts that indicate a crime has been committed and that the accused committed it. b) An accusation of a misdemeanor. (No summons is used in a criminal case.)

composition of creditors   Voluntary agreement of creditors with a debtor whereby debts due are reduced in amount and additional time may be allowed. The alternative may be bankruptcy, usually involving greater loss.

compulsory arbitration   See "arbitration."

conciliation   Efforts by a third party, commonly a professional employed by federal or state government, to persuade parties to a labor dispute to settle. He may listen to both sides and offer non-binding advice to both.

condominium   A building in which individuals own, and receive title to, separate units or apartments. Each owner is responsible for his own financing and gets income tax benefits associated with ownership. Common areas (such as the land and elevators) are owned in common by all owners of the individual units.

consequential damages   After a breach of a sales contract by a seller, the losses resulting from the needs of the buyer that the seller knew of or should have known of when the contract was made.

conservatorship   A type of guardianship established by court order whereby a conservator manages the assets and personal affairs of an adult conservatee.

consideration   The purchase price or inducement (for example, reciprocal promises) to enter a contract.

consortium   The reciprocal right of companionship, affection, and sexual relations, of each spouse from the other.

conspiracy   An agreement by two or more persons to commit a crime. In some states, one or more of the conspirators must commit an overt act (open to public view).

constitution   A written document defining fundamental legal principles for governance of the people. It may include grants of power and limitations of power.

consumerism   A social movement that seeks to improve the status of buyers and consumers in their relations with sellers and producers.

contempt of court   Willful defiance of the authority or affront to the dignity of a court, or willful disobedience of its lawful orders.

contingency fee   A fixed percentage of any judgment or recovery obtained by a lawyer for a client and accepted in full settlement for services rendered. If there is no recovery, no fee is due.

contingent beneficiary   A second beneficiary who gets the proceeds of an insurance policy when the beneficiary first named is disqualified, as when he predeceases the insured.

contract   A legally enforceable agreement to do or not to do a certain thing.

contributing to the delinquency of a minor   Any conduct by an adult that assists a person under eighteen years in any unlawful activity.

contributory negligence   The plaintiff's own negligence, however slight, that helped to cause an accident. It is a complete defense for the defendant in an action for damages in most states.

conversion   Unauthorized exercise of rights of ownership over goods of another.

convicted   Found guilty of a crime by judgment of a court.

cooperative apartment   Apartment owned by a corporation formed to acquire land and erect the building. Interested persons buy shares in the corporation to obtain the right to live in one of the units.

copyright   A monopoly right granted by the federal government to print and publish a work of literature or of art for a statutory period (twenty-eight years, renewable once). Thereafter, the work is in the public realm, and anyone may print and publish it.

coroner's jury   See "jury."

corpus (of a trust)   (Latin: body) The principal, or capital sum, of the trust estate as distinguished from income.

corpus delicti   (Latin: body of a crime) Two essential elements of every crime: (1) evidence that harm has occurred, (2) most probably because of a criminal act. It may be indicated by a corpse or burned building, for example.

corrective advertising   Advertisements required by order of the Federal Trade Commission to inform the public of errors or misstatements in earlier advertisements by the same company.

court   a) A tribunal presided over by one or more persons called judges in the case of trial courts, and justices in the case of appellate courts. b) The place where the court convenes and justice is administered. c) The judge or judges who preside.

cover   The right of a buyer to purchase similar goods elsewhere if a seller breaches the contract. He may then hold the seller liable for the difference in price and other damages.

creative labor   To bring goods into existence by personal mental and physical effort. A way to acquire property.

credit sale   A transaction in which a buyer may get possession and title to goods in exchange for a promise to pay the price later.

crime   An offense against the public; violation of a provision of the penal code.

criminal action   A trial held with a jury if desired, in which the state prosecutes a person charged with a public offense.

criminal intent   Intent to commit a crime; *mens rea* (Latin: guilty mind).

criminal law   The branch of law dealing with crimes and their punishment.

criminal negligence   Conduct that is without criminal intent and yet sufficiently careless, or in reckless disregard of others' safety, that criminal penalties are prescribed by the legislature when injury or death results.

cumulative preferred stock   Preferred stock on which agreed dividends must be paid for the current year, and for prior years if not already paid, before any payment to common stockholders. (See also "noncumulative preferred stock.")

cumulative voting   A method of voting for directors of a corporation in which each shareholder has as many votes as the number of voting shares he owns or holds proxies for, multiplied by the number of positions to be filled.

damages   Money that the plaintiff tries to recover from the defendant in a trial because of the latter's unlawful act in committing a tort or breaching a contract. (See also "compensatory damages," "consequential damages," "general damages," "punitive damages," "special damages.")

dangerous instrumentality   A gun or other object that may cause harm when given to a child without instruction as to proper use.

dangerous propensity   A child's habit that may injure others, such as throwing rocks at trains.

death taxes   Taxes imposed upon death on the estate of the decedent (that is, an estate tax on the privilege of giving) and on the gifts received by the donees (that is, an inheritance tax on the privilege of receiving).

decedent   A deceased person.

deceit   Fraudulent misrepresentation made knowingly to mislead another, who is misled and therefore injured.

declaratory judgment   The court orders nothing, but indicates what would happen if anticipated action is taken. Also called declaratory relief.

decreasing term life insurance   Provides a decreasing amount of pure life insurance without savings. Premiums remain constant as the insured grows older and risk of death rises.

decree of dissolution   A court order ending a marriage. Awarded when irreconcilable differences have caused the irremediable breakdown of the marriage, regardless of fault.

deed of reconveyance   Deed used by the trustee to return title to real property to the trustor (borrower) when he pays a loan that was secured by a trust deed.

deed of trust   A contract whereby a borrower (called trustor) gives the legal title to real property to a disinterested middleman (the trustee) to hold as security or collateral for the benefit of the lender (the beneficiary). When the loan is paid in full, the legal title is reconveyed to the trustor.

de facto   Latin: in fact, or actually. (See also *"de jure."*)

defamation of character   Promulgation of a falsehood that injures the victim's fame or reputation. May be written (libel) or oral (slander).

default   Failure of a party to do what is legally required, as to keep a contractual agreement, or to file an answer to a complaint.

default judgment   Judgment of a court awarded because the defendant failed to answer the summons and complaint or to appear at the trial to contest the claim of the plaintiff.

defective or voidable marriage   A marriage that may be legally nullified by the innocent party through court action, thereby restoring both parties to the legal status of unmarried persons.

defendant   a) In a civil trial, the person from whom money damages or other relief is sought by the plaintiff. b) In a criminal trial, the accused.

deficiency judgment   A judgment obtainable against a debtor by a creditor for the balance of the claim when sale of collateral fails to provide sufficient funds to pay the full amount due.

deficit   See "net worth."

de jure   Latin: by law, or lawfully. (See also *"de facto."*)

demand paper   Commercial paper payable at any time at the option of the holder.

demurrer   A document filed by a defendant in response to a summons and complaint when allegations of the complaint, even if true, are insufficient to state a cause of action.

deposition   Questioning under oath by the opposing attorney before the trial, of a witness or adverse party to an action, in the presence of a court reporter and his own counsel. A type of discovery procedure.

depreciated value   The value of property after deduction of a percentage of its original value because of aging and/or use.

depreciation   The decline in value of an asset over a period of time, primarily because of use and action of the elements. It is recognized through appropriate accounting methods. (See also "straight-line depreciation.")

diminished capacity   Reduced ability to exercise one's freedom of will or of choice between right and wrong (perhaps because of delusion induced by drugs or the like). It may negate the presence of specific criminal intent, such as required for first degree murder.

directors (of corporation) Persons elected by stockholders to manage and direct the business affairs of a corporation. Collectively referred to as the board of directors.

disability income insurance Insurance against the risk of disabling illness or injury that makes gainful employment impossible.

discovery procedures Methods used during the period between commencement of a lawsuit and the date of trial to learn facts about the dispute under court order. (See also "deposition," "motion to produce," "request for admission of facts," "written interrogatories.")

dishonor a) Failure or refusal to pay commercial paper when due and properly presented for payment. b) Failure or refusal of a drawee to sign (accept) a draft when presented for acceptance.

dissolution a) Legal end of a business partnership as a going concern; followed by winding-up and termination. b) Termination of a marriage relationship by court order. Called divorce in most states.

divided interest Interest in property such as a parcel of land, held separately, or in severalty, by a person—for example, by the owner of a condominium apartment.

dividend a) Profit of a corporation distributed proportionally to stockholders by order of the board of directors. b) Refund of overpaid premiums by an insurance company.

divorce Termination of a marriage relationship by court order. Called dissolution in some states.

doctrine of respondeat superior A legal doctrine holding employers liable for injuries caused third persons by their employees who are negligent and acting in the course and scope of their employment.

doctrine of sovereign immunity Traditional legal rule that "the king can do no wrong"; hence, government is not liable for the torts of its agents and employees. Modern trend is away from this.

donee The person to whom a gift is made in life or under a will.

draft (negotiable) An unconditional order in writing to a drawee, signed by a drawer, to pay on demand or at a definite time a certain sum of money to the order of a named payee, or to any bearer. Also called bill of exchange and trade acceptance.

drawee The person against whom a draft is drawn; he is ordered to pay. Also, the bank against whom a check is drawn.

drawer The person who orders a drawee to pay a draft, or who orders a bank to pay a check.

duress Threat or physical harm that deprives a person of the freedom of his will or power to choose and decide.

dwelling and contents form The form in most common use to expand the coverage of the standard fire insurance policy.

economic strike A strike for higher wages, shorter hours, or better working conditions.

emancipation Parental consent to a minor to handle his own financial affairs. It normally also ends parental duties of care.

eminent domain The inherent power of the government to take private property for the public use, upon payment of the fair market value.

employment contract Contract for services in exchange for wages or other goods. A way to acquire personal property.

enact To establish a law by proper vote of members of the legislative branch of government.

encumbrance See "warranty against encumbrances."

endorsement The holder signs his name (with or without qualifying words) on the back of commercial paper, normally to transfer title (ownership) to someone else. Negotiation requires that the instrument also be delivered. (See also "blank endorsement," "qualified endorsement," "restrictive endorsement," "special endorsement," and "warranties of endorser.")

endorsements, policy Clauses that supplement standard policies of insurance. May appear as printed forms.

endowment life insurance Combines reducing term insurance and savings, but premiums are paid for a limited number of years, commonly to age sixty-five. Then the insured may demand the face amount.

entrapment A defense to charges if the crime resulted from police encouragement, but not if police provided an opportunity or agents were available in anticipation of the act.

entrepreneur Person (or group) who assumes the risk of loss of investment in a business enterprise in exchange for the hope of profit.

equitable title Title possessed by the true beneficial owner of goods, as in credit sales where the seller may retain the legal title as security for his loan.

equity The excess of the value of property over loans or other legal claims outstanding against it.

equity, action in A civil trial held without a jury when relief sought by the plaintiff is not available at common law, as an injunction, or a divorce. (See also "law, case at.")

escrow (From Old French, escroe: roll of writings) An arrangement common in real estate transactions in some states whereby the buyer and seller (and/or the borrower and lender) designate an agent (the escrower) to carry out instructions for gathering and distributing documents and funds as necessary.

estate planning   Systematic analysis of financial assets and liabilities of the individual (or married couple) to maximize benefits obtainable from income and wealth during life (especially after retirement) and after death.

estate tax   A tax imposed by the federal government and some states on the privilege of giving property to other persons after death of the donor.

evidence   Everything that the finder-of-fact is entitled to consider in arriving at a determination of the facts.

excess liability   Payment sometimes required of an insurer beyond the face limits of the policy.

executive branch   The government department that is responsible for carrying laws into effect. (See also "judicial branch" and "legislative branch.")

executive privilege   The right of the President of the United States not to disclose information because of national security considerations, provided that there is no overriding reason for disclosure as determined by judicial review.

executor, executrix   A person named by a testator to dispose of his estate after death, as directed in his will and in compliance with law.

exemplary damages   See "punitive damages."

expatriation   Voluntary abandonment of one's country to become a citizen of another country.

express powers   Powers expressly delegated to the United States government by the Constitution.

express warranty   Warranty given by seller to buyer orally or in writing.

expulsion (from school)   Permanent removal from class, as punishment for wrongful conduct in school.

extortion   The crime of obtaining money or property by threatening injury to the victim or his family.

facility of payment clause   A provision in industrial life insurance policies that permits the insurance company to pay proceeds to the personal representative of the insured, or to any relative who pays for the funeral of the insured.

fair comment   A privilege that legitimizes certain statements on matters of public concern that might otherwise be considered defamatory. (See also "privileged communication.")

false imprisonment   Wrongful detention of a victim.

family income policy   An ordinary life insurance policy supplemented by a policy of term life insurance. A variation is called a family maintenance policy.

FDIC   The Federal Deposit Insurance Corporation organized by the U.S. government to insure repayment of deposits in member banks that fail. The maximum insured in each account is $40,000.

featherbedding   To cause or attempt to cause an employer to pay for services by employees that are not performed or are not to be performed, as by requiring unneeded extra workers.

federal   Referring to the U.S. government and its activities. The United States is a federation of fifty sovereign states.

Federal Register   Volumes containing federal written law enacted by independent administrative agencies.

Federal Reporter   Volumes containing decisions and opinions of U.S. courts of appeals.

Federal Supplement   Volumes containing decisions and opinions of U.S. district courts.

felon   One convicted of a felony.

felony   A serious crime (such as murder) that is punishable by death or imprisonment in a state prison.

fiduciary relationship   A relationship between two persons wherein one has an obligation to perform services with scrupulous good faith and honesty.

financial responsibility law   A statute requiring that, in an automobile accident, any driver not covered by insurance must post cash or bond, or lose his driver's license and vehicle registration until released from potential liability.

financial statement   A written summary of the financial condition or operating results of a business. Most commonly the balance sheet and income statement.

find   To gain possession of property by discovery. A way to acquire property.

finding   A conclusion reached by a jury or court after deliberation.

first degree murder   Murder perpetrated by an explosive device, or poison, or while lying in wait, or during commission of a forcible felony such as robbery, rape, or arson.

fixed dollar savings medium   A savings medium such as bonds, in which the interest return is prescribed by contract, and remains the same regardless of the purchasing power of money.

foreign commerce Commercial trading or transportation between the United States and any other nation. The U.S. Constitution (Article I, Sect. 8-3) delegates to the Congress power to regulate such commerce.

formal will A written will executed in compliance with law and signed or acknowledged by the testator in the presence of witnesses who also sign the document.

form prescribed by law Written expression or particular language that may be required for a valid, fully enforceable contract.

forms, policy Provisions added to expand or reduce the scope of protection provided by a standard fire insurance policy.

fornication Open and notorious sexual intercourse between two unmarried persons. A crime in some states.

franchise a) The right obtained by a person or group through contract with a manufacturer or distributor to sell a branded item in a given location. b) The right granted by government to conduct certain activities (such as gas or electric utilities) as monopolies. c) The right to vote for candidates for public office.

franchisee A person or group who obtains a franchise from a manufacturer or distributor-franchisor.

franchisor A manufacturer or distributor who grants a franchise to a franchisee.

fraud Deliberate or reckless misrepresentation made with intent to induce a victim to rely thereon and he does, to his injury.

fringe benefits Direct and indirect compensation of employees by an employer for services rendered, other than in money wages. Examples include insurance, vacations, and stock purchase plans.

fundamental rights Basic rights that a person has under the U.S. Constitution such as the rights of freedom of speech, press, religion, and assembly.

garnishment A legal proceeding in which a plaintiff-creditor gets a court order compelling a third party (such as the employer of the defendant-debtor) to pay monies earned by the defendant to the plaintiff. Also known as attachment.

general damages Money awarded by a court to pay a victim of a tort for intangibles, such as pain and suffering or mental and emotional distress.

general partner A partner in either a general or a limited partnership who has the right to share in management and has unlimited liability for debts of the firm.

general partnership   A partnership in which all members are general partners. (See also "limited partnership.")

genuine assent   Agreement to enter into a contract with free exercise of will. Not negated by fraud, duress, or similar influences.

gift from decedent's estate   Gift from the property left by a decedent, after payment of any outstanding debts. A way to acquire property by will or intestate distribution.

good faith   A general obligation imposed by the Uniform Commercial Code on both seller and buyer to practice honesty in conduct and contract.

governmental function   Traditional activity of government, such as providing police and fire protection.

grand jury   See "jury."

grand theft   The stealing of personal property of substantial value. (In California, theft of goods worth $200 or more or of certain produce with a value of $50 or more is grand theft.) (See also "petty theft.")

group life insurance policy   A life insurance policy that covers all members of a designated group, such as employees of a corporation. Usually term insurance.

guaranty   See "warranty."

guardian ad litem   (Latin: for the suit) A guardian appointed by the court to prosecute or defend any action for a minor as party.

guardianship   A court-established arrangement whereby an adult guardian is appointed to take care of the person and/or the estate of a minor.

guest   A person who rides for free in another person's vehicle. He cannot sue the driver if injured, unless the driver is guilty of intoxication, willful misconduct, or gross negligence that causes the accident and resulting injury or death.

guest statutes   Laws that pertain to guests of a driver of a motor vehicle and normally absolve him of responsibility if they are injured.

health insurance   Insurance against the risk of losses due to medical and hospital expenses.

hearsay evidence   Evidence not based on personal observation or knowledge of the witness, but consisting of repetition of what someone else has said. Generally not admissible to prove a fact, but there are exceptions.

heirs Persons designated by law to receive the estate of a decedent who leaves no will (that is, dies intestate). Generally close relatives by birth and marriage.

hoarding To accumulate idle money or other things of value.

holder in due course A holder of commercial paper who has a preferred status cutting off defenses to payment. He must (a) give value, (b) in good faith, (c) be ignorant that it has been dishonored or is overdue, and (d) be ignorant of any defenses or adverse claims.

holder through a holder in due course A holder in possession of commercial paper after a holder in due course.

holographic will A will written, dated, and signed in the handwriting of the testator. No witnesses are required.

homeowners insurance Insurance that provides comprehensive protection against fire and other listed hazards involved in owning a home.

hostile fire A fire that burns where it is not intended to be.

hot cargo agreements Agreements between employers and unions that permit workers to refuse to handle or work on goods shipped from a struck plant, or to refuse to do any work that may benefit an employer who is on the union's "unfair to organized labor" list.

hung jury A jury that cannot reach a verdict because of inability or unwillingness of a sufficient number of jurors to agree on disputed facts.

immaterial evidence Not important nor essential to the proof of facts in dispute. Counsel may successfully object to its introduction by the opponent.

immunity from prosecution The granting by a court of freedom from liability for a crime. A person who has been granted this immunity possesses no privilege against self-incrimination and may be compelled to testify about the event in question.

implied powers The authority of Congress to make laws that are "necessary and proper" for executing powers to make other laws under an express grant.

implied warranty A warranty required by law whether or not it is mentioned in a contract.

incest Sexual intercourse between relatives who are lineals or collaterals of all degrees up to and including first cousins (wherein marriage is prohibited by law).

incidental damages After a breach of a sales contract, reasonable expenses incurred by a party, as for example to inspect, transport, and care for goods rightfully rejected by a buyer.

income statement   A written statement listing the income and expenses of a business with resulting profit or loss for the period of time involved. Also called profit-and-loss statement.

incompetent evidence   Evidence that the court will not permit counsel to present during trial because of some defect relating to the witness or the evidence.

incontestable clause   Provision in a life insurance policy whereby the insurance company may not deny liability, generally after two years from date of issuance, unless premiums are not paid.

indemnification   Payment by an employer to an employee to make up for a loss suffered by the employee.

indemnify   To make good an actual loss.

independent contractor   A person engaged to utilize his own judgment and skill in performing a task as agreed.

indeterminate sentence law   A statute that provides for a range (such as one to five years) rather than a specific period of incarceration for a crime, the exact time to be determined by a designated authority after confinement begins.

indictment   An accusation of felony filed by a grand jury. (See also "information.")

indorsement   As spelled in the Uniform Commercial Code. See "endorsement."

industrial life insurance policy   A policy designed for sale to industrial workers who cannot afford conventional policies. Premiums may be collected weekly; the face amount is usually small and meant to pay for funeral expenses only.

inflation   a) A period of rising prices and wages. b) Rising prices caused by increased costs of production ("cost-push" inflation) or by increased demand of consumers for goods and services as personal incomes go up ("demand-pull" inflation).

information   An accusation of misdemeanor pleading filed by a district attorney. (See also "indictment.")

infraction   Minor crime that is not punishable by incarceration but by fine.

infringement   See "warranty against infringement."

inheritance tax   A tax imposed by most states on the privilege of receiving property from a decedent.

injunction   An order of a court of equity forbidding an action that is considered injurious to the plaintiff, when dollar damages would be unavailable or inadequate.

inland marine personal property floater   Insurance that covers personal belongings at a level close to their true value. Appropriate for valuables such as jewelry, antiques, and furs.

in loco parentis   Latin: In the place of a parent.

insanity, legal   Mental disease or defect that causes the accused to "lack substantial capacity either to appreciate the criminality (wrongfulness) of his conduct or to conform his conduct to the requirements of the law" (Model Penal Code, Sect. 4.01).

insurable interest   An interest possessed by a person who would suffer a direct financial loss if the event insured against should take place. Required if one is to buy an insurance policy.

"insurance poor"   Said of a person who has purchased too much insurance protection.

insured   A person protected or covered by an insurance policy.

insurer   A company that sells policies of insurance against specified hazards.

intentional infliction of mental disturbance   Outrageous conduct that causes mental, if not immediate physical, suffering by the victim.

intentional tort   A deliberate wrongful act that causes injury to another person, whether or not the injury was intended.

interest   The payment, usually expressed as an annual rate (percentage), by a borrower for use of a principal sum of money obtained from a lender.

interspousal immunity   traditional ban on lawsuits between spouses to avoid possible resulting disruption of family harmony. Modern trend is to allow such lawsuits.

interstate commerce   Commercial trading or transportation between or among two or more states of the Union. The U.S. Constitution (Article I, Section 8–3 E) delegates to the Congress power to regulate such commerce.

inter-vivos gift   (Latin: among the living) Gift from one living person to another; a way to acquire personal property.

intestacy   Dying without having made and left a valid will.

intestate law   Statutory prescription for distribution of a decedent's estate among heirs when he dies leaving no will.

intrastate commerce   Commercial trading or transportation within any single state of the Union. Under the Tenth Amendment of the U.S. Constitution the power to regulate such commerce is reserved to the respective states.

invest   To accumulate and place money in a variable dollar medium to earn profits or rent.

investment companies Corporations or trusts that sell shares to the public and use the proceeds to make investments, usually in stocks or bonds or both. Popularly called mutual funds; regulated under the federal Investment Company Act of 1940.

involuntary manslaughter The unintentional killing of another person because of gross negligence, or as a result of dangerous and unlawful conduct (such as killing a pedestrian while speeding).

irrelevant Not pertinent to anything of consequence in the proof of facts in dispute. Valid reason for objection to a question during a trial.

irresistible impulse The motivation whereby an accused, because of a diseased mind, could not avoid committing a criminal act even if he knew it was wrong. An acceptable test of legal insanity in a few states.

irrevocable trust A trust that may not be terminated or revoked by the trustor who creates it.

judge The officer who presides over a trial court. (See also court.")

judgment The final determination or decision of the court as to the rights and duties of the parties in a lawsuit.

judgment of nullity A court order granted a petitioner when a marriage is either void or voidable.

judgment-proof Said of a defendant from whom payment cannot be obtained even if a judgment were obtained, as when he has no liability insurance and insufficient assets.

judicial branch The government department that is responsible for determining the constitutionality of legislative and executive actions, and adjudicating rights and duties of persons who are involved in disputes. It interprets and applies the laws. (See also "executive branch" and "legislative branch.")

jurisdiction The power of a court to decide a controversy and to award appropriate remedies.

jurisdictional dispute or strike A labor dispute where two or more unions claim the right to represent the same workers, or the right to do certain jobs.

jury, coroner's A group of adults legally selected and sworn to examine evidence of the cause and circumstances of any violent or suspicious death happening within the coroner's jurisdiction.

jury, grand A group of up to twenty-three adults legally selected and sworn to review, under court supervision, evidence of alleged criminal conduct, and to indict persons whom they believe should stand trial.

jury, petit   (French: small) Same as trial jury.

jury, trial   A group, usually consisting of twelve adults but sometimes a smaller number, who are legally selected and sworn to review evidence in civil and criminal trials, and to determine the facts by verdict.

justices   Judges in appellate courts.

juvenile court   A court with jurisdiction (of a special parental-concern nature) over delinquent and neglected children.

Keogh Act   The federal law which permits a self-employed person to set aside and invest or save in an approved medium up to 15 percent of his annual income (to a maximum of $7500) free of income taxes until retirement.

kidnapping   The crime of unlawful seizure and secret confinement of a victim without his consent.

land contract   An agreement by an owner of real property to sell to a buyer who takes possession but does not get title until all payments have been made.

last will   See "will."

law   Principles and detailed rules of human conduct that are enforceable in courts.

law, case at   A civil trial held with a jury if desired, when relief sought by the plaintiff is measurable in dollar damages. (See also "equity, action in.")

legal creditor-owner   A lender who advances money for another to buy a car, or sells the car on credit, and holds a security interest in the vehicle until paid in full.

legal in inception and execution   Said of valid contracts. Thus, one may not contract to commit a crime or tort.

legal separation   A court order granted on the ground of irreconcilable differences or incurable insanity, with necessary orders for child custody and support, support of the wife, and division of community property (as in dissolution), but the marriage endures.

legal tender   Any kind of money that must be accepted by a creditor when offered by a debtor in payment of a debt.

legal title   Title to goods that gives the holder the appearance of ownership (such as security for payment of the balance of the purchase price), while another person with the equitable title is the real owner who enjoys possession and use of the goods.

legislative branch The government department that is responsible for enacting statutory laws. (See also "executive branch" and "judicial branch.")

legitimation Irrevocable acknowledgment by a natural parent that, although not married, he is the parent of a child.

letter of instructions A document prepared by a person to instruct his personal representative (executor or administrator) as to the nature and location of his assets and liabilities and suggesting appropriate action to be taken after his death. Not legally binding.

level term life insurance Provides pure insurance without savings. Usually sold for five-year periods. Renewable and convertible into ordinary policies.

liability From the viewpoint of a debtor, any claim of a creditor for payment.

libel Written defamatory statement.

licensee Someone with consent, implicit or explicit, to enter another's property.

lien See "mechanic's lien" and "warranty against encumbrances."

life insurance Insurance against the risk of loss resulting from premature death.

life tenant A person whose interest in property lasts only as long as he lives or for the duration of some other measuring lifetime.

limited defenses Legal defenses that can be asserted when a suit is brought on commercial paper and that are effective against any plaintiff except a holder in due course or a holder through a holder in due course. For example, the instrument was given in payment for goods that proved to be defective.

limited liability Restriction of liability for debts of a firm to the amount invested. Limited partners in a limited partnership and all stockholders in a corporation enjoy limited liability.

limited partner Partner in a limited partnership whose liability for firm debts is limited to his investment. His personal assets cannot be attached by firm creditors. He may not share in management.

limited partnership Partnership in which the liability of one (or more) partner(s) is restricted or limited to the amount he (or they) invested. At least one partner must have unlimited liability. (See also "general partnership.")

limited payment life insurance Combines reducing term insurance and savings, but premiums are paid for a limited number of years. Face amount is paid to the beneficiary upon death of the insured, or to the insured at age ninety-nine or one hundred.

lineals Relatives who are in a direct line of descent, as father, son, grandson. (See also "collaterals.")

listing agreement The employment contract between a homeowner who desires to sell his home and a real estate broker who is hired to find a buyer.

load The charge of approximately 9 percent made by most investment companies (mutual funds) to cover the salesman's commission and other overhead costs when shares are sold.

loan shark A person who charges exorbitant usurious interest for the loan of money, and commonly uses violence to compel payment.

loan value The sum that can be borrowed against an ordinary life insurance policy, up to the full cash surrender value.

lockout A shutdown of operations by an employer in response to union demands or to achieve other changes in an employment contract.

magistrates Judges of the justice court or other lower courts with jurisdiction over minor offenses and small claims.

malice aforethought The highest degree of mental culpability. There need not be an actual intent to kill the victim, but evil design and unlawful purpose which, if persistent, must produce injury.

malicious prosecution Taking a sham lawsuit against a victim for the purpose of vexing or harassing him.

manslaughter The unlawful killing of another person without malice aforethought. May be voluntary or involuntary.

marital deduction Deduction from the taxable estate permitted by law when a gift is made by one spouse to another.

maritime Refers to shipping and boating on navigable waters (oceans, great lakes, and rivers).

market value The price a home would bring if offered for sale in a fair market without compulsion of buyer or seller.

mayhem The crime of unlawfully depriving the victim of some member of his body, or disfiguring, disabling, or rendering the member useless.

mechanic's lien The legal claim of a contractor or worker who helped construct a building (or repair a product, such as a car). It may be asserted against the property itself for any sum unpaid. A similar lien is given by law to suppliers of materials for construction projects.

mediation Efforts by a third party, commonly a professional employed by federal or state government, to persuade parties to a labor dispute to settle.

misdemeanor   A crime that is punishable by fine or by incarceration in a county jail or by both.

misrepresentation   A lie; a false statement made intentionally, knowing it is not true. Sometimes not a lie if made innocently.

mobile home   A compact movable home. Available at a relatively low price. Generally set down in "mobile home parks" and not moved thereafter.

motion to produce   An order made by a court at the request of counsel compelling the defendant to provide specified evidence to the court. A type of discovery procedure.

motive   A reason for doing, or not doing, an act; not synonymous with criminal intent. Intent is essential for crime; motive is not.

multiple listing   An arrangement whereby many real estate brokers exchange information about a property for sale and all may try to locate a buyer. If successful, the sales fee is shared with the broker who made the initial listing agreement with the seller.

murder   Unlawful killing of a human being with malice aforethought. Usually classified as first or second degree, depending on the method used, state of mind, and so forth.

mutual fund   See "investment companies."

mutual insurance company   An insurance company that is owned by its policyholders. (See also "stock insurance company.")

naturalization   The process by which an alien (foreigner) may become a U.S. citizen.

natural rights   Rights that a person has by virtue of being human, such as the rights to life, liberty, and the pursuit of happiness.

negative injunction   An order of a court of equity forbidding certain action.

negligence   Carelessness; failure to exercise the care that an ordinary, prudent person would have exercised under the same or similar circumstances, causing injury as a proximate and foreseeable result.

negotiation   See "endorsement."

net worth   The difference between total assets and total liabilities. (If liabilities exceed assets, the negative difference is called a deficit. In a corporation, a deficit is the excess of liabilities and capital stock over assets.)

no-fault insurance   A type of automobile insurance that provides benefits to those injured regardless of fault of parties to the accident.

no-load fund An investment company (mutual fund) that sells its shares by mail and imposes no load, or sales charge, for effecting the transaction.

nolo contendere, plea of (Latin: I will not contest it) Equivalent to a plea of guilty, but cannot be regarded as an admission of guilt in a subsequent civil trial against the defendant.

noncumulative preferred stock See "cumulative preferred stock."

nonsupport Failure to contribute money in accordance with one's ability, to the maintenance of a parent or child as required by law.

note See "bond" or "promissory note."

nuncupative will An oral will.

occupancy Taking possession as owner of goods that belong to no one else (for example, wild game). A way to acquire property.

offer A proposal to enter into a contractual agreement. Made by an offeror to an offeree. (See also "acceptance.")

officers (of a corporation) Persons selected by directors and given delegated authority to manage the day-to-day business affairs of a corporation. Officers required by statute are president, vice-president, secretary, and treasurer.

off-premises extension policy Amendment of homeowners or fire insurance policy that covers loss outside of the insured home, but only up to 10 percent of the dollar value of the basic coverage.

opening statements Summaries by counsel of plaintiff and of defendant indicating what they expect to prove in the ensuing trial.

open shop A company or department where union membership is not required to get or keep a job. The employer does not necessarily bargain collectively with any union, although it may.

oppressive child labor Certain types of employment of teen-agers that are deemed to be hazardous or otherwise detrimental to their health and well-being.

ordinances Written laws of local governments, such as cities and counties.

ordinary life insurance Combines reducing term insurance with savings. Premiums are payable until death or age ninety-nine or one hundred.

ordinary or business passenger A person who pays for the service of being transported somewhere. He may legally sue the driver who negligently causes injury. (See also "guest.")

pardon Release of a convicted criminal from all punishment for his crime, including the loss of political rights, through act of the chief executive. (See also "amnesty," "commutation," "parole," "probation," and "reprieve.")

parental immunity Traditional ban on lawsuits between parents and their own children to avoid possible resulting disruptions of family harmony. Modern trend is to permit such lawsuits.

parole Release from prison during a sentence on specified conditions involving good behavior; if these conditions are violated, the prisoner is returned to complete his sentence.

parol evidence rule Legal presumption that the contracting parties have included all previous or concurrent desired oral or written understandings in the final, integrated written agreement that they sign.

participating preferred stock Shares of preferred stock, the owners of which are entitled to receive additional dividends (beyond the regular agreed amount) when payments are made to common stockholders.

partnership An association of two or more persons to carry on, as co-owners, a business for profit.

patent A monopoly right granted by the federal government to an inventor to make, use, and sell his unique product, generally for a period of seventeen years, nonrenewable. Thereafter, the idea is in the public realm, and anyone may use and exploit it.

paternity proceeding Court action to determine whether or not the defendant is the father of a child as alleged.

payee The party named in commercial paper as the one to whose order payment is to be made.

payment in kind Payment received in goods rather than money.

peremptory challenge (of juror) See "challenge (of juror, peremptory)."

perjury Lying when testifying under oath.

personal balance sheet See "balance sheet."

petit jury See "jury."

petty theft The theft of personal property of a value less than would qualify the crime as a felony.

picketing Patrolling by strikers or sympathizers at the entrances to a business plant during a labor dispute. Pickets usually carry cards urging workers to join the strikers, and urging suppliers and customers to refuse to deal with the employer.

pimping The crime of enticing a female to engage in prostitution (catering to the lust of others). Also called pandering and procuring.

plaintiff In a trial, the person trying to recover money damages or other relief from a defendant.

plea Response of the accused to criminal charges; it may be (1) guilty, (2) not guilty, (3) nolo contendere, or (4) not guilty by reason of insanity.

pleadings The complaint of the plaintiff and answer of the defendant in a lawsuit.

police power The inherent power of the government to subject individual rights to reasonable regulation for the health, safety, morals, or general welfare of the public.

policy A contract of insurance.

political rights Rights that citizens share in government, including the rights to vote and to hold public office.

poll tax A tax of a specified standard sum upon each person, without reference to income or property.

portfolio The various securities owned by a person.

possession The custody and control of property coupled with the right to use it.

power of appointment Authority given to a person (the donee) under a trust or will to designate or appoint the person(s) who shall receive specified assets after a specified event (such as death of the donee or death of the testator).

preemption A prior assertion by the federal government of authority to regulate a field (such as labor relations). States may not enact conflicting laws in such fields. (The same principle applies between state and local governments.) Also called supremacy.

preferred stock Shares that represent ownership in a business corporation and are entitled to dividends of a fixed amount before any payment to common stockholders.

preliminary hearing When an accusation is by information, an examination in open court by the judge to determine whether there is sufficient cause to hold the accused for trial.

premium The sum paid at periodic intervals for insurance coverage.

presentment for payment The act of presenting commercial paper for payment to the party with primary liability to pay.

pretermitted heir statute A statute giving rights of inheritance to children (or grandchildren) of a testator not named in the will and not provided for by settlement in life.

prima facie (Latin: at first sight) A presumption or inference (as of negligence) that may be rebutted or overcome by contrary evidence.

primary liability When a party to commercial paper is the person obligated to pay a properly presented instrument as soon as it is due, he is primarily liable (as is, for example, the maker of a promissory note).

principal a) The capital sum that earns interest or profits. b) In a crime, the actual perpetrator of it, or someone who aids him and is actually or constructively present while it is committed. c) The capital sum of a trust estate, as distinguished from income.

prior restraint Legal measures to prevent anticipated illegal conduct before it takes place, as the banning of a parade expected to cause a riot.

privilege against self-incrimination The right of any person, including one accused of crime, to remain silent when what he might say could indicate his guilt. "No person . . . shall be compelled in any criminal case to be a witness against himself . . ." (Fifth Amendment).

privileged communication Defamatory comment that can be made without fear of successful lawsuit, as in a court during a trial (absolute privilege) or about a worker between past or present employer and a prospective employer (qualified privilege, conditioned on being made in good faith about subject matter in which the parties have a legitimate interest). (See also "fair comment.")

privity of contract The relationship between two or more contracting parties.

probate The process of proving the validity of a will in court, coupled with related matters of administering the decedent's estate. Involves payment of debts to creditors and distribution of remaining assets to heirs or beneficiaries.

probation Release of a convicted criminal before sentence begins on condition of good behavior under supervision of a probation officer. If this condition is violated, incarceration begins.

procedural law Principles and detailed rules that define the methods of administering substantive law. Also called adjective law.

process Legal documents or writs used to compel a defendant in a lawsuit to answer a complaint and appear in court.

process server A person who serves (delivers) a copy of the summons and complaint upon a defendant at the request of a plaintiff.

profit The excess of revenues or receipts of a business over costs or expenses.

promissory note (negotiable) An unconditional promise in writing, signed by a maker, to pay on demand or at a definite time a certain sum of money to the order of a named payee, or to any bearer.

proprietary function A business activity of government such as running a bus line.

prosecutor   An attorney employed by the government to proceed legally against a person accused of crime. He represents the state or the people.

proximate cause   A cause which, in natural and continuous sequence, produces the injury, and without which the effect or result would not have occurred.

proxy   A written form signed by a stockholder designating another person to vote his share(s) of stock.

public defender   A lawyer provided by the community for a person who is accused of crime and cannot afford to hire his own counsel.

public use and necessity   In eminent domain, a use of value to the whole community rather than to any particular individual, but not everyone need be personally and directly benefitted.

punitive or exemplary damages   Money awarded by a court to a victim of an intentional tort, to punish the tortfeasor and make him an example as a warning to others.

purchase contract   An agreement to buy goods for a sum of money. Reciprocal of sales contract. A way to acquire property.

purchasing power of the dollar   The ability of a given amount of money to buy goods and services.

putative spouse   One who, acting reasonably and in good faith, believes a marriage is lawful, as might the second wife of a bigamist.

qualified endorsement   Endorsement of commercial paper which includes the words *without recourse*. The signer may not be held liable on the instrument unless for a breach of an implied warranty.

questions of fact   Circumstances or matters surrounding and involved in a case being tried by a court. Decided by a jury. (See also "questions of law.")

questions of law   Principles and rules of human conduct determined by the judge to be applicable in a case. (See also "questions of fact.")

quitclaim deed   A deed to real property in which the transferor gives whatever interest he may possess, which may be none. He makes no warranties and therefore cannot be held liable if the title transferred proves to be faulty.

rape, forcible   An unlawful act of sexual intercourse through force and against the will of the victim. Consent obtained by trick or threat or through the use of intoxicants or narcotics is not true consent.

rape, statutory   Sexual intercourse with a female under a specified age (usually sixteen or eighteen).

receipt of goods   When the buyer takes physical possession or control of goods. (See also "acceptance of goods.")

recognizance   A written promise by the accused, if released, to return voluntarily for further criminal proceedings.

referral sales schemes   A sales promotional method (sometimes illegal) where the price of a product is reduced to the buyer by a certain percentage, depending on the number of new customers he recruits.

registered or equitable buyer-owner   The buyer of a car on time who gets possession and use while making payments.

regulatory offense   A crime in which criminal intent is irrelevant (for example, violation of pure food laws).

reimbursement   Payment by an employer to an employee for expenses properly incurred.

reinstate   To stop foreclosure by paying all delinquent sums and related fees within a prescribed period of time. A privilege available to a borrower (trustor or mortgagor).

relevant evidence   Evidence that relates to or has a bearing upon a question of fact in dispute during a trial.

replacement value   The sum required to erect a new building of like kind and quality to one destroyed, at current construction costs.

replevin   Legal action to recover possession of goods wrongfully taken or retained by a defendant.

remainderman   The person who gets property under a deed or will after someone else has enjoyed possession and use for a specified period of time under the same document. As when a man, in his will, leaves real property to his widow for her life, and then to their children, the remaindermen.

reprieve   Postponement or stay of execution of judgment, after conviction for a crime.

request for admission of facts   Submitted to counsel by the opposing attorney before trial for the acknowledgment of facts that are not in dispute and yet are relevant and material. A type of discovery procedure.

rescission   Nullification of a contractual agreement and return of the parties to their status as it was before the agreement, insofar as possible.

residual powers   Powers not expressly delegated to the United States by the U.S. Constitution nor prohibited by it to the states, and hence reserved to the states or to the people.

res ipsa loquitur   (Latin: the thing speaks for itself) The doctrine under which negligence is inferred. To avoid liability the defendant must prove he was not negligent. Available when the instrumentality causing injury was under control of the defendant and yet injury occurred that normally would not in the absence of negligence.

respondeat superior See "doctrine of respondeat superior."

restitution Return of what has been received, as when a contract is rescinded.

restrictive endorsement Endorsement of commercial paper by signature together with words that prohibit further transfer, such as "for deposit only."

reversionary interest a) Something of value (such as the right to borrow against his policy) that a life insurance policyholder may retain when he gives the policy to another person. b) Part of the value of real property that a grantor may retain when he conveys the property to a grantee.

revocable trust A trust that may be terminated or revoked by the trustor who creates it.

riders, policy Additions or amendments that are usually typewritten and pasted to the insurance policy to modify the contract terms.

right of retraction A defense against libel favoring certain publications, such as newspapers. Even if a paper defames someone, publication of a retraction, or admission of error, may be a complete or partial defense against a claim for damages.

right-to-work laws State laws that make the union shop illegal.

Roman civil law See "civil law."

rule against perpetuities A rule of law that bars perpetuities. Any condition in a trust (or grant of land) that may deprive the owner of the power to give away or sell his interest for a period beyond any life or lives in being plus twenty-one years thereafter, plus the nine-month period of gestation for a posthumous child. Designed to keep property in commerce and under full control of the living.

rules a) Detailed laws governing human conduct. b) Laws made by administrative agencies, within the area of their expertise. c) Court orders regulating court practice or individual conduct.

sales contract Agreement to sell goods for a sum of money. Reciprocal of purchase contract. A way to acquire property.

sale on approval Conditional sale in which the buyer gets possession and right to use goods before he decides to buy.

satisfaction of judgment Proof that a debt created by judgment of the court has been paid by the defendant.

save To accumulate and place money in a fixed dollar medium to earn interest.

second degree murder Murder such as might be committed during an unjustified rage, without any deliberately formulated design to act, as in first degree cases.

secondary boycott Striking workers and sympathizers refuse to deal with third parties who buy from or sell to the struck employer. Generally prohibited by federal Taft-Hartley Act.

secondary liability When the party who has primary liability to pay commercial paper fails to do so, one or more other parties to the instrument may be obligated to pay if properly notified of the dishonor.

secured loan Money borrowed with a pledge by the borrower of specific assets that may be forfeited to the lender if repayment is not made as promised.

securities Stocks, bonds, notes, warehouse receipts, and other documents representing ownership of assets or claims for payment.

SEC The Securities Exchange Commission, a federal independent administrative agency charged with regulation of leading securities exchanges and of the issuance of securities in interstate commerce.

security agreement A legal document signed by a buyer on credit, which describes the goods that serve as security for payment of the debt.

seduction The act of enticing a person to engage in unlawful sexual intercourse by means of persuasion, payment, or promises (as of marriage), but without force. A statutory crime in most states.

segregation Isolation or separate treatment, usually unequal, on the sole basis of race, color, creed, or national origin.

self-defense, privilege of The legal right to use whatever force appears to be reasonably necessary to protect oneself from great bodily injury by an assailant.

self-incrimination See "privilege against self-incrimination."

separate property Property, real or personal, either brought into a marriage at the outset or acquired during marriage by gift or inheritance, together with the profits therefrom. Must be kept separate to retain this status. (See also "community property.")

severance damage Dollar damages recoverable because of a reduction in the value of that part of a parcel of land not taken by the government under its power of eminent domain.

sex perversion Crime that includes sodomy (carnal copulation by human beings with each other against nature—as man with man by penetration of the anus—or with an animal), oral copulation, and lewd or lascivious acts with a child.

shareholder See "stockholder."

shop right The right of an employer to use (in operation of his plant) an invention owned by an employee without payment of royalties, because the employee devised it on company time.

sight draft A draft that is payable when presented for payment (that is, on sight).

SIPC The Securities Investor Protection Corporation organized by the U.S. government to insure against loss of cash (to $20,000) and securities (to $50,000) left by customers in the custody of member brokers.

sitdown strike A strike in which workers retain possession of the employer's property. Illegal.

slander Spoken defamatory statement.

solicitation The crime of asking, encouraging, or ordering another person to commit a criminal act.

sovereign immunity See "doctrine of sovereign immunity."

special damages Money awarded by a court to pay out-of-pocket expenses (such as medical costs) to the victim of a tort.

special endorsement Endorsement of commercial paper by signature together with the words *Pay to the order of* _____ and the name of the endorsee.

specific performance Remedy available in a court of equity to get possession and title to goods that are unique, when seller refuses to deliver under a valid sales contract. Dollar damages are deemed an inadequate remedy for the plaintiff.

spouse Husband or wife in a marriage relationship.

sprinkling and accumulation trust A trust in which the trustee has discretionary authority to distribute (sprinkle) income of the trust as he sees fit among members of a designated group, or to allow the income to build up (accumulate).

standard fire policy Terms prescribed by statute in New York state and other states for inclusion in fire insurance policies.

standard nonforfeiture law Provision required by statute to be included in life insurance policies to protect the insured against forfeiture by giving him optional ways of using his cash surrender value if he defaults in payment of premiums.

stare decisis, doctrine of (Latin: to stand by decided cases) Binds an inferior (subordinate) court to follow and apply decisions and interpretations of higher courts when similar cases arise. Also called doctrine of precedence.

statute of frauds A law that requires certain types of important contracts, if they are to be enforceable, to be in writing and signed by the party being sued. Designed to discourage fraud and perjury (lies under oath) about oral agreements. Also called statute of frauds and perjuries.

statute of limitations Laws that bar legal action to punish criminals or to recover civil damages if proceedings are not begun within prescribed periods of time.

statutes Written laws of federal and state legislatures.

stock Certificate of ownership of a share or interest in a business corporation.

stock dividend Distribution of stock of a corporation as a dividend on outstanding stock.

stockholder The owner of one or more shares of stock in a business corporation. Also called shareholder.

stock insurance company An insurance company owned by stockholders. (See also "mutual insurance company.")

stock split Issuance of two or more shares for each share of stock outstanding in a corporation.

straight-line depreciation The most common method of showing depreciation. Based on the assumption that an asset deteriorates in value at a constant annual rate (for example, 2 percent a year).

strict product liability The legal doctrine under which manufacturers and middlemen who make and sell products that are defective and consequently cause injury are liable to victims regardless of lack of negligence or intent.

strike A concerted refusal by employees to perform the services for which they were hired, in order to gain improvements in wages, hours, or conditions of employment.

subornation of perjury Persuading another person to commit perjury.

subrogation The substitution of a third party for the creditor in a claim against a debtor. For example, the insurer may sue a third party defendant in the name of the insured after paying the claim of the latter against the defendant, as for damages resulting from an auto accident.

substantive law Principles and detailed rules that define legal rights and duties. Contrasted to procedural or adjective law.

summons A document issued by a clerk of the court at the request of the plaintiff when a complaint is filed. Served on the defendant, it notifies him that judgment will be taken against him if he fails to answer the complaint. Prepared by the plaintiff's attorney. (See also "complaint.")

suspension (from school) Removal from class for a definite period of time, as punishment for wrongful conduct in school.

sympathy strike   A strike called by workers in a company or department where there is no labor dispute, in sympathy and to support workers employed elsewhere.

tax shelter   An investment that has favorable income tax or death tax effects for the investor.

temporary disability insurance   Insurance required by law in some states to cover disabilities of workers that are not job-related.

termination (of partnership)   Legal end of a business after payment of debts, and distribution of capital and remaining profits (if any) to partners.

testamentary trust   A trust created by a will to take effect after the death of the testator.

testator, testatrix   Person who makes a will; person who dies leaving a will.

theft   The crime of unlawfully taking the tangible personal property of another. Generally classified as grand theft (a felony) and petty theft (a misdemeanor), based on the dollar values involved.

time draft   A draft that is payable on a certain day, or a certain number of days after the date on the instrument, or after sight (that is, after it is presented for acceptance).

tort   An offense against a private individual; a legally recognized wrong against a person or property independent of contract.

tortfeasor   A wrongdoer who commits a private injury to another person from a breach of duty recognized by law.

trade acceptance   See "draft."

trademark   A unique mark, symbol, or imprint used by a manufacturer to distinguish and identify a product. Trademarks may be registered under federal law and in many states.

trade name   A name used in commerce to identify a given firm, or products of a given manufacturer. Acquired by use.

treaty   A legal agreement or understanding between two or more sovereign countries.

trespass   Wrongful interference with the real or personal property of another. Commonly refers to entry on another's land without authority.

trial   Formal procedure before a court conducted to resolve disputed questions of fact and of law.

trial courts   Tribunals that conduct original trials.

trust   A legal relationship in which one party (trustor) transfers legal title in property to a second party (trustee) for the benefit of a third party (beneficiary).

trustee's deed   A deed issued by a trustee to convey ownership to real property to the highest bidder at an auction sale conducted after default in payments by the borrower (trustor).

undivided interest   Interest in property shared by two or more persons.

undue influence   Subtle abuse of trustful reliance on another, which deprives the victim of the freedom of his will or power to choose and decide.

unfair labor practices   Certain practices of unions and of employers that are prohibited by federal or state law.

unfair labor practice strike   A strike prompted by one or more unfair labor practices of an employer.

unforeseeable   Said of a result or effect that could not be seen or anticipated beforehand by the defendant as a reasonable person, and therefore cannot be a basis for liability if injury is suffered by the plaintiff.

Uniform Reciprocal Enforcement of Support Act   Legislation that permits distant states to proceed against a defaulting father now resident there to compel him to make payments ordered by the court for support of his children in the state of origin.

uninsured motorists insurance   Automobile insurance that protects against the risk of loss from bodily injury suffered by an insured because of the negligence of either an uninsured driver or a hit-and-run driver.

union shop   A company or department where anyone may be hired, but after a stated time (usually thirty days) a new employee must join the union or lose his job.

United States Code   Volumes containing federal statutes enacted by Congress.

U.S. Supreme Court Reporter   Volumes containing decisions and opinions of the U.S. Supreme Court. Part of the unwritten law.

universal defenses   Legal defenses that can be asserted when a suit is brought on commercial paper and that are effective against any plaintiff (for example, the defendant proves that the maker's signature is a forgery).

unqualified endorser   An endorser of commercial paper who does not add the words *without recourse* when he signs.

unsecured loan   Money borrowed on the general credit of the borrower with no pledge of specific assets that may be forfeited to the lender if repayment is not made as promised.

unwritten law Laws that are enforced by courts and found in their written opinions (cases), but not in statutes or ordinances. Also called common law.

usury Interest charged for the use of money in excess of maximum rates allowed by law.

valid Legally enforceable (as a contract, for example).

variable dollar investment medium An investment medium, such as common stock or real property, in which the return of profits (as dividends, capital gains, or rent) fluctuates with the success or failure of the enterprise.

variable life insurance policy A policy in which a prescribed minimum face amount benefit must be paid, but a higher benefit is possible if savings invested by the insurer prove to be more profitable.

venue, change of Transfer of a case for trial to another county or judicial district.

verdict The expressed decision of the jury on questions of fact submitted to it for determination, based on evidence presented during a trial.

vesting An employee becomes legally entitled to any share or part of a private pension fund before his retirement.

void Without legal force or binding effect.

voidable Subject to rescission (nullification and return to previous status) by one or both parties to a contract.

voir dire (Old French: to speak the truth) Process of questioning prospective jurors to ascertain whether they have any bias or prejudice that would make difficult or unlikely their impartiality in determining questions of fact during a trial.

voluntary arbitration See "arbitration."

voluntary manslaughter Intentional killing of another person in the heat of passion or after great provocation. For example: the killing of a third party when surprising an adulterous spouse in *flagrante delicto* (Latin: while the crime is blazing).

wage earner receivership A voluntary arrangement whereby a federal bankruptcy court approves a plan that calls for payment by a debtor in distress to his creditors, without going bankrupt. Known as a Chapter 13 proceeding. Some states have similar plans.

waive   To give up a right, such as to trial by jury.

warrant   A written authorization of a judge, or magistrate, to arrest a specific person.

warranty   a) Assurance given to the buyer by the seller with reference to the quality or performance of his product. Also called guaranty. b) Promise that a certain fact or facts are true. May be expressed orally or in writing, or may be implied by law.

warranty against encumbrances   Assurance by the seller that the goods delivered will be free of liens or encumbrances (creditors' claims) of which the buyer is not aware at the time of contracting.

warranty against infringement   Assurance by the seller that the goods sold are delivered free of any rightful claim of a third party under patent, copyright, or other legal protection.

warranty of conformity to description, sample, or model   Assurance by the seller that all goods supplied will conform to the sample or model shown at the time of the sale, or to the specifications provided.

warranty of conformity to seller's statement or promise   Warranty whereby the seller of goods who openly states or writes some factual assertion about them is bound.

warranties of endorser   Promises by an endorser of commercial paper that certain facts are true. They are implied by law unless he adds the words *without warranties* to his endorsement.

warranty of fitness for particular purpose   Assurance by the seller of goods that when the buyer indicates the purpose for which he needs the goods and then relies on the seller's recommendation, the goods will be reasonably fit for the intended purpose.

warranty of merchantability   A group of assurances by the seller of goods, including notably that they are fit for the purposes for which such goods are ordinarily used.

warranty of title   Assurance by the seller of goods that he has the title he claims to have to them along with the right to transfer or sell them.

white collar crimes   Crimes committed by persons of comparatively higher social status and economic wealth, usually without violence (such as embezzlement, fraud, and tax evasion). Contrasted to blue collar crimes such as robbery.

wildcat strike   A strike in which workers refuse to work in violation of the labor contract and contrary to union orders.

will Legal expression of a person's directions as to how his property is to be disposed of after his death. Usually written. Also called last will and testament.

winding-up (of partnership) Activities engaged in after dissolution to conclude all contracts of the firm.

Workmen's Compensation Laws under which employers must pay benefits to workers injured on the job, or to the dependents of workers killed on the job, without necessity of proof of liability in a lawsuit. Called Worker Compensation in California.

writ of execution Order of the court directing the sheriff to confiscate property of the defendant. The property is then sold to satisfy the award of dollar damages given to the plaintiff at a trial.

written interrogatories Pretrial questioning of a witness or adverse party to an action by means of written questions submitted to counsel by the opposing attorney, to be answered in writing under oath. A type of discovery procedure.

written law Rules of conduct enacted by the legislative branch. (See also "unwritten law.")

wrongful death statutes Laws that permit heirs of a person killed by wrongful conduct of another to recover damages from the tortfeasor.

yellow-dog contract A contract under which the employee agrees never to join a union while working for this employer.

INDEX

subchapter S, 361
used to defraud, 362
corpus delicti of crime, 75
corrective advertising, 199
court, 37–38
  appellate, 38
  criminal, 39
  district, 41
  divorce, 39
  federal system of, 40, 42
  justice (California), 39
  juvenile, 39, 100
  municipal (California), 39
  of appeals (circuit), 42
  probate, 39
  small claims, 39
  state system of, 39, 41
  Superior Court (California), 39
  Supreme (New York), 39, 41
  Supreme (U.S.), 42
  trial, 38
cover, 206
creative labor, 201
credit card
  duties of user, 225–26
  federal Credit Card Act of 1970, 226
  liabilities for loss and misuse, 226
  rights of user, 225–26
  Song-Beverly Credit Card Act of 1971 (California), 226
credit sale, 204
crimes without victims, 83
crime
  against property, 80–81
  against public decency and morals, 83–84
  against public health, safety, and welfare, 81–82
  against the person, 76–80
  definition of, 71
  federal and state, 85
  felony, 75
  misdemeanor, 75, 88
  parties to, 74
  punishment for, 97–98
  regulatory offense, 72
  types of, various, 84
  white collar, 73
  without victims, 83

criminal intent, 72
criminal law, 33
criminal negligence, 72
criminal trial
  arraignment, 88
  preliminary hearing, 87
  procedure leading to, 85–88
cumulative preferred stock, 305
cumulative voting, 307

damages, 38, 107–109, 206
  compensatory, 107
  consequential, 206
  definition of, 107
  exemplary, 108
  general, 108
  how determined, 113, 118
  incidental, 206
  limitations on, 116–17
  punitive, 108
  special, 107
dangerous instrumentality, 116
dangerous propensity, 116
death penalty, 90
death taxes, 374–75
debts, failure to pay, 25
deceit, 113
declaratory judgment, 7
decreasing term life insurance, 239
deed
  grant, 282, 296
  of reconveyance, 289
  of trust, 281
  quitclaim, 296
  trustee's, 289
  warranty, 296
de facto segregation, 131
de jure segregation, 131
defamation of character, 112–13
  fair comment, 113
  libel, 112
  privileged, 112
  right of retraction, 113
  slander, 112
default, 207, 280, 289–91
default, judgment, 51
defendant, 38, 99

combination fixed and variable, 304
examples of media for, 304
fixed dollar, 303–305, 309
variable dollar, 303–305, 309
involuntary manslaughter, 77
irresistible impulse to commit crime, 88
irrevocable trust, 385

joint tenancy, 295, 372
judges, 37, 39–40
judgment, 44, 62, 63
judgment non obstante veredicto (J.N.O.V.), 61
judgment-proof defendant, 108, 207
judicial branch, 7
jurisdiction, 44, 46
jurisdictional dispute, 345
jury
function of, 54, 96
grand, 45
how selected, 53
hung, 55
size of, 95–96
trial, 52–55, 95–96
voir dire, 53
when available, 52
justices, 37, 42
juvenile court, 39, 100

Keogh Act, 372, 373
kidnapping, 78

Labor-Management Relations Act of 1947 (Taft-Hartley), 341
Labor-Management Reporting and Disclosure Act of 1959 (Landrum-Griffen), 342
land contract, 282
landlord, 293
landowner's duty to
business invitee, 121–22
licensee, 121

purchaser, 287–89
tenant, 293–94
trespasser, 120–21
Landrum-Griffen Act, 342
last will. *See* will
law
civil, 33
common, 36
criminal, 33
defined, 33
ordinances, 35
procedural, 34, 101
statutes, 35
substantive, 34
unwritten, 36
written, 35
lawsuit, 38. *See also* trial
avoiding, 379
class action, 198, 210
how commenced, 44–45
steps in, 55–65
lawyer
fiduciary relationship of, 47
licensing of, 46
need for, 45–46
payment of, 48
selection of, 46–47
lease of real property, 292
legal duties of landlord, 293
legal duties of tenant, 293
legal creditor-owner, 156–57
legality of contract, 204
legal separation, 188
legal tender, 321
legal title, 204
legislative branch, 5
legitimation, 186–87
lending, 302–303
letter of last instructions, 372, 379
level term life insurance, 239
liabilities, 370, 372
liability of parties to commercial paper
primary, 320
secondary, 319, 320
libel, 112
licensee, 121
lien, 351
life estate, 297
life insurance, 238, 239–48, 372

cash surrender value, 240, 241
costs of, 243–44
decreasing term, 239
endowment, 241
family income policy, 240
family maintenance policy, 240
for children, 247
group, 247
how much to buy, 371
incidents of ownership in, 242–43, 384
industrial, 247
in estate planning, 384
level term, 239
limited payment, 240
loan value, 240
ordinary (straight), 239
reversionary interest in, 242, 384
settlement options, 242, 386–87
tax status of, 242
term insurance, 239–41
variable, 241
life tenant, 297
limitations, statute of. *See* statute of limitations
listing agreement, 274
exclusive, 291–92
exclusive agency, 291
living together without marriage
legal effects of, 192–93
rights of putative spouse, 177
limited defenses (in commercial paper), 324–25
limited liability for claims and debts
bankrupt, 227–28
government, 125
landowner, 120–21
parent, 116, 123
partner, 358
statute of limitations, 119
stockholder, 359
wife, 181
limited
partner, 358
partnership, 358
limited payment life insurance, 240
litigation, 38. *See also* lawsuit
load, 308
loan

secured, 280, 303
unsecured, 303
loan shark, 224
loan value, 240
lockout, 346

magistrates, 39
mail fraud statutes, 217
maker, 312
malice aforethought, 76
malicious prosecution, 113
manslaughter, 76
involuntary, 77
voluntary, 77
marital deduction, 372, 377–79
market value, 286
marriage, 176–82, 192–93
common law, 177–78
conciliation counseling in, 192
defective, 177
definition of, 176
legal advantages of, 181–82
legal separation in, 188–89
obligations of, 178–81
requirements for, 176–77
termination of, 187–92
types of, 176–78
void, 177
voidable, 177
mayhem, 78
mechanic's lien, 351
media, savings and investment, 303–305
mediation, 348
minors
appearance before juvenile court, 100–102
cases involving, 39
contributing to delinquency of, 83
dangerous propensity of, 184
distinction between natural and adoptive, 183–84
liability for crime, 94
liability for tort, 116, 147, 184
liability under contract, 202–203
oppressive labor of, 332
purchase of life insurance by, 236

misdemeanor, 75, 88, 97
misrepresentation
  in general, 113
  in home sales, 287–89
mobile home, 275
Monroney Automobile Information
  Disclosure Act of 1958, 219
moot question, 134
mortgage
  mortgagee, 281
  mortgagor, 281
  real, 281
motion
  for directed verdict, 60
  for new trial, 62
  to produce evidence, 51
motive, 72
motor vehicle registration
  advantages of, 156
  in relation to accidents, 156
  of equitable owner, 157
  of legal owner, 157
  procedures, 157
multiple listing, 275
murder
  attempt to commit, 73
  crime of, 76
  first degree, 76
  second degree, 76
mutual funds. *See* investment companies
mutual insurance company, 234

Nader, Ralph, 199
National Labor Relations Act of 1935
  (Wagner), 341
National Traffic and Motor Vehicle
  Safety Act of 1966, 218
naturalization, 11
negative injunction, 338
negligence, 50, 213, 338. *See also* tort
  gross, 78
  contributory, 118
  simple (ordinary), 78
negotiable instruments. *See* commercial paper
no-fault automobile insurance, 255–56

arguments against, 256
arguments for, 255
no-load fund, 308
nolo contendere, plea of, 46
noncumulative preferred stock, 305
Norris-La Guardia Act of 1932, 341
notice of dishonor of commercial
  paper, 320
nullification of marriage, 177, 188
nuncupative will, 381

obscenity, 17–18
occupancy, 202
Occupational Safety and Health Act
  of 1971, 339
offer of contract, 202
Office of Consumer Affairs (federal),
  214
officers (of corporation), 307, 358
off-premises extension, 257
open shop, 343
opening statements, 56
oppressive child labor, 332
oral will. *See* nuncupative will
ordinances, 35
ordinary life insurance, 239
owner of motor vehicle
  liability for torts of employee, 162
  liability if borrows car, 251, 253–54
  liability if lends his car, 162

pardon, 99
parental immunity, 123
parenthood
  effect of unmarried status on, 187
  how establish in absence of marriage, 186–87
  legal advantage of, 185–86
  legal obligations of, 186, 187
parents
  legal advantages of, 185–86
  liability for school damage, 147, 184
  liability for torts of children, 116,
    147, 158
  vicarious liability of, 184–85

usury, 223–25

variable dollar investment media, 303–305, 309
variable life insurance policy, 241
venue, change of, 23
verdict of jury, 54, 63
vesting, 267, 386
Veterans Administration (VA) home loan, 277
void contracts, 203
voidable contract, 202
voir dire, 53
voluntary arbitration. *See* arbitration
voluntary intoxication, defense of, 89
voluntary manslaughter, 77

Wage and Hour Law (federal), 348
wage earner receivership, 227
Wagner Act, 341
warrant for arrest, 86
warranties
   disclaimer of, by seller, 212–13
   express, 211, 212
   implied, 210–12
   in sales of goods, 210–13
   in sales of real property, 296
   in transfer of commercial paper, 315–16
warranties of endorser, 315–16
warranty
   against encumbrances, 211, 296
   against infringement, 211
   of conformity to description, sample, or model, 211
   of conformity to seller's statement or promise, 211
   of fitness for particular purpose, 211

of further assurances, 296
of merchantability, 211–12
of quiet enjoyment, 296
of seizin, 296
of title, 211
waste of real property, 283
white collar crimes, 73
wife and husband. *See* husband and wife
wildcat strike, 348
will, 370, 372, 379–84
   administrator of, 379
   advantages of, 379
   lack of, 381–83
   executor (executrix) of, 379
   formal (witnessed), 380–81
   holographic unwitnessed (informal), 381
   letter of last instructions with, 379–80
   oral (nuncupative), 381
   pretermitted heir in, 380
   testator (testatrix) of, 379
winding-up (of partnership), 357
workmen's compensation law, 268–69, 349–50
   definition of, 124
   employer defenses against, 268, 350
   who is covered, 268
writ
   of certiorari, 42
   of execution, 63
   of habeas corpus, 152
written interrogatories, 50
written law, 35
wrongful death statutes, 109

yellow-dog contract, 341
Youth Authority (California), 100–101

Computer Typesetting Services, Inc., of Glendale, California, set this book in 10-point Century Schoolbook with display type in Bauer Text Initials. Carol Schwartzback & Associates of San Francisco, California, prepared the technical art for it, and Kingsport Press of Kingsport, Tennessee, printed it.

Sponsoring Editor	Paul Kelly
Project Editor	Gretchen Hargis
Designer	Naomi Takigawa
Illustrator	Ralph Mapson